The Needle's Eye

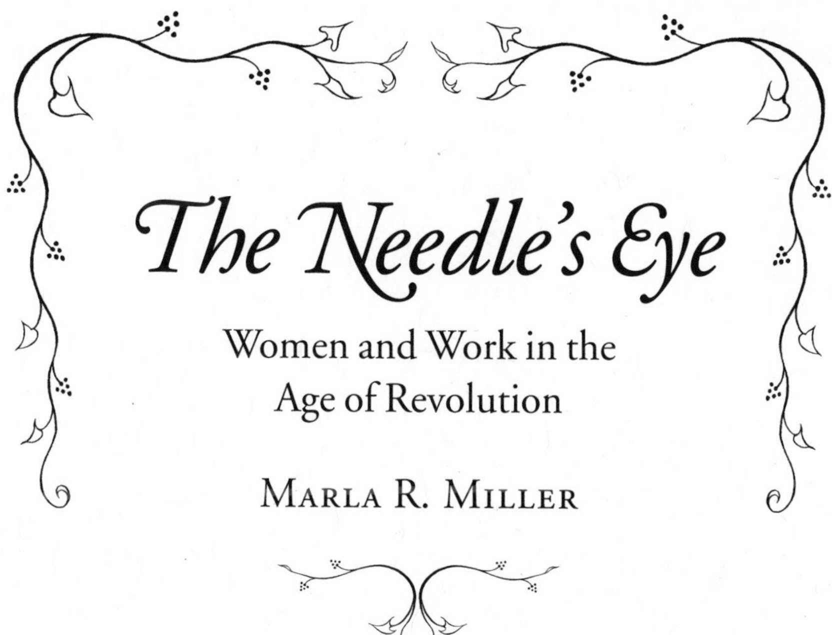

The Needle's Eye

Women and Work in the Age of Revolution

Marla R. Miller

University of Massachusetts Press
Amherst and Boston

Printed in the United States of America

LC 2006008297
ISBN 1-55849-544-4 (library cloth ed.); 545-2 (paper)

Designed by Dennis Anderson
Set in Adobe Garamond
Printed and bound by Thomson-Shore, Inc.

Library of Congress Cataloging-in-Publication Data

Miller, Marla R.
The needle's eye : women and work in the age of revolution / Marla R. Miller.
p. cm.
Includes bibliographical references and index.
ISBN 1-55849-545-2 (pbk. : alk. paper)—ISBN 1-55849-544-4 (library cloth : alk. paper)
1. Women—Employment—Massachusetts—Hadley (Town)—History.
2. Needleworkers—Massachusetts—Hadley (Town)—Case studies. 3. Women artisans—Massachusetts—Hadley (Town)—Case studies. 4. Social classes—Massachusetts—Hadley (Town)—History. 5. Clothing trade—Massachusetts—Hadley (Town)—History. I. Title: Women and work in the age of revolution. II. Title.
HD6096.H33M55 2006
331.4'8870974423—dc22 2006008297

British Library Cataloguing in Publication data are available.

This book has been published with the aid of a generous grant from The Coby Foundation, Ltd., New York.

Contents

Illustrations

Figures

Color Plates (follow page 144)

Acknowledgments

THIS PROJECT has been something like fifteen years in the making start to finish, and so these acknowledgments are unabashedly long. It seems as though I've been telling friends and family for at least a third of that time that the book is "practically done," and so it is with sincere pleasure that I at long last record my gratitude to the many people who have helped me, in ways great and small, along the way.

In these several years I have encountered a long line of librarians, curators, and administrators whose talent, dedication, genial encouragement, and general good cheer made the work I do both possible and pleasurable. During a fellowship at the American Antiquarian Society, the entire staff extended truly remarkable courtesy, but I am especially indebted to John Hench, Caroline Sloat, Georgia Barnhill, Joanne Chaison, and Laura Wasowicz for making me so comfortable there, and for pointing me toward materials I may well never have discovered on my own. At the Connecticut Historical Society, Susan Schoelwer has been especially enthusiastic about my project and its larger aims; she is one of those extraordinary object-people who make document-people like me feel as though we're all in it together. At the Pocumtuck Valley Memorial Association, Suzanne Flynt has long been a fellow traveler in the effort to untangle the mystery that is Rebecca Dickinson, and to understand the artists and businesswomen who revisited her needlework a century later; I've enjoyed her scholarly camaraderie through the years. At the Forbes Library in Northampton, Elise Bernier Feeley is a sheer marvel of efficiency and hospitality; what's more, it was she who first introduced me to the wealth and riches of the Sylvester Judd Manuscript. Kerry Buckley and Marie Panik at Historic Northampton have likewise been wonderfully alert to the documents and artifacts in their collection that bear on my work. Across the river, the staff at the Amherst College Library's Special Collections and Archives capably oversee the Porter-Phelps-Huntington papers; I cannot guess the number of hours I've spent in that comfortable reading room but am grateful to Daria D'Arienzo and Mimi Dakin for their cheerful help through the years. At the Hadley Historical Society, I will always remember with admiration and affection the late Dorothy Russell, who so cheerfully shared her own vast knowledge of local history as I undertook the research that launched this project.

A circle of textile and clothing curators, museum professionals, and costume specialists gave gladly of their time and expertise and provided me with many hours of instruction and just plain fun. A day of hands-on tutoring was wonderfully offered by the staff of the mantua maker's house at Colonial Williamsburg; I am tremendously indebted to Janea Whitacre, Doris Warren, and Brooke Barrows for a delightful February day spent together making a 1770s gown from start to (almost) finish. I am also thankful to Beth Gilgun for lending me the period-appropriate clothing that made that trip possible—and for providing yet another tactile learning experience as she laced me into my oh-so-snug jacket. This project benefited significantly from the expertise and generosity of Henry M. Cooke IV, Ned Lazaro, Aimee Newell, Pamela Parmel, and Nancy Rexford, each of whom came to my rescue at one time or another with just the right information, materials, or advice. And last, my gratitude to Lynne Zacek Bassett, for close readings of this book in various stages of development, for many hours of personal tutorial, and for her longtime support of my scholarship, is particularly profound.

Two museums have played especially pivotal roles in my development as a historian. Ever since a life-changing summer fellowship at Historic Deerfield in 1987, Norma Woods, Ken Hafertepe, Phil Zea, Joshua Lane, Amanda Lange, Edward Maeder, Jessica Neuwirth, and many others over the years have made that magical place an extraordinary scholarly resource, as well as a home away from home. Special thanks are due to Donald R. and Grace Friary for their ongoing interest in and support of my work. Most of all I would like to acknowledge a deep debt to Anne Digan Lanning, who has long shared my passion for the recovery of women's lives in eighteenth- and nineteenth-century New England; many thanks to her for almost twenty years of scholarly companionship. More material support was provided by the excellent staff of Deerfield's Memorial Libraries over the past years; David Proper, Shirley Majewski, David Bosse, Sharman Prouty, and Martha Noblick do everything excellent librarians do, and a good deal more. Of course, this project was first conceived on the porch of the Porter-Phelps-Huntington House in Hadley; I have spent untold hours in and around those rooms trying to conjure the spirits not just of Elizabeth Porter Phelps and Rebecca Dickinson but Tryphena Cooke, Peg, Phillis, and Roseanna, Persis Morse, and many other, unnamed, women who labored there. I will be forever grateful to Susan Lisk and Elizabeth Carlisle for assisting in those efforts with such enthusiasm, and for making that place so warm and welcoming through the years.

This project began as a dissertation at the University of North Carolina at

Chapel Hill, though it has roots, too, in a senior thesis at the University of Wisconsin–Madison, where Charles L. Cohen and the late and remarkable Sargent Bush Jr. first captivated me with the mystery and wonders of early America. At UNC, Professors John Nelson and Jacqueline Dowd Hall proved instrumental in the development of that project, and in my own evolution as a scholar; they are thanked effusively in that earlier set of acknowledgments, but their advice and support has continued long beyond the receipt of the degree, itself now almost ten years past, and I continue to benefit from their wisdom and encouragement. Everyone who has been through graduate school knows how important your fellow students are as well, and my appreciation and affection for my classmates Anne Whisnant, Gretchen White, Tim Thurber, Laura Jane Moore, and Houston Roberson are deep and abiding.

Two scholars have been especially important in guiding this project as well as its author. My gratitude to Laurel Ulrich is deep and wholehearted. Her reputation for intellectual generosity is legendary and well-earned; knowing what I now know about the life of a university professor, I cannot begin to imagine how she found time to read work from a student for whom she was in no way responsible—and not just once, but repeatedly, from the day that my first essay on Rebecca Dickinson arrived unannounced in her campus mailbox to drafts of this book. Through these years, her thoughtful comments and suggestions have meant as much to me as her warm personal encouragement. Kevin M. Sweeney was serving as Historic Deerfield's Director of Academic Programs that life-changing summer and had no small role in making it one. Words can hardly capture my gratitude to him for setting me on this intellectual course and for staying with me along the way. Finally, both Laurel and Kevin pointed out that the early material from which this project grew might support two books rather than one; they should rest assured that my thanks for that observation will be equally effusive in the future.

Several friends and colleagues also read large chunks of this book, and in many cases the whole thing. For their energy and support, I thank Sarah Leavitt, Valija Evalds, and again, Lynne Bassett. Pat Tracy and Christopher Clark each read the book as I was embarking on the process of revision; their perceptive comments and suggestions changed the way I thought about both the shape and the purpose of my work. Cathy Kelly gave this work a wonderfully close and insightful reading at a critical juncture in its development; her generosity, insight, and enthusiasm continue to astound me. I also managed to impose larger and smaller portions of my work on Howard Rock, Edward S. Cooke Jr., Seth Rockman, and Pamela Sharpe and am grateful to them for their astute comments and advice. Several scholars have shared findings from their own archival forays with me, and for this I am indebted to Jacqueline Carr, Mary Beaudry, and (though this has now been so long ago that she has surely given up looking for any book) Beth Nichols. Less formal but also ongoing and valuable encouragement came from Bonnie Parsons, Sherrill Redmon, Joyce Follet, and Jim and Margaret Freeman as well as Martha Lyon and Lynda Faye, for which I am also grateful.

I also feel lucky to have become part of the intellectual community that Peter Benes has gathered around the Dublin Seminar for New England Folklife; every summer—whatever the season's topic—I am energized and inspired by the conference itself as well as the principles behind it. As for my university community, I so appreciate my colleagues at the University of Massachusetts Amherst and the Five Colleges, who never fail to support my work, especially Joyce Berkman, Alice Nash, Christine Cooper, Neal Salisbury, Bob Paynter, and the members of a departmental writing group: Brian Ogilvie, Carl Nightengale, Max Page, and Kate Weigand, cheerfully hosted by the much-missed Kevin Boyle and Vicky Getis. The material that became chapter 6 was presented to the Five College History Seminar and to the members of an ongoing Interdisciplinary Seminar in the Humanities and Fine Arts; my understanding of urban women was improved by conversation with members of the Economic History and Development Workshop. Special thanks are due to David Glassberg and Barry Levy for their constant engagement and encouragement over the past several years. Bruce Laurie had the fortune (I'll let him supply his own adjective) to become my official faculty mentor on my appointment to UMass and quickly became among my most valued colleagues as well; words hardly suffice for all the advice, support, and intellectual camaraderie he has provided since my arrival on campus.

Students at the University of Massachusetts have also helped both directly and indirectly through the years, but I am especially grateful to the undergraduates in my 2003 seminar "Great History Books" (Kimberly Anderson, Jaclyn Chimeri, Nancy Edmonson, Natalie Kollman, Laura Leonard, Sarah Merva, Alannah Sharry, Max Solie, D. J. Thistle, and Gregg Ykasala) for talking over the course of a lively semester with me about things that make readers keep turning pages. Smith College student Jack Slowriver provided capable research assistance, as did Ned Lazarro while he himself was yet a master's candidate. Finally, Kate Navarra Thibodeau and Jill Ogline, graduate assistants to the UMass Public History Program, helped immeasurably by keeping many other parts of my life sane so that I could bring this project to a successful and timely conclusion.

Of course, institutional support of many kinds is crucial to any project, and I take particular pleasure in acknowledging them here. The University of North Carolina supported early research on this project through fellowships supported by the History Department as well as the Graduate School; I am particularly honored to have been a member of the first class of the Carolina/Royster Society of Fellows, as the Henry H. Dearman Fellow. A Massachusetts Foundation for the Humanities/Bay State Historical League Scholar-in-Residence Grant, Kate B. and Hall J. Peterson Fellowship at the American Antiquarian Society and Five College Women's Studies Research Center Research Associateship in 1994 all contributed to the completion of the research. More recently, a Ruth R. Miller Fellowship at the Massachusetts Historical Society allowed me to pursue related work on Boston artisans. The National Endowment for the Humanities provided crucial support, in both a summer research stipend and year-long fellowship during which I could write, as did a departmental Research and Curriculum Enhancement Leave awarded me by my colleagues at the University of Massachusetts. The University of Massachusetts Amherst Office of Research Services funded the creation of the Connecticut Valley Clothing File. I am especially grateful to Dean of Humanities and Fine Arts Lee Edwards for supporting this project in ways both tangible and intangible.

Parts of some chapters have appeared in differing forms in the *William and Mary Quarterly,* the *New England Quarterly, Dress,* and proceedings of the Dublin Seminar for New England Folklife. I cheerfully thank those journals for permission to reprint that material here. Perhaps more important, I am deeply indebted to Chris Grasso, Ann Gross, Lynn Rhoads, Peter Benes, and Linda Welter for their support and suggestions as I polished the argument and prose of those various pieces. Ann is to be doubly thanked because she also helped prepare the entire manuscript for publication at the University of Massachusetts Press, as did Deborah Smith, to whom I am also sincerely grateful; I would never have discovered my affinity for reflexive pronouns and inadvertent puns without their extraordinary attention. Kate Blackmer and Stan Sherer provided exceptional artwork, and a generous grant from the Coby Foundation funded the color illustrations that help tell the book's story. Finally, at the Press, Paul Wright, Clark Dougan, Bruce Wilcox, and Carol Betsch each helped guide this inexperienced first-time author through the publication process; I hope we get to do it again sometime. On this note about the mentoring of new writers, I would be remiss not to add here my deep gratitude to Peter Agree, who was associated with the College of Humanities and Fine Arts of the University of Massachusetts Amherst at just the right moment for me, for his sage advice and unfailing support.

Looking over these acknowledgments I apprehend how much it is true that my professional colleagues are also my best friends, and my friends and family sources of scholarly insight and inspiration. What a lovely thing it is to realize that the people I so much admire for their historical acumen, inventive scholarship, and dedication to the life of the mind are the same people whom I treasure most for their good humor, personal warmth, and political companionship. My loved ones should recognize themselves in those lines as well. Since his own work involves unraveling the history of the universe, it's not surprising that Stephen K. Peck reminds me every day how important the world beyond the academy remains; though I can be a stubborn student, I so appreciate the many things he has taught me through the years. My brother, Todd M. Miller, shows me all the time the rewards of independent discovery, of embracing new subjects and pursuing them with vigor. My father, Roger Leslie Miller, first taught me to love learning itself; to this day we share the plain fun of puzzling things out. Finally, my mother, Phyllis Arneson Miller, first led me to love the places and people of the past; if someday I become half the historian she is, then I will have accomplished something. I fondly dedicate this work to them.

The Needle's Eye

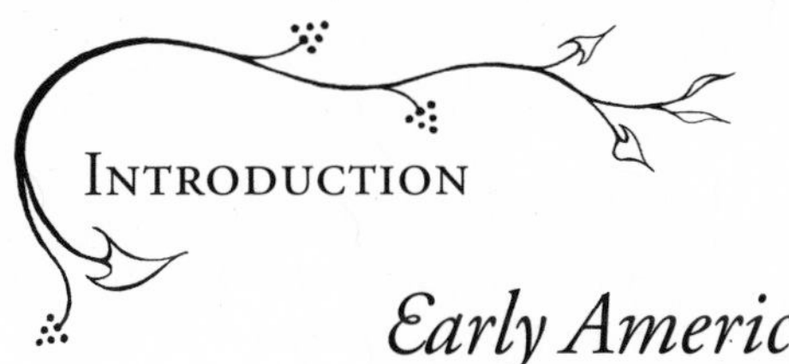

Introduction

Early American Artisanry

Why Gender Matters

Seldom does a historian find her scholarly interests reflected in the aisles of Toys-R-Us, even more rarely so those of us who study the eighteenth century. But the advent of Colonial Barbie provided me that rare instance. When I first spotted her, the historically garbed figure seemed out of place amid rows of Holiday Barbies, Dance-n-Twirl Barbies, and Gymnast Barbies. But as a women's historian studying early America I was drawn to her in both amazement and amusement. Dressed in red, white, and blue, her costume the familiar mantua, petticoat, and mob cap, she would more accurately have been named Revolutionary Barbie, I remember thinking. Most interesting to me, she held in her hand a piece of needlework. Barbie was working on a quilt square, it seemed, depicting an American eagle. Also enclosed in the box was a booklet recounting Barbie's participation in the American Revolution and explaining the small object she held in her hand. The title of the volume was "The Messenger Quilt." At first, I assumed that the usually adventuresome Barbie was involved in some sort of spy operation, cleverly inscribing and conveying military intelligence through a seemingly innocent quilt. I was disappointed to learn that the quilt simply, if enthusiastically, celebrated the signing of the Declaration of Independence with a large red, white, and blue design reading "Happy Birthday, America."

Barbie's quilt brought to mind another piece of red, white, and blue needlework announcing the founding of the new nation. Though thousands of girls have now encountered their colonial counterparts through Mattel's incarnation (as well as the American Girls popular doll "Felicity"), among the first early American women that most children meet is Betsy Ross, the alleged maker of the first United States flag. Ross has for generations been the only woman included alongside the founding fathers, her contribution to the fledgling nation her skill with a needle.[1] On any given day, close to three hundred titles concerning her crowd the nation's bookstore and library shelves, the vast majority aimed at the young adult market. She has been portrayed in films, and she has lent her name to lamps, cocktails, and sewing tables. She is one of only three historical figures immortalized as a Pez candy dispenser. Prompted first by the nation's centennial and enlarged by subsequent commemorations, the legend that surrounds Ross is both larger and smaller than the woman herself. While most popular accounts casually label her a seamstress, Elizabeth Griscom Ross Ashburn Claypoole actually worked

Colonial Barbie. Author's collection.

as an upholsterer, one of two hundred independent businesswomen in Philadelphia. Her shop thrived for several decades beyond 1776, employing over the years many young female apprentices and assistants.[2] What's more, as a resident of revolutionary and occupied Philadelphia, the nation's first capital, her association with the Independence effort—which she struggled to reconcile with her Quaker upbringing—far exceeded the making of a single flag. Betsy Ross could, and should, be remembered as representative of large numbers of female artisans and entrepreneurs in early America, but the skilled craftwork, business acumen, political conviction, and religious commitments that shaped her life are almost completely overshadowed by the aura of domesticity that has come to surround her.

When Ross's story emerged in the last quarter of the nineteenth century, it resonated with wistful colonial revival visions of early American women and their work. Needlework, at least among the white middle-class women who promoted the colonial revival, served an important purpose among Victorians coping with industrializing America. The embroidering of those tremendously popular mottoes—God Bless Our Home, Rock of Ages, No Cross No Crown—reconciled progress (in the mass-produced punch-cards through which these patterns were produced) with tradition (in the application of needlework and the selection of the messages inscribed).[3] New technologies gradually rendered decorative needlework, once the province of elite women educated in academies, the province of all. While images of Ross with the nation's first flag draped gracefully across her lap collapsed patriotism and domesticity into one compelling scene, women's personal experiences with needlework increasingly emphasized the ornamental over the prosaic.

Early American needlework has continued to be revered as evidence of the industry, taste, diligence, devotion, and resourcefulness of our colonial counterparts. These objects bring emotional comfort, too, as they harken back to a period, to families and communities, and to values that appear somehow simpler, sweeter. Since the nineteenth century, samplers, quilts, and embroidery of all kinds have enjoyed repeated revivals, each occurring amid familiar constellations of social tensions, while popular imagery associated with the Ross tale in its various incarnations, which generally supplant the upholsterer's work with that of a seamstress, has tacitly suggested that, in early America, needleworkers were ubiquitous, undifferentiated, and homogeneous. The association of femininity, needlework, and nostalgia is as compelling today as it ever was. In scenes repeated throughout museums and historic sites, docents use samplers to engage their female audience. Pointing to the small stitches and noting the youth of the stitcher, they ask women and girls to imagine performing such careful work at such a young age. The appropriate response is all but scripted: wide eyes, shakes of heads, wonder, reverence. Because needlework has for so long been for most women largely a leisure activity, we have forgotten not only that sewing was skilled work—requiring skills that not every woman possessed—but also that it was difficult, mind-numbing, eye-straining, back-aching labor.

The lack of attention to women's skilled work in clothes making stems partially from a longstanding inclination to equate skilled work within the needle trades with the everyday maintenance of a household's clothing performed by women for their husbands, parents, and children. Historians have effectively challenged myths of self-sufficiency and explored patterns of household and neighborhood production. Still, both popular and scholarly discussions of early American households too often assume that women were largely responsible for constructing their family's apparel, and textile production and clothing construction are routinely conflated in ways that seldom confuse, say, the milling of wood and the construction of furniture.[4] At the same time, as Joy Parr has observed, when it comes to the subject of work, masculinity has been so thoroughly naturalized that qualities like pride, ambition, and competitiveness are treated as if they are more obviously associated with men than women; we know less than we should about how those qualities are culturally constructed and how those constructions have changed.[5]

Put another way, while mythologies surrounding women's work have made it difficult to imagine women as artisans, popular imagery surrounding early American crafts has made it difficult to see artisans as female. Longfellow's brawny vision of the village blacksmith, or Copley's elegant portrait of the silversmith Paul Revere, leave little imaginative space for village craftswomen. John Neagle's 1826 painting of the blacksmith Patrick Lyon captures the vision shared by many Americans, then and now: Neagle depicts the broad-shouldered craftsman, wrapped in a thick leather apron, standing before a flaming forge with one hand on his hip and the other on his anvil. In the nineteenth century, the image became an oft-reproduced "icon of artisanal republicanism," a "symbolic figure representing the virtues of all craftsmen."[6] It is no coincidence that such images appeared when they did. In the first decades of the nineteenth century, as capitalism transformed artisanal trades, threatening to seize control of both "products and profits," artisans became activists on their own behalf: artisanal consciousness "crystallized" just as the "material basis for artisan unity was crumbling."[7] The independent craftsman survived in cultural productions like these if, it might have seemed at the time, almost nowhere else.

In the absence of countervailing imagery, Neagle's rendering of the heroic artisan as virtue and masculinity bodied forth has endured. Meanwhile, as the production of Americans' clothing moved increasingly from homes to factories (and eventually to factories abroad), the tasks involved in the construction of clothing faded from memory. And as dramatic shifts in the garment trades freed middle-class needles for less onerous duties, romantic images of colonial goodwives able to satisfy single-handedly their household's sartorial needs while also finding time for artistic expression thrived. In such a shadow, myths and misperceptions take easy hold and loom large, perpetuating a picture of women's needlework that distorts, even effaces, our understanding of women's artisanal work in early America. Mattel's Colonial Barbie, needlework in hand, is only one recent episode in this mythologizing. Betsy Ross's currency is undiminished as well: over a quarter of a million people seek out the Betsy Ross House every year, as curious as ever about the legendary figure they remember from grade-school pageants and sentimental prints.

Not far from the Ross house, on Elfreth's Alley, stands another historic site, a museum representing an eighteenth-century Philadelphia mantua maker's house. This site also interprets the history of Philadelphia's female

AUGUSTUS ANDROSS,

CONTINUES to carry on the Blacksmith's business in all its branches, at his old stand, a few rods west of the Court-House, and solicits a continuance of the liberal patronage of his friends, in the way of his profession.

N. B. Said Andross will forge Machinery Work to any pattern—likewise Balustrade and Iron Fences, &c. &c.

Hartford, March 29, 1819. tf 28

Augustus Andross advertisement, *Connecticut Courant,* 6 April 1819. Courtesy of the Connecticut Historical Society Museum, Hartford.

In the first quarter of the nineteenth century, as large-scale economic reorganization seemed to threaten independent artisanry, assertions of masculinity became important to artisanal identity. The advertisement, while noting the blacksmith's ability to "forge Machinery Work to any pattern," emphasizes the human strength of the artisan's body, his bulging bicep exposed by the rolled-up sleeve, and hammer held upright by a muscular forearm.

artisans but enjoys just a fraction of the number of visits the Ross house receives. Each site interprets the history of the city's skilled craftswomen, but for both, the same popular historical imagination that brings visitors to the door can make the place of artisanal skill in these women's lives that much harder to see. My main purpose in this work is to re-imagine those early American craftswomen—to move Colonial Barbie aside, to help recapture the artisanal world of businesswomen like Ross, to lead readers to the homes and workplaces of early American mantua makers. I hope to restore to historical view the legions of early American women who found livings in the clothing trades and to overturn the prevailing sense—symbolized by Colonial Barbie and the mythologized Ross—that early American needlework was ubiquitous and undifferentiated and to examine instead the complexities of women's craft production on the eve of industrialization. As Laurel Thatcher Ulrich has observed, "as yet, few historians have given serious attention to the actual structure of women's domestic burdens in early America or attempted to discover the particular conditions that may have given rise to their complaints. Nor has anyone considered working relations among women in the preindustrial female economy."[8] This study aims to help fill that gap.

Historians of women and work in the early modern Atlantic world have long been interested in tracking change and continuity within gender divisions of labor.[9] As part of a larger scholarly effort to understand, and remedy, "the persistence of women in the lowest paid, least stable and most unrewarding occupations," historians have observed the waxing and waning of women's economic opportunities in a variety of arenas.[10] Among the key insights that have emerged from this work is the extraordinary tenacity, and elasticity, of cultural constructions surrounding women and work, which have responded to economic exigency as circumstances demanded. Eighteenth-century New England, as elsewhere in the Atlantic world, was a time and place of dynamic change.[11] Ongoing, substantive transformations both encompassed and encouraged the feminization of some tasks, skills, and occupations in New England and the masculinization of others. Healing and caregiving, agriculture (especially dairying), cloth making, shoemaking, and teaching, to name only a few occupations, saw particularly dramatic reconfigurations along gendered lines in the eighteenth and early nineteenth centuries.[12] The clothing trades—among the few artisanal arenas where both men and women participated in significant numbers—afford an unusually rich opportunity to explore how assumptions about gender and work evolved during a period of remarkable flux.

Examining women in their variety of market roles in relation to one another also underscores the degree to which the work that women did and the ways that they thought about themselves as workers were interdependent. The women who populate this study are mostly rural or small-town women who augmented their household income, to greater and lesser degrees, through craft skill; they were each enmeshed, though in very different ways, in the "interlocking yet distinguishable" economies that encompassed the farms and households of early America.[13] By looking closely at relationships among women in one early American region, and even a single community—women who at first glance may look quite similar—this study seeks to add nuance to ongoing discussions of differences among women as well as inequality in early America.

This book, then, examines the nexus of social and economic relationships that surrounded works of the needle, with the ultimate aim of understanding more fully the ways in which both female and male New Englanders experienced the economic, social, and cultural changes that accompanied the evolving market economy. Early American women, including those whose work can be called artisanal, conformed to gender expectations appropriate to their age, marital status, race, and class. Underscoring the different ways in which women worked in clothing trades thus complicates simple contrasts between male and female artisanry: craftwork in early America admitted both men and women, though gender, as well as race, class, and life-cycle issues, influenced the kind and extent of one's participation in that work.

Understanding laboring women in the early New England clothing trades also contributes to the larger scholarly project of sorting out the ways in which women may have both experienced and provoked the much-discussed and so-called industrious, consumer, and industrial revolutions of the long eighteenth century. In many ways, this is a study of women and work in the Atlantic world. The scholarship of Judith Bennett, Maxine Berg, Katrina Honeyman, Margaret Hunt, Elizabeth Sanderson, Pamela Sharpe, Jan de Vries, and others has reconfigured the history of European women's labor and its relationship to the various economic, social, industrial, and political revolutions of the early modern and modern era.[14] Research on European women's work in the clothing trades, in particular, has flourished in recent years; among the most notable contributors are Judith Coffin, Beverly Lemire, and Clare Crowston.[15] Meanwhile, costume historians such as Linda Baumgarten, Claudia Kidwell, Nancy Rexford, and Aileen Ribiero have transformed the way scholars think about the production and consumption of clothing.[16] Women in Britain's North American colonies and the nation that emerged from them moved in currents of much larger streams, indeed oceans of economic and cultural change in an age of revolution. New England women understood themselves to be connected in important ways to laboring women on distant shores, and we should, as well.

In sum, the study of early American women's work in the clothing trades enables us to see economic history, labor history, and women's history across British North America from a new vantage point. Although almost all women, to be sure, worked constantly to keep their family's clothes in good order, vast numbers of women sewed for families not their own, exchanging their time and skill for goods, services, and wages. Second only to domestic service, the clothing trades were the largest employer of women in early New England and perhaps throughout Britain's North American colonies. Some women earned income on a casual basis, taking in plainwork for neighbors when the opportunity presented itself. Some completed periods of training to acquire the special skills associated with tailors (who produced formal, fitted clothing for men) and mantua or gown makers (who produced formal, fitted clothing for women). Some of those highly skilled artisans worked out of their homes; more rarely, they set up shops. Some specialized in particular items, such as gloves or stockings. Some women sold, traded, or refurbished second-hand clothing, while others labored as laundresses. Constructing and maintaining apparel consumed enormous amounts of time and attention throughout New England in the last half of the eighteenth century and the first decade of the nineteenth, drawing women into a complex economy in which they participated as (alternately and concurrently) producers and consumers, artisans and clients, employers and employees.

Women's skills with needles and shears gave them a particular place within their communities. Some became widely known makers of the region's most fashionable apparel; others took generally held skills into the homes of their neighbors. Still others served mainly as employers, and not providers, of this labor. My purpose is to plumb those hierarchies of power and skill to better understand the ways in which needlework shaped and reflected the circumstances of real women's lives, which varied significantly over time and space, by economic position and opportunity, by marital status and other life stages, by race, education, entrepreneurial talent, and technical ability; to restore skilled needlewomen to their artisanal status and to reconnect those artisans to the expanding commercial world of the eighteenth century; and to observe the century's economic transformations from the perspective of female needleworkers of varying levels of skill, experience, and independence. This, then, is a study of women, work, and the ways in which early American women's work and work identities turned on commonalities and differences that continue to challenge us today, unaided by the mythologies that elide them.

Working women's lives are notoriously hard to document, all the more so as one moves backward in time. Rarely literate, early America's laboring women were unlikely to create texts that survive for contemporary historical inspection. Traces of their work instead scatter across the letters, ledgers, and daybooks of others. At the same time, the material world they inhabited—the spaces where they lived and worked; the pins, needles, and shears they possessed; and the products of their labor—endure so infrequently that it can be hard to extract from them sufficient clues to reconstruct whole worlds of activity.[17]

The Saybrook, Connecticut, gown maker Polly L'Hommedieu Lathrop is exceptional in that her accounts for a season's labor survive, and as striking as the existence of the accounts themselves is the pride she plainly took in keeping the record: "Polly Lathrop Act Book" is inscribed no fewer than three times inside the volume's cover.[18] Gloria Main has observed the absence of account books kept by women and suggests that "few women in rural New England engaged in business on a scale or of a nature that required them to record their transactions in a systematic way."[19] Perhaps, too, women, whose educations did not typically include accounting, also found other, more idiosyncratic methods to track their debts and credits. Rhoda Childs, an eighteenth-century midwife in Deerfield, Massachusetts, for example, was remembered to have kept her accounts in chalk on the door leading to her cellar.[20] Women's uneven access to literacy and numeracy skills meant that they developed their own strategies for keeping accounts that, unfortunately, less regularly found their way into any archive.[21]

More common than volumes like Lathrop's, and more tangible (for us today) than records like Childs's, are the many account books kept by men that were also the ledgers of women. When Solomon Wright, of Northampton, Massachusetts, inscribed his own name on the cover of his accounts, the gown maker Esther Wright likewise inscribed her own, to reflect that debts recorded therein were also hers.[22] Despite the boldness of her signature, Esther Wright's identity is unclear to us today: Solomon never married; Esther is either Solomon's widowed mother, Esther Lyman Wright (1725–1815), or his never-married sister (1763–1812), also named Esther Wright. Today the volume is catalogued as the Solomon Wright account book, but his notations concerning goods and services "we" received and debts due to "us" make plain that he saw the account book as a record of shared enterprise. Similarly, the ledger kept in the 1760s by Reuban Champion is catalogued as that of a Connecticut Valley physician; the presence of transactions related to needlework long went unnoted, yet more than a third of the individuals listed in the ledger's pages were indebted to the household for Lydia Duncan

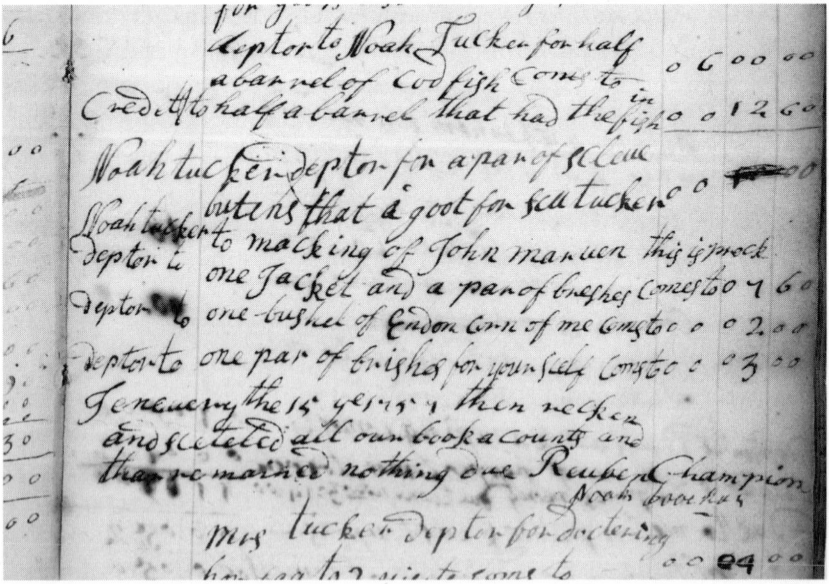
deptor to Noah Tucker for half a barrel of Codfish Comes to 0 6 00 00
Credit to half a barrel that had the fish in 0 0 12 60
Noah tucker deptor for a par of sleave butens that a goot for sea tucker 0 0
Noah tucker deptor to macking of John manuen this is mock one Jacket and a par of breshes Comes to 0 7 60
deptor to one bushel of Endon Corn of me Comes to 0 0 2 00
deptor to one par of brishes for yourself Comes to 0 0 3 00
Jenewary the 15 1775 then recken and settled all our book acounts and than remained nothing due Reuben Champion
Noah tucker
mrs tucker deptor for doctering 0 0 4 00

Reuban and Lydia Duncan Champion account book, 1753–1777. Courtesy of Special Collections and Archives, University of Massachusetts Amherst (photograph by Thom Kendall).

Accounts in this ledger show debts due to the family for "doctoring," for agricultural products, and for the making of jackets and breeches.

Champion's work making and maintaining apparel. To the names of the men and women provided services by his household, Saybrook's Reuban Champion, like Solomon Wright, sometimes appended "debtor to us," signaling his own recognition that some of the income his family enjoyed was the result of his wife's time over her needle.[23]

Additional examples are legion. The nineteenth-century Hampshire County historian Sylvester Judd could record that Sarah King Clark was a gown maker in Northampton from at least "1757 to the revolution" because her husband, William, "charged the work in his book."[24] In the account book of the Northampton bricklayer Nathaniel Phelps, roughly one in every ten of the more than one hundred accounts for masonry work contain charges for work in clothing production by his wife, Catherine King Phelps. His account book was also in part hers, the value of her time and skill assessed and charged alongside and in the same manner as his.[25] In Williamsburg, Massachusetts, Submit Williams signed her name next to entries in her husband, Joseph's account book, recording her work making clothing for her neighbors and their hired hands.[26] The ledger kept by the Hadley, Massachusetts, ferryman Solomon Cooke, which spans the years 1790 to 1814, records goods and services offered by the Cooke household to households throughout Hadley, including agricultural products from cider to clover seed, time and energy spent carting goods, tending horses, and securing animal hides, and time and energy spent making and altering clothing. The volume records the contributions that both Solomon and his wife, Tryphena, made toward their household's maintenance, the needlework being hers. But some researchers have erroneously perceived Solomon Cooke to be a tailor on the basis of these entries—an all-too-common error, I suspect, that will persist until women's formal and informal work in the clothing trades is better understood.[27]

Examples like these abound, but historians have not yet fully grasped the shared nature of such accounts. Interestingly, Solomon Cooke has also been called an innkeeper based on the presence of an inn at his home on the north bend of the Connecticut River, when closer examination makes plain that the inn was kept by Cooke's mother-in-law, Elizabeth "Easter" Newton.[28] In other words, historians, distracted by artifacts of male prerogative in colonial society and influenced themselves by the (nineteenth—and twentieth-century) notion of men's role as "breadwinners," have assumed that the account book kept by Cooke reflects primarily his labor, and that the inn in which he lived must have been under his supervision as well; the documentary evidence recording the work of Lydia Champion, Tryphena Newton Cooke, and Elizabeth Fairchild Newton has been there all along but has been difficult to uncover in records attributed to their husbands, and, when found, has been overlooked, misunderstood, and misinterpreted amid tenacious mythologies that even scholars have had trouble casting aside. The novelist Toni Morrison, writing through fiction the histories of other communities even more silent in traditional historical sources, has called her work "literary archaeology," a phrase that has seemed to me resonant with this project as well, since I, as she, have looked to "sites of memory" in order "to see what remains were left behind and to reconstruct the images that these remains imply."[29] In account books like those of the Champions and Cookes, in letters describing the newest fashions, in journals recording work hired or completed, in workspaces that still dot the New England landscape, and in surviving garments made by women with a range of abilities are shards of evidence of early America's clothes makers waiting to be recognized, analyzed, and interpreted.

The sites of memory to which we travel largely lie in western New England, alongside the Connecticut River as it makes its 440-mile trip from the Canadian border to the Long Island Sound. Though we occasionally look in on men and women elsewhere in New England, our main concern is the

Connecticut River Valley, a geographical and cultural world of its own in western New England, possibly the wealthiest gathering of communities in the region, with its own distinctive patterns of trade, settlement, social intercourse, and cultural practice. Evidence of this distinction, particularly in the context of the region's visual culture, comes down to us in reminiscences and observations of the eighteenth century. The middling and laboring men of the Connecticut Valley, we learn, were identified by the blue-and white-checked everyday shirts that they most commonly wore. When Benjamin Tappan of Boston first attended Sunday meeting in Northampton, he was surprised to find that nearly every man in the room, with five or six exceptions, had one on. "The people of Worcester County wore white shirts," Sylvester Judd further observed, "and they said they could tell a Connecticut River Valley man by his checkered shirt." [30]

The eighteenth-century Connecticut Valley that produced these distinctive wardrobes encompassed more than seventy towns between Hanover, New Hampshire, and Saybrook, Connecticut. Though the Connecticut River flows from north to south, the families streaming into the valley in the seventeenth and eighteenth centuries generally flowed south to north, as men and women made their way from coastal Connecticut upriver to Wethersfield, Hartford, and Windsor, Connecticut, to Springfield, Northampton, and Hadley, Massachusetts, and finally up to Hinsdale, New Hampshire, Brattleboro, Vermont, and points north. River communities in Connecticut were gathered together into two counties: Hartford and Middlesex, constituted in 1666 and 1785, respectively. Settled by Europeans in the second quarter of the seventeenth century, the Connecticut River Valley communities had been thriving for well over a century before revolutionary discontent began to swirl; by 1790, enumerators of the first federal census counted fifty-eight thousand inhabitants living in those two counties. To the north, Massachusetts valley towns by the end of the eighteenth century were themselves well populated, with complex economies and political networks that remained all the while connected to their neighbors to the south. When incorporated in 1662, Hampshire County took in the whole of the Massachusetts portion of the river valley (including the present-day Hampden and Franklin Counties, which hived off in 1812 and 1811), as well as the Berkshires to the west, and encompassed three towns: Springfield, Northampton, and Hadley. In 1790, Hampshire County contained sixty thousand residents in two dozen thriving towns. In the still-more-northerly reaches of the valley, the "great river" formed the border between New Hampshire and Vermont. Settled in the eighteenth century as warfare among European and Native nations subsided, Vermont's river towns, too, drew men and women from settlements to

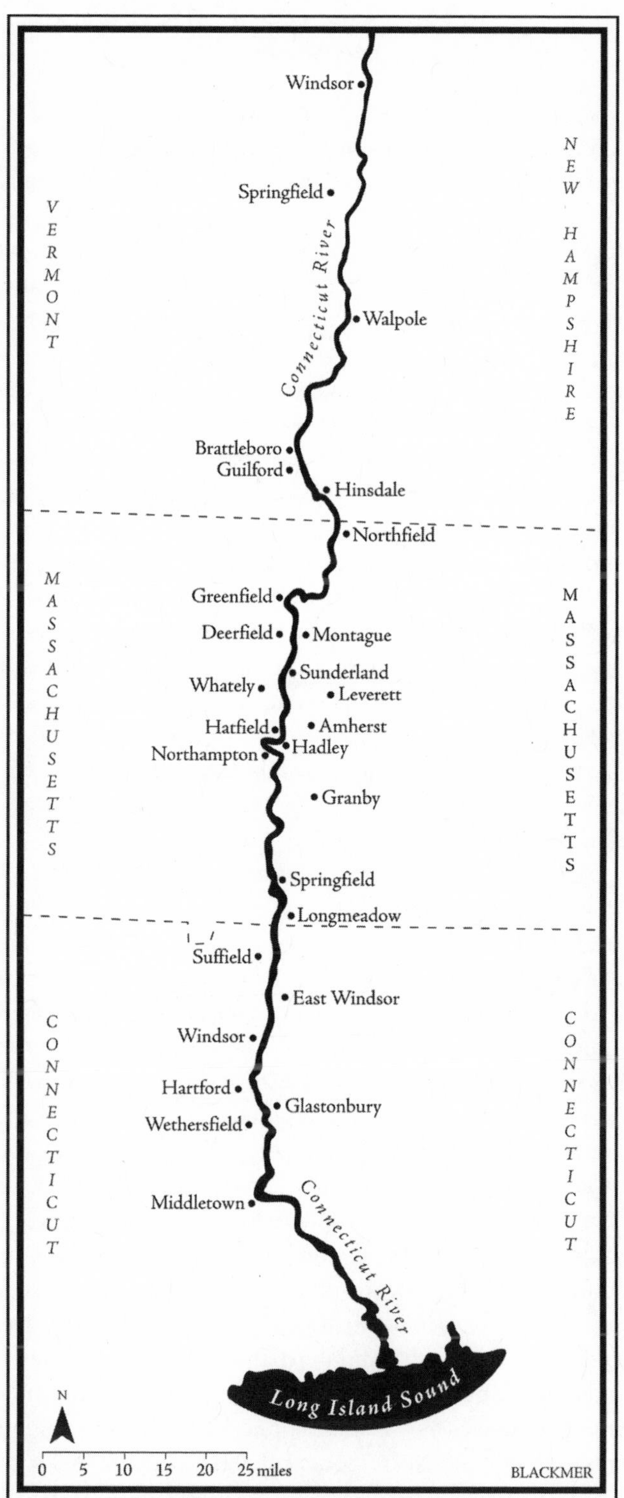

Map of the Connecticut River Valley. Kate Blackmer.

the south. Almost no European settlement had pushed beyond the Massachusetts border at the mid-eighteenth century, but following the conclusion of the French and Indian or Seven Years' War in 1763, European settlement boomed; by 1771 nearly two-thirds of the seventy-six hundred Vermonters, or about forty-seven hundred men and women, lived in the eastern half of the state, in settlements near or alongside the Connecticut, and most of those—almost four thousand—lived in river towns in the southeast corner of the state.[31]

Farming communities dominated the Connecticut Valley, thriving for centuries on the rich alluvial soil left behind as glacial meltwaters receded, leaving the fertile, easily tilled terraces that attracted early migrants.[32] As agriculture prospered, commerce flourished. Hartford and Middletown became large trading centers with an urban feel. In the 1760s, Joseph Haynes, visiting Hartford from Haverhill, Massachusetts, was greatly impressed by the "metroplous of Connecticut"; his view was shared by men and women from across the colony who looked to the capital as its most cosmopolitan community.[33] By 1770, fifteen schooners docked at Middletown; not twenty years later, George Washington would observe that Middletown, Hartford, and Wethersfield each had twenty ships at port.[34] In 1784, the Connecticut legislature granted city charters to Hartford and Middletown, together with New Haven, New London, and Norwich.[35] In 1790, forty-two Hartford stores offered a vast array of goods.[36]

Commercial sheen as well as geographical imperatives may in part account for subtle differences that separated the valley-dwellers of Massachusetts from their Connecticut counterparts. To be sure, inhabitants of Massachusetts and Connecticut up and down the river were linked by the easy geography of the river; they married one another, traded together, and shared slaves and servants, forging a larger, regional community bound together by kin and commerce. But residents of the southern state looked southward to New York for cultural inspiration, while their counterparts in Massachusetts (and to some degree Vermont as well, though Vermonters had other loyalties, too) felt the pull of Boston's commerce and culture. The gravitational force of those urban centers affected the aesthetic atmosphere of valley towns. With their state government in Hartford, men and women of Connecticut's river valley were closely attuned to the social world that swirled around centers of political power; the influence of election balls and society life reached much more deeply into the populace than it did in rural western Massachusetts—a good two days' ride from Boston—where other sources of authority proved more enduring and persuasive. As a result, Connecticut's citizens sometimes perceived themselves as more cosmopolitan than their neighbors to the north;

after a visit to Hadley, Sarah Pitkin of East Hartford grumbled about "passing so much time with Massachusetts ministers and their ministerial families" and was relieved to return home for a festive season around the capital.[37]

The chronological focus of this study is the period between the Seven Years' War and Thomas Jefferson's embargo, decades that witnessed extraordinary changes in New England's society and economy. The naturalist Stephen Jay Gould writes elegantly about cultural preoccupations with points of origin, our abiding preference for revolution over evolution.[38] We want to identify unambiguous beginnings, Gould suggests, and we want to so badly that we will do so in the face of overwhelming evidence of steady change, and great continuities. Historical scholarship is not immune from similar preoccupations: we talk about industrial, industrious, political, consumer, and market "revolutions" reshaping the eighteenth-century Atlantic world when the phenomena described unfolded over generations, if not centuries, and are riddled with ambiguities. The pace of change in every case was uneven, accelerating and retreating, advancing in fits and starts, reaching different segments of the population at different times and in different places. Indeed, it is difficult to retain these metaphors of revolution at all when continuing study has so thoroughly qualified any meaningful points of demarcation.[39]

Nevertheless, I have called this book *Women and Work in the Age of Revolution,* for the women and men whose lives are traced in these pages indeed witnessed extraordinary changes over the course of their lives, changes in their society, economy, government, and culture that they themselves perceived as dramatic, remarkable, revolutionary. The period of study chosen here encompasses change between two moments that saw acceleration and retreat in the clothing trades, from the expansion of women's participation in clothing production that attended the Seven Years' War and its aftermath to the pause in fashion during the early nineteenth century when the embargo acts squelched significant change in stylish apparel for nearly a decade. The war that followed would reconfigure American commerce and, along the way, prove an enormous catalyst for the development of ready-made clothing in the United States.

To explore the world of female artisanry before industrialization, this study examines the clothing trades as a source of employment for early American women. In undertaking such an exploration, it is important to remember that occupational titles are inexact and not entirely helpful, given the fluidities of skill that enabled women to practice a variety of tasks, movement in and out of wage work, and intraregional variation. But, generally speaking, what we understand today to be the work of a "seamstress" (the production and maintenance of comparatively simple garments) in the eighteenth-century Connecticut Valley was performed by women most often called "tailoresses." Tailors (that is, artisans who had the particular skills necessary to produce formal, fitted clothing primarily for men) were generally men, though women of equivalent skill were likewise called "tailors"; the feminine suffix, in the eighteenth-century Connecticut Valley, appears to have signaled a level of skill rather than the gender of the artisan. The period term for artisans who constructed gowns for women was generally "mantua maker," which referred to a particular style of garment once closely associated with silk from the Italian city of Mantua, though women in New England's rural communities seemed to prefer the more general term "gown maker." The work of milliners and mantua makers has always been closely connected, and women highly skilled in needlework regularly moved between the two occupations. This study is interested in women's work constructing clothing, and so observes women at work in that craft, but milliners, whose efforts were more closely concentrated on trimmings and accoutrements, were certainly important contributors to that process, especially in those years when trim and accessories were particularly crucial to a smart appearance.[40]

The book is arranged in three parts. Part I surveys the separate but intertwining worlds of clothing consumption and production in New England from the mid-eighteenth century to the eve of industrialization in the garment trades. Chapter One examines the Connecticut Valley wardrobes, their role in constructing identities, and the ways in which fashion operated to constrict and facilitate men and women's abilities to create public personas. Chapter Two then turns to the organization of the clothing trades themselves, the acquisition of skill, rhythms of work, construction methods, and other technical aspects of clothing construction. Here I show how clothing production, whether practiced by men or by women, compares to other artisanal crafts, in order to begin to sketch out the ways in which women's participation in this work both conformed to and departed from patterns observed among artisans more generally. This discussion raises questions about the way historians have thought about early American artisanry and suggests some alternative approaches that may better accommodate the full range of early American crafts.

Part II investigates more closely the array of occupations within the needle trades, from plain sewing to tailoring to gown making, and looks also at the ornamental needlework elite women, as members of the region's gentry, were obliged to complete. Because the social relations of women's work are best explored at the local level, each chapter here brings into focus the life of particular needlewomen who worked in and around a single community in the heart of the Connecticut Valley: Hadley, Massachusetts, a thriving agricultural village nestled in a bend in the river about halfway between the Connecticut and Vermont borders. The principal focus here is on six women, all of European descent, members of the Congregational Church, and more or less of a shared generation, who sustained a particular set of relationships surrounding the production and consumption of clothing. Rural women like these have hitherto been largely perceived as a fairly uniform population, their lives far more alike than they were different. But a truly attentive examination of their distinct yet overlapping worlds reveals how remarkably diverse, complex, and riddled with power relationships those communities were, how much access to skill, relative economic advantage, marriage and family, and other aspects of everyday life positioned women in relationship to one another, enlarging and limiting opportunities, shaping the trajectories of days, years, and lifetimes in ways both large and small. At the same time, each woman opens a window onto larger transformations in the economy and society, allowing us to consider the nature of the expanding market for needle skills, the family economy, and shifting gender divisions of labor at both close and wide range.

The survival of two extraordinary sources, together with unusually well preserved documentary and artifactual records in local historical societies and archives, permits such an investigation. Most important may be the memorandum book of the Hadley gentlewoman Elizabeth Porter Phelps.[41] Each week, from the year she turned sixteen until she died in 1817 at the age of seventy, Phelps sat down to record activities carried out on her large farm. She reported the numbers of hired men fed and the weight of candles dipped; she recorded the names of the women for whom she had quilted, and the names of those who had quilted for her. She noted the comings and goings of hired women who came for the week or the month or for years, as well of the arrivals and departures of needlewomen, whose tenures, generally two or three days, were shorter. Phelps also maintained through many of those same years a steady correspondence with her husband, her son, and her daughters, much of which is extant. Nearly three hundred references to needlework are found in Phelps's diary and letters, recording the services of some thirty needlewomen.

The notebooks of Sylvester Judd, the editor of the *Hampshire Gazette* and an avid local historian in the second quarter of the nineteenth century, provide the second important source. Fifty-six volumes filled with Judd's research—sometimes three and four hundred pages thickly filled with crabbed handwriting—on everyday life in colonial Massachusetts and Connecticut can be found at the Forbes Library in Northampton. While the histories that Judd wrote as a result of his researches are certainly colored by the preoccupations of his time, his transcriptions from early Northampton documents, including several account books, some of which are no longer extant, have preserved a significant body of evidence concerning trade practices in his community. Moreover, Judd's interviews with local men and women capture invaluable perceptions of post-revolutionary western Massachusetts. Though the recollections recorded in these interviews must be approached with the same cautions one would bring to oral histories taken in any era, they are nevertheless precious avenues of insight into beliefs, values, and behaviors of the day.[42]

Women in Hadley, as in other towns throughout New England, recognized certain tasks as the province of their gender, but the means by which they accomplished them varied widely and brought very different kinds of women into relationships that reflected and perpetuated those differences even as it drew them together into close, even intimate, social and economic relationships. Relative degrees of wealth as well as preference and inclination governed which labors women themselves performed and which they hired out to others. Elizabeth Porter Phelps, for example, preferred her dairy over her workbasket, employing local women to do the household's sewing and mending or saving something for her visiting daughter to complete. Her daughter preferred to do her own sewing and to hire women to perform other household chores. Though Phelps remained responsible for the cooking, cleaning, and clothing in her household, she did not herself perform all, or even most, of this labor all of the time. Like other female members of the county's leading families, she "used sometimes to work in the forenoon and dress up in the afternoon."[43]

To "dress up in the afternoon" invoked the labors of a whole range of women, from the hired help who made leisured afternoons possible to the skilled local women who cut and constructed those garments that were themselves signs of wealth, leisure, and privilege. Examining the different ways women worked (what they made, what skills and practices they used, who they worked for, and how that work was organized) allows us to explore hierarchy and power amid collaboration and cooperation within rural families as well as the communities they inhabited. Neighborhoods like those shared by the women of Hadley tend to be "treated peripherally in relation to such categories as class, ethnicity, and gender," if not "ignored entirely."[44] But neighborhoods in early America were not simply collections of people who lived near one another; they were the basis for economic and social exchange, the vehicle though which one's day-to-day life was organized, and a means by which men and women came to understand their place in larger social, economic, and political orders. As such, neighborhoods and the communities they sustained are best understood not simply as places but as a dynamic process through which values, perceptions, and relationships were continually maintained, reinvented, and transformed.[45]

Hadley, like most rural towns of the eighteenth century, was a constellation of neighborhoods. The 110 families (roughly 600 residents) who comprised the community in 1770 thought of themselves in terms of the neighborhood they lived in, from the mills to the north of the village center to Hartsbrook and Hockanum to the south.[46] The women who populate the pages that follow by and large circulated within two of Hadley's neighborhoods—the town center and the northern mill village—with the Phelps household, located about halfway between those two centers of gravity, moving within the orbit of each. Thinking of neighborhoods as process rather than place suits the ways that the families within them understood their relationships to one another and complements another historian's suggestion that we think of cross-class exchanges in early America, too, as processes—as moments in an ongoing negotiation over power, "a seemingly incessant, if often implicit, effort to redefine the conditions of their lives."[47] The women of Hadley worked every day alongside other women whose lives, choices, and opportunities shaped or were shaped by their own. At times their interests converged, and at times they conflicted. Clothing production and consumption brought women together in exchanges that could be mutually beneficial or asymmetrically advantageous. Sometimes the nature of the exchange is apparent, and sometimes it is obscure, traced in hidden transcripts perceived but unrecorded as participants assigned their own meanings to the exchange.[48] But those moments of intersection reveal how gender, class, skill, and life cycle influenced relationships among early American women.

The women we meet here—Elizabeth Porter Phelps, Easter Fairchild Newton and Tryphena Newton Cooke, Catherine Phelps Parsons, Rebecca Dickinson, and Tabitha Clark Smith—belonged to the same neighborhoods. They were in many ways alike: all fourth—or fifth-generation New Englanders, white, of English descent, and members of the Congregational Church. Their lives overlapped with and intersected one another. They took tea together and joined one another's families in times of both sorrow and celebration. They shopped at the same stores. They knew the same people. Newton, Cooke, Parsons, Dickinson, and Smith recognized one another as fellow practitioners within a common craft community. Parsons was Phelps's aunt by marriage, while the Newtons, Cookes, and Smiths were longtime neighbors at the north end of the Hadley Common. But, at the same time, their lives were very different. At times, the things that divided them were subtle: some were well acquainted with distant horizons, and others were not; some sported the newest calicos, others did not. Deeper divisions separated them as well. These women stood in dramatically different positions, for example, to the local and regional economies. They recognized wide gaps in education. They had mastered different skills and had obtained the same skills to varying degrees. Marriage and family, too, brought very divergent experiences.

These differences have themselves determined the very ways in which we can know about them at all. Elizabeth Porter Phelps left a sixty-year log of her household activities as well as a vast correspondence, preserved by descendents whose sense of family heritage was so strong that they would eventually found a historic house museum. Rebecca Dickinson can be known only through the pages of a long, painful, and pensive journal, preserved not with purpose but by chance, discovered nearly a century after her death, tucked away in an attic. Both women leave small samples of their needlework as well, but only their ornamental work was deemed worthy of historical interest: of the many gowns Dickinson made during her lifetime, not one is known to survive, but several examples of crewelwork designed to ornament her home do. Tryphena Newton Cooke appears never to have learned to write. She is known almost entirely through notations left by others—Elizabeth Porter Phelps, in her memorandum book, and Solomon Cooke, in the family's accounts—though two works of her own hand, objects lovingly made for her own children, were preserved by her family, along with stories about her passed down through generations. Easter Fairchild Newton's work is recorded mostly in Phelps's papers as well as public documents, such as the annual tavern licenses granted by selectmen. Catherine Phelps Parsons is still more elusive, known only through transcriptions of her family's accounts made in the early nineteenth century and interviews then taken with family and neighbors. Tabitha Clark Smith is the most obscure, captured largely in Phelps's record and a handful of scattered records.

Chapter Three introduces Elizabeth Porter Phelps and the ways in which needlework and needlewomen helped define relationships within her community. A farmwife and gentlewoman who tackled the everyday mending her household required while completing ornamental projects as well, Phelps was more often the employer and coordinator of the work of others, from her mother and daughters to servants in the household to local women hired to sew to skilled artisans engaged to complete more complex tasks. Phelps's farm provides an ideal environment in which to explore complex and overlapping categories of work, and complex and overlapping social and economic relationships among women. This chapter looks at ornamental needlework and a form of clothing production closely associated with the rural gentry: the creation of elaborately quilted petticoats. Here, the laborers in question are Phelps and her elite peers whose refined needlework helped sustain networks of political, social, and economic leadership among the gentry class and shape relationships between these gentlewomen and other women around them whose lives looked very different.

Chapter Four explores the ways women participated informally in the clothing trades through the work of the Hadley tailoresses Easter Fairchild Newton and her daughter Tryphena Newton Cooke, who sewed and repaired everyday clothing for families throughout their community. Their work sheds light on the opportunities women with skill, but not necessarily formal training, might find in clothing repair, construction, and maintenance and how that work bound families across economies based on the exchange of goods and skills. Such women created the expansion of household production observed by historians of eighteenth-century economies on both sides of the Atlantic.

Chapter Five turns to the production of clothing by women for women, and relationships between family life and craftwork. Surviving accounts from three generations of craftswomen in Northampton, Massachusetts, working between about 1730 and 1805—Catherine King Phelps, Sarah King Clark, and Esther Wright—illuminate a wholly female world of clients and consumers, while at the same time providing insight into the family economy as it functioned in eighteenth-century western Massachusetts. Here we examine also some of the ways in which craft skill intersected with marriage and family, through the lives of two craftswomen, Rebecca Dickinson and Tabitha Clark Smith. Smith successfully combined skilled artisanal needlework with the raising of a family, while for Dickinson, the acquisition of craft skill enabled her to remain single.

Next we consider Catherine Phelps Parsons, a skilled tailor who, with the help of a constant staff of several female assistants, made, repaired, and altered both everyday and formal clothing for men in eighteenth-century Hadley and Northampton. She was the daughter of Catherine King Phelps, a gown maker, and Nathaniel Phelps, a bricklayer—and the aunt of Charles Phelps, Elizabeth's husband. Her career in the creation of men's clothing facilitates a side-by-side comparison of women's and men's experiences in artisanal clothing production. Examining the making of men's apparel from her perspective helps place female artisans within larger spheres of craft activity in eighteenth-century New England.

Part III suggests some larger contexts of these activities, what they might tell us about the history of the consumer and industrial revolutions on this side of the Atlantic, and perhaps most important, what they might suggest about the way we think about needlework and needlewomen today. Chapter Seven charts the social and economic changes that rocked New England in the decades following the American Revolution. Here, we revisit these women and others like them and examine their lives from a different perspective, exploring how they fared as regional labor and capital markets emerged and flourished in late-eighteenth- and early-nineteenth-century Massachusetts.

The conclusion brings this consideration through the nineteenth and into the twentieth century, surveying changes in the clothing trades as well as colonial revivals in an effort to understand how the largest occupation open to women in early America has so receded from our collective view. The careers of various mythologies of early American housewifery would make for a very good book in and of itself, since the project of venerating colonial womanhood began almost as the imperial ties were thrown off. As early as the 1820s, nostalgia for the heroism of the revolutionary generation prompted Sylvester Judd to launch his researches; his feeling that the present generation of women paled in comparison to their forebears raised questions for him about the women of colonial and revolutionary Massachusetts. I choose to emphasize the parts of the story that unfolded in the last half of the nineteenth century not because they were necessarily most important in its trajectory but because those decades, particularly following the Centennial, witnessed especially vigorous efforts to remember early American women and their needlework in particular ways. Contemplating that era, if briefly, is important, because it helps us understand how such a thriving world of enterprise became so thoroughly lost to historical vision, and because it reminds us of the consequences such elisions have for contemporary American life.

Taken as a whole, this book argues that New England women in the late-eighteenth and early-nineteenth centuries participated in craftwork in ways that both mirrored and departed from the artisanal culture of their husbands and sons, revealing how the concept of artisanry as it is frequently employed often conceals more that it reveals. Along the way, this discussion also adds to a growing body of literature that suggests ways in which clothing production was already changing long before the technological and organizational developments associated with industrialization appeared on anyone's horizon, prompting and responding to larger developments in the always-shifting constructions of gendered divisions of labor. These pages also seek to probe the complex landscapes of skill and power that shaped the social relations of early American women's work, to calibrate more carefully relationships that both brought women together, and set them apart.

Part I

CHAPTER 1

Clothing and Consumers in Rural New England, 1760–1810

WHITE APRONS. When Catherine Graves was asked to recall her eighteenth-century Northampton girlhood, what she remembered most vividly were white aprons. Interviewed by the local historian Sylvester Judd in the second quarter of the nineteenth century, Graves noted that, in the 1760s and 1770s, only a handful of women had had white aprons to wear when they went out visiting; the rest wore the blue and white checked aprons ubiquitous in the Connecticut Valley. Sixty years removed, she was still able to list the families along South Street whose daughters wore white aprons.[1]

Recollections like Graves's remind us of the importance of clothing in eighteenth-century America. The white aprons worn by Anna, Rachel, and Lucinda Barnard and other young women on South Street lingered in Graves's memory because, at the time, they were important markers by which men and women—and children, too—measured their position and the position of others. In the last half of the eighteenth century, white and checked aprons, together with patterned and plain fabrics, fitted coats, imported textiles, and other elements of early American wardrobes, helped people assert and assess their place in society.[2]

"Purse and Apparel": Clothing and Its Meanings in Early New England

From the beginning of European settlement through the early national period, New England wardrobes, first, were assets. Josiah Pierce, a schoolteacher in Hadley, Massachusetts, for example, gave his hired woman, when she completed her term of service, £11 as well as "£12 O.T. [Old Tenor] in cloathing, the whole of her wages being £23 O.T."[3] Clothing also could be converted to cash to pay a debt. At auction houses, taverns, and other public places, vendue sales regularly offered clothing along with other items being sold to raise funds. When Sophia Arms died in Suffield, Connecticut, her

White apron, 1780–1800. Courtesy of the Pocumtuck Valley Memorial Association, Memorial Hall Museum, Deerfield, Mass. (photograph by Amanda Merullo).

White aprons were intended to be decorative rather than functional in the eighteenth century. Earlier in the eighteenth century aprons were vehicles on which women could display their skills in embroidery, stitching colorful floral patterns across silk backgrounds; later in the century, however, preference shifted to linen aprons embroidered with white linen threads. White aprons remained in fashion until the turn of the nineteenth century, when the empire style eliminated the natural waistline, making the apron an awkward accessory. Their decline in fashionability may also reflect changing attitudes toward women's housework in this period, as middle-class white women were increasingly inclined to demonstrate their refinement rather than their industry.

Checked apron, 1800–1840. Courtesy of the Pocumtuck Valley Memorial Association, Memorial Hall Museum, Deerfield, Mass. (photograph by Amanda Merullo).

Blue and white checked linen like that used in this apron, spun and dyed by Judith Allen Bardwell (1777–1849) of Deerfield, was a common feature of everyday life in the eighteenth-century Connecticut Valley. Men's everyday shirts made from comparable material were so closely associated with the Connecticut Valley that observers could recognize a man from this New England region by the fabric. The highly serviceable checked cloth was also popular for boy's shirts, bed and window curtains, towels, and women's aprons.

worldly goods were auctioned to offset the cost of her illness and funeral; 114 items of clothing were distributed among more than thirty of her neighbors.[4] When Elizabeth Porter Phelps of Hadley, Massachusetts, "Drank tea at Major Williamses," she reported to her diary that he was "not well—has had all his Furniture and most of the family cloaths taken for Debt and sold at Vendue."[5] The prominent military and political leader had fallen on hard times; as a result, the rich garments that had once announced his family's particular success were scattered among households throughout the county.

Vendue sales had distinct advantages for buyers, who were able to obtain high-quality clothing at prices more in keeping with their usual means. As a Middletown, Connecticut, seller whimsically noted regarding an upcoming sale, "Preserve then your cash if you'd live at your ease / at less than prime cost you may buy what you please. . . . To buy goods at half price at public Vendue / A fortune believe me will quickly ensue."[6] In the 1780s, the property of Philemon Stacey of Halifax, Vermont, was disposed of for 60 to 75 percent of its appraised value, a striped linen coat and jacket that assessors valued at £4 selling for £3, a gauze hood valued at 10 shillings selling for just 6 shillings.[7] Residents of Guildhall, Vermont, who attended the 1805 sale of John Lamson's goods watched as his "pair of new boots" appraised at $4.00 sold for $3.00, and a gingham coat assessed at $1.25 sold for one-fifth the value.[8] Vendue sales allowed sellers to raise funds quickly, while affording buyers the opportunity to obtain, ready-made, articles of apparel that might otherwise have been beyond their reach.

Bequests of apparel also demonstrate that clothing was among the valuable assets that women, in particular, could pass on. Eighteenth-century women's wills are filled with references to "best," "second-best," and otherwise enumerated gowns passed to daughters and granddaughters, sisters, sisters-in-law, and nieces. Weeks, months, and even years before their deaths, women gave careful thought to the eventual distribution of their wardrobes, wishes that were later implemented by their female family members and friends. When Mary Sedgewick of Hartford wrote her will, she anticipated one of her daughter's more immediate needs, bequeathing her own crape mourning frock, as well as a black quilted petticoat and a green riding hood. Her blue cloak went to another daughter, while her granddaughter received her "silk hood, and a paire of silk gloves."[9] In Hadley, Elizabeth Phelps routinely participated in the process of moving apparel from one generation to the next. She spent one Saturday afternoon in February 1791 "at the Generals with Mrs Hop and Judge Porters wife to help divide Mrs Porters cloathes." The day after Abigail Porter's funeral, the decedent's closest friends and relatives—Susanna Porter, Phelps, and Margaret Hopkins—gathered to divide her wardrobe among survivors. On another occasion, following the death of her sister-in-law Dolly Warner, Phelps once again, together with her friend and neighbor Esther Dickinson, "went up to divide her cloathes."[10]

Wills also contained many references to fine and everyday clothing that was passed from master or mistress to servants. Elizabeth Gunn of Montague, Massachusetts, for example, bequeathed her "every day cloths, linen and woolen" to her servants "Jana and Chloe." Rebeckah Ashley of Westfield, Massachusetts, willed her "Negro Zilpah" a feather bed and under bed, four bed blankets, all the linen and woolen sheets (except for one new woolen sheet), a silk crape gown, a black short cloak, and a "flesh-colour'd" camblet riding hood. In Wethersfield, Connecticut, when Katherine Russell willed her "Negro Woman" Chloe Prutt her freedom, she also gave her some household items "and my every Day wearing apperel and a Red Short Cloak."[11] While women like Zilpah, Jana, Chloe, and Chloe Prutt may have relished the opportunity to don the clothing of their "betters," much of this clothing may well have found its way to the second-hand trade, as the recipients converted their bequest to cash.[12]

Rewards commonly posted in the pages of a local press to retrieve lost articles of clothing also attest to the value of apparel, suggesting that it was worth both the price of the advertisement and the expense of a reward to avoid spending the time, labor, and money to replace lost items. When J. Halsey lost his brown camblet coat lined with green baize along the road between the Bolton Meetinghouse and Clark's tavern in Lebanon, he offered a reward for it in the pages of the *Connecticut Courant.*[13] In January 1792, a traveler who had "lost . . . a light coloured calico GOWN, one lawn handkerchief, and Bosom piece all Women's wear, and all tied up in a red spotted handkerchief" promised that its return would be "handsomely rewarded."[14]

Second-hand clothing circulated through both legal and extralegal channels, the constant theft of clothing further attesting to its value. Calvin Tilden turned to the pages of the *Connecticut Courant* to recover two new pairs of leather breeches, as well as a pair of white cotton stockings, a linen vest, a checked linen shirt, and other articles stolen, he charged," by James Shephard.[15] Jim, a twenty-seven-year-old African who escaped from the Westfield home of John Atwater, took so many articles that his probable appearance was hard to describe. "Tis uncertain what clothes he will wear," Atwater noted in an advertisement seeking his recovery, indicating that he "carried with him a loose coat of a butternut color with a little mixture of white, and a red plush cape, a dark brown broadcloth vest, a short blue broadcloth coat, a striped vest, a homemade butternut colored vest, a good pair of buckskin breeches, a pair of blue broadcloth breeches, a pair linen breeches, a white Holland shirt, a homespun check shirt, a brown coat, a pair brown tow cloth trowsers," and other articles.[16]

In an era dominated by political, cultural, and social upheaval, clothing also served critical public purposes. Textile production, historians have long acknowledged, drew women into the revolutionary effort, but comparatively less attention has been paid to clothing production and consumption as the products of a politics of style.[17] Among the most well-known examples is the suit of American-made wool that George Washington wore to his 1789 inauguration, produced by the newly established (and short-lived) Hartford Woolen Manufactory. Men and women throughout the new republic used clothing to assert their politics. Women of the Connecticut Valley participated fully in the boycotts organized during the imperial crisis, as well as the international political and economic maneuverings that attended independence.

After the war ended, women remained conscious of the political implications of their sartorial choices. In November 1786, more than one hundred women in Hartford, responding to the postwar economic depression and the tension swelling to the north as Massachusetts coped with Shays's Rebellion, expressed their patriotic zeal by forming an "Economical Association."[18] "Taking into serious consideration the unhappy situation of their county, and being fully sensible that our calamities are in great measure occasioned by the luxury and extravagance of individuals," the founders expressed the hope that "those Ladies that used to excel in dress . . . will endeavor to set the best examples, by laying aside their richest silks and superfluous decorations, and as far as possible, distinguish themselves by their perfect indifference to those ornaments and superfluities which in happier times might become them." The resolutions reflected the signers' sense of themselves as participants in an international network of clothing makers and consumers. They observed that "the English and French fashions, which require the manufacture of an infinite variety of gewgaws and frippery, may be highly beneficial and even necessary in the countries where those articles are made; as they furnish employment and subsistence for poor people." But, though sympathetic these individuals, they also recognized larger and more sinister interests at work; "foreign nations," they stated, were anxious to "introduce their fashions into this country, as they thus make a market for their useless manufactures, and enrich themselves at our expense. . . . Our implicit submission to the fashions of other counties is highly derogatory to the reputation of Americans, as it renders us dependent on the interest, or caprice, of foreigners, both for taste and manners; it prevents the exercise of our own ingenuity, and makes us the slaves of milliners and mantuamakers in London or Paris." For the next seven months, the women said, they would refrain from purchasing "gauze, ribbons, flowers, feathers, lace and other trimmings and frippery, designed merely as ornaments." They would reduce new purchases for weddings and mourning, eliminate purchases of new materials for routine visiting, and buy domestic rather than imported goods whenever possible. In sum, they vowed to dress simply, to limit occasions that called for fashionable excess, and to "use [their] influence to diffuse and attention to industry and frugality, and to render these virtues reputable and permanent."[19]

The Hartford Association's success is impossible to gauge—perhaps this was the year that one of the Trumbull girls famously wore the same, plain muslin dress all season long, to great local acclaim for her simplicity—and bravery.[20] Whether the signers abstained from unnecessary purchases is unknown, but their awareness of the political and economic impact of ephemeral style is striking. These women recognized the complex ways in which the lives and livelihoods of working women across the Atlantic were affected by sartorial choices exercised in western New England. On one hand, through the consumption of new goods, they furnished "employment and subsistence for poor people" in other parts of the Atlantic world; on the other hand, strict allegiance to international style made them "slaves of milliners and mantuamakers in London or Paris." Americans had articulated their need to sever colonial ties in a similar vein, unwilling to submit to political "slavery"; now the wives and daughters of the very men who guided Connecticut's role in that revolution chose parallel language to describe their own fears about the place they occupied in international economies of fashion. The Hartford declaration, which notes the ability of "foreign nations to introduce their fashions into this country . . . and enrich themselves at our expense," also points up the signers' cognizance of their own place in global economies of style, the importance of which cannot be underestimated, for the styles popular in revolutionary-era France and England came to revolutionize the clothing trades in the fledgling United States.

Refusing to capitulate to fashion's demands could be as significant as meeting them. Ministers, for example, were often noted for their sartorial *retardataire.* A striking number of nineteenth-century reminiscences record that the town's minister continued to wear breeches long after they had gone out of style, a conservatism befitting the gravity of the minister's position. In Hadley, the Reverend Samuel Hopkins wore breeches until his death in 1809, while in Stoneham, Massachusetts, the Reverend John Stevens was still hiring the tailor Polly Wiley to make breeches into the late eighteen-teens, long after his neighbors had switched to pantaloons.[21] Toward the close of the eighteenth century, some members of the New England elite found advantage in distancing themselves from the latest fashions. In Middletown, Connecticut, for example, gentlewoman Hannah Gilbert Wright posed for her 1792 portrait in large-scale floral silk that was long out of fashion; viewers, however, certainly recognized the high-quality English silk as an expensive and desirable material and with it, Wright was able to assert the appropriate, conservative appearance for a woman of her age and station.[22]

But members of the community without a comparable station to assert or protect remained anxious to maintain a fashionable appearance. In 1796, Thomas Dwight's letters home to Springfield from Boston suggest the imperative of acquiring the new styles.

> Miss Gorham and Miss Parks were as I suppose dressed *a la mode*—no waists, for these are not fashionable—a proper display of the neck with some transparent coverings over the &c &c brings you fairly to the *apron string*—it is a lamentable consideration that the sex have lost so important a part of their bodies, but it cannot be helped for fashion like Robertspierre [*sic*] & Marat deals havoc & destruction without ever assigning a reason to any tribunal.[23]

Dwight's letter captures the arrival of the so-called empire style to the Connecticut River Valley. A letter written by David Selden Jr. of Chatham, Connecticut, a few years later observes the subsequent entrance of the simple white fabrics that came to accompany the new style. Selden, visiting New York, had been asked to send home gingham but soon learned that gingham was "quite unfashionable"; he suggested that his female readers should avoid calico, too, "white muslin dresses" being "much more worn here than any other at present."[24] Thus the fad for white so closely associated with the early National period made its way from metropolitan centers to central Connecticut. Political events abroad had nurtured new styles that, when transplanted to the receptive American soil, created a transformation in fashion that would have groundbreaking implications for the needlewomen of Federal New England.

Although clothing carried critical political messages, it had more prosaic meanings as well, helping to situate men and women along social and economic continuums. The ways and degree to which that was possible were shifting toward the end of the eighteenth-century, as men and women of the new republic struggled to forge a new social order, some working to preserve long-standing class distinctions while others sought to subvert them. The circulation of clothing among slaves, servants, and members of the laboring and even middling classes complicated the legibility of a person's appearance, since people could readily acquire the visual trappings of a station to which they did not belong. Whether or not Major Williams's family found it galling to encounter their "familys cloaths" on the backs of inferiors after their wardrobe was sold at vendue, many did object to sartorial chicanery. In an economic culture in which one's credit was assessed by reputation and appearance, the ability to gauge accurately the prosperity of others was critically important.[25] The quantity and the quality of a person's apparel communicated volumes to any and all observers: strangers and friends, superiors and subordinates, debtors and creditors.

Ample evidence reveals how articles of clothing indicated membership in various social or economic groups. Men in shapeless shirts or loose frocks were instantly identified as tradesmen or laborers, for example, while a ruffle at the sleeve indicated the relative leisure of a gentleman.[26] Clothing provided identifying features just as did less ephemeral qualities of height, build, and complexion. When Dick, a "Negro Man," ran away from Abel Tillotson, Tillotson placed an advertisement seeking his apprehension and return. Describing the runaway, Tillotson reported only that he was about five feet tall; the remainder of the notice lists what he was wearing: a frock (a loose-fitting, long, shirt-like garment suitable for work), an old brown coat, an old felt hat with a leather strap around the crown, a pair of towcloth trousers, and some double-soled shoes. For observers who might help identify him, apparel was more important than physiology.[27]

Clothing, then, was among the most important means by which men and women in early New England understood how to interact with the people they encountered every day on city streets and country lanes. Reminiscing about early Northampton, Lewis Tappan recounted a handful of anecdotes that his father, Benjamin Tappan, had been fond of telling; interestingly, the subject of several of these is the different ways in which appearance could create, or counterfeit, identity. When Tappan, a young goldsmith, first moved from Boston to Northampton, he carried a letter of introduction to one of the community's leading citizens, Major Joseph Hawley. Tappan arrived at the Hawley home and raised "the ponderous iron knocker." "The door was soon opened by a man in a checked shirt and wearing a leather apron. . . . 'Is Major Hawley at home?' asked the young goldsmith. 'Yes, I am called Major Hawley,' the esteemed politician replied." Hawley was not recognized because he failed to appear in the garb of a gentleman.[28]

The startled Tappan regained his composure and proceeded with his business, but he had learned an important lesson about local culture and about the role of clothing in it. Despite Hawley's eminence as a Harvard-educated attorney, officer, and political figure, he nevertheless recognized the value of restraint. He did not flaunt his status in the cuffs and ruffles of, say, the

Boston silversmith Paul Revere; his wardrobe permitted him to signal, when necessary and appropriate, commonalities with his Northampton neighbors (in this case, the checked shirts associated with men of the Connecticut Valley), and, when necessary and appropriate, the distinctions from them that merited his authority. In Boston, Tappan too had worn "white shirts of course." But in eighteenth-century Hampshire County, he soon learned, "there were five or six men in Northampton who wore white shirts," and "they were persons who had been educated at some college." Lacking such an education, Tappan was reluctant to violate local convention. Upon "learning the custom" of his new community, and "thinking it wrong for a mechanic to ape the aristocracy of the place, [he] procured checked shirts."[29] Joseph Hawley might wear the blue-and-white-checked shirt common throughout the Connecticut Valley as he went about his daily business, but his Harvard education meant that on Sunday morning he was surely among those five or six men in white shirts. For Tappan, his own white shirts would have to lie waiting in a chest for return trips to Boston.[30]

Pressure to comply with the dictates of fashion became increasingly intense in the decades following the American Revolution. As the eighteenth century gave way to the nineteenth, consumers found themselves succumbing to fashion's demands. In 1799, one of the Heath sisters of Brookline, Massachusetts, confessed in a letter to her mother that she had, in the heat of the moment, mistakenly purchased a trendy van dyke, adding "I don't like it very well, have been almost sorry I bought it since, because I could have done without it, but I thought I must get something to make me look smart."[31] But even twenty years earlier, the pressure had begun to mount for some members of society. Young Anna Green (later Winslow), visiting Boston in the 1770s with a limited, and as it turned out, at times inappropriate wardrobe, also knew the power of clothing to communicate identity. Writing to her mother in Maine, Green expressed her horror at the prospect of having to wear her "black hatt with the red Dominie" (a hooded loose coat), for, she exclaimed, "the people will ask me what I have got to sell as I go along the street if I do, or how the folks at New guinie do?"[32] The young woman believed (or hoped her mother would believe) that the combination would have caused Bostonians to mistake her for an East Indian huckster; the embarrassment would have been overwhelming. Green's ensuing and urgent entreaty—"Dear mamma, you don't know the fation here—I beg to look like other folks. You don't know what a stir would be made in sudbury street, were I to make my appearance there in my Dominie and black hatt"—conveys the crucial role these sartorial signifiers (and goods more generally) had assumed by the end of the eighteenth century. Her mother's ignorance, due to geographical or generational distance, of "the fation" among Green's Boston peers; her daughter's "begging" to "look like other folks," to comply with fashion's dictates for her class, her race, and her sex; the certain "stir" on Sudbury Street—all of these things marked the advent of dramatic new relationships between people and material goods and the exigencies associated with them, and the centrality of appearance as a means and an end in that effort.

Wealth and Wardrobe in the Eighteenth-Century Connecticut Valley

Considering the many opportunities to transgress social codes through inappropriate apparel, it is easy to imagine a motley parade of rustics traipsing along the footpaths of western New England. But eighteenth-century wardrobes were less idiosyncratic than we might imagine. The elements comprising an ordinary outfit—breeches, shirts, vests, and jackets or coats for men; short gowns and skirts, shifts, petticoats, and long gowns for women—appeared in almost every wardrobe. All fabrics were derived from four natural fibers: wool, linen, cotton, and silk. A fifth category of materials was the leather derived from animal hides. Garments can be grouped into five broad categories: stylish, professionally rendered garments; out-of-date "finery," passed secondhand; unfashionable apparel of middling fabrics and amateur construction; worn, ill-fitting, secondhand garments; and the simply "functional" garments of laborers. Most wardrobes included examples from several categories; a person's position determined the proportion of each in his or her wardrobe.[33] Wardrobes of privilege contained the widest array of forms and materials, allowing the wearer to be appropriately prepared for every occasion. Most wardrobes were heavily dependent on imported fabrics; the few notations of "homemade" or "homespun" garments on period probate inventories suggest that garments made of textiles woven at home were the exception for many families of the Connecticut Valley.[34]

In addition to social or economic status, the nature of one's clothing was also closely associated with moments in the life cycle. The passage from childhood wardrobes to adult apparel was a moment that many families and individuals noted and recalled fondly. For young boys, it was often the transition from the gowns worn by all children to a young boys' pants that signaled a new stage of life. In his memoirs, George Howard of Windsor, Connecticut, easily summoned up the moment when boys of his generation cast off the typical "red flannel petticoat, green baize loose gown bare feet and legs [and] three-cornered straw hat," and "assumed a more significant and important bearing, jumped into Fustian breeches, mounted a round jacket, stepped into cowhide shoes, pulled a buff cap over our ears and slid proudly upon the Pond of Life."[35] The sartorial transition from childhood to womanhood was less dramatic; while boys exchanged gowns for trousers at about the age of five, girls remained in gowns throughout their lives. The style of those garments, however, did change as girls advanced in maturity, becoming longer, closer fitting through the bodice, and, before the advent of the neoclassical gown at the end of the century, more fitted through the shoulders and sleeves to direct or restrict the genteel woman's movement. Changes in adolescent apparel were not merely symbolic, however. When Elizabeth Phelps took her daughter Thankful to the local gown maker "for her to make some gowns longer," she was meeting a demand familiar to all parents of growing children.[36]

Weddings often prompted the acquisition (and creation) of clothing for the bride and groom, though the apparel worn for these occasions in the eighteenth century was not the specialized garments that emerged later. Nor were they boxed up after the wedding as souvenirs of the day. Rather, wedding finery became the couple's best garments for other occasions, from simply Sunday church services to later landmark events. Some wedding garments were so fine that they were refurbished and reused by later generations. When John Worthington married Hannah Hopkins in Springfield, Massachusetts, for example, he wore a luxurious salmon-colored silk waistcoat, its metallic silver embroidery shimmering in the candlelight. She wore a gown of English silk brocade, a rainbow of colors tracing through the weave, over a Marseilles petticoat—a petticoat quilted in the loom—both garments clearly the product of specialized workshops from across the Atlantic. Hopkins's spectacular 1759 gown was so striking that it would be worn a second time by her own daughter in 1791 and again by her granddaughter in 1824.[37]

Pregnancy marked a time when women needed new gowns to accommodate their changing shapes. A dress once owned by Betsey Barker that is housed today among the collections of Old Sturbridge Village seems to represent an alteration driven by pregnancy. Originally constructed in the last quarter, perhaps the closing decade, of the eighteenth century, the gown was later remade to accommodate the wearer's swelling figure, including a drawstring neck and open bodice that would have made nursing convenient as well.[38] As an expectant Betsy Phelps Huntington wrote her mother, "[I have] not begun to alter my blue gown into a loose dress, for I find such the most comfortable and decent for me." She continued on to say that, should she survive delivery, she might indulge and have a "handsome gown made."[39]

Mourning also prompted the acquisition of special clothing. John Ellery, planning for the mourning that would accompany his own death, bequeathed

£100 to his mother-in-law, Mary Austin, to pay for the "suit of mourning" she would require when the sad event came.[40] When Elizabeth Pitkin Porter's sister died, Patty Smith was engaged to produce a dress of black silk for the grieving sibling.[41] While the bereaved fitted themselves out with apparel appropriate to their grief, many, perhaps most, corpses in early America were dressed in "winding sheets." But some were laid out in specialized garments. Shroud making was an occupation available to both men and women in eighteenth-century England. Its history in New England is almost entirely unknown, but women like Frances Wells Miles of Greenfield, Massachusetts, who in the first half of the nineteenth century earned part of her living making shrouds, carried on a practice that was required of generations of needlewomen before her.[42]

The rate of acquisition of clothing often slowed with a person's advancing age. When Martha Newton of Wethersfield, Vermont, died in 1799, for example, much of her wardrobe was described by appraisers as "old," including seven of her ten gowns, one camblet, two checked linen, and four others of crape, calico, or calimanco. She also had a blue petticoat, a black silk bonnet, a woolen skirt, a striped petticoat, a camblet riding hood, a red cloak, a green calimanco skirt, a black quilted petticoat, a lambkin cloak, and linen short gown that were also described as old, as well as an assortment of aprons and smocks, some items valued at as little as eight cents.[43] Apparently Newton had stopped acquiring new garments some time before her final illness. Gowns described as old were likely to be in poorer condition and out of style. In Springfield, Miriam Warner was under the care of her son John for the last ten years of her life. His expenses for her maintenance, submitted to her estate after her death, show the regular acquisition of stays, shirts, aprons, gowns, stockings, and petticoats between 1762 and 1767, and then nothing at all from 1768 to 1772.[44] In her final years, Miriam made do with the things she already had.

Of the many and various early American wardrobes, the apparel of working people is hardest to reconstruct (see plate 1). Few inventories enumerate the garments of the laboring poor, and few of these objects have survived into the twentieth century. But some of the clothing worn by laboring men and women were pieces that had formerly served the middling and wealthier families who were often their employers. One might assume that the ability to purchase the services of a gown maker or tailor varied in direct proportion to a person's income, but it was not necessarily true that poorer families assumed more of their own clothing-related chores than their more privileged counterparts. Slaves and servants received cast-off clothing from their employers as well as clothing procured for them as recompense for their labor.

Like Zilpah, the enslaved woman who inherited her mistress's silk crape gown, camblet hood, and short cloak, they might acquire both fine and working clothing from their employers, which they could then choose to sell or to keep for themselves. In revolutionary Belchertown, Massachusetts, the Reverend Justus Forward billed the town for clothing he provided to a prisoner assigned to work in his household by the local Committee of Safety. Forward passed along to the prisoner two pairs of secondhand stockings for which he billed the town three shillings six pence, a pair of secondhand leather breeches for six shillings, and some "secondhand woolen mittens, half worn." He also debited his hired man, John Burt, twelve shillings for a secondhand coat that was no longer needed.[45] Elizabeth Phelps hired a tailoress to ride up and "fix an old great coat" for "Robert Fraiser a black boy [who] came to live here."[46]

Laboring men and women, whether bound or free, acquired wardrobes that were functional but not elaborate. Many advertisements seeking information about runaways include descriptions of clothing that help sketch a picture of these wardrobes: a fifteen-year-old apprentice, for example, left his Northampton master wearing a checked shirt, a striped frock, trousers, and a brown jacket. Another young apprentice, Henry Thomas, "wore away a butternut colored coat, black breeches, [and] checked linen shirt" and took with him a great coat for good measure.[47] John Barber possessed a wardrobe appropriate to a farm laborer in pre-revolutionary Springfield, comprising leather breeches, a woolen shirt and two linen shirts, a strait-bodied coat and vest, another coat, and two pairs of hose. He had a beaver hat and a larger coat—possibly a great coat—for outerwear, as well as a pair of mittens.[48] A thirty-year-old "maid servant" absconding from her duties wore a dark short gown and brown petticoat and carried with her a dark gown; a nineteen-year-old apprentice girl ran away one fall wearing a red stuff damask gown, green stuff quilted coat, a long brown cloak, and a black bonnet.[49]

The apparel of black men and women was not necessarily different from that of white men and women without resources. When Thankful Williams of Stockbridge, Massachusetts, rented the labors of Phillis from her Hatfield owner, Elijah Williams, she agreed that Phillis would be returned four years hence "in all respects as well cloathed and furnished as she was at the commencement" of their agreement; pinned to their contract is a list of apparel that describes Phillis's wardrobe: a quilt (that is, a quilted skirt), a long gown, five short gowns (the eighteenth-century equivalent of a work or everyday shirt, typically falling to the hips), six aprons, a short cloak, a pair of half sleeves, two jackets, a pair of buckles, five ribbons, five handkerchiefs, and a shoulder blanket.[50] An advertisement for two slaves posted in the *Middlesex*

Gazette gives a sense of men's everyday apparel: "Run away from the Subscriber . . . two Negro men, one aged 25 years, good looking, common stature, hair combs back, had on and took with him a felt hat, high crown, bound with ferret, snuff-coloured homespun coat with light brown lining, two black jackets, pair fustian breeches, two pairs overalls, copper Shoe and knee buckles, pair worsted stockings, and pr [ditto] linen. The other aged 22 years, about such a size and such a hat as the former, pale blue woolen coat, a striped jacket, fustian breeches, 1 pair deep woolen stockings and pair do dark worsted, wide square brass shoe buckles, hair turned back and striped trousers."[51]

The hundreds of labor contracts that survive from this period remind us that working men and women, at the close of their terms of service, acquired two suits of apparel, one fit for the workday and one of better quality, "abel for Sunday," or "suitable for Holy Days."[52] Workday apparel was generally "substantial in texture and uncouth in shape," simply cut trousers, frocks, shifts, skirts, and shirts made of leather, wool, or linen. [53] Clothing suitable for Sunday could include gowns of silk or other imported fabrics but be limited in ways deemed appropriate to the laborer's status. Typical was Fanny Gill's indenture to Adoniram and Miriam Bartlett, who agreed to provide, at the end of Gill's tenure, "clothing of all sort suitable to her Quality, fit for her to go to future Servis as an apprentice til of age."[54] The indenture of Esther Cotes to Amasa and Sarah Nims of Deerfield specifies that at close of service Esther would receive one suit of clothes for work and two for Sunday, an unusually generous arrangement, "but it is to be understood that in the latter case, the suits shall contain but one pair of stays and one quilt, and no cloak."[55]

Perhaps the most notable object associated with the wardrobes of working men in the Connecticut Valley were those ubiquitous checked shirts, like the one the eminent Major Hawley wore that startled Benjamin Tappan. Checked shirts were the single most common garment chosen to clothe men's upper bodies every day. One in three of the Connecticut Valley men's inventories surveyed for this study contain checked shirts: 21 percent are identified as linen, 2 percent Holland, a finer quality of linen, and 3 percent woolen; the fabric of the remainder was not noted by assessors.[56] For women, the equivalent of the men's checked work shirts was the checked apron, recalled by Catherine Graves as being commonplace among women of Hampshire County, and in contrast to the memorable white aprons worn by women of privilege. Women often owned several: the seven checked linen and wool aprons found in the wardrobe of Hannah Miller of Northampton were not unusual.[57]

In addition to aprons, working women's wardrobes included short gowns and skirts, more appropriate than long gowns for working in the house and fields.[58] When sixteen-year-old Polly Hall ran away from her Bernardston employers, for example, she had on a "dark brown petticoat and a short green gown."[59] Short gowns—that is, women's shirts appropriate for everyday work—were considered appropriate working apparel for women of all classes, though women of comparative privilege changed out of their "morning," or working, clothes in the afternoon, when friends and neighbors, or more formal company, might come visiting. When the Windsor gentlewoman Lydia Ellsworth died, she had a dark short gown "new, not made up" awaiting the attention of a needlewoman.[60] Short gowns in the Connecticut Valley were generally made of linen (24 percent), often striped, or wool (9 percent), though short gowns of baize, cotton, and calimanco, in red, brown, and green, were also seen.[61] Not surprisingly, dark patterns were favored over light for these garments usually intended for the kitchen rather than the parlor. By 1781, however, women had begun to wear short gowns of calico, a desirable cotton import; nearly one in four of the total number of short gowns listed in inventories between 1760 and 1808 were made of calico, though here, too, dark patterns were much preferred to light.[62]

Women throughout society—workers as well as their employers—sought to acquire the cottons increasingly available from India.[63] English social commentary was greatly preoccupied with the ability of hired women to replicate the appearance of their superiors; theaters routinely seized on the phenomenon—or the fear of it—in comic scenes involving mistaken identities. But emulation worked both ways, as fashions moved from the elite classes to the working classes and from the working classes to the elites.[64] The caraco, for example, a jacket worn by genteel women, evolved from a garment common to working-class wardrobes, while the raised skirts of polonaise gowns alluded to laboring women's tendency to hike up their skirts to keep them clean and dry. Laboring men's garments influenced the development of the frock coat popular among genteel men by the end of the eighteenth century. And Thomas Dwight, living in Boston, described another such instance in mail sent home to Springfield in the 1790s: "late letters from England say that the gentlemen of that country all wear check'd shirts, in honor of the navy who have performed such prodigies—those who do not wear whole shirts of that kind have a bosom of chex—you may not perhaps see the foundation of this compliment unless previously informed that both officers and soldiers from the admiral to the private where check'd shirts when at sea—as indeed do all the other seamen."[65]

The wardrobe of middling households elaborated on the basic wardrobe of laboring people, similar forms rendered in somewhat larger numbers and better fabrics and generally maintained in better condition.[66] A man might possess two or three pairs of breeches (often one of leather), a frock, two or three shirts (at least one but probably more checked, for everyday use, and another of better quality, perhaps Holland, for Sunday), one or two waistcoats, two or more coats (of lesser and greater quality, sometimes with matching vest or breeches or both), and some heavier outer garment, such as a great coat. Finally, a hat, usually beaver, was essential to most men's wardrobes. In Vermont, Matthew Patrick had two suits, each apparently worn as a complete ensemble assessors of his 1789 estate found a "best suit, coat, waistcoat, breeches and shirt," and a "second best suit, coat, waistcoat, breeches and shirt." Patrick had four pair of stockings, one thread (that is, cotton) and three yarn (probably wool). For special occasions, there was a waistcoat with silver buttons, but for workdays, he likely turned to his old jacket and breeches. Patrick also had two hats, one white and one black, a pair of shoes, and an old pair of boots.[67] Charles Evans of Brattleboro, Vermont, had two brown close-bodied coats. He had two vests, one striped and one black, and a pair of black breeches. Three old pairs of breeches and an old undervest also lay in his trunk, as did three pair of old trousers, suitable for work days, together with a pair of woolen overalls. A new pair of drawers had recently been acquired, supplanting an old pair. Two cotton shirts probably served him for most days, though a finer, Holland shirt was probably reserved for Sundays. Three old shirts could be paired with the worn trousers when he needed to be in the field. Finally, for outerwear he had an old gray surtout and a newer blue great coat. As was true of most men's wardrobes, his great coat was by far the most valuable item, worth more than £2 at the time of his death, more than twice that of the old surtout.[68]

A typical middling woman's wardrobe contained three to six shifts, two or three petticoats, three underpetticoats or skirts, perhaps quilted of silk or wool fabrics or of linen and wool blends, such as striped linsey-woolsey, several short gowns, a cloak or cloaks, and assorted caps, kerchiefs, and aprons.[69] The wardrobe of Rachel Parmenter of Hinsdale, Vermont, suggests what such constellations of clothing might look like. Parmenter owned three short gowns, one each of wool, linen, and calico, that she might wear with either her red or her yellow skirt. A woolen apron protected her clothing from dirt, soils and stains.[70] She had one long gown, worth more than ten times any of her short gowns, suggesting it was very fine, or very new, or both. When it was chilly, she wrapped herself in a shawl. Two yards of chintz in her possession suggest that she was contemplating an alteration or addition to her wardrobe. But Parmenter, like the majority of working women, spent most of her days in a skirt, short gown, and apron. Abigail Wells of Northampton owned two woolen gowns as well as two calico gowns, beneath which she might add either of two quilts, or two petticoats. She also had seven shifts, a pair of stays, five aprons suitable for work days, a Holland apron that she might pair with her finer gowns, and a silk hood and apron for special occasions. She also had a camblet riding hood, seven caps, and an assortment of handkerchiefs.[71] A step better was the wardrobe assembled by Elizabeth Lyman of Hadley. At the time of her death Lyman possessed two silk gowns and a silk cloak, three calico gowns, and gowns of chintz, bombazeen, silverett, and camblet. A scarlet cloak was available for traveling abroad, as well as a second, less valuable cloak and a riding hood. She also had two quilts and two shirts, as well as five aprons, for everyday wear, and a silk apron for better occasions (see plate 2).[72]

The wardrobes of the "better" classes were, not surprisingly, even larger (see plate 3). People of means had could acquire and maintain a larger number and greater variety of garments from which to choose, and found it markedly easier to keep up with new fashions Women like Lois Morton of Hatfield, who had a dozen gowns and another half-dozen petticoats, were more able to respond to shifts in fashion, to have garments in the colors most favored from season to season, to alter sleeve lengths, widths, and shape to comply with current trends, to add and subtract the appropriate trimmings; men with a dozen or more shirts could always appear with their clothing neat, clean, and in good repair.[73] They too could keep up with developments in the cut of cuffs and ruffles and could more easily afford to acquire coats and waistcoats in the fabrics favored each season, as well as the services of a tailor who could render the subtleties of the preferred cut of the moment.

The wardrobes of the gentry, however, were not simply larger than those of their neighbors. They also were distinguished by their quality. The dress of the region's best families—most familiar to us today in the portraits by artists such as John Singleton Copley and Ralph Earl—included a higher proportion of garments that were made professionally, as signaled by their texture, color, and fit.[74] The higher the quality, the greater the likelihood that a garment had been produced in a commercial establishment of high repute. Apart from the degree of luxury signaled by the fiber (the quality of woolen and linen fabrics ranged widely, while silk and cotton were imported from Asia), the smooth, uniform feel of some fabrics indicated that the carding, weaving, and fulling required to create them was accomplished outside of the home, and probably across the Atlantic. Particularly complex weaves and finishes also indicated European production.

Color too was crucial to codes of appearance. Those in Northampton's meetinghouse who were not garbed in check distinguished themselves with yards of fine white linen: "the genteel image required [that] fine white fabric met suit or dress, revealing that the immaculate body was covered by a film of white cloth."[75] Elite women distinguished themselves with white, too, at the neckline and in the sleeves—evidence of their ability to acquire fine linen fabrics and their ability to keep them clean, both by refraining from soiling them and by having access to help in laundering them. Those glimpses of white were set off by the smooth textures and rich colors of imported satins and brocades. Color was not the object here—both men and women recognized the value of restraint, of choosing subdued, restrained hues—but when color was employed, its tones were deeper, richer, and truer in the garments of the gentry.[76]

In the eighteenth-century "theater of artifice," equal emphasis was placed on theater and artifice; that is, the eighteenth-century European worldview valued artificiality as evidence of humanity's ingenious manipulation of the natural world.[77] The muted, earthy tones of much everyday clothing, reflecting that world, were the products of local vegetable dyes. Another grade of fabric was colored with dyes that were objects of long-distance trade. More important than color, however, was pattern. While local dyers with access to imported dyestuffs, including cochineal, logwood, and indigo, could produce varied and vivid hues, they could not replicate printed cottons like chintz and calico, the woven patterns of brocades, damasks, and paduasoys, or the embossed patterns of moirés, all popular fabrics among the late eighteenth-century rural gentry. Technological innovation had made possible these textiles and the designs they carried. The result was a new wealth of bright fabrics bearing intense patterns that were naturalistic (in that they most commonly carried designs comprising vines, leaves, and flowers) but emphatically not natural. Copley's portrait of Dorothy Skinner, for example, depicts the large-scale floral silks, of sprightly colors on a light ground, that were popular in the middle decades of the century, while Hannah Wright's lush golden-colored silk damask, captured by Ralph Earl, suggests how the fabric's visual richness and weight could affirm a family's wealth and position.[78]

Still more than materials, style, cut, and fit became of acute concern. As the eighteenth century progressed, elite men and women began to look for ways to subvert the attempts of aspiring neighbors to emulate their style.[79] Sumptuary legislation had failed to regulate the appearance of masters and servants; the prohibited goods were too alluring, and too readily available, to be kept away from the middling classes. At the end of the eighteenth century and beginning of the nineteenth, war, embargoes, and blockades disrupted trade enough that the substance of garments became politically charged. Those desiring expensive fabrics occasionally found them to be inappropriate, or simply inaccessible, and so increasing significance accrued to style. The gentry developed new codes of conduct and dress that hinged not merely on the acquisition of goods but also on special knowledge about how to use them. The result, in men's clothing, would be an aesthetic of restraint that gave elites an opportunity to demonstrate republican virtue, escape some of the pressures of consumer culture, and at the same time assert their social superiority.

The images and descriptions of elite men and women that survive from the period preceding this sartorial republicanism convey the full effect of elite wardrobes, providing glimpses into the appearance of the gentry at its height and the impression those ensembles made on less privileged observers. When Roger Wolcott of Windsor went riding, for example, which he did several times a week in the mid-eighteenth century, he "never appeared abroad but in full dress," including a scarlet broadcloth suit, a long coat with wide skirts, "trimmed down the whole length in front with gilt buttons, and broad gilt vellum button holes, two to three inches in length." The cuffs, too, were wide and ornamented with matching gilt buttons, while the waistcoat's skirts were richly embroidered. Ruffles at his neck and lace over his hands completed the outfit.[80] Wolcott's appearance reflected the central traits of elite wardrobes. The scarlet fabric, ample materials, gilding, ruffles, lace, and embroidering all signaled Wolcott's secure position at the peak of local and regional networks of authority.

The wardrobe of Wolcott's Windsor neighbor Elizabeth Newberry suggests the female equivalent. When she went out, Newberry might choose from among her blue broadcloth "cloak and head," another "homemade" blue cloak, a silk cloak, a red cloak, a riding coat, a red camblet short cloak, or either of two short calico cloaks. For her head, she might select one of two silk bonnets, a silk hood, or choose among more than a dozen caps. She owned several gowns, including one of black taffeta and others of russell, calico, silk crape, and chintz. Her everyday apparel included a brown gown, a long loose gown, and others described as "homemade striped" and "old calico." Her petticoats were crimson-colored, scarlet, white, striped, red, and plain. For work days, she had a calimanco or linen short gown. Like many other women, she had an assortment of aprons, some for work and some for show: on the finer end was a short silk apron and another of laced lawn. If the day's events called for her better apparel, she might put on one of four Holland aprons; if it was a day for working around the house, any of the six checked, coarse or plain aprons would do. Beneath her garments, depending on the weather, she could choose any one of her two woolen shifts, two cotton shifts, or six linen shifts; rarely, one suspects, did she resort to one of the old or plain shifts folded in a drawer. One of seven pairs of stockings covered her legs.[81] The 1784 inventory of "Madam" Sarah Porter of Hartford and Hadley includes a cloak and two gowns of calico; it also reveals that she at one time owned at least two gowns of Alapeen—a rare and costly fabric that appears in the estate of only one other Hampshire County woman. Other expensive garments in Porter's wardrobe include and a quilted silk petticoat assessed at thirty shillings and a gown of black paduasoy assessed at £4.[82]

While probate inventories can capture a picture of wardrobes as they lay in drawers, trunks, and chests, no longer to be opened by their owners, a nice sense of such wardrobes in action can be gleaned from contemporary correspondence, such as that of the prosperous Heath family of Brookline and Portsmouth. In the fall of 1786, for example, one of the daughters wrote to her sister that she had gone visiting "to Mrs Sherburne's Thursday."

> [I] did not think of seeing any body there [she continued], wore striped calico round gown, black gauze handkerchief, beaver hat, Mrs Goddard wore calico gown and coat, black hat and muslin handkerchief. . . . [Friday] we spent the afternoon at Mrs Palmers, Mrs Goddard drest her[self] as she did the day before, I wore calico gown & coat, muslin handkerchief, lawn apron & beaver hat. . . . Phoebe Sherburne came in here the day before yesterday to look of my Hat to see how the crown was [reas'd] in she & Sally have new white Hats to day, have been to meeting, wore muslin gown & pink coat, & black vandyke. The other evening . . . Fete Meseroy came in with a loose gown on, said she had been ironing all the afternoon.[83]

Other young women were equally watchful of their wardrobe's reception. Young Anna Green Winslow, who had traveled to Boston in 1772 to attend school, subsequently recorded her sartorial triumph.

> I was dress'd in my yellow coat, my black bib & apron, my pompedore shoes, the cap my Aunt Storer sometime since presented me with (blue ribbons in it) &c. & a very handsome loket in the shape of a hart she gave me—the past pin my Hond Papa presented me with in my cap, My new cloak and bonnet on, my pompedore gloves, &c, &c. And I would tell you that for the first time, they all lik'd my dress very much. My cloak and bonnet are really very handsome, & so they had need be. For they cost an amasing sight of money, not quite £45, tho' Aunt Suky said, that she suppos'd Aunt Deming would be frightened out of her wits at the money it cost.[84]

Fashion Information and the Eighteenth-Century Consumer

Increasingly important in achieving gentility, along with the sometimes "frightening" amount of capital, was the acquisition and allocation of cultural capital, that is, an informed eye that could recognize and replicate prevailing taste and style in the selection of fabrics and the cut in which the ensuing garments were rendered. As greater numbers of people gained access to the fabrics, colors, and styles of the gentry, the gentry sought additional means by which to identify themselves and to deny others access to their circle. Creating this new genre of knowledge and then restricting access to it was "the great trick of the elite," who had the time and resources to devote to acquiring this information for themselves.[85] The production of gentility depended on access to special forms of information, by both producer and consumer.

In part, deploying one's understanding of fashion encouraged some self-policing. While members of the rural gentry expressed their access and entitlement to authority through the acquisition of material goods, any hint of excess risked quick and certain censure.[86] This was something Elizabeth Phelps knew, or at least of which she was reminded: "Monday Mr Phelps carried me to see Mrs Colt—settled I hope more firmly a friendship begun before—heard from her the vanity of great appearances—may it be a warning from her never to value myself for grandeur."[87] "A few cursory remarks made accidentally by a friend" furnished Abigail Lyman with much food for thought when her "attachment to worldly goods" was pointed out to her: "I thought I was long since convinced 'that our life consisteth not in the abundance we possess' yet I find I have been desirous of accumulating this superfluous fullness—and have freely gratified my taste in dress perhaps beyond the dictates of prudence and without conforming to my husband's purse."[88] Perhaps Lyman's acquaintance and Phelps's neighbor were simply making general observations, or perhaps both young women appeared in need of words of caution. Lyman, tellingly, recognized a "prudence" apart from the strictly financial consideration of her husband's purse, and certainly, since their neighbors' daily attire was largely composed of wool, linen, and leather, the colorful imported silks and cottons these more prosperous women donned must have drawn notice. Both women, however, found the warning apt. Lyman resolved to "be more guarded in the future."

Choosing wisely for Phelps, Lyman, and other women like them meant negotiating the dazzling array of goods that flooded Connecticut Valley shops. For their clothing, men and women of the Connecticut Valley were eager to purchase the wares of local shopkeepers, some produced locally or regionally, and others the stuff of global commerce. The advertisements published by local merchants alerting residents to goods "lately arrived" suggest that these shops offered dozens of different fabrics in a wide range of quality, pattern, and color. More than a hundred different fabrics appear in Connecticut Valley inventories from the last half of the eighteenth century and first decade of the nineteenth.[89] Of gowns whose materials are identified by court-appointed assessors, the largest proportion by far (19 percent) were made of some variety of silk—including lustrings, taffetas, satins, and, more than any other, silk crape (11 percent).[90] Two dozen types of linen were available to the colonial consumer. A glimpse into the contents of one eighteenth-century shop conveys the extent of the choices available to the discerning shopper. By the 1760s Elisha Pomeroy's Northampton shelves groaned with the weight of about twenty-five hundred yards of fabric, including broadcloths, serges, kerseys, shaloons, tammys, durants, fustians, camblets, cambleteens, calimanco, calico, satin, and dozens of other varieties of textile, in colors from black, blue, and brown to pink, yellow, and crimson, in patterns from striped to spotted, and in qualities from coarse to fine.[91] This selection was not unusual and only continued to expand: at the turn of the century, Nathan Bolles's Hartford shop likewise offered broadcloth in blue, buff, drab and scarlet; flannels; baizes; black, pink, and green moreens; camblets; russells; shalloons; and buckrums.[92] He carried tammy in pink, blue, green, black, and mulberry, and durant in black, blue, pink, green, and red-brown. Customers could choose blue velvet or black calimanco, as well as an assortment of crapes and sarcenets. For customers in search of pattern, he offered a dark chintz as well as olive, red spotted, and lite -sprigged, as well as spotted and sprigged calicos and stamped cambric.

Whereas the fabrics available to rural women were mediated through the selections of shopkeepers, the styles in which they were rendered were not. Shifts in fashion generally reached New Englanders by one of four sources: written information, such as instructions supplied in correspondence, and, eventually, in the press; the gowns in up-to-date urban fashions worn and carried in trunks by women traveling from the cities to the countryside; merchants or artisans whose work brought them into contact with prevailing styles in other communities, regions, and countries, which they then carried along with them; and word of mouth. In an era before the advent of patterns as we know them today, style and literacy went hand in hand; fashionable women needed to be able to read the descriptions of costume creeping into the pages of the local press and to write descriptions of the styles they had seen and have those descriptions read by others.[93] Such correspondence was enhanced by travel. Men and women who had the privilege of travel conveyed information to others whose horizons were more narrow, providing them with an opportunity to observe even as they themselves were observing. The cumulative effect of these encounters was ultimately to transmit dispatches both verbal and visual between metropolitan Europe and its colonial hinterlands.[94]

Word of mouth was the most prevalent means by which women received and disseminated information. In contrast to men, who gathered information from conversation, but also correspondence, newspapers, pamphlets, and other published sources, women's information networks were firmly grounded in face-to-face encounters.[95] Gown making multiplied the opportunity for these exchanges; rural artisans were important links in the chain of communication from style centers. But word of mouth is also the least reliable means by which to convey information, an especially salient point when it comes to fashion. Misinterpretations inevitably occurred along the route, as women of varying levels of skill essayed to approximate urban style. As stylish garments were in turn approximated by others and so on, rural facsimiles—modified and inflected by the overt preferences of rural men and women—became gradually removed from their originals.

In larger cities, merchants and mantua makers played a large role in the dissemination of trends. Some women "lately arrived" from European centers of fashion were more aware of emerging styles; others advertised their close connection with European fashion through the receipt and display of dolls clothed in styles currently popular abroad.[96] But more often, fashion news traveled by less direct routes, entering from abroad through port cities and making its way to the countryside on the lips of traveling men and women and in the letters and goods they mailed home. Thomas Dwight, for example, while serving as a legislator in Boston, undertook a good bit of shopping on behalf of his family, as well as their circle of friends, at home in western Massachusetts. A memorandum written on the eve of his departure for the capital set the tone for the remainder of his tenure: "Get for Miss Buckminster and send by the first stage 2 yds scarlet satin or 12.5 yd Scarlet lustring. 1 pr riding gloves (short, not pink) fashionable."[97] Sometimes, goods traveled both directions, as when Hannah Dwight sent her bonnet back to the city with her husband, where the keeper of his boardinghouse had agreed to "undertake to transmute or transform your bonnet in the shape a la mode if the silk will admit of it."[98] In 1799, "a vessel which lately arrived from England with a number of passengers" brought "a cargo of new fashions—the brim of a gentleman's hat is not wider than a common hair ribbon—helmet cap or horseman's caps are all the rage for the ladies—black stocks (stuffed with larger puddings) are coming fast into vogue with the gentlemen—ladies wear the same when in mourning and some of them when not—as gentlemens fashions I am pleased with it—black suits my delicate complexion, and saves a deal of hard labor to the laundress."[99] Dwight's own source was often "late letters from England," which kept him and other New Englanders apprised of current fashion before it even arrived on the city's docks.

In rural communities, gown makers were mediators of innovations introduced by others; they were not the arbiters of fashion that their nineteenth-century counterparts would become. Urban traders, though, familiar with the trends popular among their customers and the tradespeople who served them, regularly communicated that information to their more rural clientele, and so influenced the purchases that they carried home. When Esther Williams of Deerfield asked her husband to send an order to the Boston merchant Samuel Eliot for satin, bombazeen, and appropriate trimmings for a cloak, Eliot replied that he was unable to find any of the latter fabric: "Bombazeen being an article formerly used for mourning and mourning being proscribed, there is none to be had."[100] Eliot reported that he had sought the "advice of Mrs Eliot and two milliners with regard to quantity and quality," and that the three women suggested that persian would be at the time "more fashionable." At the urging of the milliners, Eliot added their recommendation that the "head of the cloak, if made fashionable, must be large."[101] Abigail Lyman also received instruction by proxy, from both a Boston craftswoman and her friend and peer Rebecca Salisbury. Lyman wrote her husband, "If you find it convenient & get me a Cloak—let it be a long cardinal—& get me a pattern & directions how to make it of a Milliner according to the latest fashion which Rebecca will inform you—& also what trimming will be best."[102] In Northampton, either Abigail herself made up her new garment or else she relayed the instructions she received to another, more local craftswoman.

Correspondence among fashionable women regularly conveyed specific instructions that could be implemented by local artisans. "If you know of any new way to make gowns," Betsy Phelps Huntington asked her sister-in-law Sarah Phelps, then living in Boston, "be so kind as to describe it to me."[103] Sometimes that reporting even arrived third-hand. Visiting New London, Connecticut, in spring 1804, Patience Langdon wrote her sister in South Wilbraham, Massachusetts, *"I am told that* the latest fashion for making gowns is for the trail to drag as long as the gown is from your shoulder to the floor and be entirely square[.] Short sleeves are most worn here in white gowns" (emphasis added).[104] It would be left to her sister Sophronia to try to interpret and implement this information correctly. In 1798, young Elizabeth Southgate Browne sent "gown patterns" to her mother, together with detailed directions toward the successful reproduction of the garment in question: "the one with a fan back is meant to meet just before and pin the Robings, no string belt or anything."[105] In another letter, she explained that "long sleeves are very much worn, made like mitts; crosswise, only one seam and that in the back of the arm, and a half drawn sleeve over and a close, very short one up high, drawn up with a cord."[106]

While the vast majority of written descriptions of clothing were contained in private or semi-private correspondence, a nascent fashion press did play some role in apprising rural women of urban style. Though female literacy was not widespread until the end of the eighteenth century, those Connecticut Valley women who had enjoyed access to education did watch the Boston and Hartford papers carefully, and when possible, used these bulletins to guide their own purchases.[107] Abigail Lyman combed the pages of the *Columbian Centinel* before writing to her husband, frequently in Boston on business, advising him of her needs. In one letter she wrote, "You will find Black Bo[rmast] for Mamas gown at Ann Bents, No. 50 Marlboro Street . . . as I observe she publishes it."[108] In another, she asked her husband to procure a pair of slippers, "pritty good ones," because she could not "get any in this town worth buying." This letter, dated 29 May 1797, was written a mere five days after the *Centinel* was published in Boston; Lyman had clearly turned to its advertising pages as soon as it arrived, read the notices with care, and dashed a letter off to her husband immediately, hoping to reach him in time to secure the wanted articles.[109] With luck, she would have her new slippers—nicer than any available locally—in a matter of days.

Craftswomen, too, carried fashion as they traveled from place to place, encountering new styles that they then incorporated into their own repertoires. Sometimes this travel was international; in revolutionary-era Hartford, for example, Mary Gabiel stressed her Parisian origins to draw business away from Mary and Jane Salmon, whose Boston training must have (for Connecticut consumers, at least) paled in comparison.[110] In Boston another Parisian emigrant noted that she could provide "all that concerns ladies dress" in fashions popular in France.[111] J. Ritchie Garrison has observed the importance of "tramping" among men learning the carpentering trades, suggesting that the time they spent working in the shops of other builders provided more than simply opportunities to find more work and income; the exposure to new techniques and trends also provided a substantial portion of their education and training.[112] Young female apprentices moved less often between craftswomen, but craftswomen, too, moved between communities, and in so doing widened their range of experience. Use of the popular phrase "lately arrived" appealed to the urban mantua makers, who drafted advertisements to the local press as much as it did other artisans, as it signaled their recent familiarity with prevailing fashions in their country or city of origin. Among women in the clothing trades, the quality of having been "lately arrived" could prove to be their strongest selling point, even as they worked to establish themselves among a new and, they hoped, long-standing clientele.

Forays from rural and small-town communities to city centers provided amply opportunity to glean news of styles. "Formerly there was a fashion of wearing masks made of silk velvet and made stiff with paper," one resident of eighteenth-century Northampton recalled. "There was a hole for breathing and places for the eyes—a few had them in Northampton—some of Mr. Edwards' daughters, it is said, and Ebenezer Phelps' wife used to wear a mask [when] she rode out." This woman remembered, "Mrs. Edwards used to go to Boston (so said) once a year, and bring home the fashions!"[113] As a young woman, Elizabeth Porter traveled with cousins to see the spring elections in Boston and to visit family and friends in Hartford and Middletown. As the fashion of wearing masks suggests, trips like these served as reconnaissance missions, after which gentlewomen communicated to their home communities the latest developments in urban style through their personal appearance and their correspondence.

When Betsy Phelps went from Hadley to visit her brother Charles at college in Cambridge, her mother, Elizabeth, asked her to "take a little notice how such things are made if you can."[114] Later, while living in Litchfield, Connecticut, Betsy wrote to her mother, "if Sally [Charles's wife] can send me a fashion, or a gown to look at by you, I will send it home by my father and be very much obliged to her."[115] The clothing of these gentlewomen often served as patterns, or models, for others.[116] One summer afternoon in July 1798, Phelps noted in her memorandum book that "Dr. Porter's wife and young widow Gaylord" [a local gown maker] had come by "to fix a gown for Mrs Porter by one of Betsys."[117] While in Boston the previous fall, young Betsy Phelps had patronized one of the roughly one dozen mantua makers then working in Boston; six months later, Lucretia Gaylord would try to duplicate the work of that Boston mantua maker in a gown for Charlotte Porter.[118]

It is difficult to know whether these rural women successfully imitated urban fashions, or even in what manner they attempted to. European style migrated quickly and easily to colonial urban centers and surely took no longer to find its way to the countryside. But the degree to which it was transformed along the way remains murky. For example, the estate inventory of the Hatfield gentlewoman Lois Morton indicates that she owned a gown made of cheney, a worsted fabric more often used in urban settings for furnishings, and especially bed curtains.[119] Morton had an extensive wardrobe at the time of her death, comprising more than one hundred articles of clothing, and eighteen gowns, of lustring, chintz, calico, calimanco, russell, crape, cambleteen, wildbore, and cotton. What prompted her to select cheney on one occasion for her new garment? Was this fabric perhaps considered more versatile by women on the periphery of urban fashion? Several passages in the correspondence of Betsy Phelps Huntington suggest that there was at least a perceived gulf between the city and the countryside. When a friend of the Phelps family staying in Boston wrote home to his wife in Hadley that he had asked Betsy to help him purchase the fabric for a broadcloth cloak that she had requested, the woman worried that he had mistakenly suggested that superfine broadcloth was wanted, when only a "good fine wool, not the first quality" would suffice. She promptly made a point of speaking to Betsy's mother, Elizabeth Phelps, who then conveyed the correction to her daughter, hoping that she had intervened in time.[120] Similarly, when writing to her brother in Boston to request the purchase of a beaver hat, Betsy suggested that he need not overspend, as "a cheaper one would answer as well as any here in the country."[121] Conversely, in December 1797, upon returning to Hadley after a visit to Boston, she laughingly reported to Charles their mother's fear that one new fashion that she had brought home from the city "should frighten some out of the house of worship."[122] Twenty years later, when Charles Porter Phelps brought home his second wife, Charlotte Parsons, from Boston and Newburyport, her first appearance at the Hadley church was similarly memorable, certainly to Phelps's nephew Theodore Huntington, who later recalled that "she was very much dressed, indeed her costume was so altogether beyond that of our people, that to my youthful eyes it was very near the ridiculous."[123]

Such observations remind us that the Congregational meetinghouse was among the most important stage sets in a community's "theater," that Sunday services were sartorial as well as spiritual events. According to oral tradition, when, in about the 1770s, Madame Wyllys appeared at Hartford's North Meeting House in a calico apron, the garment was "then so new and stylish" that the women around her "could not fix their minds on the sermon."[124] This tale may well seem to be nothing more than the sort of charming anecdote that appealed to nineteenth-century local historians, but evidence suggests that some parishioners were sufficiently distracted by the clothing around them that they remembered it many years later. An elderly Solomon Clarke never forgot the Sabbath Day impression made by Asahel Pomeroy, keeper of Northampton's principal public house: "I remember well his stately form, standing in his pew, facing the choir, back to the pulpit, his ponderous watch seals hanging from his vest."[125] When Lucy Watson gave her "recollections and notices of Dress" from her Walpole, New Hampshire, childhood, she remembered that "the most dressy lady at church was Mrs Levitt, the Minister's Wife." Levitt "alone went to church without a bonnet, and holding a fan before her face, as was then the fashion of the Seaboard." Watson summoned memories of "Col. Bellows' daughter and her two half sisters," who "wore black silk bonnets in much of the plainness of the present Quaker bonnets, but having a bow in front." "The gayest ladies then wore black silk hats with flat crowns and large brims—Set so much on the front of the head, and rising behind, as to leave the back of the cap, Expos'd. White, or colored bonnets, were not seen. All the rest of the dress was very very gay."[126] Sixty miles south, the minister's wife was more reluctant to stand out from her community. When Sabra Cobb Emerson left Boston to join her husband, John, in the wilderness settlement of Conway, Massachusetts, she brought with her a silk umbrella, but when she noticed that no other Conway families possessed such an accessory, she put it away, never to be carried again. She later used the silk to make bonnets. The women of Conway, however, worked a little harder to make a good Sunday show: oral tradition preserved there records that women would travel to church in their everyday clothes, and then, before entering the meetinghouse, change into their finer apparel "under the sheltering branches of the Chestnut tree at the foot of Rice Hill."[127]

While the meetinghouse may have been the high court of fashion in eighteenth-century Massachusetts, high style in eighteenth-century Connecticut was more closely associated with politics, with election balls and the Hartford Assemblies possibly the most fashion-forward events in the whole of the Connecticut River Valley during the Revolutionary and Federal eras. In 1790, one prominent Hartford observer boasted, "Our assemblies are most brilliant, and . . . at the last there were forty Ladies in most superb attire."[128] Though women and men from rural Massachusetts traveled to Boston for annual elections and fitted themselves out for the occasion, for the genteel residents of the Connecticut Valley, Connecticut's Election Day, held annually on the second Thursday in May, was an important social event. A ball was held on the evening following the election, and another the following Monday, the latter being "more select."[129] When Hannah Smith of Glastonbury described her early efforts to prepare for a ball, she reported, "We are very busy preparing for the election having five girls to fix out, some of them old enough to think their clothes must be made in the very newest fashion and their bonnets made at Hartford, so we have been obliged to get them"[130] In western Massachusetts, where, as we have seen, Sarah Pitkin grew bored spending time with ministers and their ministerial families, there seems to have being nothing comparable to the Election Ball and similarly festive events.[131] The Hartford Election Balls and associated assemblies were the pinnacles of fashion in the Connecticut Valley of the Federal era, the place that style was set and set in motion.

THE FASHIONS introduced in the Hadley meetinghouse struck some observers as frightening, ridiculous, or overly pious; indeed Betsy Phelps's mother teased that the gowns her daughter returned with from Boston might cause a riot. Instead, however, Charlotte Porter affirmed Betsy's taste by acquiring a similar gown for herself. Now at least two Hadley women sported the new style, helping to popularize it in the area. At the same time, the woman who copied the gown, Lucretia Gaylord, learned the fashion, thus further facilitating its adoption into the local lexicon of design. Meantime, in Connecticut, the local assemblies proved critical venues at which new fashions were introduced and observed, to be replicated time and again in households up and down the Connecticut River. Transmitting information in this way, through a series of face-to-face exchanges, was in keeping with long-standing custom that regularly engaged women in local information networks. The spread of female literacy would soon provide greater numbers of women with direct access to more cosmopolitan vistas through newspapers, magazines, and books, but for now, a series of mediations like this one most often conveyed the fashions of Paris, London, New York, and Boston to the New England countryside.[132]

The process by which women and men constructed their wardrobes, and their identities, was complex. People needed tools to accomplish their goals. Consumers gathered fashion information through their correspondence and the press, but perhaps the most important tool was the looking glass. Elisha Pomeroy anticipated this need as early as the winter of 1761, when he stocked his Northampton shop with thirty "pocket looking glasses"; men and women, no longer tethered to any particular spot on the landscape, required portable means by which to inspect their appearance, to make sure that the image projected outward matched their interior sense of themselves.[133] At the end of the century, the desire to scrutinize one's appearance had by no means abated. In the fall of 1797, eighteen-year-old Betsy Phelps visited her brother at Harvard and acquired fashions that were still unknown, but would become known, in her native Hadley. The young gentlewoman from the countryside spent a good deal of time that season observing, noting what kind of stockings were worn, what cut of sleeves were preferred, which style of hat was most genteel, and which merely serviceable. Two years later she would return to outfit herself for marriage and housewifery; by then she would be well familiar with the goods carried in the Boston shops. But on this early foray, she was still something of a novice. And when she arrived in the city, late in the month of August, she realized that she had forgotten something essential to her sojourn there. She quickly wrote home to her mother, requesting that she promptly send the "little looking glass that stands on my dressing table."[134] The emerging gentlewoman was monitoring the process of her own self-fashioning and would need it.[135]

Chapter 2

Needle Trades in New England, 1760–1810

In fall 1800, Frederick Wardner left the Windsor, Vermont, shop of Isaac Green with two and a quarter yards of coating for a surtout, having paid thirteen shillings six pence. Along with the cloth, Wardner had bought a dozen and half coat buttons, three skeins of thread, linen to line the sleeves and pocket, and a yard of flannel for the interlining. He took the cloth to Thomas Welch, a tailor who measured him and cut the pieces for the new overcoat, charging two shillings for his work. Wardner then carried the several pieces to Catherine Deane, a tailoress who made up the garment. She charged five shillings to assemble the coat, apply the buttons, and press the finished garment.[1]

To attain the tasteful appearance he desired, Wardner drew on the expertise of at least three people in his community whose contribution to the production of the new coat lay within a complex economy of skill, time, and talent. Men like Thomas Welch performed the more technically demanding tasks of cutting and turning coats, jackets, and overalls.[2] As Isaac Green's account books reveal, several women in the town, like Catherine Deane, made and mended coats and overalls and performed plain sewing. Lovice Simmister, for example, sewed up fustian overalls for Wardner "after they was cut out," possibly also by Welch, and Oliver Barrett's wife offset her household's debts to Green by making shirts, at three shillings six pence. Phebe Hill's attempt to do the same was less successful; Green gave her the pieces of a pair of breeches already cut out and credited her three shillings for making them up, noting, however, that they were "very poorly" done. Thereafter, Hill was engaged to sew only "coarse" shirts.[3] Polly Hastings, in contrast, performed a variety of jobs for Green, making and mending shirts, breeches, jackets, and overalls. Her ability to alter jackets, turn coats, and make surtouts allowed her to turn her sewing skills to steady advantage.

Deane, Simmister, Hastings, and Hill had counterparts throughout New England. To be sure, as daughters, wives, and mothers, women contributed mightily to the construction and preservation of their family's apparel. Their work is not to be treated lightly: keeping a family clothed depended heavily on unpaid labor within the household, as women laundered, mended, altered, and constructed many of the garments that their families needed from day to day. Most women's "housewifery" required a basic familiarity with clothing production and maintenance. Short gowns are a good example of the sort of garments, including also shirts, skirts, and shifts, whose cut and construction were "universally understood." These common everyday women's shirts were made from a full width of material cut in one piece that stretched from the waist at the back, over the shoulder, to the waist in the front, thereby avoiding the need for shoulder seams. An opening was cut to create the neckline, and rectangular pieces of material were then attached on either side to create the sleeves. "Significantly," Claudia Kidwell points out, "this was a two-dimensional use of textiles. The final fit of the garment was not achieved principally through the cut of the material." Instead, a rough, loose fit was achieved through the addition of either pleats or casings with drawstrings. A whole genre of apparel—men's shirts, women's shifts, robes, banyans, and other similar garments—were conceived principally as combinations of rectangles. These were the garments that most women learned to make.[4]

Another genre of apparel, including men's coats and women's gowns and stays, involved a far more sophisticated understanding of clothing construction—knowledge of physiology and a feel for mathematics as well as materials and motion, that is, of the particularities of given fabrics as they assumed fluid three-dimensional forms. The skills that separated amateur from master carpenters mirror similar distinctions between amateurs and specialists in the clothing trades; needleworking artisans, like their woodworking counterparts, "worked with complex geometry and measurements"; clothing construction, like housebuilding, "was more than a matter of manual dexterity and knowledge of [materials]. It required advance thinking skills and an understanding of three-dimensional relationships."[5]

Legions of women took their skill with a needle and shears to the marketplace to meet the demand for clothing and to augment their household income. Some women worked as tailoresses, making and mending the household linens and everyday clothes whose maintenance consumed much of a woman's time in early America. Others cultivated special abilities and worked as gown makers, stay makers, and tailors, providing specialized skills to the men and women of their communities. A survey of the structure of the clothing trades in early New England suggests that clothes making involved divisions of labor along gender lines as well as economic and social opportunity, age and marital status, and even race. The work engaged a variety of people—some with little skill, some with more, some professional artisans—who acquired and applied craft skills and knowledge and moved through their various communities as need, opportunity, and inclination dictated. Sorting through the various ways in which women and men participated in clothes-making occupations suggests a more nuanced understanding of craft skill than long-standing definitions of artisanry have so far encouraged, revealing multifaceted communities of practice that engaged laborers of greater and lesser skill in tasks and activities that turned on the gender of a given garment's maker as well as its eventual user. What's more, the gendered compositions of each of these trades were in flux throughout the eighteenth century—developments that engage our attention in subsequent discussions. But first it is important to sketch the general outlines of these occupations as they emerged in early modern Europe and unfolded across early American communities.

Gender and the Needle Trades in the Early Modern Atlantic World

In some ways, the participation of eighteenth-century New England's working women in cloth and clothing production comes as no surprise: women have long been associated with fiber arts.[6] Reasons for the ancient association of women and needles are easy to find; the tedious processes involved in cloth as well as clothing production—often requiring relatively little attention but a good deal of time—were compatible with child care. Yet historians generally agree that women's significant presence in skilled clothing trades during the late eighteenth century and early nineteenth was a relatively recent phenomenon in western European societies.

Though European women had traditionally sewn for their families, professionally made clothing for both sexes was largely the province of male artisans, especially in urban areas, from about the thirteenth century (when the cloth and clothing trades fell under the control of guilds) to the seventeenth century. At issue were methods of cut, construction, and closure. Women's garments were generally loosely shaped and fastened with drawstrings and pins, while men's garments required a closer fit and the more difficult production of buttons and buttonholes. Women's formal clothing, however, involved complicated architecture and required the special skills of a tailor. Long accustomed to this arrangement, tailors exerted great energies to protect their trade from independent female labor. Guilds defined apprenticeships, determined who could serve them, and set and enforced standards of quality. They also required that production occur in public workshops.

Empire-style gown and detail of seam, 1800–1815. Courtesy of Historic Northampton (photographs by Stan Sherer).

This gown from Hadley, Mass., illustrates both a desire to comply with prevailing fashion and the consequences of misjudgment managing one's materials. The garment's maker failed to bring her materials together effectively at the long center seam, creating an awkward pattern down the front of her gown. For comparison, see the well-executed seams of the tailor-made striped silk frock coat on page 173.

Because tailors jealously guarded the "mysteries" of clothing construction—that is, the technical and conceptual abilities to construct apparel—most women lacked the specialized knowledge needed to create garments that required attention to fit.

This division remained in place until the seventeenth century, when women asserted their right to participate more fully in the making of clothing. European women had long been active in needle trades, particularly as the wives and daughters of tailors routinely contributing their skills and labor to their family's upkeep. But during the late seventeenth and early eighteenth centuries, they pressed for greater autonomy and independent artisanal status as well, gaining ground in the making of men's clothing and largely capturing (except for the most formal apparel) the making of clothing for women and children. In the Netherlands, male tailors successfully protected the core features of guild status but could not prevent the steady growth of women working in clothing trades.[7] In Brittany, the number of women tailors rose over the first half of the eighteenth century. The tailor's guild in Nantes, France, reluctantly began admitting women in 1733, a change in policy that simply reflected the growing number of women who had entered the field without anyone's permission; if the guild hoped to exert any control at all over these artisans, they had first to bring them under the umbrella of guild oversight.[8]

The pressure to admit women to the clothing trades emerged as female sewers came to dominate a new trade, mantua making, generated in part by the advent of a new fashion. When it emerged, the mantua (originally a sort of loose coat falling open to reveal a skirt, usually worn over a matching or contrasting petticoat) represented a "revolution in women's apparel."[9] Formal attire for women previously involved a heavily whaleboned bodice and a long-trained skirt that was attached to the bodice with hooks or buttons. The mantua, a one-piece gown worn over a separate bodice, transformed both production and consumption. Support was no longer fixed in, and so required by, each particular garment but was supplied by a separate article, the stays. The new garment demanded comparatively less skill to make, required less fabric, and provided more comfort; it was therefore more accessible to larger numbers of consumers, who could now appropriate high fashion without so clearly transgressing prescription for their class or station. At the same time, because the new style evolved from loose, informal "gowns of undress" that had long been the province of seamstresses, the construction of this form, simply in new and richer materials, did not violate standing prescriptions regarding female participation in the clothing trades. The advent of this new fashion would transform the clothing trades. Needlewomen seized the opportunities this development offered. The new style of gown was promoted vigorously by aspiring needlewomen who saw in the fashion a chance to garner a good deal more business, opening a channel through which they would ultimately gain control over the construction of nearly all women's garments.[10] And as needlewomen tapped into a growing market, their customers, who included wealthy and powerful aristocratic women and others who aspired to look like them, acquired a "vested interest" in these craftswomen's "independence and success," a development that would affect the outcome of the challenges that ensued as men in the clothing trades struggled to maintain control of production.[11]

The widespread popularity of the mantua significantly advanced the prospects of enterprising women across Europe, who assumed control of most semi-skilled needle work and gained nearly sole authority over the making of women's gowns as well. The *couturieres* guild in France acknowledged fifteen hundred *maitresses* in the capital city by 1745, a number that would double by the outbreak of revolution.[12] Tailors retained authority over the making of men's fitted clothing (including coats, suits, vests, and breeches), as well as women's riding habits, which resembled men's suits in appearance and construction, but women generally came to be the primary sewers of both men's and women's working clothing and of women's fitted clothing.[13]

Several social, economic, political, and cultural factors contributed to these transformations. Women's infiltration of clothes-making crafts resulted in part from larger constrictions of opportunity. As scholars studying women's occupational prospects in a variety of times and places have observed, women came to dominate needle trades only as they were squeezed out of a much broader range of occupations. Before the late seventeenth and eighteenth centuries women could be found working (with varying degrees of autonomy) at a wide variety of tasks in a range of fields, apprenticed as blacksmiths and barbers, plumbers and joiners, fishmongers and upholsterers. But, as early as the fifteenth century and accelerating into the eighteenth, massive economic reorganization caused the supply of laborers in all fields increasingly to exceed demand for their services.[14] Craftsmen sought to protect their trades and launched efforts to reduce female competition. Apprenticeship and guild membership was increasingly limited, while restrictions were placed on women's independent production; the employment of female workers was discouraged, controlled, or simply prohibited. The result was that, by the late eighteenth and early nineteenth centuries, the range of possibility for female artisanal activity had sharply narrowed. But that same constriction of opportunity produced expanded roles in the trades that remained accessible.

Economic and cultural rationales worked together to effect these changes. The argument that clothes making was an appropriate occupation for women irked tailors, because casting sewing as appropriately feminine cast them as necessarily effeminate. Tailors found themselves on an uncomfortably ragged edge of the traditional sexual division of labor in which "women tend to process 'soft' materials (cloth, leather, reeds), while men process 'hard' materials such as metal, wood and stone."[15] Tailors did occasionally work with leather, the "hardest" material of which clothing (e.g., leather breeches) was constructed, which contributed to the division of labor between male and female clothing producers, but, to these men, the distinction was not clear enough for comfort. Moreover, because tailoring did not require a dedicated site or separate workshop and was associated closely with work performed in the home (which was already becoming defined in Europe as not-work), men in clothing production received very little respect for their skills. In the hierarchy of London trades, tailoring fell just above the work of common laborers, together with that of porters, coopers, bakers, butchers, weavers, sailors, gardeners, and masons. All "hard-working manual jobs, some were quite skilled but all low in status, the pay usually poor and irregular."[16] In his mid-century guide to trades, Robert Campbell rose to their defense, though weakly, insisting that the tailor is "not such a despicable animal as the world imagines; that he is really a useful member of society."[17] But the same qualities that defined needle trades as appropriate for eighteenth-century women made them emasculating for eighteenth-century men. That derogatory view of tailoring helped clear the way for greater female participation in the trade.

From the earliest days of New England's colonization, then, the tailors, milliners, and mantua makers who came to Britain's North American settlements brought with them expectations about men and women's participation in the clothing trades. Very little is known about either tailors or mantua makers in early New England. Though women tailors do not appear in seventeenth-century sources, both men and women do appear as mantua makers. John Richards was a mantua maker in early eighteenth-century Hartford, while in the 1720s and 1730s, "Mrs E.A." from London advertised in the Boston press that she "designs making Mantos and Riding Dresses" as well as "all sorts of Millinary work"; she also offered her skills as an instructor in the art of dressing heads and cutting hair.[18] About the same time, Richard Bassett and his wife, from the "Court end of London," also advertised their shared enterprise; in addition to mantuas, they offered "all sorts of gowns, petticoats, Spanish flies, mantels, velvet hoods and mantel hoods, high crowned hats and cloaks."[19]

As the eighteenth century wore on, a thriving world of clothes-making artisans hummed along throughout New England. Just as European gown making was transformed from a trade controlled by men to one dominated by women, in New England, men like Richards and Bassett were the exceptions; by 1789 (the first year that Boston published a city directory), all of the city's (advertising) mantua makers were women. And New England women, like their counterparts elsewhere, would press to expand their role in the skilled making of men's clothing, too. At the same time, other women, without specific training in any clothing trade, continued to ply their needles in less formal ways. The clothes-making trades in New England, then, reflected the larger sweep of change transforming practices across Europe but responded, too, to particular circumstances closer to home.

The Spectrum of Needleworkers in Rural New England

Men and women throughout New England seem almost perpetually engaged in the production and consumption of textiles and clothing, within their own households and in the households of others. The enormity of work involved in creating even a single garment is so staggering that it can be difficult for those of us accustomed to simply purchasing the finished product to take in.[20] A good sense of the process as it stood at the close of the eighteenth century can be gained from the diary of Elizabeth Fuller, a fifteen-year-old girl from Princeton, Massachusetts. In February 1791, Fuller spent three days (beginning on the ninth) picking wool that had already been designated for a coat for her father. She began to break the wool on the twenty-second, working through about four pounds a day for three days. On 1 March, her mother began to spin the wool for the coat, which occupied her for several days over the next three weeks, until she finally finished on the twenty-fifth. A woman arrived in April to warp the loom with the thread (which had been dyed blue, apparently by someone from outside the household), which Elizabeth finished drawing in the next day. She wove about two yards each day that she worked on it, and "got out the piece" on the morning of 14 April 1791. Her father then carried the wool fabric to "Mr. Deadman's," probably to be fulled. In June she records, "Ma cut out Pa's coat" and, later, that her mother was sewing it up. In July, Elizabeth began the process all over again, "picking blue wool for Pa's surtout," which too would be broken, spun, woven, cut, sewn and fulled during the next few months, until it was finished the following October.[21]

While Mrs. Fuller possessed sufficient skill to cut her husband's coat without resorting to the help of a tailor, the amount of clothing required by New England families was simply too great, and the range of garments too broad, for the demand to be met solely by women working to supply their own households. Thousands of young women contributed to the work of textile production by hiring themselves out as spinners, while, by the close of the century, both women and men in New England worked at weaving. But clothing production (and maintenance) engaged another work force of tailors, tailoresses, gown makers, stay makers, milliners, and laundresses. Long before Catherine Deane picked up her needle, a dense network of artisans and laborers flourished across the region. Occupations within the clothing trades were not distinct. Though each trade required command of particular skills, some skills were shared across the clothing trades, and some practitioners might master skills associated with more than one trade. Rather than trying to identify specialized trades, or to create artificial categories within those trades, it is both more helpful and more accurate to think of a craft's practitioners as falling along a "range . . . based upon training, tools and task difficulty."[22] Better still is to envision multidimensional communities of practice that engaged men and women of greater and lesser skill in a variety of associated occupations in ways that could change shape over the course of individual lives and circumstances. Put another way, clothes making encompassed a range of skills, some shared, others not, and most involving novices, amateurs, and specialists.

In communities along the Connecticut River, a tailoress was akin to what we today might call a seamstress (a word that, along with its companion, "sempstress," appears infrequently in manuscript sources from the Connecticut River Valley). Semi-itinerant in that they traveled locally, lodging for several days at a time in the home of their neighbors and employers while they went about their business, these needlewomen took widely held but well-developed skills into the households of others. Their work required no particular training, unlike that of tailors and gown makers, but it did demand a good deal of practice, and it would be incorrect to categorize these women as "unskilled" workers. Clothing in early America, as we have seen, was a valuable asset, and great care was taken to prolong the lives of individual garments. Tailoresses generally performed tasks required to produce and maintain the most common garments for men and women (as well as children of either sex): shifts, shirts, skirts, frocks, jackets, trousers, and other garments constructed largely in two dimensions that required little attention to fit. Keeping these garments in good order was no small undertaking. Everyday life in early America was hard on clothing: cloth was regularly stained, soiled, and discolored, torn or worn through at the elbows and knees; seams split, hems frayed, and buttons went astray. Laundering could stress both materials and construction. At the same time, clothing had to change with the bodies it covered; garments were enlarged and cut down, reshaped and resized, and sometimes converted altogether from one thing to another, men's coats cut down to clothe boys, quilts converted to skirts, skirts converted to quilts, and so forth. The best needlewomen could make alterations and repairs, and render them invisible, too.

Many New Englanders owned one or more garments of better quality. For women, these garments were gowns that fit snugly through the bodice, shoulders, and arms before cascading gracefully to the floor. The construction of gowns, unlike that of skirts and shifts and other two-dimensional garments, demanded special training and expertise. A gown maker had to be able to solve a series of challenging mathematical problems in order to persuade flat textiles to conform gracefully to curved surfaces, such as the negative curvature of the back.[23] Since many middling women owned only a single gown of good quality, or acquired such gowns infrequently, they were rightfully loath to risk cutting into expensive fabrics themselves. When Catherine Parsons—among the most active tailors in Northampton—needed new silk gowns for herself and her daughters, she purchased the skills and experience of the Northampton gown maker Esther Wright to make them up. She also employed the gown maker to cut the pieces for a pair of stays, though she did not ask her to assemble them.[24] Parsons's choice reminds us that occupations within the clothing trades, though related, were not interchangeable. Tailoresses, tailors, gown makers, milliners, and stay makers specialized in different aspects of clothing production and possessed specialized knowledge appropriate to those tasks.

The construction of so-called polite clothing required, in addition to an understanding of the human form, an understanding of and familiarity with many different fabrics that allowed the gown maker to turn the special properties exhibited by expensive materials—the gloss of calimanco, the weight of paduasoy, the luster of satin, the stoutness of ducape—to best advantage. As one skilled (though not necessarily specialized) needlewoman warned a younger novice at the work, "Did you consider that silk does not stick to you like cambric[?] it sets off and needs to be longer than anything else."[25] The younger woman's inexperience nearly caused her to cut her pieces too short; were it not for this timely warning, yards of fabric would have been ruined. Technological advances in textile production raised challenges for eighteenth-century gown makers. When large-scaled patterns gained popularity, for example, special skill was required to ensure that repeating rhythms of vines and flowers were shown the advantage of both the fabric and its wearer as they stretched across a tightly fitted bodice and cascaded down the bell of the skirt. Cutting and positioning fabric in this way is a challenge, but good gown makers could do it while also making the most of expensive materials.[26]

Expense did not necessarily deter a person from hiring skilled help to complete an article of clothing; purchasing the labor of a practiced artisan typically represented just 5 to 15 percent of a garment's total cost. The nine yards of pink durant that the Hadley gentlewoman Elizabeth Porter Phelps acquired in 1788 cost eighteen shillings; at that time the cost of cutting and making a gown was normally about two and a half shillings, or just under 14 percent.[27] Catherine Phelps Parsons paid three shillings each for Esther Wright's time and talent in 1791; the price of silk that summer was typically between six and eight shillings a yard. The Greenfield tailor Silas Wells charged one shilling six pence to cut a coat, but ten shillings six pence to cut and sew the garment from start to finish.[28] Similarly, merely cutting out and not making up that same gown could cost as little as nine pence.[29] In these instances, the labor may not even have included basting (that is, using long, loose stitches to tack the cut pieces together in their proper relationships, in preparation for sewing), suggesting that little effort was put into fit. Reluctance to cut into the best materials one could secure—whether store-bought or homemade—when more experienced help was so affordable, was merely practical. One poorly planned cut could easily ruin yards of fabric.

Consumers who secured the services of skilled artisans also saved time. Clothing production was enormously time consuming, drawing even adept needlewomen away from other necessary chores. Women turned to gown makers when they needed to have a garment completed more quickly than their time permitted. Thus, when Sophronia Beebe of South Wilbraham needed a new gown, her sister Patience suggested she have it made by "Mrs Clark," who, she noted, "will I dare say make it fast enough for the cash."[30] Tailors, too, routinely emphasized the speed with which they worked, offering in their advertisements such standard assurances as "short notice" and "with dispatch." Burrage Dimock, a tailor in Connecticut, raised the bar for everyone when he guaranteed "coats made in 12 hours notice!"[31]

Finally, as Claudia Kidwell points out, "homemade clothing must have looked homemade"; that is, the garments produced when an untrained hand simply replicated the shapes and seams of some picked-apart garment answered the basic need to cover the body but probably little else.[32] While certainly talented home sewers routinely produced serviceable, even stylish apparel for themselves and their families, slouching jackets, wrinkled shoulders, misapplied ornament, and uneven hems signaled the work of amateurs, whose training in clothing construction was limited to the copying of other garments that were professionally rendered, or, among less fortunate families, from garments that were themselves only poorly made. The ability, or lack thereof, of some men and women to hire an experienced needleworker was readily apparent in the cut of their clothes, and so too was their ability to achieve some semblance of gentility on ready display.

For these reasons—to conserve the value of their material, to spare the time demanded by a host of other household chores, and to achieve an appearance reflecting some greater measure of refinement—many women turned to others for assistance in the construction of even everyday clothing.[33] Stylish clothing (which made up a very small part of a working woman's wardrobe, a larger part of a middling woman's, and a still larger part of the wardrobe of a woman of the rural gentry) required higher levels of skill that were beyond the fundamental skills most women mastered. Artisans who knew how to cut a well-fitting garment were essential not only in cities like Boston and Hartford but in the New England countryside as well. By the middle of the eighteenth century, most rural New England communities had access to one or more skilled tailors and one or two gown makers, plus dozens more who took in sewing as a means to contribute to their household income.[34]

In addition to making and altering gowns, some needlewomen also constructed that essential women's undergarment, stays. Stay makers were important contributors to clothing and clothing construction, and their craft closely linked to gown making, since gowns required the structured foundation stays provided. Several layers of linen beneath a final, top fabric were stitched together to provide stiff support, the shape of the stays primarily provided by closely spaced channels filled with reed or baleen (whalebone). At the same time, stays, which pressed women's bodies into the shape and carriage of gentility, were essential instruments of genteel deportment. For most of the eighteenth century, the wooden busks inserted in pockets running the length of the stay's center contributed to an erect posture and also prevented women from bending at the waist; movement from the hips or knees was considered more elegant.[35] Since a good deal of force was required to push whalebone through the channels or to stitch through the leather with which the stays were bound, stay making was widely considered primarily a male trade. Campbell's *London Tradesman* asserted that "the Work is too hard for Women, it requires more Strength than they are capable of."[36] In rural New England, however, many craftswomen made stays in addition to gowns, including Catherine Phelps and Sarah Clark, who charged over three times more for stays than for a gown. Rebecca Dickinson, Anna Phelps, and others also made stays.[37]

Closely related to the production of clothing were laundresses, who contributed to clothing maintenance. Though both white and black women worked as washerwomen in the eighteenth century, laundresses in Federal-era New England appear to have been drawn disproportionately from the population of freed slaves. Women of the rural gentry, in particular, often hired black women from the area to come in and do their washing. In Hadley, Elizabeth Phelps recorded that the former slave "Old Phillis" (whose name, coincidentally, is the same as that of the younger woman who belonged to Phelps' household) washed for them, as did another, unnamed, black woman, while one Native American woman is recorded as having toiled especially diligently making soap. This Phillis was also hired to wash for the Porters in town. Betsy Phelps Huntington, too, while in Litchfield, Connecticut, specifically mentions hiring black women to wash. Peggy Browning, a former slave of Connecticut's Wadsworth family, remained on the property after manumission, taking in laundry to support herself.[38] Even in Hadley, the heaviest, dirtiest labor—hefting multiple buckets of water, moving washtubs, carrying wood, building and maintaining fires, making soap, scrubbing clothes, heating and lifting cumbersome irons—seems to have been reserved (at least by women of the local gentry) for women of color.[39]

Women regularly acquired and deployed a range of skills related to the overlapping occupations of the clothing trades. In every community on any day an observer could find women helping friends, neighbors, and relatives in informal exchanges, whether related to the clothing trades or to other work, that stood outside any real or metaphorical marketplace. But that exchanges such as these occurred within kin groups and between neighbors does not necessarily mean that they were only gestures of mutual aid among women. Within households and extended families, transactions regularly occurred "within the calculus of monetary exchange even when cash did not change hands": sons kept accounts of their mother's room and board, sisters on the work they performed for their brothers, nephews, and nieces. This was a "culture in which almost everything, including the mutual support offered kin, had a price, even if the bill was not immediately forthcoming."[40] Diaries, correspondence, and interleaved almanacs are filled with notations in which women are recorded as having sewn garments for their cousins, brothers, uncles, aunts, nieces, and others, labor that was regularly figured within larger patterns of exchange and indebtedness among families and neighbors.

The Acquisition of Clothes-Making Skills

For most women and some men, transformation from novice to knowledgeable sewer began in childhood. When they were barely six or seven, girls and occasionally boys began to learn the fundamentals of sewing. They were tutored first in the simple care of their tools, in how to keep their sewing box or basket neat and orderly, and they were reminded of the importance of keeping a watchful eye on one's thimble and needle.[41] Sewing samplers allowed girls to practice their cross and running stitches, before moving on to the whipstitch and back stitch. When ready, they were given easy projects of mending, darning, and sewing simple seams. As they grew older, they learned to handle a pair of scissors and were eventually allowed to cut textiles. Because cloth production required an enormous investment of time and resources and the constant care of cloth and clothing was imperative, the ability to prolong the life of a garment, to mend, alter, or remake worn or outdated clothing was among the earliest skills most women acquired.[42]

Young women mastered progressively demanding tasks. The basic elements of clothing construction formed a part of every woman's education in domesticity, and most women were able to cut and construct many of the articles their families required. Elizabeth Fuller, growing up in central Massachusetts in the 1790s, records the cutting and sewing she and her sister Sally did for a variety of garments during one busy month: "made myself a shift"; "made myself a blue worsted [petti]coat"; "[helped Sally] make me a brown woolen gown"; "Sally cut out a striped lutestring gown for me"; "I cut out a striped linnen Gown"; "Ma cut out a Coatee for me."[43] The diary of Sarah Snell Bryant of Cummington, Massachusetts, which opens in 1794 when Bryant was a young wife and the mother of small children, records the vast amount of sewing required to keep a household's clothing and linens well supplied and in good repair. In the first decade of her journal, she produced hundreds of garments for herself, her husband and children, her parents and brothers, and many members of her community. For her family alone her output included more than a dozen shirts a year and a nearly equal number of trousers, as well as several pairs of breeches and overalls and, on average, seven men's and boy's jackets, three short gowns, three long gowns, a like number of skirts and petticoats, and a host of new aprons, stockings, gloves, drawers, and frocks every year. Roughly one day in every three saw her picking up her needle to attend to clothing needs; if one includes time spent producing and maintaining household linens, and also days devoted to textile production, then her responsibilities with regard to cloth and clothing required attention six days in seven for the whole of this decade, and likely the decades to follow were little different.[44]

While the sheer quantity of Bryant's needlework reminds us of the enormous time and energy clothing production consumed, her diary indicates that her work was of high quality as well. She handled materials that ranged from those of her own spinning and weaving to Italian striped silks, stamped muslins, chintzes, satins, and velvets, and she could construct garments that ranged from women's waistcoats and petticoats to short gowns, loose gowns, and robes, to outerwear such as cloaks and surtouts. Men's garments at which she was equally adept included jackets, breeches and pantaloons, frocks, overalls, great coats, and spencers.[45] She also spent time altering and mending. On more than one occasion she "ripped a coat to pieces" to "turn" it, that is, to reverse and reconstruct the pieces to draw more wear from the materials. She put new seats in old breeches and once cut apart an outdated or perhaps damaged dimity gown to preserve from the remaining fabric a short gown and petticoat. When her father brought home an old coat "to make the boys some cloths," Bryant wrested from the material a pair of trousers and two jackets for her sons, Austin and Cullen.[46] In the hill town of Cummington, Sarah Bryant could well supply the needs of her own family and often those of her neighbors too.

Even the creation of the simplest clothing, however, demanded, or certainly benefited from, greater levels of skill if a woman wanted to cut lengths of valuable textiles as efficiently and effectively as possible. Anna Green Winslow of Boston recalled that, though she had either purchased or produced a piece of linen large enough to make a dozen shifts, her aunt "could cut no more than ten out of it."[47] A better needlewoman would have conceptualized the most efficient configuration of shapes before cutting. Even should the cutter plan more skillfully, just one mistake could ruin yards of fabric. As Huldah Sheldon wrote her daughter Lucy, "I shall send the muslin you mentioned next week by mail. You will see I cut William a shirt from one of the breadths, and fear I have spoiled it, but since I do not know what use you want to make of it, shall send as is."[48] Betsy Phelps happily reported to her brother that the piece of Holland that he had purchased "makes nine shirts—instead of six," suggesting that a skilled hand had cut the linen to better advantage than he had anticipated.[49] Skilled cutting meant knowing precisely how much fabric a given garment should require; overestimating meant overpricing, and artisans who suggested that clients acquire more fabric than was in the end required were open to accusations of incompetence if not fraud, suspected as they were of designing to keep scraps for themselves. Underestimating, however, could be just as disastrous, if the cutting, once begun, could not be completed as planned

Learning to cut and sew the fundamental pieces of a working wardrobe was part of most women's training in housewifery, but some women sought out special clothing-related skills through apprenticeship, allowing them to earn livings as artisans in the clothing trades. As essential feature of artisanal studies has centered on the acquisition of craft knowledge, generally through master-apprentice relationships in which novices are understood to obtain the skills necessary to succeed at a given craft under the tutelage of an accomplished practitioner.[50] But the traditional model may not reflect the way many artisans actually mastered a given craft. Rather than absorbing primarily the knowledge of one's employer, many aspiring artisans, male and female, acquired their skills through increasing engagement in communities of practice.[51] Our search for and reading of these contracts themselves, which necessarily reflect contemporary emphasis on the teacher's effort to transfer his or her knowledge to the student, may reveal more about contemporary notions of skill and training than conventions in the early modern world. An alternative model views craft learners as members of artisanal communities. Aspiring craft practitioners began with little or no expertise in a given area and gradually, from their masters or mistresses as well as others more experienced than themselves (whether journeymen in the formal sense or simply others more practiced and adept), accumulated conceptual and manual skills that set them apart from the majority of their neighbors. They practiced those skills and acquired others. Eventually, they became known as specialists, in the neighborhood, in the community, and even perhaps the region, prompting others to seek out those special skills and exchange other goods or skills of value for them.

Long-standing conceptions of apprenticeship may limit full understanding of the acquisition and dissemination of early American craft skill in other ways as well. For example, by far the largest number of surviving indentures for young women, in Europe or America, indicate that the young girls in question were to learn "housewifery." This stipulation, however, can be misleading; housewifery could mean craft involvement along with general household labor. Eighteenth-century households did not draw distinctions between domestic and craft labor as sharply as we do today; the general upbringing of children inevitably meant some exposure to the artisan skills in the family.[52] Thus, by emphasizing one model of instruction, we may well be missing the whole picture of craft training.

Artisans, then, were not just individuals who had completed the terms of an apprenticeship contract. Any man or woman who knew how to make objects that others judged to be "aesthetically, functionally, and economically acceptable" was an artisan.[53] Thus, if we expand the definition of craft skill beyond the mere mastery of a specific set of manual operations and concepts transferred whole from expert to novice to include the acquisition of special abilities not widely shared in a given community that allows one gradually to assume a larger role in a community of practitioners, we can enlarge our understanding of skill as well as what constitutes artisanal labor.[54] We can also move beyond static and hierarchical dichotomies that too often separate domestic and artisanal work, recognize formal as well as informal learning, and envision a more complex enterprise involving larger worlds of family and community relations. This broader and more flexible conception is especially useful in rural settings where agricultural work remained central to most families' economic activity and artisans' opportunity to specialize was constrained by the comparatively limited nature of local markets.

This expanded definition of craft skill also conforms more closely to the acquisition and application of skill among women in the Connecticut Valley. Scattered references throughout account books, daybooks, and diaries indicate that rural women took on trainees whom they considered apprentices. The Hatfield gown maker Rebecca Dickinson, for example, recorded the visit of her "former 'printis," Patty Smith, in the pages of her diary and recalls going herself to "learn the trade of gownmaking."[55] The accounts of Sarah Clark of Northampton contain her credit for having made a gown for "Eben Clark's wife's apprentice."[56] Catherine Phelps Parsons's daughter described her mother's several assistants as her "apprentices."[57] In none of these cases do documents survive that affirm a legally binding relationship of the kind traditionally understood as an apprenticeship. But recognizing only those bound by a specific legal instrument (in which they typically agreed to serve an employer in the exercise of some handicraft, art, trade, or profession, for a certain number of years, with a view to learn its details and duties, and in which the employer is reciprocally bound to provide instruction) may arbitrarily exclude most young women, and perhaps some young men, not because their status as learners of a craft was not recognized in their day but because the legal instruments were reserved for young men whose economic, civic, and political identities required it. Unknown numbers of young women, then, completed periods of training in the clothing trades that, while acknowledged as apprenticeships by participants and observers alike, left no paper trail. Among the women of the Connecticut Valley, however, even when no written agreement was drafted, the apprenticeship relationship was recognized by the artisan, the novice, and the community at large.

Girls and young women also did complete more formal apprenticeships. These periods of training were established by written agreement, some of them voluntary and arranged by parents and others involuntary and assigned by selectmen or overseers of the poor.[58] In rural areas, voluntary apprenticeships seem to have lasted for about a year. When Silas and Anna Graham of Wethersfield, Connecticut, bound their daughter Anna to the Glastonbury tailor Asa Talcott, like the parents of Clarinda Colton of Springfield who bound her to the Deerfield tailor Ithamar Burt, they sought to provide their child with training in a craft that they hoped would afford an ongoing source of income.[59] Most surviving indentures, however, document compulsory apprenticeships that generally bound the apprentice until he or she reached the age of majority. Seven-year-old Rebeccah Baxter of Middletown, Connecticut, the daughter of Hannah Barstow, was bound to an apprenticeship in the tailoring trade with Elijah Treadway and was obliged to remain in Treadway's household for eleven years, until she reached the age of eighteen.[60] In Connecticut in 1788, the Middlesex County court suggested that Middletown's board of selectmen "put and bind Elizabeth Fisher, daughter of Christopher Fisher late of said Middletown deceased who is one of the town poor" as an apprentice to Ephraim and Beulah Merriam of Wallingford. The Merriams agreed to provide Elizabeth with training in the "art of mantee making in all the parts thereof" as well as the "art of good housewifery with some instructions in reading & writing." In 1804, Middletown selectmen bound an impoverished thirteen-year-old, Lucinda Cone, to the widow Clarissa Redfield, who promised to "give said Apprentice a Bible, and to Board her whilst learning a Trade (Mantu-Maker or Taylor)."[61] But such agreements between local overseers or selectmen and mantua makers or gown makers were unusual. Among the eleven hundred boys and girls bound out by Boston's overseers of the poor between 1734 and 1805, only two of the girls had contracts that specifically indicate they were to be taught this trade: Ann Crowmartie was bound to the mantua maker Ruth Decosta in 1769, and Ann Wilkinson was bound to the mantua maker Martha Mellens in 1784.[62] Many of the girls whose contracts noted only household chores may have been exposed to aspects of trades practiced within their new households, but most apprenticeships in which young women were explicitly bound to mantua makers or gown makers appear to have been voluntary arrangements sought by parents anxious to provide their daughters with marketable skills.

Although the Hatfield gown maker Rebecca Dickinson records having "gone" somewhere to learn the trade of gown making, she recorded neither the duration of her own apprenticeship nor the durations of the apprenticeships she directed. But there seems to have been a wide range in the recorded duration of apprenticeships, probably reflecting a wide variety in the rigor and extent of the training offered. As a feature of a compulsory arrangement, Elizabeth Fisher's term of seven years "to learn the trade of mantee making" was probably a function of her age more than the time required to master her craft.[63] It seems more likely that the young Hampshire County women who aspired to the trade completed a period of training more like that supervised by the tailor Catherine Phelps Parsons, that is, between one and two years.[64] Between 1800 and 1810 Margaret Booth of Longmeadow kept a constant stream of young women on hand, for about a year at a time, usually beginning in December or April. Polly Chaffee, Sarah Kilbie, Mary Bliss, and Mercy Cooley—these young women and others may have spent that year helping Booth with her work and learning something of the needle trades themselves.[65]

Like tailors' apprentices, the aspiring gown or mantua maker absorbed much of her training through observation. Although in general, an apprentice initially spent her time running errands and doing odd jobs around the workplace—tending hearths, cleaning the shop, sorting and organizing threads, buttons, fabrics, and measurements, and keeping tools in good repair, all the while gaining exposure to the routines of the trade—she might soon begin to accompany her mistress to the homes of clients, observing as she measured bodies, cut materials, and constructed garments. As time went on, the apprentice would learn how to measure clients, noting lengths on strips of parchment that would determine the shapes and sizes of the garment's pieces. She might begin her sewing by helping to stitch long seams. Perhaps the application of trimming would follow and then some of the discrete tasks of assembly, such as attaching sleeves to the bodice of a garment or sewing a surtout's long seams. Finally, she would assist in the crucial work of fitting garments. Rebecca Dickinson's apprentice, Patty Smith of Hadley, underwent just such training. Patty was the daughter of Warham and Martha Smith; her father, a merchant, was among Hadley's wealthiest men.[66] In November 1785, when Patty was seventeen, she accompanied Dickinson to the Phelps home to watch her go about her work there. By July 1787, she was entrusted with the making of a mourning gown for the elderly Elizabeth Pitkin Porter. Eventually, like her mentor, she obtained continuing employment in the Phelps household at Forty Acres. Perhaps she was hired at the suggestion of Dickinson herself, in the hope that Smith could replace her work for the family in her old age. If Dickinson did recommend Smith for hire at Forty Acres, the referral would be consistent with the familial network through which many women entered the Phelps home as needleworkers. And other Dickinson protégés may eventually have found work at Forty

Acres as well, thanks to craft or kin connections. Rebecca's sister Anne Dickinson Ballard placed her daughter Rebecca with the gown maker so the young woman might learn to cut garments. Apparently the younger Rebecca took to the trade, for almost twelve years later she went to Forty Acres to work for the Phelps household.[67]

For both tailors and gown makers, as for other craft practitioners, continuing experience—their ongoing participation in communities of practice—"supplemented the basic technical foundation acquired" during apprenticeship.[68] As we have seen, some craftswomen did travel to new places, bringing new fashions along with them. But whereas men in the clothing trades (as in woodworking trades) expanded their knowledge and improved their skills by tramping, moving from place to place, serving as journeymen to established tailors around the region, women more typically learned from clothing that had done the traveling. When in the summer of 1798, twenty-one-year-old Lucretia Smith Gaylord accompanied her client, Charlotte Porter, to the home of Elizabeth Phelps "to fix a gown for Mrs Porter by one of Betsy's," she studied the work of her counterpart in Boston and then approximated the new style to the best of her abilities. In the process, she acquired new knowledge and skills that she could then offer to other women in western Massachusetts.[69]

Rhythms of Work

Although the means by which men and women attained artisanal status differed, once established they operated in much the same way, combining their skilled work with their household and farm chores. In rural New England, few could afford to specialize in just one product; the market was just too small. Rural artisans "mustered a livelihood from several activities within a local agricultural economy." William Mather of Whately, Massachusetts, for example, worked as a cabinetmaker, housewright, brickmaker, mason, glazier, wheelwright, and farmer, as well as filling a number of town offices.[70] In a similar fashion women blended skilled sewing with other income-generating activities, as well as their regular household chores. Working as a tailoress or gown maker provided a way for young single women and wives to contribute to their family's income, and for never-married women and widows to earn modest livings.

Artisanal activity fluctuated over the course of the agricultural year. Cabinetmakers, who often had their own fields to tend, produced less furniture for their local clients during the late spring, summer, and fall, the peak seasons of the agricultural year.[71] Among specialists in the clothing trades, the pronounced variation of demand typically produced months of unemployment broken by times of overwork. Clothing needs were necessarily attended to when time and income permitted. In weeks devoted to planting and harvest, people's minds were in the fields; tattered breeches or worn vests would have to wait. For the Deerfield tailor John Russell, the spring planting seasons and the months of harvest were the least active periods for his shop; Russell produced the bulk of the year's clothing during the late summer, fall, and winter.[72] Entries in the diary of Josiah Pierce of Hadley—which contains references to Pierce's clothing consumption, as well as to the work of his niece Esther, a tailoress—suggest that peak months of clothing production were November and January, when the harvest was in and spring planting had not yet begun.[73] Beginning in July, cresting in November, and continuing on through February, tailors attended to the many clothing needs of their communities. For the more socially attuned, these were also seasons during which more formal attire was in greater demand.

The same rhythms of the agricultural year consumed the attentions of gown makers and their clients, but women may have focused on their clothing needs at other moments than did men. Tabitha Smith's work for Elizabeth Phelps suggests that rural women turned their attention to their wardrobes most often during the summer months once the fields were sown and the gardens planted, but before the late summer and fall harvests would set them to other tasks. While some activity occurred in every month, most of Phelps's gown acquisition and alteration took place in June and July, with somewhat less activity in May and August. The accounts of the gown maker Esther Wright suggest that women purchased much of their clothing in the late spring and early summer. In 1790 Wright made more gowns in May, June, and July than she did in the rest of the year combined; the following year, she made almost half of the year's total in those months.[74] Although gown making (and alteration) was the principal activity of the summer, in the winter, the demand changed. Those summers that saw Esther Wright busily producing gowns for her community were not interrupted by the making of heavier articles; not a single frock appears in her accounts for the summer of 1790, and only one appears in the summer of 1791. Conversely, in the winter months outer garments were attended to. She made four frocks in January 1791 alone. Dickinson also noted on more than one occasion that the week before Thanksgiving was an especially busy time and November in general a hurried season, a rhythm confirmed by the accounts of Esther Wright.[75] On 15 November 1790, Wright's accounts debit Joseph Hutchens for the making of a gown and two frocks. On the nineteenth, Joel Wright engaged her to cut a frock, and on the twentieth, she made two gowns for the family of Eben

Wright. That same day, Simeon Bartlett also hired Wright to make a gown. Wright may have felt she had her hands full when Supply Clark arrived four days later with material for his wife's riding hood.[76] At times gown makers found themselves simply too busy to take on additional work and so faced what must have been the painful prospect of turning away work that they could only wish would come in at a more even pace: Ruth Pease of Blandford, Massachusetts, writing during a visit to Hartford in the winter of 1812, on more than one occasion recorded having been, as on this February afternoon, "unsuccessful in my applications to mantua makers." The following day Pease revisited the mantua maker, and "after some delay . . . found that it was in vain to think of getting a gown cut and basted. The one on whom I depended was ill. The others were engaged."[77]

Though less remunerative than the creation of new garments, alterations were common and necessary, and often sustained artisans throughout the year. Of the twenty-one gowns Elizabeth Phelps makes reference to in her diary, the gown maker Tabitha Smith created or altered fourteen of them, producing gowns of calico, lustring, stuff, and chintz. In addition, she made or altered more than twenty gowns for Phelps's two daughters, sometimes converting a garment of the mother's to a gown for a daughter.[78] Often, this work was required in order to adapt clothes to the changing bodies of growing girls ("Tuesday Thankful and I at Mrs Smiths for her to make some gowns longer for Thankful"), pregnant women (an expectant Elizabeth Whiting Phelps Huntington wrote home that she had "not begun to alter my blue gown into a loose dress, for I find such the most comfortable and decent for me"), aging women, and so on.[79] Changes in women's bodies, whether for growing girls, pregnancy, or aging, were, as we have already seen, perhaps the most common and compelling reasons to extend the life of a garment. But shifting fashions also accounted for many alterations. Toward the end of the century, for example, America's interest in the French Revolution produced a corresponding revolution in silhouette. And when European fashion—inspired by democratizing political impulses and an international fascination with all things Greek and Roman sparked by the unearthing of Pompeii—urged women to don revealing sheer white gowns that suggested columnar marble statues brought to life, a major overhaul of American women's wardrobes became necessary.

Seeking this slimmer form, Elizabeth Phelps engaged a young woman to "make [her] lutestring gown plumb," that is, to reduce the bell shape of the skirts, formerly popular because they emphasized horizontal lines, in favor of a narrower garment that emphasized the vertical.[80] That the gown was then about twelve years old suggests the degree to which alterations could extend the life of expensive garments; indeed, Phelps's wedding gown was made and remade three times in forty-two years. Created in 1770, it was altered eighteen years later, in 1788, and again in 1812, for the now-elderly Phelps, or perhaps it was too "made plumb" to suit her then-thirty-three year-old daughter Betsy Whiting Phelps Huntington. In all, three needlewomen (that we know of) collaborated on the gown over its lifetime: Rebecca Dickinson created a garment that lasted some eighteen years, Molly Wright of Northampton extended its life for another twenty-four, and Hannah Stockwell of Hadley further prolonged the life of the garment, though we do not know for how long, in 1812, four decades after its original construction.[81]

Alterations also became particularly important during periods of political and economic upheaval. At the onset of the Seven Years' War, Esther Edwards Burr wrote, "Rain all day, and so dark that we could hardly see to work, and *propor for the times,* I have my old raggs about me, trying to make one new gound out of two old ones" (emphasis added).[82] A month after Esther Burr found herself trying to splice together a new gown, she wrote Sarah Prince with an apology for slighting her correspondence: "so busy about some tayloring that I must beg to be excused. You must know that I am the Taylor. I'm altering old cloths which is very hard work."[83] During the Revolution, when the interruption of trade with Britain meant a shortage of imported textiles, old dresses were again pressed into additional service, and women with the skill to extend the lives of garments were in high demand. Elizabeth Phelps turned over a spate of alterations to Tabitha Smith in the 1780s, perhaps reflecting some difficulty in acquiring new textiles.

Finally, there was the work of simple maintenance. Such work proved the mainstay of rural artisans. Needleworkers spent a good deal of their time maintaining garments, with tasks that included simple repairs to damaged apparel and alterations to extend the fashionability of a garment, to modify it to fit the changed body of its owner, to adapt it for another wearer, or simply to squeeze a few more seasons' life from it, "turning" the pieces of coat to conceal worn fabric and expose fresher material. In Glastonbury, most of Asa Talcott's income was derived from his work restoring and altering clothing.[84] Indeed, like woodworkers, blacksmiths, and other artisans, tailoring and gown-making artisans depended on repairs for a large share of their work.

The spaces in which this work was performed varied widely. Unlike furniture makers and silversmiths, who relied on sizable tools and machinery, from lathes to forges, artisans in clothing production could carry out their work, which was ad hoc and versatile, in a wider array of spaces. To be sure, tailors' shops were present on the New England landscape. Eighteenth-century tailors rented shops in commercial buildings, erected small structures on their home lot, installed shops in ells attached to their houses, or simply dedicated a corner of their living spaces to their craft work. In Hartford and Boston, tailor's shops could be found throughout the commercial district. While acquisition of a dedicated site surely reflected some measure of artisanal achievement, most tailors, male and female, appropriated spaces in and around their homes, either in addition to or in lieu of formal shop space, or worked in the homes of clients. By the close of the eighteenth century, the celebrated 1648 brick Pynchon mansion in Springfield had come to house the tailor shop of Jeremiah Snow.[85] Few such shops remain intact in the communities along the Connecticut River, but some evidence survives to hint at what they looked like. In Granby, Massachusetts, for instance, Homer White's shop occupied an ell attached to his home; he later moved to a dedicated shop space (see plate 4).[86]

In 1772, one Boston "tailor and habit maker" alerted potential customers that he would travel to "gentlemen's houses" to secure their patronage. And in rural western Massachusetts, Sylvester Judd notes, "some tailors formerly went from house to house, making garments," adding, "it was so in my younger days," about 1800.[87] Needlewomen, however, were, on the whole, less likely than men to work in shop settings. If a large table could not be dedicated to the work, planks on trestles provided table space, while work-in-progress could be hung on pegs around the craftswoman's home.[88]

A clothes maker's needs were simple: a well-lit space with broad tables on which to cut and sew fabric, irons and access to a fire on which to heat them, and shears, needles, and pins were the essentials. The senior artisan principally required shears with which to cut fabric; assistants responsible for the assembly of garments used shears, scissors, thimbles (generally of steel and open at both ends, as opposed to the closed thimbles of brass, silver, and occasionally gold used by domestic needlewomen), and large and small needles. Pins came in many sizes and served many purposes. (While they were certainly tools associated with sewing, they were also an essential part of a woman's wardrobe; often pins were a garment's primary method of closure and fastened handkerchiefs and other modesty pieces in place as well.) Long slips of parchment were required to record measurements, though some tailors simply found paper where available, tearing up strips of the local newspaper or using other discarded pieces. An assortment of irons was necessary to press finished fabrics and to press down seams; press boards on which the ironing was done could be as simple as boards laid on trestles. A clothes frame might be employed to store finished garments and a stiff clothes brush to free clothes from dirt and dust.

Inventories of several eighteenth-century tailors in the Connecticut Valley reveal that such tools required little in the way of capital. In the 1770s, Robert Corsill of Springfield owned a tailor's goose, a pair of shears, a pair of hand irons, and a box and heaters, valued together at £2 6s. 6d. Tables on which he laid out yardage for cutting, shop boards on which to sit while sewing, a clothes frame, and other related equipment were appraised at £1 7s. 8d.[89] George Herbert of Deerfield owned tools appraised in 1786 at a mere 12s., roughly the same value as just two of the six chairs scattered around his home. His shop tables, clothes frame, and other shop furniture was valued at another £1 7s. 6d., for a total of just under £2.[90] In 1787, Joseph Slack of Windsor, Vermont, owned equipment that was similarly valued at 12s. 8d.; his iron goose, shears, bits and bodkins, chisel, brush, and press boards were equivalent in value to his saddlebags and bridle.[91] The Hartford shop of Thomas Gross contained a "shop table" valued at 1s. 6d., and a small assortment of irons (one goose worth 6 s., and another worth 2s. 6d.) and shears.[92] In 1812, Jonathan Root's shop contained one small table, as well as a single pair of shears, a goose, and a clothes horse.[93] Nehemiah Street's 1791 probate inventory gives a larger sense of the goods as well as the tools that the Farmington artisan kept on hand: one large shears, one goose, two gross of sleeve buttons, fourteen stock buckles, a hundred yards of shoe binding, nearly five dozen vest buttons, two and a half dozen coat buttons, four dozen yellow buttons, and thirteen bags of death—head buttons valued at £1. Fabrics in the shop included scarlet broadcloth, black velvet, green Persian, white sarcenet, a small assortment of calicoes and callimancoes, and plain and figured gauze.[94]

Among Connecticut Valley artisans, the outlay required for tailoring tools was comparable to that required for saddlers and shoemakers; in the 1760s, generally between £2 and £3 or less would allow an aspiring needleworker to acquire the necessary equipment.[95] By comparison, the Springfield blacksmith John Day owned an anvil worth £5 13s. 4d., and another, smaller one worth £1 13s. 4d. His tools were valued at another £8 18s. 6d., and his shop building itself still more. At the same time, his competitor James Warner owned a shop and tools worth over £30.[96] But that the cost of tailoring tools was small does not mean that they were widely owned. Of some three hundred inventories taken in seven Hampshire County towns during the last quarter of the eighteenth century and first decade of the nineteenth, only one contains a pair of tailor's shears. Just twelve, or 4 percent, contain a tailor's goose, a long, thin iron used to press seams; by contrast, box irons appeared in nearly 1 in 5 household inventories, while flat or sad irons turn up in equal numbers. No more than 15 percent contained shears of any kind, and two-thirds of these were valued at less than 1 shillings.[97] Almost half were worth 6 pence or less, suggesting that the shears most households owned were of comparatively poor quality; tailor's shears were typically worth about 2 shillings, and sometimes 5 shillings or more.[98]

Construction Methods and Other Technical Aspects of Clothing Production

Constructing a garment in early America, as now, began with lengths of two-dimensional fabric that needed to be cut into specific shapes and assembled before they could be transformed into three-dimensional garments.[99] Following the steps associated with the making of a gown from start to finish conveys the various skills required by successful artisans. The gown maker first considered the fabrics at hand and assessed their properties with respect to the garment to be constructed and the size and shape of the person who was to wear it. Do patterns need to be accommodated among the various pieces? How might the weight and drape of the selected fabric affect the finished garment? How might the finished garment conceal flaws in the wearer's body or enhance attributes? Having considered these and other questions, the artisan was ready to start fitting the garment to the wearer, a process that began with the draping of the lining material on the intended wearer's body.

For most women's gowns, the bodice lining was cut first, forming a foundation on which the bodice would then be draped and sewn.[100] These linings, generally of muslin or linen fabrics, were most often cut directly on the body of the garment's intended wearer, to insure the closest possible fit.[101] Next, the gown maker had to make some choices about the finished garment—the silhouette it would have, the location and methods of closure, and so forth. A gown might float freely from the shoulders to the floor, or it might conform closely to the body. It might close entirely in the front, or it might remain open to reveal a stomacher. The English gown, in which a series of pleats were stitched down across the back, allowing the material to hug the trunk of the body before releasing into the folds of the skirt, was popular in the second half of the eighteenth century. Pleats were important tools because their method of construction, folding the material accordion-style and then stitching the folded fabric in place, allowed the gown maker to preserve without cutting as much as possible of the original textile, a practice that also preserved the client's ability to remake the garment in the largest range of future alterations.[102]

"Patterns" of the eighteenth-century were not the paper models familiar today. Instead, gown makers based new garments on past experience. A strip of paper or parchment provided a means by which to note and track lengths,

"Ladies Dress Maker," from *The Book of Trades* (1804), 30–31.

As the published caption for the image reads, "The plate is a representation of a mantua-maker taking the pattern off from a lady by means of a piece of paper, or cloth. The pattern, if taken in cloth, becomes afterwards the lining of the dress."

measurements in inches being largely unknown before the early nineteenth century. In June 1789, when Tabitha Smith "took measure" for Elizabeth Phelps's daughters' new gowns, she was replacing old lengths with new ones.[103] Betsy and Thankful had had new gowns from Smith the previous May, but they were growing girls (ten and thirteen years old, respectively) and those old measures would no longer do.[104] The measurements helped Smith determine how much fabric she should cut for the new gowns. She relied on no published pattern for the gowns' form; instead, she based these garments on other ones she had made, taking into account any new requests from Phelps. Using the measures as her guide, Smith pinned, cut, and stitched her way to the finished garment. For the bodices, she draped and fastened some thin, malleable material—usually paper or a filmy fabric like muslin—over her clients' shifts and stays. This step generated information from which to cut the gowns' fabric, and, if cloth, provided the eventual garments' lining.[105] Such "patterns" could be basted together for one, and perhaps several, fittings before the scissors were picked up and the intended cloth cut up. A "pattern" for a gown might also be created from an old garment left by the client, or from paper or cloth patterns retained from an earlier garment. The gown maker then assessed how to cut her pieces to make the best use of (that is, use the least amount of) her client's expensive fabrics. The client and craftswoman might have a several fittings in which the size and location of the pleats, the angle and shape of sleeves, and other features would be determined and sewn in. The client might contribute to the assembly process, particularly in the comparatively less skilled stitching of long seams. All in all, it was a time-consuming process that meant much shared time and space between client and craftswoman.

Having determined the style desired and cut her fabric appropriately, the gown maker was then presented with the task of assembling her pieces. Eighteenth-century clothing was constructed with only a few different types of seam stitches, but which stitch to use at any moment was determined by the seam's role in the overall architecture of the garment in question, and particularly how much stress the joint was likely to receive. The choice of stitch also depended on whether or how often the garment was likely to be laundered and whether the garment was likely to be taken apart for later alterations. As Linda Baumgarten and John Watson explain, "shirts and shifts were sewn with fine backstitches and then felled to enclose all raw edges. Linen selvages were joined by butting and whipstitching them closely. This process not only saved expensive fabric but also resulted in sturdy garments that could withstand washing. Men's fitted coats, waistcoats, and breeches were sewn with sturdy backstitches that withstood the strain of movement. The lining and fashion fabrics were also joined together with attention to an economy of motion on the part of the maker. As Baumgarten and Watson also point out, "separate facings were seldom used two hundred years ago. Rather, linings extended out to the edges of the garment, where they were turned under and stitched to the fashion fabric. This process was often done with a stitch that resembles slanted hemming stitch on the lining side but forms running topstitching on the fashion fabric side. This stitching method sews the top parts together and top stitches in one operation."[106]

The cutting of a garment and its assembly were two separate processes, not always performed by the same hand. On many occasions, rural gown makers simply basted the garment together, leaving the more tedious stitching of seams to the client, who performed this labor herself, assigned it to a daughter or a servant in her household, or hired out this task too, to a local seamstress or tailoress. Ruth Pease of Blandford, Massachusetts, hoped while visiting Hartford to get a gown "cut and basted"; but she was unsuccessful in finding a craftswoman who was not already oversubscribed.[107] On another day, she had more luck, as she "rode into Springfield to get a gown basted &c" and was home before tea.[108] In 1776 Wethersfield, Connecticut, the tailor Oliver Talcott charged Elizur Burnham's household two shillings six pence for "part making a gown and cloak" while in 1783, Ephraim Baker paid a shilling "to cutting and basting a gown."[109] In Northampton, the gown maker Sarah Clark's activities in the 1760s, 1770s, and 1780s included "cutting out," "making," "making over," and "altering." Clark also charged for gowns made "in part," suggesting that some women elected to do as much of their own sewing as their time and talent allowed.[110] In 1807, Elizabeth Phelps hired Olive Dickinson "to cut and baste a callico gown."[111] Elizabeth Huntington occasionally cut her own gowns but then employed other women to sew them up: "last thursday Chloe came and made my gown, & I like it much."[112]

Once the basic garment had been constructed, additional time and skill was necessary to apply the appropriate trimmings. Since cut varied little across garments, fashionability through most of the eighteenth century was largely derived from the choice of fabric and the application of trimmings. Common forms of embellishment in the 1760s and 1770s included robing, ruching, ruffles, fringe, and flounces. In the 1780s, when style was largely determined by an abundance of trimmings, milliners, whose skill in the ornamentation of hats and other sorts of headwear gave them additional experience in this area, became especially important. The production of the trim itself involved special skills. Robing, for example, was created with long strips of fabric that had been "pinked" on either side to form a decorative profile.

To create these strips, the artisan used a small pinking tool, a metal instrument molded on one end with the pattern to be cut. The fabric to be pinked was folded and placed on a surface that could bear repeated hits (like a leather pad on a hard surface); the artisan began striking the pinking tool with a mallet, creating with each blow a small segment of patterned ribbon. The amount of trim applied to a gown varied widely, depending on the current fashion and the financial resources of the client, from simple embellishment at the sleeves or neckline, requiring about four feet of robing, to long serpentine strips twice that long applied to the length of the bodice.

As the eighteenth century gave way to the nineteenth, and the rococo styles of the Georgian era were supplanted by neoclassical simplicity; in gowns, the significance of trimmings receded as preference shifted to sparer forms. The radical change in silhouette that occurred beginning in the 1790s presented a serious technical challenge, as clothing producers contended with a gradual shortening of the waistline. By 1800, gowns were gathered just below the bust, which, together with the increasing preference for plain white fabrics, created a columnar appearance meant to allude to ancient Greek statuary (see plate 5). The new fashion was strictly adhered to; one Massachusetts correspondent described three sisters who were almost in uniform in their muslins: "the three miss Davises looked as if they were born at a birth, they looked of an age, and dress'd exactly alike, [with h]andsome mouse-colour'd hats, & veils, mouse colour'd ribbands round their little, slender waists. . . . [T]heir bows were tied exactly alike [and] didn't vary half quarter of an inch." [113] Needleworkers, asked both to create new garments and to alter old ones to conform to prevailing fashion, struggled to master this new cut, a chore that for some artisans generated a good deal of business.

David Lazaro has traced the ways in which artisans struggled to adapt to the challenges that accompanied the shift to the neoclassical style, developing new technical skills along the way. As he observes, "mantua-makers chose many different ways to fit 1790s gowns. Some modified the earlier use of stitched-down vertical pleats, continuing the custom for fitting gowns that was established at the end of the seventeenth century. Others employed seams, which began to appear only at the end of the decade, and would become universal by the first few years of the nineteenth century, when tailoring women's garments gradually became more accepted." The unidentified maker of a gown in the collections of the Pocumtuck Valley Memorial Association struggled to bend her skills to the new fashions, accomplishing fit through the use of forty-six pleats stitched down the back of the bodice when seams would have been "easier and faster" and would have produced a "cleaner, slimmer line" as well.[114]

By the turn of the nineteenth century, these lightweight gowns were the order of the day and presented little mystery to their makers. The impact of this dramatic change in silhouette on the artisans who produced it is explored in a later chapter; for now, it is important simply to note that the introduction of these new styles required the mastery of new skills. Clothing construction was by no means self-evident in early America; different sorts of garments demanded different sorts of skills. Even individual elements of construction, from buttonholes to seams and pleats, demanded specific conceptual knowledge and technical abilities. The creation of the region's wardrobes depended on an array of laborers, men and women whose skills were simultaneously distinct and overlapping. For women who worked before, beyond, and in the absence of marriage as tailoresses; for tailors, gown makers, and stay makers who secured training in the "art and mystery" of skilled needle trades; for women obliged to provide clothing for their families, apprentices, and farm laborers; for others whose obligations extended to more ornamental stitching; and for the recipients of all of this labor, making clothing was indeed a business never done.

Part II

CHAPTER 3

Needlework of the Rural Gentry

The World of Elizabeth Porter Phelps

IN THE LATE summer of 1769, the young Hadley gentlewoman Elizabeth Porter rode from Forty Acres, her farm north of the village center, into town, to the home of her cousin Sarah Porter Hopkins. She came to assist in the quilting of Sarah's new black calimanco petticoat. During the three days that she stayed with the Hopkins family, other young women came to help with the quilt. Doubtless tea and cakes were enjoyed, and pleasant conversation shared; meanwhile, the petticoat was completed. On Friday, Porter rode home, and on Sunday she recorded the gathering in the pages of her journal: "Wednesday went to quilt upon a black Calliminco coat for Mrs Hop[kins]—in the afternoon Miss Sally Woodbridge of Hatfield and Miss Betty Williams and others of our own people. Thursday in the afternoon Miss Betty and Miss Sophia Patrage from Hatfield—Fryday I returned."[1]

Elizabeth Porter's entry tells us what she considered important to remember about the event: that she had been gone from her home from Wednesday to Friday and that during that time she had helped produce the new quilted petticoat of black calimanco that Sarah Hopkins would be wearing around town. She also thought it important to note the names of some of the other women who had participated—Sarah Woodbridge, Elizabeth Williams, and Betty and Sophia Partridge—and to mention unnamed others of her "own people," the kinship, social, and economic communities to which she and her family belonged.

What Porter's entry omitted is equally significant. Most important, she left out the work of other women not of her "own people" who also contributed to the quilting. In the days before the quilters arrived, for example, someone had readied the materials for the quilting. Three to four pounds of wool had been washed and scoured in soapy water, rinsed (several times), and laid outside on the ground to dry. Then it was carded and set aside for batting. Meanwhile, another series of jobs had produced the linen or wool fabric that would be used for the backing. If linen was used, then flax had

Forty Acres, Hadley, Mass. PPHP. Courtesy of Amherst College Archives and Special Collections.

This early twentieth-century view of the Phelps home shows the 1752 main block (at right, with c. 1799 alterations to left), the c. 1770 ell that extends to the rear, and the long c. 1797 ell that housed a large kitchen and dairy on the ground floor, with garret space for servants above. A woodshed and corn barn lead to the carriage barn at the end of the building.

been soaked, scutched, heckled, carded, spun into thread, and woven on the loom; if wool was used, then the material was cleaned, carded, spun, and woven.[2] When the quilting was at hand, the lining of the quilt was laid out and about a half-pound of wool for each square yard of lining spread carefully across, so that the batting would be even. The desired pattern was drawn on paper (a task requiring considerable expertise, especially if the pattern was elaborate), and then transferred to the quilt top.[3] The three layers were basted together and put on the frame. At the same time, Hopkins and her help—perhaps Naomi, her' "maid" around this time—cleaned the house and prepared beds and bedding for lodgers. They also readied the room where the quilting was to take place, bringing chairs in and moving chairs out and setting up the roughly ten-by-ten-foot quilting frame in the center of a well-lit room—perhaps the south parlor of her newly built home.

Sarah Hopkins made sure that her family and friends would be there to help. The names of the women recorded in Elizabeth Porter Phelps's journal are those of the "River Gods" and other, lesser elites—the handful of families, like the Porters, who possessed the Connecticut Valley's political, economic, social, religious, and cultural authority. These are the women of "our own people" that Porter recognized. Sarah Hopkins was the daughter of a selectman and justice, Eleazer Porter, the sister of another selectman and justice, "Esquire" Eleazer Porter, and the wife of Hadley's minister, Samuel Hopkins. Her first husband was the town's previous clergyman, Chester Williams of the powerful, and power-brokering, Williams family. When Williams died, she married Hopkins, his successor as minister, and remained at the center of Hadley's ecclesiastical, cultural, and economic authority. Sally (Sarah) Woodbridge was the daughter of the Reverend Timothy Woodbridge. Betty Williams was the daughter of the economic and political powerhouse Israel Williams. Betty and Sophia Partridge, cousins of Betty Williams, belonged to yet another River God family, that of Oliver Partridge and his wife, Anna Williams Partridge, of Hatfield. Oliver Partridge was a colonel, high sheriff, and justice; Anna was the daughter of the Reverend William Williams of Weston and the granddaughter of the Reverend Solomon Stoddard of Northampton and the Reverend William Williams of Hatfield.

On the morning of the quilting, Elizabeth Porter made sure that her family's slaves and servants would keep the household running smoothly in her absence. Once satisfied, she changed out of her work clothes into something more appropriate for a few days of visiting and set out for town. Meanwhile, Sarah Hopkins, too, dressed to receive guests and made sure that the hired girl or girls had finished preparing hasty pudding, butter, molasses, breads, and cakes and pies and had readied the tea set. Porter arrived, as did others, and, after a flurry of welcomes, the quilting was under way. Later that day, Sally Woodbridge and Betty Williams ferried over from Hatfield to help with the project. Perhaps they, like Porter, stayed overnight. They quilted the following day, too, with the added assistance of the Partridge girls, who were perhaps encouraged by their Hatfield neighbors to join the gathering. As the quilting along the edges of the large frame was completed, the women rolled the materials under. Gradually the frame's parallel strips moved inward, and the chairs on which they rested moved nearer. After several such rolls, the women finished quilting. Porter remained another night and perhaps helped Hopkins restore order to her home. On Friday she returned to Forty Acres, anxious to see what had been accomplished in her absence. Back at the Hopkins house, the quilting was cut from the frame. More work remained before the garment was finished. A piece of unquilted material needed to be sewn to the top edge of the quilting to form the waistband. Pocket slits were cut into the quilting and then bound with silk tape. The rectangular piece had to be sewn together to form the shape of a skirt, and, finally, tapes to tie the petticoat closed had to be sewn into each side, and more tape sewn along the bottom hem. Only then would Sarah Hopkins be ready to display the new and beautiful product of those few days' labor (see plate 6).

In her single, brief entry, Elizabeth Porter hints at a world of activity linking households throughout her community that resulted in a single black petticoat. Many women contributed to the making of the garment—young and old, black and white, some working at leisure, some working for income, and some whose labor was controlled by others. But the diarist recorded only the activity of women like herself, whom she and they recognized as "our own people." The elision reminds us how notoriously underdocumented the lives of working women in early America are and how our historical perspective is necessarily skewed by the records and perspectives of the comparatively privileged women who left behind documents for later generations to study. It helps explain why this study of working women in the clothing trades pauses first to consider the lives and needlework of genteel women. Because it is largely through their records, mainly the diaries, letters, and ledgers they left behind, that we can learn anything about the often-nonliterate women they employed, it is almost impossible to tell the stories of early America's working women without conveying something about these genteel women, who will come up again and again in the pages to follow.

EXPLORING THE lives of genteel women and the needlework they produced also reveals how ornamental needlework sustained an elite culture that preserved and advanced the authority of the region's wealthiest families and how those families were inseparably bound to communities of working women whose labors made elite culture possible. The quilting of these fashionable petticoats was both functional and ornamental; while the making of these skirts involved tasks common to the making of other simple garments, the application of decorative quilt patterns engaged specific manual skills as well as fashion knowledge and aesthetic sensibilities. In other words, this was work that was simultaneously practical and ornamental. To consider the ways in which quilting illuminates differences among women is to turn mythologies of the craft inside out, since quilting has long been associated with democratizing forces in American women's lives, more often a metaphor for connection than for difference. From the nascency of feminist scholarship, images of needlework and textile production, with references to "weaving" together "threads" of experience or "piecing together" "the patchwork of women's lives," have remained enormously popular among scholars interested in women's experiences. The compositional look of quilts, especially in the late 1970s and early 1980s, became commonplace in women's history publications; photographs of bed quilts and quilt squares, as well as graphics inspired by the design vocabulary of quilting, graced the covers of dozens of early women's history journals and monographs.[4] Such allusions proved compelling and appropriate feminist symbols because they celebrate, redefine, and reclaim a task traditionally performed by women. They prompt connections between traditional women's crafts and the "craft" of contemporary women historians and honor the creativity, artistic expression, and resourcefulness women have demonstrated in a variety of places and circumstances.[5]

Myths surrounding needlework have carried and created special burdens in American women's history. Quiltings, for example, have been depicted as wombs of women's culture, sites of female unity through which intergenerational wisdom is passed.[6] As Elaine Hedges explains, the pieced quilts made in the nineteenth century and celebrated in the twentieth "validated the dailiness of women's lives, and their unappreciated household labor; their scrap content was seen as analogous to the often fragmented, interrupted nature of those lives; the quilt's nonlinear, nonhierarchical design structure of repeated blocks, as well as the cooperative work methods of the quilting bee, were seen as attesting to feminist ideals of equality, and of mutuality and cooperation among women." Furthermore, Hedges points out, the warmth quilts provide cued associations with 1970s feminist "ethics of nurturance and caring," while "the very process of making a quilt—combining separate, disparate pieces of cloth into a new, unified whole—powerfully served as symbol for the new wholeness and unity, both individual and collective, and the political solidarity that was, of course, the goal of the feminist movement."[7] Quilting has also served more conservative needs in American culture, helping capture and express some wistful longing for a less complicated, less divisive past. Since the first "New England Kitchen" appeared in the mid-nineteenth-century, quilting bees have been staples of historic tableaux.[8] As the author of one essay exclaims, "no other craft or art form is more closely identified with the values that define this country: . . . freedom, democracy, equality, home, community, and individual expression."[9]

But the quilting of popular historical imagination does not usually capture the whole history of the work. As Sally Garoutte has observed, many quilts dating from this period were not unusually warm, "containing as they do only the minimum amount of filling to show off the quilting."[10] Quilts were not regarded as necessary to equip warm and comfortable Hampshire County beds; in the last half of the eighteenth century, bed quilts were acquired only after blankets and other bedding had been obtained. In the eighty-two probate inventories taken in the Hampshire County towns of Hadley, Hatfield, Amherst, and South Hadley between 1770 and 1800 that enumerate bedding, half contain no quilts at all, and only nine list more than one, suggesting that quilts were reserved for the "best bed" in a house, while sheets, coverlets, blankets, and bed rugs warmed the rest.[11] The most basic bedding seems to have been sheets and blankets; if any additional textile was present, it was most popularly a coverlet. These eighty-two inventories contain 181 blankets, 127 coverlets, 50 quilts, and 42 bed rugs. Forty-one inventories contain no quilts at all. What's more, when quilts did appear in early New England homes, they were—at least in the eighteenth century—not typically the pieced variety so often imagined but rather "whole cloth" quilts, where the ornamented expanse of sheen and color was itself an artifact of the household's relative success. When worn as a petticoat, the quilt took on still other meanings involving the wearer's class, her cultural sophistication, and her place in social orders large and small.

There is much to be gained by dismantling the romance that surrounds the American quilt—beguiling as it may be—and mythologies that both evince and elide women who worked to complete them. The bee itself and other reciprocal exchanges of work have in recent years come under closer historical scrutiny, revealing the significant role such events played in forging and sustaining cognitive and structural order, how the exchanges therein—products of far more subtle and sophisticated motives than mere neighborliness—were key mechanisms through which a person's sense of his or her relationship to the community was defined and clarified.[12] The perceived ubiquity of needlework, too, has obscured important, asymmetrical relationships among women, and quilting, perhaps the most familiar form of women's needlework, has been among the main culprits in that obfuscation. Recognizing that quilts were not as widely possessed in colonial rural America as has generally been believed makes it harder to see them as emblems of classlessness; that they were rarely pieced but more often topped with costly stretches of imported fabrics dispels the aura of frugality while throwing light on the close relationship between quilting and commerce.[13] If quilting is to continue to provide a useful metaphor for women's lives, we must expand its utility and see it also as evidence of privilege, denoting differences in women's access to certain symbols of affluence and femininity. Enlarging our view of quilting to encompass laboring women employed in eighteenth-century London quilt warehouses, consumers of quilts who lived on the western fringe of the British empire, women who quilted beautiful and elaborate petticoats for themselves, and women whose labor in other rooms within and beyond the house made that quilting possible, helps us to see quilts and quilted petticoats as the products of intersecting revolutions in manufacturing, in commerce and consumption, and in social and labor relations. Quilting can certainly continue to be an effective metaphor for interconnectedess among women, if we can overcome the implication that that interconnectedness comes on even footing.[14]

The production of quilted petticoats was one means by which women contributed to the distinctive quality of their own wardrobes; they undertook other sorts of ornamental needlework as well: embroidered scenes and family coats of arms, completed at female academies throughout New England, were brought home, mounted in costly gilded frames, and displayed prominently in the parlors of the region's most powerful households, announcing to all visitors that this was a family of distinction. For centuries, young women of Europe's upper classes had practiced tatting, tambour work, lace making, and embroidery to ornament garments and household furnishings. These "accomplishments," together with the tools employed to produce them, helped communicate, and create, their elite status.[15] But the needleworks of young privileged women are perhaps more interesting for their significance within elite culture. As we examine this work, we catch glimpses of the women who helped make that possible, especially the hired girls and enslaved black women who labored in the households of these elite women. Together, these objects suggest the broad range of needleworks, from the spectacular to the mundane, that were present in eighteenth-century New England, and so also suggest the broad range of needleworkers enmeshed in their production.

Almost thirty years ago, Nancy Cott suggested that "the characteristic 'work' of unmarried women of the elite consisted in maintaining social contacts," but surprisingly little scholarship has examined closely the ways in which that work was carried out.[16] Needlework—in young women's academies, in genteel parlors and on genteel bodies—was an important part of that process. Female members of the New England gentry assumed responsibility for the same needle chores carried out in households throughout their communities, though the means by which they accomplished these chores differed, in ways that were closely related to the special duties associated with female gentility, particularly surrounding the production of ornamental needlework. Although the general categories of work required to run a household varied little whether the work was at the top or near the bottom of the local order, that position helped to determine the manner by which the family's women accomplished those tasks. The genteel circle who labored over Hopkins's petticoat helped produce the privilege the minister's wife enjoyed. If such women did not, typically, construct their own "best" gowns, they did, as we see in a later discussion, enrich them with ornamental embroidery, drawing on skills cultivated in the elite academies. But quilting petticoats also provided a vehicle for other kinds of important work planting and cultivating lines of association among influential families. Quilted petticoats, then, provide an unusual opportunity to explore the collaborative needlework of local gentlewomen and its role in the assertion and maintenance of their family's status.

Needle Work, Needle Art, and Women of the New England Gentry

While quilting, especially of bedding, has clearly captured an important corner of American historical imagination, other forms of early American needlework are probably more familiar to contemporary museum goers, and it is worth pausing briefly to consider them as artifacts of genteel womanhood and objects of genteel labor. Ask someone to imagine a piece of colonial needlework, and she will surely envision some form of sampler or perhaps a piece of crewelwork or embroidery, a bed hanging teeming with cascading vines and flowers, or a worked scene of idyllic rural life. Such extraordinary displays of needle skill were no less impressive in the eighteenth century than they are today: the artistry and intricacy of these objects of display were intended to impress observers, and they succeeded.

The skills associated with these more ornamental forms of needlework are not necessarily separate from the work of clothing production. Consider, for example, the spectacular floral and pictorial designs Abigail Wadsworth and Mary Wright Alsop, two Connecticut gentlewomen, embroidered on linen gowns.[17] These elite women, and others like them, employed skills acquired in female academies to embellish their apparel, displaying simultaneously their skill, wealth, and leisure. Those crewelwork pieces are important artifacts of other aspects of the clothing trades, too, since they emerge from elite women's ability to hire the labors of others to complete the more practical kinds of needlework necessary to maintain their households. Crewelwork in particular allowed its practitioners to transform needlework from a tedious chore to an art form; the extraordinary undertakings that survive in contemporary museum collections must have been enormously satisfying to their creators, marks of aesthetic achievement and evidence of remarkable endurance and commitment as well as a noteworthy allocation of time and energy unavailable to many neighbors.[18]

The acquisition of the special skills required by ornamental works like these was part of genteel women's general education. Girls might work one or two samplers between the ages of five and nine, polishing literacy skills at the same time they mastered an array of practical and decorative stitches. They might then progress to fancy embroidery. Even girls who attended academies only briefly often returned home with an example of ornamental needlework.[19] In Hartford, the school of the Patten sisters—Ruth, Sarah, and Mary—attracted young women from across New England. Their pupils' days were "divided between study, painting, embroidery, and some needlework. Each young lady had a handsome framed piece" to present to her parents when she retuned home, since embroidery was considered an "indispensable accomplishment."[20] Surviving needlework from schools around New England attest to the importance accorded needlework in young women's educations, their meticulous stitching and artful composition evidence of the dedication and training that young women poured into these objects. Most familiar among works of schoolgirl art are pictorial embroideries on silk, many of which illustrate biblical passages or convey scenes of rural simplicity. These beautiful objects have prompted a good deal of scholarly inquiry that need not be summarized here.[21] It is sufficient to note that many such works were completed by Connecticut Valley girls while attending school in Boston, Hartford, Litchfield, Norwich, Deerfield, South Hadley, and elsewhere.

One project that was particularly popular among young women of wealthy New England families finishing their education was the embroidering of a family coat of arms. These heraldic needleworks, generally worked in gold, silver, and colored silk threads on a black, diamond-shaped ground, are among the most impressive examples of needle art. Expensively framed and displayed in a home's most public spaces, they signaled the owner's wealth, education, leisure, and privilege, communicating a family's ability to do without a daughter's labor while she attended school and to select and enroll her in a school filled with well-heeled students. The working of the piece conveyed a family's membership among the leaders of society, while the heraldic imagery signaled the supposed duration of that membership. At the same time, the products of these young women's labor allowed select citizens of the colony and then early republic to assert their English heritage. As Betty Ring has observed, "undeterred by either republicanism or nationalism," these objects represented a desire, among New England's elite, "for purely English emblems of family pride and prestige."[22]

Connecticut Valley women embraced this work alongside their counterparts elsewhere in New England. A truly spectacular embroidered coat of arms is among the exceptional needlework completed by the Northampton gentlewoman Esther Stoddard. Anne Grant of Windsor, Connecticut, too, produced a remarkable heraldry. Grant attended the Boston school of Janette Day with the daughters of John Hancock and other notables; having purchased more than 110 skeins of silk and 80 yards of silver and gold thread, Grant finished her heraldry during a three-month stay in the city in 1769.[23] Jerusha Mather Williams executed a coat of arms while a student at the Patten sisters' school; perhaps she later conveyed these skills to her own students at Deerfield Academy.[24] In the 1770s, Mary Porter, who was shipping goods down river from Hadley in preparation for setting up housekeeping in New Haven, wrote to her fiancé to alert him to the arrival of two bureaus, one of which contained an important addition to their new home: "I would remind you (for fear the wagonner will forget it) that my coat of arms is done up, in one of these cases."[25] Twenty years later, when Mary's daughter married James Hoyt, she too was concerned about the safety of her own needlework. Writing to her parents from Rocky Hill, Connecticut, she asked them to send along her bed, bedstead, and tester frame, her chest and trunk of clothing, and her eight cherry chairs, adding "My Coat of Arms had better not be left at [New Haven]." She suggests that "perhaps it can go in a box with your picture," hinting that needlework from both the mother and daughter traveled together from one home to the next.[26]

An unfinished piece of heraldic needlework begun by Jerusha Pitkin in the 1750s suggests that some women's desire to complete these symbols of affluence was not sufficiently strong to carry them through. Her needle, still threaded, rests in the black satin ground, and never-opened skeins of silk remain wrapped in their London labels.[27] Once married in 1760, Pitkin apparently found other uses for her time. A similarly unfinished work by Pitkin's cousin Elizabeth Porter Phelps, who was ten years younger, suggests that she too lost interest before the work was completed (see plate 7).[28] Family lore holds that Phelps took up this work again at the end of her life, and that her death in November 1817, shortly before her seventieth birthday, interrupted its progress. Since heraldries were long out of fashion by this time, it seems plausible that this by-all-accounts industrious woman, who had married Charles Phelps in 1770 and in the decades following had run a large and productive household, was, though increasingly confined to bed, striving to remain productive by picking up work laid down many years earlier, when she, like Jerusha Pitkin, was a young gentlewoman cultivating the accomplishments of her station.

Such elaborate needleworks were time-consuming and signaled periods of relative leisure among the women who completed them. When Abby Wright "called in Springfield to see a piece of needlework lately executed at a celebrated school in Boston," she learned that "the expense of the limner in drawing and painting was $8 and six months were spent in Boston working on it."[29] Even the small workbag that Abigail Lyman of Northampton embroidered as a gift to her friend Rebecca Salisbury consumed the better part of four days.[30] Such objects also marked young women as well-traveled, known and knowledgeable beyond the boundaries of their home towns. Like quilting, they implied a certain mobility but a still broader one. The desire to acquire training in the ornamental art of embroidery brought together young women from throughout the region, forging ties among them no less significant than those their husbands and brothers forged in the halls of Harvard and Yale. As members of a larger community of elite women extending from New Jersey to Vermont, they made contacts throughout the region that would eventually draw together men from throughout the region as well.

Ann Grant, coat of arms, c. 1768, and detail of stitching. Courtesy of Historic Deerfield, Inc., 1391 (photograph by Penny Leveritt).

This coat of arms was embroidered by Ann Grant (1748–1838) of East Windsor, Conn., while she was attending Ann and Elizabeth Cumming's school in Boston. Genteel families across New England embraced these allusions to English aristocracy in the middle decades of the eighteenth century. The gold and silver threads together with the expert selection and execution of stitches conveyed to viewers the maker's taste, education, and privilege.

Acquiring the skill and talent to produce ornamental needlework could prove crucial to building these alliances. When Abigail Brackett of Boston married Erastus Lyman and moved to Northampton, embroidered needlework provided her entry into local society. In the months following her arrival, the young bride felt unable to penetrate Northampton's social circles, particularly since her husband was eighteen years older than she, and his peers more like her parents' than her own. She eventually found a solution in the working of two embroidered landscapes with Sarah Hunt, one of the set of young Northampton gentlewomen "whose Mothers [she] more commonly visited. "My motive for first having them drawn was to gratify Mrs. S. & I have thought till now that would be the only end they would answer—but as [Sarah Hunt] has one to finish, and having nothing more important to demand my leasure at present, we have agreed to work together."[31] Initially she proposed to undertake a project that would "gratify Mrs S." (possibly Deborah Snow, who taught embroidery in Boston from the 1780s through about 1803), but Lyman soon realized other advantages from her needlework.[32] She and Sarah Hunt, the daughter of Ebenezer Hunt, an influential apothecary and physician in the town, worked together almost every day, and soon Lyman recorded in the pages of her journal, "It is not long since I mention'd . . . that I had no particular friendship or intimacy with any—this can no longer be affirmed with truth." Indeed when she finished the first pattern, "The Shephard," she wrote that she would much regret the completion of it, had she not another left to work.[33] While working her embroideries, Lyman forged the first of several important friendships with other prominent Northampton families.

This effort to create and maintain social ties should not be taken lightly. In part, the importance of these activities within communities of elite women can be seen in the way they encouraged each other across generations and within peer groups. Elizabeth Porter to be sure, was urged by members of her family to attend the neighborhood quiltings, and a cousin, Sarah Porter Hillhouse, encouraged her granddaughter by praising her for undertaking a new needlework project: "I am glad to hear you have begun another piece of work and approve of the object."[34] These words must have carried weight with the little girl, who was so enamored of her grandmother that she begged her mother to make her matched clothing and liked to amuse her parents by pretending to be Grandmother Porter climbing into bed. While women in the Porter family transmitted among themselves an appreciation for the importance of needlework, Abigail Lyman grasped its importance in forging social relationships: Lyman noted that she hoped to "profit" by her conversations with Sarah Hunt, and though she meant that she wished to gain from

Hunt's "entertaining and instructive conversation," there were other profits to consider as well. Families like the Hunts were important connections for the Lyman family business. They were people Abigail could not afford to slight.

The elaborate ornamental needlework produced by women of the New England gentry that attests to ties among these women of privilege are closely associated, too, with women whose lives were far different but inseparable: the enslaved women who made this ornamental work possible. Among the most notable producers of crewelwork in early New England was Mary Wright Alsop, who was born in Middletown, Connecticut, in 1740, the only child of Joseph Wright, a prosperous farmer and brickyard owner, and Hannah Gilbert Wright.[35] At fourteen, she was sent to Rhode Island for an education, probably attending Sarah Osborn's school there in Newport. In 1754, she produced a pastoral canvas based on the shepherdess motif popular among eighteenth-century gentlewomen and later, an extraordinary series depicting the four seasons. In the late 1750s, she also completed a slip seat for a roundabout chair, as well as several pocketbooks for her father and others. After her wedding in 1760 to Richard Alsop, a highly successful merchant and importer of West Indian goods, several of these important pictures ornamented the couple's north parlor. More than fifty years after Richard's death in 1776, the pictures continued to decorate the walls of Mary's home. Mary Alsop raised ten children in the 1760s and 1770s, yet she continued to produce a prodigious amount of needlework. Richard Alsop's 1776 inventory includes eight mahogany chairs with worked seats, as well as two worked fire screens. That steady production of sophisticated ornamental work is inseparable from the family's access to slave labor. Before Richard's death, the Alsop household included at least two enslaved men, Acra and Quash, and a woman, Catherine Barrett. By 1790, five slaves helped care for Mary's large family. Catherine Barrett would be freed in 1794, while Mary's 1795 will instructed her children to continue to provide for an "aged Negro" named Jenny. A notable number of these spectacular pieces of needle art were products of slaveholding families: the Porters and Pitkins, Wolcotts and Williams—the same families who secured elite educations for their daughters, and the metallic threads and gold frames those educations required, also embraced forms of labor that were both signs and means of privilege.[36]

The Collaborative Work of Quilted Petticoats

As the wife of the Hadley lawyer, selectman, justice, representative, and deacon Charles Phelps, Elizabeth Porter Phelps had a social position to maintain as a leading member of the Hampshire County gentry. One important expression of that status was gathering with other women of similar status to collaborate on the ornamentation of quilted petticoats.[37] The costly materials of which these objects were made, the special skills and knowledge of prevailing fashion required to produce them, and the time involved to complete them—each forms of luxury and privilege—demonstrated to the community one's superior social position.[38] At the same time, the gatherings that produced them strengthened the kinship and cultural ties that bound together the political, social, economic, and cultural elite. This work did produce items of practical value yet also signaled and perpetuated their participants' status as members of the local gentry.

A la mode in the Connecticut River Valley since the second quarter of the eighteenth century, quilted petticoats were visible in the opening at the front of a woman's gown and beneath the folds of the skirt when pinned up to accentuate the hips.[39] Occasionally worn over hoops, panniers, or some other means of broadening that horizontal line, quilted petticoats helped women achieve a refined silhouette: broad through the shoulders, narrow at the waist, and widest in the full and circular drape of the skirt. The design of petticoats varied, but generally they carried an elaborate border around the hemline, the most visible part of the garment and hence the portion executed with greatest attention to display. The most complex ornamentation usually occupied the front of the garment, filling the space revealed by the open gown. Large, normally concealed areas were filled in with a pattern less complicated than that of the borders, such as rows of shells, squares, diamonds, or ovals.

The material of which the petticoat was constructed contributed to its cachet. Silks have always been expensive, luxury materials, valued for their sheen. Their luster was replicated in cotton chintz by glazing and in worsteds (including the highly popular calimanco) by pressing. Silks also permitted greater indulgence in color. Petticoats in eighteenth-century Hampshire County were generally of darker hues—more than two-thirds of the quilted petticoats listed in inventories between 1760 and 1820 were practical (and restrained) colors, such as black, brown, or blue—but occasionally they appeared in greens, reds, yellows, and pinks.[40] In Hartford County, Connecticut, petticoats were distributed more evenly across the color spectrum, blues, browns, and blacks competing for attention with reds, yellows, greens, purples, and whites. In Connecticut, striped petticoats were by far the most prevalent, though women also wore them with flowered, sprigged, and other patterns.[41]

Quilted petticoats, like the bed quilts with which they are so closely associated, served multiple functions, from the utilitarian to the symbolic, and providing warmth was not their primary function.[42] Tellingly, these decorative skirts were usually worn above garments more appropriately designed to keep the wearer warm: linen or wool shifts, plain cloth petticoats, and at times utilitarian quilted underpetticoats. Though these fine quilted petticoats did provide some additional comfort, they were more important as objects of fashion and as objects produced by gatherings of the local elite.

Some of the quilted petticoats that graced Connecticut Valley laps were imported, the product of female quilters laboring in large workshops in London, where they were seated around frames, earning a shilling a day to produce garments sold at retail or wholesale in London shops or exported to the colonies.[43] Beginning in the late 1600s, manufacturers had discovered that quilted petticoats were "ideal commodities": these drawstring skirts were unusual in that they could fit a variety of figures, and so were among the few garments that could be made for sale to distant and unknown consumers. At the same time, while the petticoat, a staple component of women's costume, was unlikely to go out of fashion as a form, the quilting patterns and materials were wholly responsive to changing preferences in color, fabric, and pattern.[44]

Quilted petticoats of tammy, horsehair, calimanco, and silk from London and Bristol arrived in Boston and New York shops from at least the late seventeenth century. Cost varied widely depending on the materials. The Boston trader Hannah Boydel sold quilted persian gowns and green camblet quilted petticoats for as much as five pounds.[45] Merchants also sold quilted petticoats by the yard, enabling a woman to purchase the quilted materials and sew up the finished petticoat more quickly.[46] The quality of these garments could be quite high; costume historians have observed the "superb craftsmanship" associated with quilted clothing that came out of sophisticated London workshops in the middle decades of the eighteenth century. As evidence that "only craftspeople with considerable experience could create" some of the complex quiltings that survive in collections in the Metropolitan Museum of Art in New York City and London's Victoria and Albert Museum, Kay Staniland points to the "fineness and regularity" of the stitching, which in some cases used twenty-two running stitches per inch on corded quilting, when a more usual number for wadded quilting was nine stitches per inch.[47] Clearly, some quilted garments produced in metropolitan workshops were aimed at a luxury market, but they represented only the high end of a vast world of professional, wage-earning quilters.

Drawing the patterns for this elaborate needlework also provided some women with comfortable livings. Robert Campbell's 1747 *The London Trades-*

man suggests that women able to "draw shapes and figures upon men's waistcoats to be embroidered, upon women's petticoats, and other wearing apparel" could charge "large prices"—as much as thirty shillings a week at a time when domestic servants generally earned just three or four. The workwomen who executed these designs, however, earned considerably less: Campbell also indicates that quilted petticoats in that city "are made mostly by women, and some men, who are employed by the shops." These laborers "earn little," Campbell observes; the work is "nothing to get rich by, unless they are able to purchase the materials and sell them finished to the shops which few of them do." "They rarely take on apprentices," he continues, "and the women they employ to help them, earn three to four shillings per week and their diet."[48] On this side of the Atlantic, women also offered quilting skills to neighbors. When Elizabeth Foote of Colchester, Connecticut, drew a quilt pattern for her neighbor Mrs Blush (for either a skirt or a bed quilt), she was repeating a scene played out time and again in New England communities as women skilled at this task shared their abilities with others. New England women could also earn a little income doing the actual quilting for neighbors; Jonathan Judd, a bachelor in South Hadley, for example, hired Eunice Lyman to quilt for him (presumably on a bed quilt), in return for which she took goods out of his shop.[49]

In the eighteenth century, then, women on either side of the Atlantic could purchase ready-made quilts produced by quilters in metropolitan workshops or purchase the skill and time of neighbors to draw the design or execute all or part of the quilting. But many women, too, chose to quilt for themselves at home. Perhaps their most important tool was the quilt frame. The frames themselves were fairly straightforward affairs: generally four strips of wood about one inch thick, two to four inches wide, and nine to twelve feet long, with a one-inch width of heavy cloth securely fastened along the edges.[50] To these, the edge of quilt was either pinned or basted. The four corners of the frame were held together with pegs through holes, bound together with ties (or, later, with iron clamps), and then the whole supported on the rails of four low-backed chairs. These simple devices—strips of wood with fragments of fabric still attached—rarely found their way into probate inventories. In 1760s Hartford, Connecticut, the Porter family's quilt frame was worth just 1 shilling 6 pence (equal to the value of a cradle or a cheese tub; slightly less than that of their four milk tubs), while upriver in Northampton, Elisha and Esther Pomeroy possessed a quilt frame valued at 4 shillings when Elisha died in the spring of 1762.[51] Esther Williams of Deerfield had a quilting frame when she died worth $1.75 (by comparison, her pine kitchen table was worth $1.00, and her dressing table $3.00). In her will,

Williams indicated that her household furniture was to be divided between her daughters. Polly (Mary Williams Ashley) took home her mother's quilting frame, to be put to use in her own busy household.[52] It is nearly impossible, however, to determine from probate inventories the number of New England households that possessed quilt frames, since daughters like Polly often retrieved their mothers' quilt frames long before any court-ordered assessors found reason to knock at the door.

In eighteenth-century New England, quiltings allowed women to gather together to work and socialize. Indeed, Elizabeth Porter Phelps in her youth was regularly "called to quilting"—the only kind of needlework she performed that required her to travel, sometimes reluctantly, out of her home and into the homes of others. In the years before her marriage, she performed 92 percent of her quilting activity in the homes of others; twenty years later, she performed most of her quilting in her own home, while during these years her daughters, Betsy and Thankful were, as Elizabeth Phelps had been, "called to quilting."

When the quilting was nearby, women could conveniently walk from house to house, while access to sleighs, carriages, and other means of transportation allowed some women to travel farther with ease and to avoid arriving in bedraggled skirts and dust-covered shoes.[53] The use of carriages to cover spatial distances, however, also reflected and created social ones. Though walking between households was certainly feasible for these women, most of whom lived within two or three miles of one another, riding in carriages enhanced their status and prestige. A striking correlation exists between the quilters recorded at the Phelps house and the owners of carriages listed in Hadley's tax valuations. Sylvester Judd notes that, at mid-century, the only carriages in Hampshire County were those owned by Moses Porter of Hadley (Elizabeth's father) and another by Israel Williams of Hatfield (that "monarch" of Hampshire whose daughters quilted with Elizabeth.[54] If Elizabeth Porter enjoyed one of the few such comfortable conveyances in her childhood, she was equally well provided as a young wife: Charles Phelps purchased a new carriage in Boston the week that he and Elizabeth Porter published their marriage banns.[55] By 1791, the family had also acquired a stand-top chaise, which after 1795 was housed in a structure built to shelter their several vehicles.[56] Other members of Elizabeth Phelps's quilting circle, the majority of whom came from the Warner, Hopkins, Shipman, and Porter families, also enjoyed this amenity. Elisha Porter's family owned a riding chair at least by 1763, the Kelloggs in 1768. By at least 1785, the Reverend Hopkins had a chaise, as did Eleazer and Susanna Edwards Porter and Jonathan and Mary Graves Warner, whose son Lemuel married Dorothy Phelps,

Elizabeth Porter's sister-in-law. William Shipman had a riding chair.[57] Sylvester Judd lamented in the second quarter of the nineteenth century that the women he remembered from his childhood could be seen on horseback "every hour of they day"; they "mounted and dismounted" horses "without aid" and "had not the helpless appearance" of privileged women of his day.[58] Phelps and her peers had been among the first to embrace those new forms of conveyance, as well as the definitions of genteel womanhood that arrived with them.

Women of the rural gentry certainly could afford to purchase the stylish, imported quilted petticoats made in London workshops; they could also have purchased the materials and labor required to complete them. So why, we might ask, did they devote so much time and energy to the production of fine quilted petticoats? Quality, in part, provides an answer, since even the most attractive mass-produced quilted petticoats often lacked the tell-tale detail of home-sewn garments.[59] Beautiful, richly detailed petticoats represented local design and local labor, conveying crucial information about the wearer, her financial resources, and the ways she could choose to allocate her time. But also worth noting is the degree to which collaborative quilting itself was valued by women of the rural gentry. The work of this sort of quilting was almost always bound up with social activity. Betsy Phelps Huntington confirmed what a "dull business" quilting by herself could be, while less than 5 percent of Elizabeth Porter Phelps's references to quilting refer to what appears to have been her quilting alone. One study of New England quilters found only 6 percent of diary entries recording quilting indicate that the diarist was working alone.[60]

Because of the larger purposes of collective quiltings, however, it seems likely that these events made their way into women's various forms of records and memoranda for their social aspect. Records like Ruth Henshaw Bascom's diary, which records when groups of fourteen to twenty-one Leicester women came to "assist . . . with quilting," may tell us as much about how women thought about collective quilting as they do about the role such gatherings played in production.[61] The quilting of elaborate petticoats made of costly materials certainly expressed the same "kinship, group cohesion and cultural leadership" as the stately mansion houses in which they were produced—and, as material products and symbols of the female members of the rural gentry gathered together, in ways perhaps much more literal than a common affinity for gambrel roofs or pedimented doorways.[62]

The collaborative work of quilting and other such gatherings began long before the participants arrived. Susanna Edwards Porter's sister, Esther Edwards Burr, a native of Northampton, found herself "extremely ingaged" preparing for a spinning frolick. She begged her friend Sarah Prince to forgive her for slighting their correspondence, explaining that she had been busy "making cake for spinning frolick today" that "is to be attended tomorrow and several days after I suppose." Putting on the frolic had Burr "almost wore up to the hub."[63] Quiltings were little different: the materials for the work had to be gathered and prepared, the house had to be cleaned and readied for visitors and overnight guests, refreshments had to be made, and the several components of the quilt had to be assembled and then put on the frame.

In part, a woman's ability to devote an afternoon or more to quilting and other kinds of ornamental needlework depended on her household's access to other labor. As one Northampton quilter recalled, "plain or straight work"—that is, quilting in its most basic form, along parallel lines—could be finished in a day, but such speed was rare when the highly decorative patterns that ornamented finer garments were involved.[64] Since hospitality of high quality was an integral part of reciprocal work bees like quiltings, feeding and entertaining participants appropriately (and cleaning up afterward) became essential to any gathering's success. Such imperatives invoked other series of tasks in the household hosting the event; at the same time, attendees had to make sure more routine labors around their own homes continued.[65] Among the eighteenth-century New England gentry, such labor was supplied by enslaved and hired laborers. When Elizabeth Porter Phelps attended quiltings in Hadley, her slave Peg remained at Forty Acres to see to ongoing chores at home. Peg, along with her two daughters, Phillis and Roseanna, had worked for the Porter household for nearly her entire life. Of the five young women who attended Sarah Hopkins's quilting on that August afternoon in 1769-Sally Woodbridge, Betty Williams, Betty and Sophia Partridge, and Elizabeth Porter—each, as well as the hostess, lived in homes with black slaves. Sarah Hopkins had received her first husband's slave woman, Phillis, as part of his bequest; after Sarah married her husband's successor in the pulpit, he moved into the house that Sarah and Phillis kept.[66] Oliver and Anna Williams Partridge had an enslaved husband and wife in their household, and Israel and Sarah Chester Williams during their marriage owned several men and women, including Kate, and at about the time of this quilting, Blossom.[67]

In fact, though less than one-tenth of the New England labor force was enslaved, most of the River Gods and their families had slaves, generally an adult man and woman. Throughout Hadley, Hatfield, Deerfield, Northampton, and Amherst, a handful of black men and women lived and worked in the households of a handful of wealthy English families. Each of Hadley's first three ministers owned slaves. Of these, Isaac Chauncey owned Arthur

Prutt, his wife, Joan, and their seven children, who would eventually be sold into neighboring households, including that of Moses and Elizabeth Porter.[68] The Reverend Jonathan Ashley of Deerfield and his wife, Dorothy Williams Ashley, at one time or another owned at least three slaves: Jenny, her son Cato, and another man, Titus.[69] Fully half of the men in the powerful Williams clan were slave owners.[70]

Many of the women with whom Elizabeth Phelps quilted through the years came from slave-owning families. Betty Chauncey joined Phelps's quilting from time to time; her father, Josiah, owned at least one enslaved woman by the 1740s.[71] The household of Phelps's friends Penelope and Patty Williams by the 1740s and 1750s included at least one enslaved woman and one enslaved girl, while Sally Goodrich appears regularly among Phelps's fellow quilters; her father, Aaron, was also among Hadley's slaveholders.[72] Even after the demise of slavery in Massachusetts, these families continued to draw on the labor of black women, and in ways closely related to quilting: "Yesterday," Phelps wrote in the fall of 1802, "mrs lawyer [Abigail Phillips Porter, the wife of the attorney Elisha Porter] sent her black girl up here on foot to invite me to help her quilt—& I went."[73]

The care with which Phelps recorded this and other visits in the pages of her diary suggests that these quiltings must be located within general patterns of visiting in early America, an activity that, as Karen V. Hansen has suggested, bridged and blurred what we have come to call the "private" and the "public," creating an intermediate, and intermediary, sphere that she terms the "social." Visits were fundamentally public encounters that occurred in traditionally private spaces.[74] The flow of traffic between influential households was one significant means by which the social, economic, and political networks that comprised Hadley's public arena were created and sustained, a fact of which these women were ever aware. One study of work and society in rural Massachusetts, attempting to distinguish these "frolics" from other sorts of market transaction, points out that these events never appear in the columns of account books and suggests that people simply kept a "mental tally" of their neighbors' participation.[75] But the tally might not have been mental at all: women may not have kept account books recording the exchange of goods, cash, or services, but their diary narratives recording the arrivals and departures of friends, family, and strangers are account books of another sort, in which reciprocal obligations were tracked and remembered. Diaries retained an accounting of social obligations, as well as the work that was accomplished within them. Certainly both visits and the recording of them was serious business. "Madam" Sarah Porter kept in the pages of her almanacs a careful record of visits to and from her home on the Hadley common, while Northampton's Abigail Lyman's first journal registered "the people I had visited & who had visited me," which invitations she had accepted, and which she had declined.[76] Phelps's desire to track the quilting she and her daughters contributed to their community is evidence of the special significance of this labor and suggests another reason that women's diaries are more likely to contain references to collective than solitary quilting; it affirms Catharine Anne Wilson's insight that "reciprocal work operated much like a bank, in which all made their deposits and were then entitled to make their withdrawals or acquire small loans."[77]

Elizabeth Porter Phelps's memorandum book, too, preserves the steady stream of company that flowed from Hadley center to Forty Acres and back again. Once married, Elizabeth and her husband, Charles, remained in the home of Elizabeth's birth, enabling the bride to continue patterns of hospitality familiar from girlhood; in any given year, two hundred visitors might cross their threshold.[78] That socializing was an important obligation among women of the rural gentry, and that it could prove hard work, is captured in Betsy Phelps Huntington's concern that her husband's Connecticut parishioners might fault her for failing to endure the "drudgery" of visiting.[79] Elizabeth Phelps, too, wrote her daughter late one August that there had "not been any women to see her" in some time; she was a little surprised and embarrassed by the lack of company ("don't tell of it," she asked her daughter), but confessed that her husband, Charles, saw one "good reason why": "I owe visits to all."[80] Phelps's neighbors had surely been noting those reciprocal obligations as carefully as she and found Phelps overdrawn on her account. Visits carried an exchange value less tangible than that of goods or labor but no less significant. Through the daily, weekly, and yearly rhythms of visits, "people . . . publicly exchanged the goods of the world at large"—tea and cakes to be sure but also the use of a shared yet select world of material goods. Visits provided an opportunity to view, handle, and enjoy one another's imported "set of China dishes—best sort," to demonstrate and acquire knowledge of the current fashions and forms in tea equipage and to demonstrate and acquire knowledge of the rules for proper tea-drinking etiquette: where, how, and with whom you should sit, what subjects you should and should not discuss, how you should handle a teacup properly, and how you should indicate that you have finished.[81] The table on which the tea was served provided a focal point for these various kinds of exchange, the effort and expenditure to acquire stylish, specialized tea tables and stands indicating that Connecticut Valley elites "took these events, which both defined and maintained social boundaries, very seriously."[82] To use one another's carved, upholstered, and matched sets of furniture, the travel to and from one another's homes in expensive carriages—the material appointments of visits enabled members of the rural gentry to share the accoutrements of gentility, to enhance their sense of commonality, and to distinguish themselves from neighbors who were unable to acquire these goods and were unfamiliar with the rituals associated with their proper use.[83] For most of the community, who had little access to these houses' formal spaces, the sheer scale and elaboration of the façade told them everything they needed to know; visitors of comparable station, however, "would have found the specialized goods and luxury items more important to their estimation of [a family's] refinement and gentility, and to their comparison to their own social positions."[84]

The importance of quilting in that effort is made clear by the attention paid to it by Elizabeth Porter's female relatives. After the death of her father, and given the often fragile health of her mother, her extended family assumed much responsibility for her upbringing. They saw to it that she traveled with her cousins to meet family, friends, and associates in Boston and Hartford, and they attended to her formal and practical education, tutoring her in the finer points of polite behavior. Particularly anxious that young Elizabeth attend to her quilting responsibilities was her father's sister, Phebe Porter Marsh. Phebe's husband, Samuel, had assumed some legal liability for young Elizabeth when in the months following her father's death he co-signed her guardianship papers, but Phebe Marsh made sure that her niece was learning her familial roles and obligations. On more than one occasion, Elizabeth recorded that her "Aunt Marsh came up here and would have me go quilt."[85] Marsh hoped to instruct Elizabeth in the importance of demonstrating her family's commitment to and respect for these ongoing working relationships; the rising gentlewoman's presence was necessary to affirm her own household's status in the community.[86] Other relatives, too, made sure that Elizabeth attended these gatherings, as when "Aunt Porter came here to stay to have me go to quilting for Miss Patty upon a crimson duerant."[87] Her Aunt Porter rode up to Forty Acres and spent the day caring for Elizabeth's ailing mother so that the younger woman could be present at what she perceived to be an important gathering, but from which "Aunt Porter" herself could be absent.

In the years just before and just after her marriage, Elizabeth Phelps quilted for both her immediate and her extended family. Gradually, however, she devoted less and less time to projects not intended for her own household, and apparently less energy to the production of petticoats. Almost 40 percent of her references to quilting are clustered in the four years prior to her marriage. After the birth of her first child, references to quiltings in which Phelps herself participated decline by about 75 percent, and after the birth of her second there is no reference to her quilting for seven years.[88] She continued to quilt on occasion, but these projects tended to be both with and for members of her immediate family: her sister-in-law, her mother, and her children. When Elizabeth attended Sarah Hopkins's quilting in 1769, she and Sally Woodbridge were the oldest, at twenty-two and twenty-three. Betty and Sophia Partridge were thirteen and fifteen years old, respectively, and Betty Williams was sixteen.[89] As these women aged, their daughters assumed their places around the quilt frames of Hampshire County. Beginning about 1793, when her daughters were twelve and sixteen, most entries in Phelps's diary noting quiltings recorded the activity of these young women: "Girls at brother's to quilt," "girls quilting at Esq. Porters with many others," "girls quilting at Judge Porters."[90]

To be sure, quilting could be a time-consuming, monotonous chore best tackled by groups of women working together. But collective effort was not necessary to complete the task, suggesting that quiltings served purposes beyond the strictly functional. Cooperative sewing brought together families with shared, and sometimes divergent, and even divisive, interests. When women of the Porter, Phelps, Williams, and other elite families gathered around the quilt frame, longstanding associations were affirmed, and new ones begun.[91] New arrivals to the community and new generations of participants were incorporated into the group, perpetuating enduring values and codes of behavior. Tensions may well have simmered beneath the surface, but attendance at the quilting itself continued to assert group identity and belonging.

Mothers and daughters of the rural gentry may have had other reasons to take an interest in quiltings. One Hampshire County quilter recalled that often, when a quilting lasted for more than one day, "married elderly women" would gather for one, and "younger ladies" another, suggesting some planning and intention associated with the separate gatherings.[92] And of course the teas and dancing that often followed the close of the workday were opportunities for young men and women to meet one another and to cultivate romantic relationships. Historians have made much of the politically astute alliances formed between powerful Connecticut Valley families but give surprisingly short shrift to the agency of the young women participating in this process. At quiltings young women were able to meet the young men who were the brothers, cousins, and friends of their fellow quilters and to assess their prospects.

As much as anyone, then, young women performed the work of establishing, maintaining, and extending family position. By the time Elizabeth

Porter had changed her name to Phelps and had become the mother of her own girls, little about these quiltings had changed. New generations of young women gathered together in the homes of their mothers, aunts, and neighbors and under their guidance, learned to quilt, to visit, to take tea, to flirt, and to marry wisely. Seated around the quilt frame, these women drew closer and closer together, the circle drawing tighter and tighter, as the quilt neared completion; ten feet shrank to eight and then to six and four. At the center of the circle lay the object that would be the enduring symbol of that collaborative work to present and future communities. Quilting drew together the circle of Hampshire County gentlewomen—"others of our own people"—in a shared work that helped insure the continued prosperity and influence of their families. The petticoat that was finally cut from the frame was but one of the products of this important collaboration. In the same way, the elaborate pictorial needlework completed by young women of elite families and displayed proudly in those families' parlors performed cultural work of their own, forging ties that bound together the region's most influential families.

While these young, well-off girls in the Connecticut Valley quilted and embroidered, their black and Native American counterparts—who themselves sometimes appear in these embroidered pictures, tending to their mistresses—executed the heavier labor required to run the household. Elite needlework engaged the labors of white women, too, domestic servants whose efforts in other rooms of the house made more leisurely projects possible. At the same time another work force of needlewomen contributed to the production and maintenance of elite households' wardrobes, to enable other women to "dress up in the afternoon." White servants and hired needlewomen, black slaves and laundresses, Native American workers: all of these women's labors contributed to the production of the ornamental needlework that reflected and perpetuated elite culture in early America. Though their work is unattributed, they are present in these objects.

The unique needlework completed by women of the rural gentry, made possible in part by their ability to purchase the labor and skill of other sorts of needlewomen, has something important to teach us about the clothing trades in early America, and the way needlework figured into the lives of very different sorts of women. Women of the rural gentry were responsible, as mistresses of households, for clothing acquisition and maintenance, and they employed a wide variety of strategies to meet that obligation. But they had other duties as well that were important in larger constellations of skill, status, and clothing in early New England. The production of elegant quilted petticoats was one way that women of privilege acquired a wardrobe that distinguished them from others in their community. In this regard, they were clothing producers of special skill who obtained their training not through apprenticeships and labor contracts but within the tutelage of elite communities, among their "own people." At the same time, these quilted petticoats, and the process of their production, proved an essential means by which elite families sustained authority. As such, they are evidence of unpaid, but nevertheless essential, work performed by local gentlewomen toward their family's prosperity.

Chapter 4

Family, Community, and Informal Work in the Needle Trades

The Worlds of Easter Fairchild Newton and Tryphena Newton Cooke

THE INN at the south end of the Hadley common catered to polite travelers, men and women traveling to and from Boston by carriage or coach. The inn at the north end of the Hadley common tended to serve a rougher crowd, mainly ferrymen who worked on the river. Among other skills, Tryphena Newton Cooke, daughter of the innkeeper Elizabeth "Easter" Fairchild Newton, learned to manage the rowdy behavior of the raftsmen. According to family tradition in Hadley, tired of one man's coarse and constant overtures, she finally took a swing at her tormenter, knocking him down. Startled, he rose to his feet, sputtering that "he would only submit to that because she was a woman." Cooke allegedly retorted that she would not have stood as much as she had unless she *was* a woman.[1] While the story is surely at least partly apocryphal, there was something about the character of Tryphena Cooke that her descendants hoped to remember in its telling. She was, it seems, patient to a point, shrewd, strong of will and of shoulder. She was also acutely aware of some special burdens of womanhood. And she was plainly the sort of woman who knew what needed to be done, and did it.

The life stories of Easter Newton and Tryphena Cooke—innkeepers and tailoresses both—provide an unusual opportunity to look closely at women's informal work in the needle trades. When not taming rowdy raftsmen, Tryphena contributed to her family fortunes by the more sedate work of sewing. Easter, too, saw both tailoring and innkeeping as means to settle debts and generate income. Like thousands of other New England women, married and single, they took their skill with a needle into the marketplace to contribute to their family's well-being. Easter Newton was tailoring in Hadley at least as early as 1771, when her family's account with Josiah Pierce was

The Cooke family home. Courtesy of the Ashfield Historical Society.
The c. 1800 home as it appeared at the end of the nineteenth century.

credited for her "making a coat"; like Catherine Deane, Easter Newton here was likely assembling ("making") a garment that had already been cut by a tailor.[2] In 1779, she made her first overnight visit to Phelps's home, where she tailored for two November days.[3] Tryphena Newton enters Elizabeth Porter Phelps's record in December 1786, when, at the age of twenty-two, she spent several days at the Phelps farm mending and sewing for the household. She left on Thursday, 21 December, and Phelps duly noted the visit in the pages of her memorandum book the following Sunday. Tryphena appears in Phelps's notations again only a handful of times, the last on a Thursday in October 1791, when, now "Mr. Solomon Cooke's wife," she arrived to "fix Reuban" (one of Phelps's hired hands) some clothes. Tryphena Newton Cooke would not be mentioned in those pages again until the summer of 1805, when Phelps recorded her death and funeral; Easter Newton continued to sew at Forty Acres as late as January 1812, when she came to "fix a short coat" for the gardener, John Morrison.[4]

Easter Newton, Tryphena Newton Cooke, and Elizabeth Porter Phelps are as entwined in the present as they were in the past. In eighteenth-century Hadley, such women knew each other well: Easter and Tryphena depended on Phelps for part of their families' livelihood, while Phelps depended on both women to help her meet her obligations as the mistress of a large farm.

Today, it is only by considering these women and the documents they left behind together that we can derive a fair picture of any of them. That Tryphena Newton nearly disappeared from Phelps's accounting when she changed her name to Cooke is not unusual; the needlewomen, skilled and unskilled, mentioned in Phelps's voluminous record largely vanish from that text upon marriage, with Easter Newton among the few exceptions. After Tryphena married Solomon Cooke, a ferryman, Phelps rarely recorded her coming to sew for that household. Other sources tell us that Tryphena Cooke's family—her mother, Easter, her husband, Solomon, and probably her children—together ran their family's inn, in a house that still stands on the banks of the Connecticut River.[5] From these facts and from Phelps's memorandum book, it would be easy to conclude that Tryphena engaged in tailoring as a young unmarried woman but generally dropped out of paid work once marriage provided new occupations and responsibilities. The Cooke account book, however, offers another view of her labors and makes plain that she sewed for the Phelps household at least as many times after her marriage as she did while single. Among other things, the account book enables us to compare Phelps's record of the semi-skilled needlework she hired with Tryphena Cooke's record. Perhaps more than anything else, these sources taken together remind us how easily the work of laboring women is elided. Though we have Phelps's memorandum book, an extensive and seemingly exhaustive record, the young needlewoman is omitted from Phelps's narrative accounting once marriage changed the circumstances of her labor; though we have an account book kept by Tryphena's husband, the needlework recorded therein has been both overlooked and misunderstood. If read with care and attention to evidence of both absence and presence, these documents illuminate intersections of household, community, and marketplace that shaped rural Massachusetts at the close of the eighteenth century.

Open almost any Connecticut Valley account book kept during the last half of the eighteenth century or the early decades of the nineteenth and you will find references to women sewing. Ledgers teem with examples of women who paid for groceries, labor, and services, as well as consumer goods, by mending, making, and altering simple and complex garments for others. At mid-century, in Deerfield, Massachusetts, Elizabeth Corse earned income mending jackets and making breeches, coats, and "Indian Shirts" for Elijah Williams, in exchange for goods from his shop.[6] In the late 1780s and 1790s, in Longmeadow, Massachusetts, Lucinda Cooley earned a shilling a day tailoring for one and two weeks at a time.[7] In the 1790s, in Suffield, Connecticut, Mehitable Kellogg, a widow, offset her debts to the physician Apollos King by making and turning jackets, coats, and breeches.[8] In Saybrook, Connecticut, and West Springfield, Massachusetts, Lydia Duncan Champion worked alongside her husband, Reuban, a physician and merchant.[9] Like Catherine Deane, Lovice Simmister, Phebe Hill, and Polly Hastings, in Windsor, Vermont, who added to their household income by turning their needles to profit, she brought in her fair share of the household's income through her work cutting, making, altering, and mending garments. Of the one hundred accounts maintained in the Champions' ledger, Lydia's needlework appears in roughly one-third.

This chapter, then, surveys women's work as tailoresses in rural New England. We begin by looking more closely at the work of tailoresses surveyed in Chapter 2 and then return to the story of Easter Newton and Tryphena Cooke and the ways in which needlework contributed to their households' concerns while embedding them in their community's economic and social networks. Easter's work at both sewing and innkeeping suggests how needlework could be one of several means of support for New England families. Tryphena's work, and Solomon's accounting of it, were also common features of New England life at the turn of the nineteenth century. Together, the two women's lives illuminate the contours of semi-skilled needlework—labor that was at times impromptu and informal but also accomplished and purposeful—as an occupation for eighteenth-century rural New England women.

Plainwork

Much of the clothing made and repaired in early America in some way involved the remunerated labor of semi-skilled needlewomen. More women may have worked in the clothing trades than in any other occupation except, perhaps, domestic service. Tailoresses generally stitched articles of clothing for men, women, and children that did not involve the complicated cutting or fitting that more skilled artisans (tailors, gown makers, and stay makers) were trained to do. They might cut out and construct simple garments, mend and alter garments, or assemble garments already cut out by more skilled artisans, conserving the time of others better allocated to other tasks. When, for example, Betty Potter, a hired woman in the Hollister household in Glastonbury, Connecticut, needed a new gown in the spring of 1793, neither she not her mistress spent time bent over a needle; instead, a local needlewoman, Esther Smith, was employed to make it up, charging two shillings six pence for her work.[10]

The most challenging alteration projects tailoresses undertook involved cutting down men's coats and breeches to clothe the "rising generation" or remaking their shabby or outdated garments to give to hired men. Alterations also helped prolong the life of more costly garments; for example, the strength of eighteenth-century silks, the ample materials with which these garments were made, and the large, loose stitches with which some parts were assembled meant that gowns of this expensive fabric could be made and remade to adapt to changing fashion, or changing figures. Tailoresses participated in the production of new clothing as well, cutting and sewing shirts and shifts, for example, or assembling garments already cut by a professional, as Catherine Dean and Lovice Simmister did for the men of Windsor. Having "your work cut out for you" was no mere metaphor: tailoresses were often called upon to sew together pieces of a new garment only basted together by tailors or gown makers, whose special skills were unnecessary for this more routine labor. Although stitching did not require the cultivated expertise that cutting did, producing the hard-wearing seams demanded by clothing intended to withstand years of steady use did require skill. Men's shirts and women's shifts, for example, were worn through the workday and as nightclothes and so required firm stitches and strong, well-finished seams.[11] The work of tailoresses may not have been especially arduous, but it was tedious and time consuming and did demand some skill and ingenuity. One shirt or shift took several hours to sew by hand, from the cutting of the individual pieces to the stitching of long side seams to the addition of gussets and sleeves to the finishing of hems, with decorative flourishes, such as ruffles, sometimes adding to the task at hand.

The work of tailoresses was closely linked to that of other laborers. Early American households turned on three general categories of work: textile production and maintenance, food preparation and preservation, and cleaning and general upkeep. Women hired and performed (both intermittently and for long terms of service) many different kinds of help. Spinners and weavers helped produce household textiles. Some hired women contributed to the ongoing production of dairy and poultry products for the market and for use at home. Others assisted with day-to-day chores around the home. In the hill town of Cummington, Massachusetts, for example, Sarah Bryant's hired women washed and ironed, scoured pots and floors, spun wicks and made candles, and hatcheled and spun flax for linen, which they also bleached.[12] Elizabeth Phelps set her hired women to work washing woodwork, cleaning out the buttery, scouring floors, feeding farm laborers, and butchering hogs. They performed much of the daily work to put food on the table and the larger efforts of food preparation and preservation, especially around harvest time, when dozens of hired men needed to be fed. They knitted, spun, washed, and made soap and probably assisted with mending and sewing chores as well.[13]

In their efforts to accomplish all of this necessary work, housewives balanced their resources accordingly, constantly weighing inclination and ability against availability and expense. When Phelps lost her hired woman Zerviah, she thought she could "get along pretty well if there wasn't any sewing to do."[14] In the summer of 1800, Hannah Smith of Glastonbury wrote her mother, Abigail, that she had engaged a girl for a year, and so she did "not mean to do any hard work," although she had "had eno to do for Zephina to get her ready to go out of town to school and I have had Patience Munn here to help me sew for her."[15] Though domestic servants contributed to the completion of sewing chores, many employees had their own sewing to worry about: as Betsy Huntington wrote home to her mother, the hired woman Polly "helps a great deal," but she "must keep her sewing—she has brought enough of her own to last till spring. . . . [N]ext week I intend to get somebody to come and make Mr H's shirts and my shifts."[16] In Hatfield, Mary Graves Miller recalled that when she was a young wife in the early nineteenth century she had "fourteen in family, six of whom were apprentices, and my hands were full. I could not bear hired help; they were mostly poor stick, down at the heel, with heads like an oven broom. So I put out my sewing, and got black Cynthy for washing and great day's work."[17]

Miller's reluctance to keep hired girls reflects specific changes in domestic service that had taken place in the decades following the American Revolution, but her strategy in balancing the sets of chores revolving around sewing, laundry, and the other work of the household was an old one. Women throughout New England had long employed different strategies to accomplish these tasks and allocated their resources, financial and physical, appropriately. To be sure, these various sorts of work and workers were very different, but women assessed their need to employ needlewomen and domestic servants in tandem, weighing the services that each performed and the wages that each commanded. For their part, working women, too, chose which sources of income they preferred, also to suit their own abilities and needs, though circumstances of class and race might circumscribe their options. What emerges is an image of the wide variety of ways in which New England women acted as employers and employees, products of their differing positions within the local economy. As that local economy changed, so too did women's opportunities, constraints, and relationships to one another.

Mary Miller managed her household responsibilities by employing nearby women to take in her sewing and laundry, freeing her own hands for other labors on the family farm. Hiring this sort of help, as Faye Dudden has pointed out, "was not a carefree undertaking, but it probably involved less friction" than engaging domestic servants to perform what she calls "non-market women's work."[18] Hiring women to spin, weave, or launder or employing tailoresses to sew involved less subjective measures of the amount of work or its quality than general household chores. What's more, it did not require forging and maintaining ongoing day-to-day relationships: when the tailoress completed her work, she moved on, to be asked again or not depending on the needs and satisfaction of the mistress of the house. Hired women, by contrast, had to be instructed, nurtured, corrected, and praised. As Elizabeth Phelps advised her daughter, managing hired women was a chore—and skill—that required "a great deal of flattering and scolding," which, she added, "you know I could administer very handily."[19]

Thousands of stitches were required to keep a household's clothing and textiles in good order. "I have made since you left here twelve shirts & [shifts]," Phelps wrote to her daughter in the spring of 1803, and "knit almost three pairs of cotton stockings besides the socks and mittens and all the other mending which has never been properly clear'd off, since I came [home], till very lately the shirts that you work'd some upon are recon'd in. [N]ow there remains about 6 or 8 frocks & trowsers to make and repair which as soon as my thumb is well, will be attended too."[20] To survive from season to season, breeches, shirts, and stockings required not only "prudent management" but also frequent darning, patching, and underlaying.[21] On top of this came the construction and maintenance of many household textiles, including curtains, sheets, pillowcases, and other household linens. Elizabeth Porter Phelps found such work mind-numbing. In a letter to her daughter, she reported that she regularly dozed off while trying to keep up with her plainwork: "I've been trying to get my mending and work so forward, as I dare take time to write . . . I have been kniting on a mittin and churning alternately till at the last calculation I've had more than thirty naps and now I shall try writing and churning."[22] Six months later, she wrote, "tis now a little past 3 & I've been mending stockings near two hours, & am so sleepy, must try whether this business will keep me awake."[23]

Phelps apparently had little patience or stamina for the monotony of stitches required to keep a household clothed, and perhaps little talent for it as well. While her daughter Betsy was at home, it appears that the younger woman, who preferred the more sedate work of sewing to the more vigorous work of the kitchen, assumed many of these chores. "I feel as I could go along considerable well, if there was no makeing or mending," Elizabeth told Betsy. "When you come, you can sew, & I can do the work."[24] While she was still living at home, young Betsy Phelps had helped clothe the Phelps men: her correspondence with her brother teems with references to her work supplying and maintaining his wardrobe, including making and mending five and six shirts at a time.[25] Typical is the July 1796 letter that Betsy sent her older brother Charles, away at Harvard. "Mr. Hopkins is so obliging as to take charge of two shirts, your finest," she wrote, but "they are not wash'd for we had to finish making them this morning." She apologized for not having completed his "others" but assured him that they "shall soon and send them by the first safe opportunity." The next April, they were at work once more making shirts for Charles: "As to your shirts, you shall have them as soon as possible—we shall go to work immediately upon them." When the shirts finally left Hadley, on 30 May, she enclosed with them a note boasting that she had made his shirts "with my own hand."[26]

Betsy's boast suggests that Charles would easily conclude otherwise, that is, that not all of the sewing she sent him was of her doing. Elsewhere she wrote, "your piece of holland makes nine shirts—instead of six."[27] A skillful cutter had wrested more shirts from the materials than either of them had anticipated. Was that hand eighteen-year-old Betsy's, or one of the many experienced needlewomen that the family employed? Or had the length of Holland gone to a local tailor to cut? And who provided the labor required to sew up these several garments?

There was no difficulty in finding local women to take on this work. In towns throughout New England, families traded goods and services, their exchanges tracked in accounts often extending over several years, and only intermittently reckoned. As families acquired the goods they needed and desired, they indebted themselves to kin and neighbors; in return, they exchanged products of their own labor and skill. Clothing production and maintenance generated demand and involved skills that many women could supply. Most of those employed at the Phelps house are traceable to a dense network of Anglo-American laborers from local families, mostly young women, mostly unmarried. Unlike Phelps's domestic servants, without exception drawn from hilltowns or communities that lay along the highway between Hadley and Boston, her needlewomen hailed from their immediate community. Of the twenty-five tailoresses named in Phelps's diary whose hometowns can be identified, twenty-one were from Hadley and Hatfield, with the remainder from the bordering or nearby communities of Granby, Amherst, Belchertown, and Northampton. Not coincidentally, all of these women were enmeshed in the local credit economy.[28]

These tailoresses illustrate the interpersonal character of New England's female clothing trades. Since women seeking help with sewing could not, in most instances, turn to the local press to find the names of dependable women available for hire, they turned instead to friends, relatives, and other needleworkers for suggestions. Some young women, like Betty and Tryphena Newton, came to perform needlework through the work of a parent. Betty Newton accompanied her mother to Forty Acres nine of the twenty-two times that Easter came to work at Forty Acres, and she came on her own, as did Tryphena, to sew and occasionally to weave. While family ties brought new generations of women into the clothing trades, they also brought together craftswomen and clients. Members of Phelps's social and family circles introduced one another to the needleworkers they had engaged, as on the August afternoon that Phelps's daughter Betsy brought her friend Fanny Lyman to Hadley "to get some taylouring done at Mrs. Smiths."[29] In the spring of 1778 Phelps's sister-in-law, while staying with the Phelps family, "sent and brought up Molly Marsh to taylor," after which Molly and her sister Mabel began sewing regularly for the Phelps household.

Within communities of working women in early America, the type of work a woman was likely to do and the conditions under which she labored were shaped by race, class, and geography. Tailoresses, for example, were drawn primarily from a given community's white population.[30] In Connecticut Valley account books kept in the last half of the eighteenth century and first years of the nineteenth, references to women of color working in needle trades are rare. Instead, enslaved women worked as domestic help, while free women of color usually worked as laundresses, not needlewomen.

Anglo-American women in need of an income had a wide range of occupational choices, though as we have seen, the women who worked and lived as Hadley's domestic servants were drawn from a different geographic and economic pool than were Hadley's needlewomen. At the same time, however, the employment of tailoresses and the hiring of household help were linked in part because tailoresses' labors helped remunerate those hired men and women. Labor contracts stipulated that laborers receive, at the end of their tenure, two suits of apparel, one appropriate for church and another for everyday use. Fulfilling their end of those bargains often meant, for the wives of employers, hiring yet another, more temporary laborer to help with the sewing. In the fall of 1803, Prince Cooley carried a note from Charles Phelps into the Porter shop asking that the bearer be allowed "cloth for a coat, waistcoat and pantaloons, and shirt, with the necessary trimmings—also a hat and one pr stockings" and that the expense be charged to Phelps's account.[31] Cooley had completed his term of service and would return to Forty Acres with the materials from which one of his suits would be made; he would soon find himself clothed from head to heel. But before these lengths of cloth could be called a suit, the pieces would have to be cut out and sewn up—tasks that likely brought to the Phelps home at least one, and maybe more, local women. Similarly, Simon Baker of Walpole, New Hampshire, was just ten years old when he was bound to Charles Phelps for a term of almost eleven years, to expire when he turned twenty-one. Baker's contract required that he at that time be provided with "two decent suits of apparel, one for Sabbath and one for work." Baker fulfilled his obligation, and, in turn, Elizabeth Phelps fulfilled hers: when, on 19 March 1777, Baker signed off that he had received two sets of breeches, shirts, jackets, and stockings, his legal relationship with the Phelps household ended.[32]

Such obligations as providing clothes for laborers required Phelps to engage local tailoresses. A year after Baker left, for example, she asked the local tailoress Lydia Smith to show her how to make a pair of breeches for a workman.[33] Maintaining clothing for hired men and women consumed a significant amount of an employer's attention. Tryphena Cooke charged Charles and Elizabeth Phelps for making coats for their "boy," Reuban (an orphan brought to the farm at the age of five), as well as the hired men Whitney and Gastens.[34]

Making clothing was more lucrative than cutting or altering, because it took more time and energy. In one year, for example, Lydia Champion earned £12 13s. making three pairs of breeches, two jackets, two coats, and a pair of trousers, and just over £2 for cutting out three great coats, six pairs of breeches, five jackets, two vests, a coat, and "cloes" [clothes]. Champion was prepared to cut breeches of leather and deerskin when called upon but more commonly cut clothes out of various linens and woolens. Her repertoire in terms of making up garments was similar: largely coats, breeches, vests, and jackets, as well as great coats. The tasks she performed, and the income they generated, varied widely, from 2 and 3 pence for cutting out vests and breeches to sums as high as £3 10s. for making up a jacket and breeches from start to finish. Champion's annual earnings varied widely: they sometimes totaled more than £14, though her average annual earnings for the decade following her marriage were closer to about £4.[35]

What prompted women to begin sewing for households not their own? For most tailoresses, sewing helped offset the ordinary debts of everyday life. In Hadley, for example, Moses Gunn's household settled a debt to Josiah Pierce for legal work "by his wife making a coat for Jonah, by ditto for Samuel and Jacket for Samuel, By making a jacket for Jonah, by making breeches for Jonah and Samuel, [and] by making a jacket for myself," earning on the whole 12 shillings 6 pence.[36] Similarly, in Windsor, Connecticut, Anna Cook, a widow, offset her debts to the tanner Jerijah Barber (for shoes, as well as molasses, rice, and sugar) "by work done tailoring."[37] Silence Bartlett was eighteen when she began tailoring for Daniel Worthington. Her father, Caleb Bartlett, who owned little real estate, swept the floors of the Hadley meetinghouse for additional income. In 1770, during the time Silence was tailoring for Worthington, her father's estate was assessed at £52, the town's median in that year.[38] Tailoring for Daniel Worthington allowed Silence to contribute to the Bartlett family fortunes. For both employees and their employers, the ongoing need to secure goods and services from the community prompted and sustained relationships.

Economic crisis—most commonly the death of a male provider—also drew women into tailoring. Lucy Nash of Granby, Massachusetts, was hired "to taylor men's clothes" in the same year that her father, Eleazer Nash, died insolvent. Her mother, Phebe Nash, being "greatly straightened," appealed to the probate court judge to permit her to keep "some part of the movables as the law in such cases directs."[39] He allowed her their pewter, a table and three chairs, cookware, three beds and bed linens, and a chest of drawers to store them in. As an afterthought, he added above his signature a spinning wheel and reel—probably in acknowledgment of her need of those tools to contribute to her family's support. Meanwhile, her eldest daughter, Lucy, went to work at tailoring. Robert Blair St. George has suggested that local elites' use of local craftsmen to produce "public artifacts . . . fulfilled a moral responsibility to lend public support to their neighbors."[40] William Hosley suggests further that, "in addition to providing a means to work off debts, the community elite . . . were anxious to promote harmony by keeping the home team at work and on the field of play."[41] It seems likely that tailoresses were hired for similar reasons. Family crises like those experienced by the Nashes brought women into new economic relationships; Phelps's decisions about which needlewomen to hire when were surely in part guided by her knowledge of the needs of women and families throughout her community.

Happier occasions also drew women into clothing production. A noticeable number of sewers were working on the eve of their weddings, suggesting that New England tailoresses channeled particular energy into earning extra income in the months prior to marriage.[42] Molly Marsh of Hadley tailored regularly for the Phelps family into the fall of 1781, when she declared her intention to marry Joseph Field; Betty Newton lodged twice to tailor in January, again in April, and twice more in May before she married Moses Kellogg in October.[43] In anticipation of establishing a new household, prospective brides acquired kitchen equipment, crockery, glassware, and linens, and other goods. Their work could offset the household's additional debts with local artisans and shopkeepers as the family prepared for the upcoming event.

The range of goods needed is captured in careful inventories fathers kept of objects purchased for their daughters. The record made by Preserved Wright of Northampton when his daughter Sarah married Asahel Clapp suggests how these purchases were distributed across local and distant sources. The long list included a feather bed, bolster, and pillows; yards of ticking, sheets, and pillowcases, along with thirty-five pounds of feathers; towels, table cloths, and napkins; a brass kettle, a pot, a disk kettle, a frying pan, and a warming pan; basins and other earthenware; a quart pot; a candlestick; two knives; six spoons; three bowls and six trenchers; six London plates with six matching platters; three pint basins; a brass skillet; a pair of box and heaters; a pair of hand irons; shears; two trammels; two porringers; a slicer and a pair of tongs; a chamber pot; a bailing pot, kettle, and skillet; a tankard; a flesh fork and skimmer; a chopping knife; and a looking glass. All of those things were purchased in Boston. From local sources came a wool wheel, a flax wheel and reel, a chest with two drawers, two chaff beds, pails and tubs for butter, cheese, and bread-making, six black and white chairs, five hundred pins, a barrel, a broom, and a bible. Fabric purchased locally included yards of taffeta and damask, as well as drugget quilt for a pillion; fabric from Boston included, along with the ticking, several yards of calico (an extremely fashionable fabric in this period that may have been for her gown), and fifteen yards of some print along with rings, tape, and binding for bed curtains. About two-thirds of the expense for Sarah's "setting out," then, went to Boston merchants and artisans, with the remaining third spent locally, incurring debts that could be offset by the labor of any family member, including the soon-to-be bride.[44]

Household, Community, and the Needlework of Easter Newton and Tryphena Cooke

Looking closely at the sewing performed by Easter Newton and Tryphena Cooke helps place this aspect of the clothing trades in the context of community. Tryphena was born in 1764, the third of Francis and Easter Newton's five children. Francis and Easter named their daughter after a woman praised in the New Testament (Romans 16) as among those who "work hard in the Lord," and there is little doubt that Tryphena worked hard in both her spiritual and her secular realms. She had two older sisters, Betty and Eleanor, a younger sister, Sally, and a younger brother, Francis Junior. The Newtons were among those families who migrated westward with each generation, ever in search of new opportunities. Francis's parents were born in Marlboro, Massachusetts, but moved to Leicester, where Francis was born. When he married Easter Fairchild in 1753, the two were in Belchertown. They lived for a time in Granby and around 1770 moved to the north end of Hadley's West Street, where the Connecticut River swings into the broad arc that encircled the eighteenth-century village.[45]

Housewright, wheelwright, and farmer Francis Newton appears never to have found the success he was seeking. In 1770, as he approached his fortieth birthday, his estate was valued under £30, notably less than the town median of £52.[46] The family's circumstances over the next several years are difficult to puzzle out, but by the end of the decade, Francis and Easter Newton were searching for ways to augment their meager income. At this point the four girls were able to contribute to the household income, but little Francis, born in 1774, was still too small, and with neither the means to purchase acreage nor the familial labor to farm it, the Newtons looked to other occupations. In 1779, they began tavern keeping, and around the same time, Easter Newton became a regular presence at Forty Acres. When they were old enough, Easter's daughters Betty and Tryphena accompanied her. Betty had been weaving there from the time she was fifteen, and later, especially in the early 1780s as she was nearing twenty, she and her mother sewed regularly for the Phelps family. After Betty married, her younger sister Tryphena assumed Betty's place at Forty Acres until her own marriage in 1790.

Many women appear, like Betty and Tryphena Newton, to have undertaken this type of sewing while unmarried. Betty and Tryphena Newton, Molly and Mabel Marsh, Patty Smith, and others largely cease to appear in Phelps's journal (as needlewomen, at least) once they were married. Of the twenty-six women mentioned as tailoring at Forty Acres, twenty-one were unmarried at that time (another three cannot be identified). In part, being single allowed women the flexibility to spend several days in the homes of their employers. The image of the itinerant artisan is of course familiar and extends accurately to needlemen, who as tailors and journeymen traveled from town to town to obtain work, but it is not appropriate among rural New England's needlewomen, at least if by itinerant we mean an occupation that involved both travel and some speculative risk.[47] Tailoresses often remained a day or two in the homes of their employers, but their itinerary was hardly uncertain. Rather, they sustained their craft among a local and established clientele not from one dedicated site but from a chain of local sites only temporarily dedicated to the work. Some sense of this movement can be seen in the diary of Josiah Pierce. Pierce's niece Esther came to live with him in May 1764. On 7 September of that year, he records that she "begins my great coat." On the fourteenth, she finished it, and the next day, began another. She finished that one on the seventeenth, and the following day traveled across town to Ebenezer Marsh's, where she sewed for four days. Between 22 September and 10 October, Pierce records that she returned home, left for Deacon Smith's (across the green from Marsh), returned home, left for Jon Cooke's home on the "middle highway" that ran through the center of town, returned home, and then went again to Cooke's. In the spring, Pierce notes other similar series of brief visits by his niece to households around the town common: four days at the Kellogg house, another four at Oliver Warner's, and then three at Enos Cooke's.[48] Young women, likewise, lodged in the Phelps home for several of days at a time, normally spending two nights in the home of their employer. Typical were weeks when, as Elizabeth Phelps recorded in October 1816, "monday tuesday daughter Hun[tington]: had a girl here 2 days to taylour."[49]

While at first glance, however, Phelps's memoranda may appear to show that most women who sewed for income were single, Phelps's book together with records from the Newton and Cooke families tell us not that sewing was the particular province of unmarried women but that unmarried women were more likely to work in the homes of their employers, and married women were more likely to work in their own homes. Easter Newton is one of the few women found sewing in the home of her employer with any regularity after her marriage, journeying often to Forty Acres. Much of that work, however, was accomplished during her widowhood. Consistent with Phelps's records, which mention only a visit from Tryphena after her marriage, the Cooke family ledger indicates that after her marriage Tryphena continued to take in making and mending and even increased her attention to this work, once she began raising her own family.

When fifty-year-old Francis Newton, like Eleazer Nash, died insolvent, Easter, struggling to settle the debt-ridden estate, petitioned the courts for permission to sell some real estate to raise funds.[50] Judge Eleazer Porter directed Newton's neighbors Enos Nash and Warham and Chileab Smith to assign Easter's dower rights, preserving for her use one-third of the family home: "the south lower room of the great house, and the whole of the kitchen & south half of the cellar, and the whole of the barn." As the estate made its way through probate, Easter petitioned to retain some of her household goods. Like Phebe Nash, she was allowed beds, linens, a chest of drawers, and the minimum kitchen equipment, as well as a foot wheel and a great wheel to enable her to continue spinning flax and wool.

Though Easter had begun to sew for the Phelps family as early as 1779 (and was sewing for other neighbors as early as 1771, when Josiah Pierce acknowledged her four shillings six pence credit for making a coat), her work at tailoring increased its pace in the early 1780s as she adjusted to widowhood.

In 1781, she traveled regularly to Forty Acres to help the Phelps household prepare for the coming winter, and she returned twice in January as well. The following year, too, saw a series of summer and fall visits, and the spring of 1783 was an especially busy season. Elizabeth Phelps was planning a trip to Boston, while her daughters, Betsy and Thankful, were preparing to attend school in Amherst, events that could account for the extra attention to their apparel. The spring work of the farm together with the declining health of her slave girl Phillis also demanded her attention. In early April, the household began to make soap; the following week Lucy Marshall arrived to begin weaving while Phelps sent for Phillis's grandmother, Peg, to help care for the weakening child. The same weeks that saw repeated visits of the Newtons found Elizabeth Phelps anxiously attending to the young girl. Phillis died on the last day of April 1783 and was laid to rest at a funeral at Colonel Porter's house on the town common. Easter and Betty arrived once more to tailor the next day.[51]

The years to come gave Easter Newton both pleasure and pain. In November 1783, her eldest daughter, Betty, married Moses Kellogg Jr., whose father was a former selectman and among the town's wealthier residents. That same year, Eleanor married Jonathan Cook Jr., an apparently well-educated man who in time became a physician. But neither of Easter's elder daughters would live to raise their families; Eleanor died after less than a year of marriage, and Elizabeth died in the winter of 1790. For whatever reason, Easter did not continue to work under the Phelps family roof during these years; in fact, she did not travel to Forty Acres again until November 1807, when Elizabeth wrote her daughter Betsy that "our friend Mrs Newton" had come to "fix Robert" (one of their hired boys). Elizabeth added that she had "been able to work with her" for a bit, after which Charles took her home. She returned to sew twice more, on both occasions to alter coats for the Phelpses' hired men.[52]

Clearly, Easter Newton had become more than an occasional employee for Charles and Elizabeth Phelps; she had become a "friend." Elizabeth had attended the funerals of Betty Kellogg and Eleanor Cook, and later she would care for Tryphena in a time of need. In the small community of Hadley, the distance between families like the Newtons and the Phelpses was not always great, as relationships extended over generations. When Tryphena became a wife and mother with a family of her own to support, Charles and Elizabeth concerned themselves with the new household as well. Solomon and Tryphena regularly found themselves financially obligated to Charles and Elizabeth, and so Elizabeth hired Tryphena to help her repay her debt and provide her with the additional income she needed to keep her family afloat, and in doing so helped to maintain between the two households a harmonious and ongoing relationship.

Tryphena Cooke's skills appear to have been fairly broad. She earned most of her income for "making" breeches, trousers, and overalls, as well as shirts, jackets, waistcoats, coats, great coats, and surtouts. She occasionally performed alterations, "letting out" and "turning" coats, mostly for growing boys, though she occasionally produced clothing of better quality, such as the waistcoat she completed for the college-bound Pierrepont Porter, the sixteen-year-old son of Eleazer Porter. She also continued to sew for the Phelpses' hired hands. Though Phelps last noted Cooke's arrival to sew in October 1791, when she came to "fix" that coat for Reuban, her own family's accounts show that in 1792 and 1793, for example, she made two coats, a waistcoat, and a pair of trousers for hired men at Forty Acres. By and large, the garments that passed through Cooke's hands were everyday clothing whose usefulness was extended by alterations or repair. Only very rarely does the Cooke ledger note her work cutting garments; the two jackets and coat she cut in the spring of 1791 for John Montague's three-year-old child, Zebina, are almost the only references to cutting in the entire volume, and then for a toddler's garments. Cooke may well have lacked skill in this area; for example, she made two shirts, a pair of trousers, a jacket, overalls, a fine Holland shirt, and a coat for Solomon Parker but does not debit Parker for the cutting of any of those garments. Her earnings for making garments like these hovered around two and three shillings. On two occasions garments brought as much as six shillings: a jacket for Elisha Smith in 1796, and a "sterat boddey coat" (straight-bodied coat) for Levi Gale in 1793.[53]

The work Tryphena Cooke did bound her family's livelihood with that of others. Sometimes families intermingled accounts at the local merchant's shop; Enos Smith, for example, for whom Cooke had apparently done nine shillings' worth of sewing work, gave her a note for William Porter, asking him "please to let the bearer Mrs Cooke have 9/ [goods valued up to nine shillings, charged to Smith's account] out of your store."[54] Running accounts between households like this and others captured in the Cooke account book also illuminate the ways in which community members relied on one another for the goods and services they needed to sustain themselves and their families. Cooke's tailoring was one means by which she and her husband settled accounts with family and neighbors. Solomon Cooke's brother Andrew, for example, supplied the household with rye and corn by the bushel; in return, Tryphena kept his wardrobe in good order, making him trousers, waistcoats, overalls, and great coats. In all, more than 120 men and women, ranging in wealth and status from Eleazer Porter to the freed slave

Joshua Boston, exchanged goods and services with Solomon and Tryphena Cooke during the twenty years of accounts that appear in their surviving ledger.

This record, though fragmentary, of Solomon and Tryphena Cooke's exchanges with Charles and Elizabeth Phelps reveals that their relationship was ongoing.[55] Around the same time, for example, that Tryphena made the two coats, a waistcoat, and trousers for the Phelpses' hired men, Solomon sold the household three animal hides. When the two families reckoned accounts in January 1794, the Cookes still owed the Phelpses a balance of 15 shillings 5 pence. Over the next year, Solomon earned 1 shilling leading a horse to or from the ferry. He also carried two more hides to Forty Acres, one weighing fifty-nine pounds, worth nearly the whole 15 shillings, and another smaller hide worth 10 shillings. Still, by January 1795, the Cooke family—now enlarged to include a toddler, Elizabeth, and an infant, Tryphena—was yet deeper in debt to Charles and Elizabeth Phelps, owing them 3 shillings 9 pence. In November and December, as they and Charles Phelps prepared to reckon accounts, Tryphena labored diligently to work off the balance. She made a great coat, a waistcoat, a pair of trousers, and two coats for hired men, earning altogether £1 toward relieving the debt. When Solomon contributed a calf skin, the Cookes finally "ballanced all accounts" with Charles Phelps on 15 January 1795, a month before Tryphena delivered her fourth child. Further transactions with Phelps brought in a few shillings now and then; Tryphena made a coat and other clothes for the hired man Whitney in 1797, and again for Reuban in 1798. The families balanced accounts again in February 1801. These last accounts were less systematically settled, perhaps suggesting that the two families' later dealings required less rigorous and regular scrutiny.

Indeed, relationships between families constantly fluctuated in response to changing circumstances. For example, just as marriage altered the physical circumstances of Tryphena Cooke's sewing, changes in her family's needs altered the quantity of work she took on. She was married in January 1790, and her first child, a son, was born the following November. Six more children would follow. Before her children were born, Tryphena Cooke sewed very little—only one or two entries each year record this work, and her earnings were slim. Perhaps in these years she was making cider, helping around the inn and tavern, and performing some of the other work for which Solomon charged in his book. But as her family grew, Tryphena sewed heavily, earning an average of nearly £2 a year. In 1793, with an infant and a toddler and another child on the way, she reached a peak earnings of 69 shillings, or more than £3. Interestingly, these are the same years that the couple seems to have been making some improvements to their home. In March 1792, the household accounts contain debts associated with the framing of a barn. In August 1794, Solomon's brother Elihu Cooke was credited for three weeks' work at Solomon's house "soring a winder hole in a garret," and in December, he was paid for painting.

After 1797, Tryphena's charges in Solomon's accounts dropped off sharply, though it is hard to say why. By the end of that year she had four small children, but before long she would have three more, and her children had not previously prevented her from taking in sewing. Perhaps the work of the inn replaced her sewing.[56] At the same time, the sewing needs within her own household were increasing. For example, Tryphena Cooke provided clothing and maintenance for her own family's hired help, Solomon Parker and Jemima Boynton. When "Sol" needed a new pair of trousers, unlike Elizabeth Phelps, who hired local women to maintain her help's clothing, Tryphena provided the labor to accomplish the task, while her husband charged the work against the servant's accounts in his book.[57]

Family fortunes for Tryphena Cooke also meant shifting skills and experiences, turning to both needlework and tavernkeeping as circumstances allowed or demanded. As we have seen, her life at the inn taught her how to keep the peace, an important skill when town selectmen could deny licenses to anyone whom they believed incapable of maintaining an orderly house.[58] Here, as she had when she began her needle work, Tryphena worked alongside her mother. Easter Newton first worked at tavernkeeping with her husband, Francis, in 1779 and 1780. In 1781, after his death, she obtained a tavern license in her own name and continued to receive licenses for nearly twenty years, until 1810.[59] Though the house was long been remembered as Cooke's inn, it seems unlikely that Solomon Cooke and his mother-in-law were competing for customers; instead, the structure that housed Easter Newton's business was likely Tryphena and Solomon's home. Solomon's father, Andrew, had purchased this, the last house lot along the river, in 1795, and the new house was built not long after, and perhaps almost immediately, since in 1796 Widow Newton sought to expand her clientele by purchasing advertising space in the columns of the *Hampshire Gazette,* promoting auctions at her public house.[60] The two-story, five-by-four bay Federal-style house on the banks of the Connecticut River was a convenient stopping place for men and women traveling by ferry over the river, often guided by Solomon.[61] No account book detailing life at the tavern is known to survive, but Easter Newton's series of licenses together with oral tradition that remembers Tryphena in the barroom suggest that mother and daughter played central roles in the daily operation of the tavern, while the ferryman Solomon Cooke seems to have spent his time on outdoor jobs.

In 1805, at age forty, Tryphena Cooke died after an extended battle with breast cancer. In the final months of her life, the family inn became a site of religious and social gatherings: in April 1804, Elizabeth Phelps attended a religious meeting and found "more than a hundred people there, notwithstanding there are almost every night meetings . . . twice every week—all sorts attend."[62] Later that month the Phelpses attended a singing meeting there.[63] Ailing by December 1804, Cooke suffered with the disease through the spring and into the summer, when Charles Phelps visited and prayed with her. The first Sunday in June Charles and Elizabeth stopped in after services to pray with her once more. Nine days later, they attended her funeral. The minister, who acknowledged Cooke's long illness, took as his text Philemon 1:23: "For I am in a strait betwixt two, having a desire to depart, and to be with Christ; which is far better."[64] Solomon, left with a houseful of children between the ages of fifteen and two, soon remarried. His son Solomon eventually took over management of the business, and, when he died, his wife, Clarissa, continued on, the third in three generations of women to run the inn at the north end of the Hadley common.[65]

Tryphena Cooke's needlework exists for us today in the breach between two very different sources, both of which capture more shadow than substance. Only two pieces by her hand are known to survive: a shirt and a bonnet she made for her son Samuel.[66] From the memorandum book of Elizabeth Phelps we catch a glimpse of a young unmarried needlewoman journeying up to Forty Acres to tailor. But Phelps's text misleads us. Tryphena Cooke is one of many women whose needlework vanishes from Phelps's memorandums, although Phelps continued to employ her skills. What changed was neither the amount of work nor the nature of it but rather its location, as we learn from Tryphena and Solomon Cooke's record, which places Tryphena's skills within the context of her larger community. From this record we learn that women worked at tailoring throughout their lives.

In part then, both Easter Newton and Tryphena Cooke offer examples of the growing numbers of women moving into the clothing trades during the eighteenth century. Account books like Tryphena and Solomon Cooke's remind us to be more attentive to the legions of references to sewing that fill eighteenth-century ledgers. As Gloria Main points out, "when nominally feminine tasks became important to household income, men undertook a share of the responsibility, even if only to keep track of the profits."[67] Tryphena's entries provide evidence not only of her own patterns of work but also of its significance within the Cooke family economy.

In Tryphena Cooke's accounts we also see a reflection of the rising numbers of New England women who were earning livings from clothing

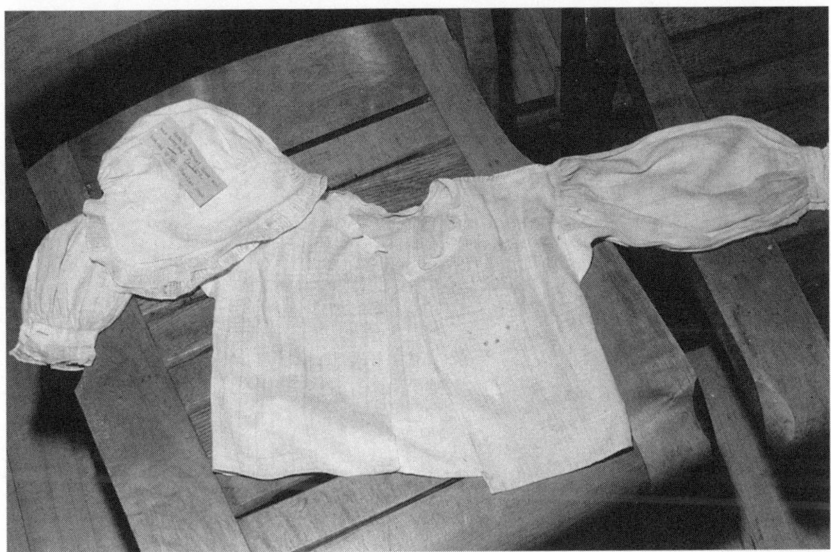

Needlework by Tryphena Newton Cooke, 1790–1805. Photograph courtesy of Wadsworth Atheneum Archives (Great River Archives), Hartford, Conn.

A child's bonnet and jacket are all that appears to have survived to the present from the needle of Tryphena Newton Cooke. This photograph was taken in the 1980s during fieldwork for an exhibition; the location of these garments is no longer known.

production in the eighteenth century. Reconfigurations of household and community labor drew some women's energies away from the tasks surrounding clothing production and maintenance, creating opportunities seized by others. At the same time, a plentiful labor force, for the most part female, was progressively linked to burgeoning demand. As more people demanded new garments in new forms and new fabrics, more hands were required to produce them. The blossoming consumer revolution, then, also helps explain women's entry into the paid labor force, though women like Cooke were of course consumers as well as producers. To purchase the new luxuries making their way up the Connecticut River, women looked for opportunities to earn cash or to gain credit at local shops. When Easter Newton settled a debt to Josiah Pierce by making a coat, or Tryphena Cooke exchanged her skill with a needle for goods out of William Porter's shop, she rehearsed a scene that would be repeated, on ever-larger scales, throughout the town, county, and region.

CHAPTER 5

Family, Artisanry, and Craft Tradition

The Worlds of Tabitha Clark Smith and Rebecca Dickinson

THE ENTRY in Elizabeth Porter's memorandum book for 20 November 1768 reads: "tarried at home because of a heavy snow storm—sacrament day. Monday near night went into town and brought one Tabithy Clark to taylor for us—Wednesday night carried her home and went to Mr Porters tarried there til Friday night—helpt quilt upon a brown coat for Molly Dickinson all Thursday night. Fryday I helped Miss rebeckah Dickingson make a gown for me. Spent the Eve at Mr Hop, returned home. Satturday this day one and twenty years of age."[1] Like most women during most weeks, on that day, Elizabeth Porter (later Phelps), Tabitha Clark (later Smith), and Rebecca Dickinson found themselves with needle in hand, performing familiar tasks. The quilting of petticoats for young women like Molly Dickinson regularly filled festive afternoons for young Elizabeth Porter, as they continued to do following her marriage to Charles Phelps, and would for her daughters, Elizabeth and Thankful, as well. Tabitha Clark, then on her first visit to the Porter farm, would become a regular presence at Forty Acres, as Elizabeth Porter Phelps engaged Clark's services many more times over the next twenty years. Dickinson, a thirty-year-old unmarried woman already well known for her skillful gown making, also visited the farm often in the last decades of the eighteenth century as a respected artisan and as a welcome guest.

If their stitches now seem identical, the stitchers were not. Tabitha Clark's needlework produced income for her family, while Elizabeth Porter's needlework, often ornamental, usually signaled, as it did on this occasion, an opportunity to cultivate relationships with women of comparable social and economic status. Both women would eventually marry, and for Elizabeth Porter Phelps, time spent quilting elaborate petticoats gradually gave way to overseeing the needlework of others. Tabitha Clark Smith, in contrast, continued throughout her life to work in the clothing trades, eventually replacing Rebecca Dickinson as the artisan most responsible for maintaining the Porter and Phelps women's wardrobes. Marriage for Clark meant less a change of duties than a change of venue, since she no longer journeyed out of her home with her needle. Dickinson, however, was more highly skilled than either Clark or Porter, at least in the winter of 1768; her apprenticeship in the complex physical and mental operations of cutting fabric rendered her services uncommon and valuable in Hampshire County. Because she was unmarried and self-supporting, her training proved especially important. As she recorded in the pages of her journal, "my daily bread depends upon my labor."[2]

Dickinson's and Smith's craft brought them into economic relationships with women like Phelps, to be sure, as well as with tailoresses like Easter Newton and Tryphena Cooke, who often found employment in the construction of garments once the gown makers had finished their work. In small towns, craftswomen surely were familiar with the abilities of local needlewomen.[3] But Dickinson and Smith occupied a space apart from Easter Newton and Tryphena Cooke, and Elizabeth Phelps, too. They possessed craft skills that none of these other women had mastered, creating, altering, and maintaining gowns for Elizabeth Phelps, her mother, and her daughters, as well as other local families. Dickinson and Smith were members of communities defined by geography—Hatfield and Hadley, as well as the larger community of Hampshire County towns along the Connecticut River and in the surrounding hills. But they were also members of a community of artisanal women who inhabited the eighteenth-century Connecticut Valley. They knew of—and perhaps learned from and competed with—other gown-making women from those towns, including Catherine King Phelps, Sarah Clark, and Esther Wright in Northampton, Lucy Sheldon in Deerfield, and Mary and Jane Salmon in Hartford. They also learned from, and competed with, artisans from distant places—mantua makers in Boston and Hartford, even New York and London, who also attracted the patronage of their most privileged neighbors and between craft skill and family life, artisanal and family identity, and other features of potential clients.

Dickinson, Smith, and their craftworking colleagues provide points of entry into the worlds of clients and craftswomen that surrounded rural New England gown making, illuminating intersections of eighteenth-century community life. These women's lives shed light on the female and family economies of late eighteenth-century rural New England. Gown makers sustained economies in which clients and craftswomen together were consumers and conveyors of fashion. At the same time, these craftswomen maintained households as well and saw their work as an important asset to the family livelihood.

Gown Making as a Trade for Women in Eighteenth-Century New England

In the eighteenth and nineteenth centuries, many craftswomen practiced millinery and mantua making together. Milliners made hats and headdresses, which demanded familiarity with a wide array of trimmings, from ribbons, tassels, and lace to flowers, feathers, and other kinds of ornament. For that reason, milliners generally carried these sorts of shop goods, as well as other small accessories, such as mitts, gloves, caps, sashes, scarves, shawls, aprons, handkerchiefs, hoops and panniers, cloaks and mantles, and canes, fans, umbrellas, and parasols. Milliners and gown makers shared a need to understand the modish application of trimmings—ruching, robings and ruffles, fringe, bows, paste ornaments, and other embellishments, to be applied, as fashion warranted, to sleeves, skirts, petticoats, and bodices. The two closely related occupations commanded the highest status, and the greatest income, not only in the women's clothing trades but in the female labor market more generally.

While milliners concentrated on creating stylish headwear and trimmings, gown makers or mantua makers mastered special skills related to the construction of fashionable women's garments. Through formal and informal apprenticeships, gown makers learned, for example, how to apply a flat, inert surface tautly yet malleably around the width and breadth of a living, moving form.[4] Social skills, however, were equally important, and those appropriate to this line were underscored in period trade manuals. In 1747, for example, Robert Campbell counseled prospective artisans and their parents that the main requirement of the mantua maker was an ability to "flatter all complexions, praise all shapes" and be the "compleat Mistress of the Art of Dissimulation." Bound to discover her client's "deformities," she must have the prudence to keep silent about flaws in a given figure along with the ability to conceal—and transform—them.[5] Those responsibilities drew craftswomen and clients into especially intimate relationships. To meet these highly personal demands, successful artisans cultivated discretion and diplomacy alongside their needle skills.

At the same time, they necessarily attended to changing fashions, keeping abreast of new developments throughout the Atlantic world while assessing which would gain favor among their local clientele. Much of a gown maker's trade was shaped by her neighborhood, by the aspirations and preferences of the women around her, their financial resources, and their ability and desire to conform to prevailing fashion. Gown makers depended on a steady circle of patrons, who recommended their work to others in their social circle. The *Book of Trades* attests to the importance of word-of-mouth testimonials: "Young women ought, perhaps, rarely to be apprenticed to this trade unless their friends can, at the end of the term, place them in a reputable way of business, and can command such connections as shall, with industry, secure their success." Happily for prospective artisans, however, the "business requires, in those who would excel in it, a considerable share of taste, but no great capital to set up in it."[6]

In short, trained gown makers offered their manual and conceptual expertise and their taste and time. In communities throughout New England, women could be found who had become the community's local expert in the construction of fashionable, fitted clothing. A small number established shops, while others—a large majority of the gown or mantua makers in eighteenth-century rural New England—turned skill to profit among circles of neighbors. In Northampton, Catherine King Phelps and Sarah Root Clark supplied their neighbors with garments through most of the eighteenth century; in surviving accounts from the 1790s alone, Esther Wright cut, basted, made, and altered more than 180 gowns, cloaks, stays, and other garments for residents of that community.[7]

Gown or mantua making lent itself well to the income-generating strategies long embraced by New Englanders. Like most rural artisans, including carpenters and housewrights, women who knew how to construct women's more formal clothing paced that work amid the larger routines of the agricultural year, combining farm work with craftwork. Elizabeth Foote, for example, is known to historians of early New England and of early American needlework mainly as the maker of a spectacular bed rug, one of three extant rugs made by the Foote sisters of Colchester, Connecticut.[8] But Foote's extraordinary bed rug is not the only evidence that she knew her way with a needle; she also earned income as a gown maker. In March 1775, for example, Foote records that she made two gowns for the Welch family, earning seven shillings six pence. In two weeks one April she made two gowns for Amos Wells's little daughters and cut out two loose gowns for them as well, "fixed and partly made" a gown for Lydia Wells, made at least two gowns and possibly more for Lieutenant Levy Wells's wife, and made a gown for Nab Fox, who appears to have resided in the Wells household. The following months she records working on gowns for other neighbors as well—Bethiah Kellogg, Molly Caverly, an infant child in the Martin household, Noah Foot's "girl," and Abner Hills's family, where she "fix'd two gowns at 6 [pence] per gown," later adding still three more gowns to the Hillses' wardrobes. Foote also did a good bit of other textile-related work, spinning and weaving for households throughout her community and drawing the pattern for a quilt border for Mrs. Blush. Her journal suggests that she also made and sold cheese and did general housework for her neighbors.[9] Thus, gown making was for Elizabeth Foote one source of income among many. At the same time, for the women of her neighborhood, paying Foote to help with clothing was one strategy by which to meet their own obligations. Foote may never have completed an apprenticeship in gown making; she did not work at the trade exclusively, nor did she maintain a dedicated site in which to practice her craft. By many definitions, she would not qualify as an artisan. But she clearly had skills that were valuable to Colchester families and membership in the community of practice that encompassed Colchester's clothes makers. Like other rural women (and men) with some artisanal ability, she did not rely on a single occupation but instead found income and support through a variety of activities carried on simultaneously, seasonally, or from time to time.

The gown maker's craft involved, as indentures of the day traditionally indicated, mastery of the "art and mystery" of clothing construction—skills that included the art of diplomacy as well as the mystery of clothing construction. A successful gown maker was able not only to produce and reproduce gowns in the latest fashions but also to fit and flatter all body types, from short, stout Elizabeth Porter Phelps and robust Experience Richardson, who weighed over two hundred pounds ("God enables me to cary about a Great heft," the pious diarist noted, "but the heft of sin I beare is much heavier") to the Davis sisters of Portsmouth, New Hampshire, wiry young women with figures like "button wood sticks."[10] The means by which gown makers acquired those skills varied widely, though, unlike apprentices in the making of men's clothing, who might learn their craft from a man or a woman, aspiring gown makers in the eighteenth century learned their craft almost entirely from other women. Some young women learned under the tutelage of a mother already versed in the trade; others gained entry into the craft through formal or informal apprenticeships, some arranged by parents, others by local officials. In 1769, thirteen-year-old Ann Cromartie, bound to the mantua maker Ruth Decosta by the Boston Overseers of the Poor to learn the "Art, Trade or Mystery of a Mantua Maker," served a term of nearly five years, until she reached the age of eighteen, while Ann Wilkinson, bound similarly to Martha Mellens, labored for three years before her release in December 1787.[11] In 1788, Elizabeth Fisher of Middletown, Connecticut, entered into an agreement with Ephraim and Beulah Merriam of Wallingford, binding her to the Merriams for seven years, during which she should "learn the trade of mantee making." [12]

The construction of clothing for women was carried out in a primarily female world of clients and craftswomen, and laborers with a range of skills. Though traditionally women obtained outerwear (and fashions based on outerwear) from male artisans, most of their clothing acquisition was accomplished among other women. Surviving accounts associated with Catherine King Phelps, Sarah Clark, and Esther Wright list the female clienteles that they served. Catherine Phelps made gowns for Mary Phelps, Major Pomeroy's daughter, Thankful Pomeroy, Roger Clapp's daughter, Jonathan Strong's wife, and women in Samuel Clapp's family and Deacon John Clark's family. More rarely did Phelps undertake assignments like the "suit of clothes" she produced for the tailor Samuel Pomeroy in 1731.[13] Similarly, her successor, Sarah Clark, worked within a circle of Northampton neighbors, producing garments for a range of recipients from the infant Jared Clark to the elderly Abigail Baker. Clark sewed for more than fifty individuals in more than twenty families. Though she occasionally made clothing for men—supplying, for example, Thomas Starr with long breeches each year—she generally made and altered gowns and cloaks for the women of these households. Approximately 25 percent of her gown-making activity was intended for married women between the ages of eighteen and sixty, with a slightly larger percentage for unmarried women in that same age range. Another larger category of recipients, comprising more than a quarter of the total, were children under ten. About 10 percent of the gowns Clark made went to girls between the ages of ten and seventeen, with the remaining 5 percent to elderly women in her community, the small number probably reflecting the decreasing clothing acquisition of women in those years.

Records from the eighteenth and early nineteenth centuries reveal the variety of garments and tasks that gown makers undertook. Sarah Clark earned most of her gown-making income making and altering gowns of linen, but she also made riding hoods and cloaks, cut and made loose gowns and wrappers, made and altered stays, and, on at least one occasion, made a "shepherdee" for a member of the Alvord family. She could also produce men's garments, including breeches, trousers and overalls, shirts and frocks.[14] Esther Wright, working in the 1790s and beyond, also earned most of her income cutting, basting, and making and altering gowns, including gowns of comparatively costly fabrics like calico and silk, though she also cut, made, and altered stays; cut, basted, made, and made over frocks; made, altered, and made over long and short cloaks; and made and made over slips. While Wright occasionally made finer garments, like the silk gown and coat she produced for a member of Samuel Clark's family, often she remodeled garments brought to her by women anxious to prolong their use. Approximately one in five of the gowns Esther Wright treated were altered, made over, or simply had "work done," which typically meant simple repairs. In November 1796, Samuel Clark's wife engaged Wright to make a new gown, paying the going rate of two shillings six pence for the service. But while she was there, Clark also had her make over a cloak and two gowns, one of silk, paying her another five shillings for the additional work.[15]

Few sources survive to suggest how many projects gown makers and tailoresses took on at one time. For Tabitha Smith of Hadley, two days seems a typical amount of time between clients' visits. In August 1784, for example, Elizabeth Phelps went to Smith's on a Wednesday "to get her to do some tayloring" and went "Fryday in the forenoon down for it." On another occasion, in 1790, she and Betsy rode down "Tuesday . . . [to] Mrs Chileab Smiths to get her gown made. Thursday Betsy and I down again for it."[16] The number of hours spent on a project depended on its complexity and the gown maker's skill and speed. Also important was the number of hands available to help, whether a gown maker worked alone or had the assistance of daughters or apprentices to help sew the long seams, and otherwise contribute to the process. In 1784 Smith's daughters were not yet old enough to help. By 1790, however, Lucretia, who would years later become a gown maker herself, at nearly thirteen was surely an asset to Tabitha's work.

Evidence from the accounts of Sarah Clark and Esther Wright afford some insight into the earnings of a skilled needlewomen. In the 1750s and 1760s, Sarah Clark charged between two shillings and two shillings four pence to make a gown for an adult woman. Some clients, like Marah Brown, a servant living in the home of Deacon Ebenezer Hunt, asked Clark to make her two gowns "in part." Clark charged slightly over a shilling each for this service. Brown hired just enough skill to render the parts of the garment beyond her own capability, and by providing what skill she could—probably completing the long seams of the gowns skirts—she saved half the labor costs of the new garment. The charge for altering such a gown was generally a shilling or slightly more—about half the cost of construction—while the charge for merely cutting it was generally only six pence or about a quarter of the cost of construction. Simpler garments brought in even less; in 1766, for example, Clark cut three wrappers for only five pence. To make cloaks and riding hoods Clark sometimes charged a good deal more, from one shilling six pence to three shillings and more, perhaps reflecting the time involved in sewing long seams. On the one occasion that Clark was asked to produce a shephardee, she charged seven shillings six pence, the most charged for any single article in her accounts. Making and altering gowns, cloaks, and hoods for adult women comprised almost half of Clark's overall business. The remainder, about one-third of her overall activity, involved making gowns for girls seventeen years old and younger.[17] Thirty years later, Esther Wright charged similarly. In the 1790s, she typically charged two shillings six pence to make a gown for an adult woman and roughly half that to alter one, though sometimes as little as six pence. Gowns of high-quality fabrics like silk or calico cost more—usually three shillings, or 20 percent more. Cutting alone was still far cheaper than sewing; Wright charged just six pence for her skill with the shears a shilling or a shilling two pence to cut and baste, or assemble, a new garment.[18]

Women with the ability to make stays could earn considerably more for their construction. Trade books of the eighteenth and early nineteenth century suggest that stay making was a man's craft, but New England women were making stays at least as early as 1730, when Catherine Phelps produced a pair for someone in the neighboring household of Roger Clapp for which she charged twelve shillings. A gown at that time might cost between four and seven shillings.[19] Stays were worn by women of all ages; Sarah Clark's accounts document her making stays for girls as young as twelve-year-old Anna Clark, though most recipients for this labor were women in their twenties and thirties.[20] Sarah Clark charged ten shillings for a pair of stays.[21] In the 1780s and 1790s Esther Wright charged six shillings for making stays, more than double her rate for making a gown.[22] As preferences shifted from the highly structured bodices of the mid-eighteenth century (which could mean, for the artisan, producing and assembling ten to twelve panels, each consisting of multiple layers of lining, boning, and exterior fabric, tedious stitching of the many channels—sometimes more than one hundred—that held the stiffening material, creating two set of eyelets for the lacings, and binding the outside edges with leather) to the gentler silhouette of the neoclassical style, the structure of and demand for foundation garments like stays changed in ways that affected the income generated by their construction.

A gown maker's potential earnings were at least in part determined by the community's access to other comparably skilled women. One brief, dramatic battle between gown makers competing for customers erupted in Revolutionary-era Hartford when Mary Gabiel, a mantua maker from Paris, began advertising in the *Connecticut Courant.* In May 1775, she announced, "MARY GABIEL, Mantua-maker and milliner from Paris, informs the Ladies of this Town, and others, that she makes all kinds of Ladys gowns, Caps, Bonnets, &c, and dresses Lady's heads in the *neatest and newest* French Fashions. . . . She also washes all kinds of fine linens, gauzes, laces, &c. She may be found at the house of the Widow Patten in Hartford." She repeated her advertisement the following week and again at the end of the month. In October, an even larger advertisement informed the public that "MARY GABIEL, Milliner from France" continues in her trade, while "Dr. Gabiel" also indicated that he would shortly be opening a French School.[23]

Two sisters who had been operating their own successful shop in Hartford, Mary and Jane Salmon, unmarried at ages thirty-two and twenty-nine, respectively, followed Gabiel's second announcement with a notice of their own: "MARY AND JANE SALMON, from Boston, hereby inform the Ladies in this and the neighboring towns that they make the newest fashioned bonnets in the neatest manner and any sort of caps at the same reasonable prices they have been accustomed to in times past. They likewise make cloaks, &c."[24]

Gabiel responded immediately: the 4 December edition of the *Courant* ran another advertisement, again reminding readers of her French origins. Perhaps the Salmons got wind of this notice, because they, too, reran their ad in this issue. But that, unfortunately, is the end of the story. After this episode, none of these women remained in Hartford. Perhaps Gabiel failed to find the success she sought in the valley's largest port, since she does not seem to have remained and was apparently long gone by the time the women of Hartford, in 1786, declared their intent not to become "the slaves of milliners and mantua-makers in London or Paris."[25] The Salmon sisters, too, ultimately left Hartford and returned to Boston, where they purchased the front end of a brick mansion on Washington Street.[26]

Gabiel and the Salmon sisters were not the last Hartford gown makers to use their association with centers of fashion to draw clientele. At the turn of the century, "Mrs Mather" entered Hartford's artisanal circle with a similar ploy. Following a "long residence in New York," Mather informed readers, she had "an arrangement with some ladies for the receipt of the first fashions." In later years, the Lincoln sisters and the Barnards vied for local patrons in Hartford. The Lincolns were on Pearl Street, near Burr and Company; the Barnards occupied the former stand of competitor Chloe Filley at the corner of Main and Theatre. Each partnership regularly posted notices of their skills and availability in the local advertising columns, sometimes within days of each other, suggesting that these women were well aware of their competitors' actions and strove to match them.[27]

Family circumstances affected how women practiced their craft. The marital status of gown makers who were single, unlike that of married women, for example, permitted them to travel to obtain work. Though the geographic and economic scope of a gown maker's trade is difficult to assess, the range of travel to clients by unmarried gown makers seems to have been similar to that of rural New England tailors, or perhaps somewhat more narrow. Studies of other trades have suggested that rural artisans usually found the largest number of their clients in their own community but that they drew a significant proportion from surrounding communities as well and occasionally had transactions with more distant customers. The account book of the early nineteenth-century Whately cabinetmaker William Mather, for example, reveals that of the more than 230 clients Mather served, 35, or 15 percent, were from outside Whately, and only 7 were from towns that did not border Whately. Likewise, of the more than 310 clients the Deerfield tailor John Russell served, 53 percent came from Deerfield and 47 percent from the surrounding towns.[28] From Hatfield, Rebecca Dickinson traveled to nearby towns such as Hadley, Conway, Amherst, and Northampton and occasionally farther, including one trip sixteen miles west to Williamsburg.[29] She could visit several customers in one trip, as she recorded doing in October 1787, when she stopped at Mrs. Cleman's house, Captain Chapin's, Mrs. Wells's, and Captain White's.[30] Business and pleasure no doubt mingled as Dickinson visited friends, family, and old and potential clients in her travels around the county.

Another point about family roles among gown makers is worth noting here. Although this observation is impressionistic, the number of needlewomen for whom birth order can be identified who were eldest daughters is striking. Both Patty Smith and her mentor, Rebecca Dickinson, were the first daughters in their families. The gown maker Lucretia Smith Gaylord was the first daughter born to Tabitha Clark Smith.[31] Elizabeth Foote was the first child born to Israel and Elizabeth Kimberly Foote. In Bernardston, the mantua maker Anna Connable Wright was the eldest daughter of Samuel and Rebecca Ryther Connable. In Northampton, the mantua maker Sarah King was the eldest daughter of Daniel and Mary Miller King. In Granby, Lucy Nash, a "tailor of men's cloathes," was the first daughter of Eleazer and Phebe Kellogg Nash. Eleanor Strong, apprentice to the Northampton tailor Catherine Phelps Parsons, was the oldest in a family of largely daughters, as was her co-apprentice, Martha Alvord. In Hartford, the mantua maker Chloe Filley was the first child of Mark and Eleanor Bissell Filley.

Perhaps the younger sisters of these women learned and practiced trades as well, but no evidence of their work survives in the historical record.[32] But perhaps too there was some preference for equipping eldest daughters with some marketable skill beyond common housewifery. Initially, this theory may seem counterintuitive; surely the eldest daughter was the one most useful to her mother, assisting with household chores and minding younger siblings as the family continued to expand. Nevertheless, the number of female artisans in rural New England who were first daughters is striking.

Striking, too, is the number of businesses operated by sisters.[33] In the 1770s, Mary and Jane Salmon opened their shop in Hartford. In 1809, Mariah and Ann Bennett, skilled in "Needlework, Millinery and Mantua-Making," informed "the ladies" of Hartford that they would "make gowns, bonnets, caps," and other items in the "newest fashions." In 1812, "Mary Barnard and sisters" announced that they had "commenced the mantua-making and millinery business in all its branches." They would supply the newest fashions at the shortest notice and take in plain sewing.[34] In 1813, Mary and Betsy Lincoln opened a shop.[35] These sisters may have been the daughters of the Mrs. Lincoln who in December 1811 announced in the pages of Hartford's *Courant* that she has "resumed her business of mantua-making and millinery" at her home, "Ladies Pelices, Habits, etc. cut to order."[36] The following April, she repeated her notice, adding that "she will be particular in obtaining the latest fashions, and unremitting in her endeavors to please those who favour her with their orders." Finally, she notes that she also offers "plain sewing done in the neatest manner"—this service quite possibly the work of young needlewomen-in-training Mary and Betsy.[37]

The rearing of artisanal daughters raises important questions about craft lineage and its place in the female world of gown making. The family and descendants of Catherine King Phelps offer some answers. An active gown maker in at least the 1720s, 1730s, and 1740s, Catherine King was born in Northampton in 1701. When she was twenty-three years old, she married James Heacock, but he died only a few months later. In 1730, she married Nathaniel Phelps, a mason from Northampton and a widower with three young children. Their first child was a daughter, Catherine; later they had another daughter and a son, Charles. Charles Phelps was a highly successful artisan in Hampshire County (his grandson would marry Elizabeth Porter) whose clients included the area's political, military, and social leaders. But Catherine King brought advantages of her own to the marriage, apart from her artisanal skill. She had inherited a good deal of wealth from her father, who died in 1720, from her late husband, and from his father, who died in the late 1720s, leaving his former daughter-in-law a generous bequest. When her brother John died in 1745, he too left her a significant bequest.[38]

Catherine Phelps's inheritances and the income she earned as a gown maker enabled her, as her granddaughter later recalled, to fulfill her "desire and ambition," to "furnish her house as well as her sister Experience," who had married the prosperous trader Timothy Dwight. Her comfortable do-

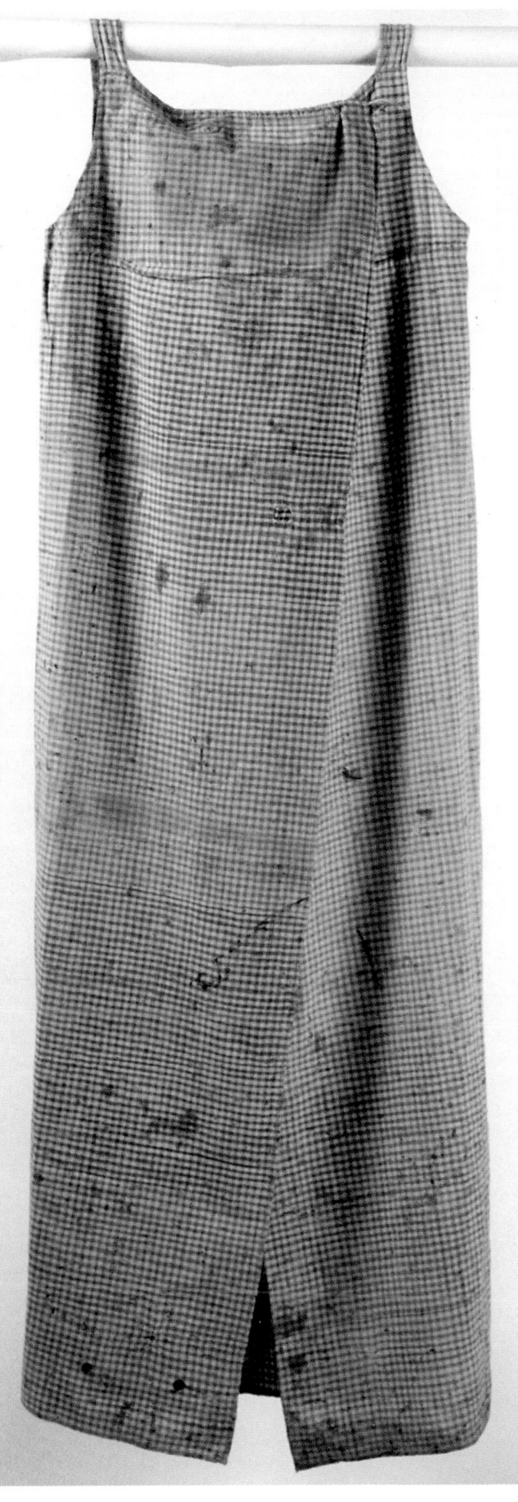

Plate I. Checked smock, late eighteenth century. Courtesy of the Pocumtuck Valley Memorial Association, Memorial Hall Museum, Deerfield, Mass. (photograph by Amanda Merullo).

Smocks, used to protect one's clothing while undertaking messy household chores, were damaged over time. This rare example of a woman's everyday work clothes is made of the blue and white checked cloth that was also commonly employed for women's aprons and men's shirts. The several stains and patches suggest the hard use such garments saw; however, the seam under the bustline suggests that the garment was intended to conform to the silhouette popular toward the end of the eighteenth century, indicating that even work clothes responded in some ways to prevailing fashion.

Plate 2. Diadema Morgan's gown, 1785. Courtesy of the Pocumtuck Valley Memorial Association, Memorial Hall Museum, Deerfield, Mass. (photograph by Amanda Merullo).

Diadema Morgan (1764–88) wore this blue wool open robe when she married Northfield's Phineas Field in 1785. Gowns like this one represented the best apparel middling women and men acquired; after her wedding, Diadema would not fold the expensive garment away as a sentimental souvenir but would wear it to meeting on Sunday and for other special occasions as long as it remained stylish. Such garments were altered when necessary to accommodate changing fashions, changing bodies, or a new wearer. Note that the bodice is made so that the wearer pins it, edge-to-edge, at the center front. The close fit is achieved in part through the center back (in a style called *en fourreau*, or the English back), where the maker cut the pleats in one with the skirt, laid in place over a linen lining, and stitched down so that two box pleats release into the skirt just below the natural waistline. The maker used an underhanded hem stitch to attach the bodice to the lining, back stitching at the underarm attachment, and a running stitch of approximately eight stitches per inch on the seams. (See Baumgarten, Watson, and Carr, *Costume Close-Up*, 24–28, and Lazaro, "Construction in Context," 16–19, cited in chapter 1.)

Plate 3. Mary Floyd Tallmadge (1763–1805), by Ralph Earl, 1790. Courtesy of the Litchfield Historical Society, Litchfield, Conn.

As costume historian Aileen Ribeiro has written, "The portrait of Mary Tallmadge is monumental in every way; the costume is almost regal in tone" (Kornhauser, *Ralph Earl*, 173, cited in chapter 1). The gown she wears displays the exceptional artistry of some unknown mantua maker; the open gown and matching petticoat of blue satin are ornamented with robings of gathered satin trimmed with matching cords and buttons. Two rows of gathered and pinked satin trimming embellish the petticoat's hem as well, while the sleeves are accented at the elbow with additional satin trim.

Plate 4. *L'atelier de couture*, by Antoine Raspal, c. 1760. Courtesy of Musée Reattu, Musées d'Arles.

This painting shows a shop interior in eighteenth-century France, but the details would be similar to such shops throughout the Atlantic world at that time. Shop employees range from mature women to young girls learning the trade. They work around a large table, suitable for cutting cloth, well-lighted by a large window. Work-in-progress hangs from pegs on the wall. Both the mistress of the shop and her young apprentice elevate their laps by resting their feet on footstools. Even the young women working at the table rest their feet on the basket beneath.

Plate 5. Cotton muslin dress, 1805–1810. Courtesy of the Connecticut Historical Society Museum, Hartford.

This hand-stitched cotton muslin is unlined. It was probably worn by Charlotte Perkins (1790–1873), daughter of Enoch and Anna Pitkin Perkins, when she attended the Hartford Dancing Assemblies in 1805. Very different in terms of both embellishment and construction from the fashions that preceded them, neoclassical gowns like this one represented a significant departure for women in the clothing trades, who cultivated new skills (and abandoned others) in order to meet consumer demand.

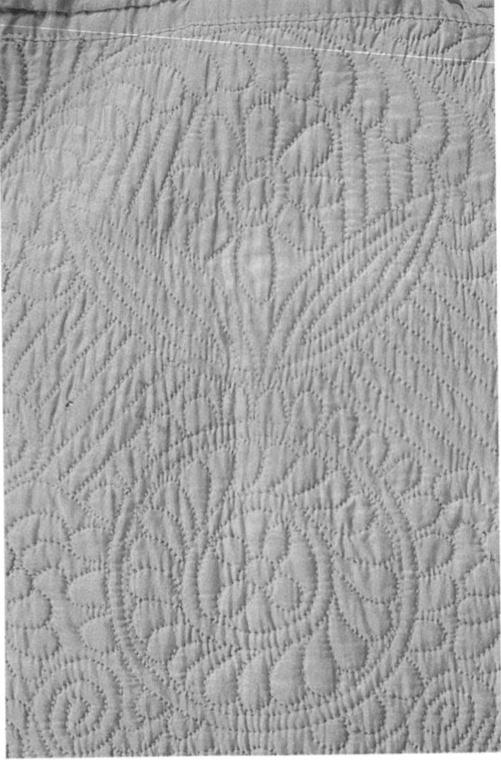

Plate 6. Quilted petticoat, c. 1730–1740, and detail. Courtesy of Historic Deerfield, Inc., 200.72.3 (photographs by Penny Leveritt).

This yellow silk taffeta skirt, lined with plain woven blue wool, reveals the expertise and care of its quilters in the dense design of scrolls, medallions, and floral elements. Both quilting and seams contain nine to twelve stitches per inch. Gold silk braid was applied to the hem for added effect. A series of pleats was introduced to create particular fullness at the wearer's hips, in accordance with prevailing fashion which encouraged some women to wear panniers. The skirt's makers left the top of the garment unquilted, and folded the end of the fabric over before stitching.

Plate 7. Elizabeth Porter Phelps's heraldic needlework, 1760–1817. PPHP. Courtesy of Amherst College Archives and Special Collections.

James Lincoln Huntington recalled that his ancestor was working on this in the twilight of her life in the early nineteenth century, but it is likely that she was then picking up a project laid down years earlier, when heraldic needleworks like this one were fashionable among young gentlewomen. The quality of the work and her lack of interest in completing the piece are evidence perhaps that Phelps had less enthusiasm than Ann Grant (see figures pages 99) for mastering the subtleties of embroidery.

Plate 8. Rebecca Dickinson, head cloth. Courtesy of the Pocumtuck Valley Memorial Association, Memorial Hall Museum, Deerfield, Mass.

This head cloth was completed in 1765 by Rebecca Dickinson, a twenty-seven-year-old gownmaker from Hatfield, Mass. Embroidered textiles like this one were enormously popular among eighteenth-century white women. Originally inspired by the vibrant fabrics that English traders brought back from the Far East, the cascading vines, flowers, leaves, birds, animals, and other motifs common in these works allowed a woman to display her technical skill and artistic sensibility as well as her ability to devote time to their completion. Women embroidered bed hangings such as this one, as well as pockets, petticoats, and chair seats. Although Rebecca Dickinson was a formally trained maker of women's clothing, none of the garments she created are known to survive; instead, her family preserved several examples of her ornamental needlework, including a set of bed hangings, a coverlet, and a firescreen. Her diary survived by accident, discovered several decades after her death in the garret of her last home.

mestic environment included at least one slave. In 1747, she was widowed a second time when Nathaniel died after a lingering illness. She then married Gideon Lyman and lived with him for almost thirty years, until his death in 1775 left her a widow once more. Toward the end of her long and productive life she moved in with her daughter, the tailor Catherine Phelps Parsons. She died in 1791.39

Another member of Catherine King Phelps's extended family also worked in the clothing trades. Esther Lyman Wright, born in 1725 to Gideon Lyman and Esther Strong Lyman, was twenty-two when her widowed father married Catherine Phelps. Though no confirming documentary evidence survives, it seems possible, even probable, that Esther Lyman learned the work of clothing construction from her stepmother, though she may of course have obtained her skills elsewhere as well. About 1747, Esther Lyman married Selah Wright, who died in 1786. Whether or not Esther practiced her craft during the years of her marriage is not known; no account book associated with Selah and Esther Lyman Wright has been found. However, after her husband died, Esther moved in with her son Solomon. The account book the mother and son kept together from the 1780s to the early 1800s shows her working vigorously at her trade.[40]

Artisanal skill in the Phelps family can be traced through the sons and grandsons of the Nathaniel Phelps who was among Northampton's original settlers, migrating north from Windsor, Connecticut, in 1655. These sons and grandsons were for generations successful masons, stonecutters, and silversmiths.[41] Phelps family masons built chimneys for some of the most powerful households in the county. At the same time, several women in the family were known for their mastery of needle skills. Abigail Lankton, sister of the Nathaniel Phelps who married Catherine in 1730, was a local shoemaker. Catherine and Nathaniel secured training for their daughter Catherine Phelps Parsons in the tailoring trade. Their son, Charles, married a gown maker, Dorothy Root (and their son Charles wed Elizabeth Porter in 1770). It seems possible that Root obtained her training from Catherine King Phelps, bringing her into contact, and a romantic liaison, with Charles. When Root died in 1777, Charles Phelps proposed marriage to another gown maker, Rebecca Dickinson (who declined).[42]

The chain of skill that traces through the women of Catherine King Phelps's extended family suggests that familial ties were important to women in the clothing trades.[43] That dynasties appear to have occurred infrequently, or with less prominence, among needlewomen, however, than they appear to have among families like the four generations of Northampton blacksmiths among the Pomeroy men may stem more from the character of the trade itself than from anything about female artisanry or economic culture. Tailoring, for example, with its minimal capital investment, was less likely than other crafts to see sons bound to a family trade.[44] Furthermore, the lack of lineage among artisanal women may be present but difficult to see. Even though the daughters of craftswomen learned skills from their mothers that they would use to work at clothing production, just as the sons of craftsmen learned skills from their fathers, the consequences of marriage makes these women harder to trace. The familial line linking those masons who share the name Phelps and the lineage of blacksmiths in the Pomeroy family are easy to spot in the historical record, but the prosaic fact that women artisans changed their names upon marriage renders those relationships invisible. During her lifetime, Catherine King was a widely recognized gown maker in Northampton. She changed her name three times during her life, to Heacock, Phelps, and Lyman. Her daughter, Catherine Phelps, later Parsons, also took up a needle trade, which she then shared with her daughter Experience Graves.[45] Although such genealogies can be difficult for contemporary historians to piece together, the shared familial identity of these mothers and daughters was readily apparent to their friends and neighbors. As Edward Cooke observes, for artisanal families, craft skills provided "both a livelihood and a legacy." Knowledge and tools alike became assets "transmitted through the family network." Just as artisan fathers bequeathed both skills and tools to succeeding generations, so too did artisan mothers.[46]

Artisanry, Marriage, and Family and the World of Tabitha Clark Smith

Catherine King Phelps and Sarah King Root Clark were married women in the years they were actively pursuing their craft. Their accounts, intermingled with those of their husbands, suggest some of the ways in which artisanal women contributed to the needs of their families. Other sources clarify other aspects of the world of rural craftswomen in the last half of the eighteenth century. The memorandum book and correspondence of Elizabeth Porter Phelps, which offer glimpses into the world of Tabitha Clark Smith, for example, allow us to consider the artisanal relationship between craftswoman and client more deeply and also to contemplate more fully the world of married artisans, whose work was embedded in larger contexts of family and community.

By the summer of 1769 when Tabitha Clark entered the pages of Elizabeth Phelps's memorandum book—"Thursday Tabitha Clark taylored here. Fryday went to work in town"—she was about nineteen years old.[47] Born in Uxbridge, Massachusetts, around 1750, she was the daughter of Robert and Ann Tefft Clark, who had moved to Massachusetts from Rhode Island shortly after their marriage in 1739. Tabitha was the fifth child of six, three sons followed by three daughters. How she came to be living in Hadley by the 1760s is unclear, but her move may have been associated with her father's death in 1753; her mother, a forty-two-year-old widow with six children under fourteen, remarried quickly and followed her new husband to the Springfield area. By 1769 and over the next several years, Tabitha Clark journeyed about three times each year to the Phelps home to perform some service for that household, sometimes altering a gown, sometimes creating one, like the brown silk crape gown she made for Elizabeth's mother in the spring of 1772.[48]

Marriage and motherhood affected but did not necessarily disrupt those patterns. In March 1775, when she was nearly twenty-five, Tabitha Clark married Chileab Smith, who was born in 1746, the eldest son of Windsor Smith. In April, she and Chileab stood in the broad aisle of the Hadley Congregational Church and "made their confession for the sin of fornication," she being swelled to eight months' pregnancy, though she and Chileab had been married only a few weeks.[49] The Smith family was one of the largest in Hadley. Samuel Smith, a leading citizen in Wethersfield, Connecticut, had been among the original settlers when Hadley was founded in the 1660s. By the time Chileab married Tabitha, Smiths had been a regular presence on the select board for more than a century, deacons of the church, and leaders in the local militia. Windsor Smith was a local merchant of some standing; he and his eldest son, Chileab, operated two mercantile concerns, in Hadley and West Ashley, trading in English goods—mostly hardware, rum, and sugars—and livestock. Smith's shop also imported through New York a variety of English fabrics, including kerseys, serges, flannels, broadcloths, calicoes, chintzes, and velvets. His inventory also included such fashionable accoutrements as muslin and silk shawls, silk gloves, and expensive trimmings for women's gowns, like black and white laces and edgings, as well as crockery and glassware.[50] The Smiths' home lot was on the west side of the Hadley common, on the north end by the river. When Andrew Cooke purchased a lot on which to settle his son Solomon and Solomon's wife, Tryphena, he purchased it from Windsor Smith's family and built the house that would become the Cooke tavern just north of the Smiths' home.[51]

In the summer of 1775 Phelps observed that Tabitha Smith was sewing up at the mills (a neighborhood today known as North Hadley). After her marriage, however, Smith does not reappear in Phelps's records with any regularity until 1783. Her work habits had changed; like Tryphena Cooke, she apparently no longer journeyed out of her home to sew, or at least she did not go again to the Phelps home. In August 1784, for example, when Elizabeth Phelps rode to Smith's on a Wednesday "to get her to do some tayloring" and went "Fryday in the forenoon down for it," the gown maker had four children between the ages of nine and sixteen months, and was five months pregnant with a daughter, Joanna.[52] When in the spring of 1790 Phelps and her daughter Betsy rode down "Tuesday . . . [to] Mrs Chileab Smiths to get her gown made," the craftswoman had six children.[53]

Artisanal women moved in and out of their trade as necessity and opportunity dictated; marriage appears not to have signaled the same rupture of work cycle among these needleworkers that it would for their nineteenth-century counterparts.[54] At the time of Tabitha Smith's marriage, for example, the peak of her craft activity still lay ahead. She worked most often at home, enabling her to see clients and care for her children at the same time. Furthermore, she sometimes turned clients away; Phelps was occasionally told that Smith simply "could not attend," forcing her to return another day.[55] Like other married gown makers in the rural Connecticut Valley, Tabitha Smith worked in the homes of other women before she married, and afterward brought other women into hers. Sarah King Clark appears to have worked steadily through two marriages. Born about 1728, she married Simeon Root some time before 1741. He died about a decade later, leaving King with a year-old son, Elihu. In December 1757 Sarah married William Clark. Their first child together, another Sarah, was born in the fall of the following year and would be followed by four more children; the last was born in July 1770. Clark farmed and drove fattened cattle to Boston, while Sarah continued to make clothing, perhaps in the shop (formerly that of a weaver) that stood on Clark's property, or perhaps in the family home. In 1768, the year of her greatest gown-making activity, Elihu was seventeen and her other children all between the ages of ten and four.[56]

Of the twenty-one gowns Elizabeth Phelps refers to in her memorandum book, Tabitha Smith created or altered at least fourteen. In addition, she made or altered more than twenty gowns for Phelps's two daughters, as well as some for Phelps's mother, Elizabeth Pitkin Porter. From the 1760s to the turn of the century, Smith produced flattering garments in ducape, calico, lustring, stuff, chintz, and figured Italian silk. Smith's familiarity with a wide range of fabrics was no doubt enhanced by her husband's trade. Her work complemented his. Chileab Smith carried in his shop a wide array of yard goods imported from London and New York, including superfine broadcloths and cashmeres, serges, kersies, shalloons, durants, striped and plain calimancoes, russells, velvets, dimities, and velveteens. Consumers acquainted with Tabitha Smith may have found themselves directed to Chileab's shop when in search of appropriate materials, while consumers acquainted with Chileab Smith & Co. may have learned of Tabitha when inquiring about a skilled woman who might fashion for them the desired garment.[57]

Almost ten years passed between Tabitha Clark Smith's wedding and the date of her next appearance in Phelps's journal; another seven years separate that reference from the next entry in which she appears. During those years she may or may not have been working for women other than Phelps. During the 1790s, however, she seems to have worked for the Phelps family with greater regularity, particularly producing and altering clothing for Phelps's daughters, Betsy and Thankful. If the gown maker had withdrawn somewhat from trade, the reason for her return to her craft at this particular time is hard to tell. Though she had lost two sons in infancy in the years immediately preceding her return, she continued to bear children in the years to come and, at the same time, continued to pursue her needlework, now with five children, the youngest six months old.

Smith's return to the pages of Phelps's memorandum book may well reflect less the effects of continued child-bearing than the maturation of both women's daughters. Betsy and Thankful Phelps were "entering society," in quiltings, weddings, and social events around Boston, at their Amherst academy, in dancing school, and during visits to friends and family in Hartford and Boston. Their need for appropriate attire may have prompted Phelps to reacquaint herself with Tabitha Smith and her needle skills. At the same time, Smith began to draw on the skill and labor of her three daughters. Smith performed the greatest number of services for Elizabeth Phelps in 1792 and 1793; in 1792, her eldest daughter, Lucretia, was sixteen, Lucinda eleven, and Joanna nine. Lucretia was at the age of apprenticeship, and she apparently received her training under her mother's tutelage. By 1798, Lucretia Smith Gaylord had become a gown maker to whom Hadley women turned, as her mother had been before her. It was she who had come to the Phelps home to inspect a gown Betsy had bought in Boston so she could make one like it for Charlotte Porter.[58] But in 1792, the three girls could sit at their mother's feet, sewing the long seams that brought together the pieces Smith had cut out, enabling her to increase the number of women to whom she could offer her skills. Far from a liability, Smith's growing family was the asset she needed to expand her activities.

Lucretia Gaylord's husband, Samuel, belonged to one of the county's most influential artisanal families. Her father-in-law, Samuel Gaylord Jr., was a well-known woodworker in Hampshire County who built houses in the summer and made and repaired furniture and farm implements in the winter.[59] Conservative in his design, Gaylord served the needs of wealthy farmer-merchants with a preference for tradition. He was aided, no doubt, in securing that clientele by his fortunate marriage to Penelope Williams, an influential local gentlewoman who was among Elizabeth Porter Phelps's dearest friends; in fact, Gaylord completed several of the renovations to the Phelps home in the 1770s and 1780s. His son, Samuel III, contributed to his father's business until his untimely death fourteen months after his marriage to Lucretia prevented any extended legacy. Lucretia served the sartorial needs of those same farmer-merchant families, at the same time extending her mother's legacy, stepping into a circle of clients already in place. Lucretia's sister-in-law, Elizabeth, or Betsy, Gaylord, also gained skill in gown making. Nine years old when her brother married Lucretia, Betsy may well have enjoyed the tutelage of Lucretia or even of Tabitha. By 1809 Betsy Gaylord, at twenty-five, was also sewing for the Phelps family.[60]

Although both Tabitha Smith and her daughter Lucretia found spouses whose businesses advanced their own, we cannot assume that such relationships were necessarily harmonious. How women's craft identity functioned alongside other identities grounded in marriage and motherhood is hard to tell. Did intrafamilial tensions affect the working relationships of couples like Catherine and Nathaniel Phelps, Tabitha and Chileab Smith, and Lucretia and Samuel Gaylord? Men's use of collective language—"our" or "us"—in the pages of their accounts suggest that they saw their family's debts and credits as shared resources and shared obligations, but it is impossible to generalize about the authority these women exercised over their income.

In this case, Tabitha's relationship with a client is easier to track. Evidence from Elizabeth Phelps indicates that her association with Tabitha Smith encompassed more than just business, that they nurtured a long relationship and that an intimacy developed between Phelps's daughters and "Mrs Tabitha." In places like eighteenth-century Hampshire County, the social distance between clients and craftswomen was often slight. The two families did business together; Chileab Smith traded with fellow merchants Eleazer and William Porter, carting their freight with his from Hartford and Middletown to Hadley and trading salt, sugar, rum, iron, corn, flax seed, textiles, trimmings, and other goods.[61] The Smiths were among the few Hadley families who approached the Phelpses in terms of sheer material wealth. In 1799, for example, Chileab Smith and his son paid $199 in taxes. Only five households paid more, and Charles Phelps Jr. and his son had the largest bill due at $535.[62] Born in 1747 and (about) 1750, respectively, Elizabeth and Tabitha were also roughly contemporary; Elizabeth married five years earlier than

Tabitha but both women had their first child in the 1770s. The Phelps girls began accompanying their mother on errands to the Smith home as early as 1788, when Betsy was nine and Thankful eleven. Smith watched them grow into young women—and watched them carefully, since their changing figures required additions and alterations to their wardrobes. The girls regularly "tarried" at Smith's house and occasionally helped her quilt. They attended the wedding when Lucretia married Samuel Gaylord and came to the funeral when Chileab died, leaving Tabitha a widow. Betsy Phelps seems to have been especially fond of the gown maker; some suggestion of her continued affection might be read in a letter in which Elizabeth told her daughter the happy news that "Mrs Tabitha," then a widow, might "be invited to change Smith for Ward."[63]

The Smiths were intimately connected with other households as well. When Judge Porter asked Chileab Smith to assist with the settlement of Francis Newton's estate, for example, he may have been acknowledging a particular familiarity between the Smith and Newton households. The two families lived in the same neighborhood on the north end of the town center, and Tabitha Smith and Easter Newton both worked in the clothing trades. In April 1786, Chileab Smith purchased the two-thirds of the Newton house and about half an acre of land that were put up for auction, for £8 10s.[64] Just over a year later, Chileab sold the half-acre of land back to Easter for £9. Without more information it is hard to know what to make of these transactions, but it seems possible that the Smiths, in purchasing part of Newton's home, were trying to help her remain there as she entered widowhood.

For Tabitha Smith, Lucretia Gaylord, and other women like them, artisanal work was generally compatible with their work as wives and mothers; marriage did not transform their labor patterns in the same ways that it did or could for other working women. And the work complemented, even advanced, their social position among other leading artisan and merchant households, as well as the rural gentry. For these women, skills in cutting, fitting, and sewing were assets that could be picked up and laid down as circumstances warranted. For women who never married, however, who never gained the assistance of partners or children, artisanal skill offered other advantages, including possibly the opportunity to remain single.

Artisanry, Singlehood, and the World of Rebecca Dickinson

Unmarried at fifty-one, Rebecca Dickinson believed that her "story frights half the women of the town."[65] Whether or not her story actually frightened her neighbors, it is today both moving and instructive. As a craftswoman,

Dickinson was not so different from Tabitha Clark Smith or Catherine Phelps Parsons; her work with pins, needles, shears, and irons was identical, and many of the same themes that trace through their lives in the trade trace through hers. What divides Dickinson's life from those of other women is not skill level or social class: it is that she, unlike the large majority of her neighbors, never married. Her journals preserve the toilsome "journey of life" of a woman struggling to "act her part alone," without benefit of male resources. "I am apt to be greatly Puzled to find me Self here alone," she wrote one summer evening, "but i know the matter is a Secret to me."[66] Unraveling that "secret" consumed the better part of the nearly five hundred entries in her journals. More than any other single factor, Dickinson's "failure" to marry governed her experience as a woman and as an artisan in colonial New England in ways both great and small. A "fish out of water," a "sparrow alone on a rooftop," she was aware of nothing so much as her own aberration. "How oft they have hissed and wagged the head at me," she wrote, "by reason of my Solotary life."[67] Dickinson's unmarried state was without doubt a source of unending pain, but it was also a source of opportunity and satisfaction.

For some women in early New England, singlehood and artisanry went hand in hand. The popular image of the spinster seamstress is grounded in both myth and reality. Throughout the eighteenth and the nineteenth centuries, the needle trades were especially attractive to unmarried women. Anecdotal references to elderly unmarried needlewomen are commonplace in eighteenth-century manuscripts. For example, Abby Wright of South Hadley recorded an encounter with "Old Miss Susan" of Wethersfield, Connecticut: "She came in to see me a few minutes while her goose was heating. She plies her needle with as much assiduity as ever."[68] Women like Old Miss Susan could be found in every community. Without husbands, unmarried women often found themselves dependent on the continued generosity of aged parents or married siblings—a situation many found at best precarious, at worst humiliating. A trade mitigated financial dependence, as well as feelings of vulnerability, depression, and loneliness. Dickinson had counterparts in every town in the county, unmarried women who supported themselves with needlework. Among them were Esther Wright in Northampton, Elizabeth Macomber and Mary Lee in Amherst, Kate Catlin in Deerfield, and Polly Lathrop in Saybrook. Moving through her life without the usual cycles of marriage, child-rearing, and widowhood, Dickinson felt herself superfluous in a world of pairs, as the pages of her own journal testify. For women alone, gown making could provide relief from days of isolation, a sense of productivity, a source of self-esteem, and an outlet for creative sensibilities. What's more, for Dickinson, her trade was her sole means of support.

The eldest daughter of Moses Dickinson, a farmer and dairyman, and Anna Smith Dickinson, Rebecca was born 25 July 1738 in Hatfield. As the eldest child, she surely helped raise her younger sisters and brothers; by Rebecca's eighteenth birthday, she had five siblings: Samuel, Martha, Miriam, Anna, and Irene. During her youth, Rebecca learned the trade of gown making. As time went on, each of her sisters married. Martha moved seventy miles north, to Bennington, Vermont. Anna left for Pittsfield, almost seventy miles west, while Irene moved to nearby Williamsburg. Samuel and his wife, Mary, established their home just over the Hatfield line in Whately and continued in the dairy business. Only Miriam stayed close by, moving a few doors south to the tavern owned by her husband, Silas Billings. Meanwhile, Dickinson remained in the house in which she had been born. She worked at her trade, helped with the growing family, and remained active in the "busi scenes of life"—all the while moving beyond the usual age of marriage. Then when it seemed that she should have a chance finally to "change her name," she felt the "bitter blow" that "robbed her hopes" for marriage, a family, and a home of her own. Whether marriage rejected Dickinson or Dickinson rejected marriage is impossible to tell, and not relevant here; for the moment, it is important simply to place Dickinson in the context of her community, a woman living on her own in early rural New England.

Dickinson was an active artisan in the Hatfield area by the late 1750s and continued to work regularly at her trade through at least the 1780s. In her diary she frequently mentions "invitations" to work in surrounding Hampshire County towns, including Hadley, Conway, Amherst, and Northampton, suggesting that she had no need to solicit clients. That she was selected to create the gown of dark brown ducape in which Elizabeth Porter married Charles Phelps indicates Dickinson's gown-making skill; despite Porter's access to port towns from Hartford to Boston, she chose to have this important gown created by a local woman whose skills were known and respected throughout the county.[69]

By the time that she fashioned Phelps's wedding gown, Dickinson was thirty-two years old. It had been nearly two decades since she and "Catte Graves" had embarked on apprenticeships in the gown-making trade that, Dickinson wrote, had been "of unspeakable advanta[g]e" to her but of "no Servis" to Graves, who had since married and raised a large family.[70] That Dickinson continued to practice her trade while her co-apprentice abandoned this work is suggestive. Graves may have worked at her craft in the years prior to her marriage. Her skill with a needle may have helped her to find a suitable mate, since parents apprenticed daughters with some hope that a trade might render them more productive, and hence more desirable, as wives. Eighteenth-century English parents recognized the advantage of training daughters in prestigious trades like mantua making and millinery work, and it is likely that this strategy influenced their counterparts in the colonies as well.[71] But for Dickinson, apprenticeship did not attract a marriage partner.

Rebecca Dickinson lived in Hatfield and worked regularly in the bordering communities of Hadley and Whately but recorded in her journal occasional trips slightly further afield, too, east as far as Amherst and west to Williamsburg. Other patterns widened the artisan's range of influence without requiring that she travel. She often met potential clients, for example, when she worked at Forty Acres. On one such occasion Elizabeth Porter Phelps recorded that "in the Eve Miss Rebeckah Dickinson came here to make a pair of stays for my mother and alter a gown. Tuesday Mrs Crouch and Moses Kellogg's wife came here—jest at night Polly came to do some business with Miss Rebeckah . . . I went [into town] returned that night found Rebeckah gone home. Fryday she came over again—in the afternoon called upon us Esq. Porter with his wife soon left us—Gideon Warner's wife came for a visit. Just at night came up Mrs Porter and Mrs Colt, Polly and Nabby all for Huckleberrying—presently up come Miss Pen to see Miss Rebeckah—this day Miss Pen set out for home for Pomfret. Sat Miss Rebeckah went home soon after dinner."[72] Some women clearly made it a point to come up to the Phelps house while Dickinson was there, as did Polly Porter and Penelope Williams. But it is also possible that Mrs. Crouch, Mary Sheldon Kellogg, and Mary Parsons Warner as well as Mrs. Porter and Mrs. Colt consulted with Dickinson while visiting; they may at least have seized the opportunity to secure a place on Dickinson's schedule. Penelope Williams then carried the fruits of Dickinson's labors back to Pomfret, Connecticut; "Mrs Colt," probably a member of the Porter family from Springfield, may have done likewise.

Perhaps it was her ability to flatter the short, plump figure of Elizabeth Porter Phelps that rendered Rebecca Dickinson a favorite tradeswoman at Forty Acres. Dickinson often produced apparel for special occasions, such as the August afternoon she "was at Sister bilings to fix Patte Church and Bets Huntinton for the we[dding reception] of oliver hastings."[73] The frequency with which weddings follow Dickinson's visits suggests that for these occasions, too, Dickinson prepared gowns for Phelps.[74] On one occasion, after a visit from Dickinson, Phelps wrote: "in the afternoon Mr. Phelps and I went to Mr. Chester Williams weding to Loice Dickinson of Hatfield. Thursday miss Pen was married to Sam'll gaylord, Timothy Eastman to Anna Smith, Eaneas Smith to Mary Dickinson, Hannah Montague to one Isaiah Carrier of Belchertown—so much for one day at Hadley."[75] On another occasion, Dickinson labored at the Phelps home for the better part of a week prior to Elizabeth and Charles Phelps's departure for Boston during spring elections, suggesting that she was engaged to help Phelps prepare to socialize in elite Boston circles as well.[76]

Unlike her counterpart Tabitha Clark Smith, Dickinson had no husband with whom to negotiate household expenditures: she controlled the income that she earned, though that income is difficult to ascertain, since no ledgers from the family are known to survive. She does, however, appear in the account book of the Hatfield merchant Oliver Smith. The purchases she made—seven yards of callimanco and half a yard of cambleteen, amounting to ten shillings seven pence—were debited to Dickinson's account and credited by Mary Smith, for whom Dickinson had performed some service, recorded elsewhere.[77] Some sense of the income she may have earned can be gleaned from the account book of another gown maker, Polly L'Hommedieu Lathrop.[78] Although Lathrop, unlike Dickinson, did marry, she was widowed at a fairly young age and never remarried, and so she was a self-supporting artisan for the remainder of her long life. Born about 1768, Lathrop came to the colony in 1776 when her parents, Giles and Esther L'Hommedieu, fled Long Island during the American Revolution. They appear to have gone first to Middletown but later moved east to Norwich, where Polly met Lynde Lathrop and married him in 1795. Soon widowed, Lathrop spent the remainder of her life, like many unmarried women, migrating from house to house, sometimes boarding, sometimes staying with relatives.

Accounts from 1803 and 1804, when Polly Lathrop was living in Saybrook, capture a year in her life; that "Polly Lathrop Ac^{t} book" is inscribed three times on the cover hints that this was perhaps the first such volume she opened. A small pocket is carefully stitched inside the first page to hold loose items. Her tally for those years lists thirty-two gowns, two cloaks, five frocks, two bonnets, eighteen shirts, four pairs of trousers, and two full suits of clothes for thirty-four women and seven men. She earned 3 shillings for each gown—4 shillings if the gown was made of silk. Alterations brought the same 3 shillings. For a short gown, Lathrop charged slightly less, 2 shillings 6 pence. Frocks also ran slightly less than gowns. Men's shirts, like women's gowns, brought in 3 shillings each, and trousers from 1 shilling 6 pence to 2 shillings 4 pence. The total amount earned for 1803–4 was £5 14s. At that time she was living as a boarder, with a woman she refers to as Mrs. Latimer, in a house where her brother Ezra occasionally boarded as well. Entries for the next decade are less systematic but show Lathrop at work altering and making gowns, frocks, waistcoats, petticoats, and jackets, mostly, these records suggest, as part of her payment for room and board.

While gown making may have been among the better prospects for women who had to earn a living, the income it provided was highly unreliable. The uncertainty plagued Rebecca Dickinson, who bemoaned the threat that slack periods and the irregularity of employment posed to her security. "How times vary with me," she noted one November afternoon, lamenting "how hurried" she was "formerly at this Season of the year."[79]

Aging and illness affected her income, as well as her peace of mind. Even when in relative good health, more and more often she found herself unequal to the demands of her craft. Dickinson recalled wistfully those years when she had been "hardly too scared to walk too miles afoot," but now, she fretted, "old age has Crept up," the number of potential clients necessarily declining as her geographical range narrowed.[80] As she aged, she grew increasingly concerned over recurrent bouts with the "Collick." During the winter of 1787, illness and "Physick overdoing" caused her to faint. Alone in the house, she took to her bed, but this only created anxiety over her financial affairs: "have had an invitation to goe to Hadley to work but no Strength to move and must be Content with what is ready earnt by me since my health and my Strength is gon i would beg of god that my Estate may be a comfort to me now in the time of old age."[81]

Whether or not Dickinson's "estate" adequately supported her, the apprehension she experienced in regard to the sources of her continued support is undeniable. As she prepared to receive her mother one winter, she anticipated her arrival with some hesitation, remarking "how we are to live i cant see."[82] On another occasion, she was "awaked by a dream i thought that i had Stole from mrs hurberd but knew my Self to be innocent but my Credit was a going," suggesting that anxiety over financial security ruled her consciousness both day and night.[83] Another journal entry from those months captures vividly the specter of unemployment and the tremendous relief of steady income: "god has in great mercy this Summer back given me work he heard my Cry and has sent imploy for my hands the god who heard my Cry has given me work."[84]

Her "Cry" is understandable: she well knew the precarious economic situation other unmarried women endured. A few days later she observed: "this week died at Hadley . . . a girl of about thirty years of age well and dead in a week She had no home but was Driven from one brother to another and lived with her Sisters Some of the time." On another occasion she noted: "this Day have heered of the Death of Patty Lymen above thirty years of age . . . a Disconsolate girl . . . when i Compare my life with many of my acquaintences i am Content and well i may be there is no unmaried woman who has a hous to Shelter my goods in when others run from Place to Place not knowing where to goe nor what to Do."[85]

The parents of unmarried women often made provision for them in their wills, generally a room reserved for them in the home of a sibling or some form of financial or in-kind support. At the time of his death, Moses Dickinson, however, had provided for each of his daughters equally, suggesting that Rebecca was then able to generate sufficient income to support herself; Anna Smith Dickinson, too, distributed her "wearing apparel and household furniture" equally among her four daughters. Furthermore, Rebecca may never have received her father's legacy: while Moses had specified that his son, Samuel, would receive and distribute the funds from the estate, Rebecca was her brother's second-largest creditor at the time of his death—he owed her more than ninety-seven dollars. At some point, Moses Dickinson did give his daughter a parcel of land in Williamsburg, perhaps with the idea that she could rent it or convert it to cash. But Rebecca was still in possession of this property at the time of her death, having never been in straits so dire, it would seem, that she was forced to sell it.[86] Despite the constant lamentations in her journal, Dickinson was clearly not poor by any definition of the word; what is striking, then, is the acute sense of vulnerability that she could not shake, the fear that she could at any moment be reduced to utter dependency.

Singlehood and artisanry had psychic as well as economic costs and benefits. Slack periods meant not simply a loss of income but a loss of companionship: on one Friday afternoon in November 1787 Dickinson wrote, "this Day I am out of imploy the week before Thanksgiving . . . how like a being forsaken i live here alone nothing to do but sit and mope the time away." Though work distracted Dickinson from her chronic loneliness, outings into her community sometimes grieved her. "It is not worth my while to go from the hous [she regularly observed] it is So lonesome to return here again."[87] Weddings were a prime source of employment and an equally sure source of pain. Of one upcoming celebration, she wrote, "fifty copples are to be there this evening how gay the assembly will look but I have no Part no Portien there."[88] The extraordinary pain such events produced is captured in another entry, written after the wedding of yet another neighbor:

> [A]bout Dusk or the Edge of the evining Set out to Come home to this lonely hous where i have lived forty nine years lonesome as Death . . . to ruminate the Strange thoughts and Schemes with which this mind of mine has Surmised to think on the many wais Contrived by me for a Portion in the world and with the world and like the world but after all here alone as lonely as tho i was Cast out from all the rest of the Peopel and was a gasing Stock for the old and young to gaze at . . . Came home Crept into my window and fastened up my rome reeled Down by my bed and after a Poor manner Commited my Self to god . . . [o] my Poverty as to the things of time when other Peopel are a Seeing there Children rejoicing with one another im all alone in the hous and all alone in the world."[89]

Evidence within those same pages of proposals of marriage declined to suggest that Dickinson was not so anxious to marry that she would accept any suitor who came her way.[90] Nor did those "dark hours" come every day. Her spirits seemed to rise and fall with her employment, probably because work allayed her fears about the future and kept her busy in the present. When her work was plentiful, she remarked "how my time flies." Gown making provided much of Dickinson's social life and created a role for her in the community that in part filled the place of familial roles. For women like Dickinson, singlehood and the trade of gown making, which lent itself easily to an intimacy between craftswomen and their clients and community that could result in an honorary or symbolic familial status. Like Tabitha Smith, Dickinson found friendship in her client Elizabeth Phelps. The Phelps papers record a growing familiarity between the two women. References to "Miss Rebecca Dickinson" give way to "Rebecca Dickinson," "Rebecca," "Becca," and by 1808, "Aunt Beck," an appellation embraced throughout the community of Hatfield.[91]

Indeed, as an artisan with access to homes throughout the area, Dickinson may well have been an unusually important disseminator of public opinion in Hatfield. Her trade gave her access to the interior, even intimate spaces, of the community's most respected families. Eighteenth-century communities recognized the potential risk of gossiping employees; apprenticeship contracts regularly stipulated that an apprentice agree to serve a master "well and faithfully, and not reveal his secrets."[92] While the reference usually signals tricks of the trade, secrets were easily had. Catherine Parsons Graves, for example, daughter of Catherine Phelps Parsons, remembered a customer who was "a great news gatherer," who "used to sit with the tailor girls for news."[93] Needlewomen who traveled from house to house penetrated the façades their social superiors presented to the larger community and thus became ideal channels through which information and opinion flowed.[94] Gossip "constituted the mainstay of community discourse in antebellum New England," providing a means by which to establish and enforce codes of behavior.[95] Whether Dickinson persuaded or influenced others, she most certainly gossiped.[96] When Asa Wells married Bets Smith in Hatfield, Dickinson recorded both local gossip and her own role the multiple conversations that disseminated it when she wrote, "it is agreed by all Peopel there never was a Copel married with So Poor a Prospect of gaining livelihood."[97] In his 1910 history of Hatfield, Daniel Wells records that "as she traveled from house to house about her work, she acquired a fund of information concerning her neighbors that was unequalled by any other person. A gift of making pithy, epigrammatic remarks caused her to be regarded as something of an 'oracle.' "[98] Samuel D. Partridge, a life-long resident of Hatfield, remembered Dickinson as a "very intelligent woman" whose sayings "were frequently repeated" by townspeople.[99] The flow of information between clients and craftswomen did not imply an equal relationship; needlewomen may well have chafed at this aspect of their work, which required them to listen deferentially to their client's conversation whether or not they found it interesting.[100] Yet access to elite conversation could also supply the artisan with useful information on a host of subjects from what is considered stylish in the world of consumer goods to more personal details about to the financial circumstances or romantic prospects of clients and neighbors. Potentially, Dickinson could define public opinion as she commented on the lives of the families whose houses she entered.

Whether the information gleaned empowered women like Rebecca Dickinson, the conversations that unfolded over long afternoons of stitching and fitting certainly comforted Dickinson, who wrote, "How the person lives who lives alone god only knows there is no one in the world loves Company more than me but it is gods will or im quite undon Surely it is more than i can Doe to Submit to it."[101] Excursions to Jesse Billings's blacksmith shop "to have some work done by him mending my tools and tools to use this day" enabled her to stop at the Billings tavern and visit with others in town that morning as she made her way to her client's home.[102]

At age fifty-six, Dickinson once again "resigned" herself to her singlehood, sighing, "i have this Day Concluded that i must finish my Dais with the title of old maid an uninvied title but Surely there is no hope for me." Over time she had become increasingly reconciled to her unmarried state: "My bou[g]hs have been trimmed of[f] but the tree is not hurt . . . tho i Stand in the forrest with my branches of[f] and look not like the rest of the trees yet my mounten Stands Strong." Her lack of children notwithstanding, she "stood strong," confident that through her singlehood God would "Surely bring [her] feet to the gate of heaven." "There is a great many family blessings i know nothing of," she wrote, "but the gifts of time alwais bring Sorrow along with them a numirous family and a great Estate bring a great Consern upon the minds of the owners more than a ballence for all the Comfort that tha bring." Throughout her life, Dickinson struggled to cling to that insight, to look at a neighbor and conclude that "she has her fortun i mine very different and both right."[103]

Artisanry played no small role in that unfolding of events and the formulation of that conclusion. Dickinson's career had enabled her to fend off the poverty so often associated with singlehood, to withstand the loneliness and sense of purposelessness that she battled daily. It may well have been her artisanal skill that permitted, or even encouraged, her to resist offers of marriage and to find a more favorable position in her community than the "uninvied," "formidable" title of "old maid" invited. "To old people who remember her," the Hatfield historian Margaret Miller wrote in 1892, "or knew her by hearsay, she was a 'Saint on Earth," a 'marvel of piety.'" Others remembered her as the "most industrious woman that ever lived."[104] And industrious she must have been, and imaginative as well: surviving examples of Dickinson's careful and inventive needlework hint at both a commitment to craftsmanship and expression of creativity that rendered her trade a source of pride and an outlet for artistic sensibilities (see plate 8). Her craftwork and artisanal identity provided the main means by which she formulated a place in her community, her public identity, and perhaps a good deal of her private one as well. Her artisanal skill contributed to her ability to make a considered decision; the income it produced provided financial independence, while the social interaction helped to alleviate her often intense loneliness, mitigating her discontent and allowing her to refuse marriage proposals when a woman in more serious financial or emotional straits might have accepted out of sheer desperation.

There is little evidence about when Dickinson retired from her trade, though an entry in Elizabeth Phelps's journal suggests that she may have continued to influence clothing production in at least the Phelps home even after she stopped sewing. In July 1787, Phelps wrote: "Thursday the Widow Hubbard, the Widow Ellis and Becca Dickinson all here from Hatfield. Becca stayed—the rest went home. Fryday she and I went into town at many places." The following week Phelps and her husband rode into Northampton to "get a black gown" for Phelps's mother, whose sister Bidwell had died. Perhaps Dickinson helped Phelps select the appropriate fabric and trimming for this mourning garment while the two women were shopping. That Dickinson's apprentice, Patty Smith, arrived Saturday to sew the gown suggests the extent to which Dickinson continued to participate in gown making at Forty Acres, this time in an advisory role.[105] Dickinson's journal makes no reference to her craft after 1790, and entries in the Phelps diary after this point do not specifically mention gown making. Though she would live for many more years, Dickinson was by this time in her early fifties and perhaps found the strain of close needlework increasingly difficult. An entry describing how Dickinson's mother, Anna, in a "puzzling fit" had broken Dickinson's spectacles suggests that her work had taken its toll on her eyesight.[106]

"My days glide quietly along," Dickinson wrote in the summer of 1794. "Found in the spirit of thy holy day," one Sunday afternoon, she rededicated herself "to live in the light of Spiritiall life hopeing waiting doeing gods will to the end of my mortal life is the Desire of rebeca Dickinson."[107] In March 1815, she fell and injured—perhaps broke—her hip; by then her perambulations had been largely confined to the home of her nephew and his family, who had taken her in.[108] At the end of the year, on New Year's Eve, Rebecca Dickinson "finished her course with joy" and was laid to rest among her family in the Hatfield burying ground

THE ACQUISITION of special skills afforded gown-making women particular places in their families and communities, bringing them into intimate relationships with households throughout their neighborhoods, towns, and regions. Like "Aunt Beck" Dickinson, some artisans formed close connections with leading households. Clients became friends, and a world of female clients and craftswomen a source of artisanal pride, craft expression, and economic advantage. Marriage and family shaped those activities, allowing women like Dickinson to remain unmarried while proving an additional asset to already prosperous households like that of Tabitha Clark Smith. Smith, Catherine King Phelps, Sarah King Clark, and Esther Lyman Wright each drew on craft skills to enhance their contribution to their household's well-being. In some cases, craft identity was more stable than marriage, as women like Catherine King Phelps practiced her trade through partnerships with three successive spouses.

Craftswomen whose conceptual and manual clothes-making abilities exceeded those of clients like Elizabeth Phelps or tailoresses like Easter Newton and Tryphena Cooke nevertheless shared tasks, knowledge, and work spaces with a range of other local needleworkers, creating a community of sewing women whose daily work brought them into close connection. In other ways, however, gown makers' heightened skill level gave them more in common with other artisans, including women who successfully established themselves as tailors, or skilled makers of men's clothing. Both gown makers and tailors acquired and cultivated the ability to create fitted and more fashionable apparel; Tabitha Smith and Rebecca Dickinson found counterparts in tailors like Catherine Phelps Parsons, who primarily constructed clothing for men and who grappled with comparable challenges in terms of materials and construction. In a world of male masters, clients and competitors, however, they also faced challenges of their own.

CHAPTER 6

Gender, Artisanry, and Craft Tradition

The World of Catherine Phelps Parsons

IN THE 30 January 1769 issue of the *Connecticut Courant,* Robert Robinson, a tailor in Hartford, gently mocks the gentlemen of the town for allowing their "cloathes" to be made by women. Asking readers to "count up the cost / and see how many pounds you've lost" by allowing women to cut their clothes, Robinson notes that any man of "wit . . . loves to see his coat cut fit." The disgruntled craftsman would have been no happier upriver; in 1769, "nearly all the men's clothing" in Northampton, Massachusetts, "was made up by women," including Catherine Phelps Parsons, who, for more than forty years in the last half of the eighteenth century, enjoyed a thriving tailor's trade in the growing commercial center.[1] Born in 1731, she was the eldest daughter of Catherine King Phelps and Nathaniel Phelps. Her mother and her sister-in-law, Dorothy Root Phelps, were gown makers, and she passed her skills on to her daughter Experience, as well as dozens of other young women. The craftswoman was the sister of the Northampton bricklayer Nathaniel Phelps and the aunt of Elizabeth Phelps's husband, Charles.

Parsons, according to Sylvester Judd, was for many years the only tailor, male or female, working in Northampton. She catered to a distinguished clientele, making the bulk of the vests and breeches worn on town streets in the years surrounding the American Revolution.[2] The political, economic, and social leaders of the community and "a few others" had their finest apparel made in Boston but obtained their coats, vests, and breeches from Parsons.[3] She also made and repaired clothing for Northampton residents at the other end of the spectrum; town accounts in the 1770s show debts to Parsons for her work clothing the town's poor.[4] This female maker of men's clothing is never called a "tailoress" in early sources but is always referred to as a tailor (and her employees as the "tailor girls"). No records survive to document how Parsons received the training that allowed her to embark on a long career as one of Northampton's most prominent artisans,[5] but she was certainly notable for the training she gave others: she had so many apprentices that all of

Northampton's needlewomen in the first part of the nineteenth century owed their training to her.[6]

Much of what we know about Parson's work comes from partial transcriptions of the Parsons household account book and oral histories taken by Sylvester Judd. No surviving evidence suggests that Parsons kept a separate account of her labor; rather, she and her husband, Simeon Parsons, appear to have tracked this work alongside others performed for their household. When Catherine married Simeon, she underwent the transformation that all women of her generation experienced with marriage: the loss of her legal identity, now subsumed under that of farmer Simeon Parsons. Under the laws of coverture, married women like Catherine Phelps Parsons could not execute contracts, convey property either brought to marriage or acquired thereafter, or serve as executors of an estate. Their ability to control the use of real estate became circumscribed. She could not sue clients who had failed to pay her or be sued for debt. A woman working among men, Catherine Phelps Parsons proved no exception when it came to the law; she could not execute contracts or collect outstanding bills without the cooperation of her husband.[7]

Parsons's work, then, allows us to compare women who made clothes for women, and competed only with other women, with those who made clothes for men, and competed with men, revealing how shifting divisions of labor unfolding across the eighteenth-century Atlantic world looked as they emerged in rural Hampshire County.

WOMEN TAILORS were not especially common across New England, though neither were they especially rare. They can be found in Northampton records at least as early as the 1710s and 1720s and continue to appear continuously thereafter; Hampshire County women who stated their occupation as tailor before the county's Registrar of Deeds during the third quarter of the eighteenth century include Esther Graves in Greenfield, Martha Nash in Hatfield, Lydia Kellogg in Sunderland, Mary Smith in Granville, and Jemima Woolworth in Longmeadow.[8] In Deerfield, Susanna Allen was recognized by the courts as a "single woman and taylor."[9] Moreover, husband-and-wife teams worked collaboratively in communities throughout the Connecticut Valley; John and Hannah Russell appear to have worked together in their Deerfield shop, Hannah taking over the shop's affairs after Jonathan's death, while, similarly, in Glastonbury, Connecticut, Annar Talcott assumed charge of the Talcott tailoring shop after the death of her husband, Asa. In Granville, John and Mary Smith were both working tailors in the 1770s.[10] In 1772, Esther Harrison appealed to the Overseers of the Poor in Boston to obtain the release of her children from the city's almshouse. She had found a good master to take in her son and needed her daughter at home to care for her other children, she asserted, so that she could work at her trade as a tailor.[11] And Robert Robinson's 1769 complaint suggests that women were threatening his livelihood there.

Women artisans were less likely than their male counterparts to lease shop space, advertise in the local press or business directories, or assert their artisanal identity in legal documents after marriage, so it is impossible to determine with any degree of accuracy the numbers of New England women who worked in the clothing trades, steadily or intermittently, or practiced as skilled tradeswomen; the records are simply too scattered and too slight. Instead, it is more helpful to think in general terms of the characteristics of the trade and of the supply of, and demand for, artisanal skill in individual communities. To thrive, artisans such as silversmiths and cabinetmakers, whose goods and services were comparatively expensive and not essential, required large, prosperous populations, while makers of simpler, inexpensive, and more necessary products could be found in most towns. The demand for clothing was universal; most New Englanders, at one time or another, found occasion to purchase the services of a tailor or gown maker, either to secure new garments or to prolong the life of old ones, and the cost of these services was often small. That being so, nearly all communities in early New England had, by the middle years of the eighteenth century, and probably earlier, one or more practicing tailors and gown makers at any given time. Large towns might have more. Northampton toward the end of the eighteenth century, for example, with a population of just over sixteen hundred, had four or five working tailors and several gown makers. Gown makers were almost universally women, while tailors were more often men, though not exclusively.

Judd's claim that Parsons was her community's only tailor appears to have been somewhat exaggerated; other sources show clearly that Parsons faced several male competitors, some fairly transient, others less so. The pages of the *Hampshire Gazette,* as well as extant account books, reveal men and women working simultaneously in the needle trades. What varied, it seems, was the nature of their preparation for the trade, the physical setting in which they carried out their labors, the role craftwork played in their families' larger economic objectives, and the ways in which they were compensated for their skill and time. That Parsons is the only one to endure in the community memory probed and preserved by Sylvester Judd in the early nineteenth century, however, suggests something about her comparative significance among the town's post-Revolutionary tailors. When men and women recalled the means by which clothing was obtained in the late eighteenth century, most remembered Parsons, a fact that casts a slanting light on the share of that market she once garnered.

Men and women gravitated to needle trades for similar reasons, but while tailoring offered men one comparatively accessible route to tradesman's status, it was among the few avenues open to women. In other words, the same factor that made tailoring attractive to some men made it feasible for some women: it was among the least costly routes to an artisanal craft, requiring very little capital and equipment.[12] The tools of the trade (mostly needles, thimbles, scissors, and pins, as well as an assortment of irons) were small, inexpensive, and easily acquired, and fees for apprenticeship were usually lower than in other more lucrative trades requiring more expensive tools and more elaborately fitted shops.[13] A minimal initial investment equipped one to solicit clients. As an eighteenth-century London playwright put it, "The Tailor's trade no ample fortune needs: / Soon as the suit's bespoke, the cloth you buy / When made, deliver'd, and the cash is paid."[14] Most tailors did not maintain inventories of fabrics or finished goods. Instead, clients generally secured the materials, from cloth to trimmings, and sometimes even thread. The artisan supplied only his or her talent and labor, time, and a set of fairly inexpensive tools.

Moreover, to prosper, the successful tailor had to be "a nice cutter and finish his work with Elegancy."[15] An adept artisan also cultivated a keen eye and quick judgment about how a suit of clothes might cover flaws in a client's form, posture, or movement and accentuate his or her finer qualities. "Any bungler," Robert Campbell pointed out in his 1747 advice manual, "may cut out a shape where he has a pattern before him but a good workman takes it by his Eye in the passing of a chariot, or in the space between the Door and the Coach." Moreover, he or she must be able not only "to cut out for the Handsome and well-shaped but to bestow a good shape where Nature has not designed it; the Wry shoulder must be buried in Flannel and Wadding; he must study not only the Shape but the Common Gait of the Subject."[16]

The means by which men and women acquired those skills differed. Young men apprenticed almost exclusively with other men, while young women who sought training in the tailoring trade routinely apprenticed with either men or women. Women who apprenticed with men are better documented than those who trained with women. Apprenticeships in the needle trades, as discussed earlier, like apprenticeships in general, fell into two categories: voluntary agreements arranged by parents or guardians, and involuntary agreements assigned by selectmen or Overseers of the Poor. Though young girls were often apprenticed to learn housewifery skills (which may or may not have included craft skills), others were bound to artisans and sometimes specifically to learn the trade of tailoring. Silas and Anna Graham of Wethersfield bound their daughter to the Glastonbury tailor Asa Talcott, while the parents of Clarinda Colton, of Springfield, bound her to the Deerfield tailor Ithamar Burt. In making these arrangements, the Grahams and the Coltons sought to provide their daughters with training in a craft that they hoped would afford an ongoing source of income for their present and future households.[17]

Catherine Phelps Parsons's daughter recalled that her mother "commonly had three or four apprentices, and sometimes more."[18] Early in Parsons's career, one apprentice was Eleanor Strong, whose parents, Caleb Strong, a local tanner, and Phebe Lyman, were prominent citizens of Northampton. Martha Alvord, the eldest of the five children whose parents were Saul and Martha Alvord, also "learnt of her to make garments."[19] Among Parsons's last apprentices was the early nineteenth-century Northampton tailor Esther Pomeroy, only daughter of Heman Pomeroy and Esther Lyman Pomeroy. Alvord and Strong, fellow apprentices, were both born in 1747, fully thirty years before Pomeroy's birth in 1777. Well over one hundred young women may have learned their trade from Parsons in the four decades that she was in business. Those who stayed at home (as Alvord and Strong surely did) worked one year, while those who lodged with Parsons worked eighteen months, providing her with additional, now-skilled labor to offset the expense of their room and board.[20]

As Eleanor Strong's training suggests, some young women who completed some formal apprenticeship to a needle trade brought an inherent advantage to the marketplace, in that they were often the daughters of middling and more prosperous artisanal and professional households. That a family's social and economic position shaped a child's social and economic opportunities is unsurprising, and consistent with long-standing practices across the Atlantic. European families of higher economic status tended to apprentice daughters to mantua makers, while families of average or below average means trained daughters in plain sewing, a less prestigious trade.[21] For aspiring middle-class parents, skilled trades offered some prospect of social advancement.[22] Information on the families of many Hampshire County needlewomen is too scant to analyze systematically, but women of special ability in clothing construction often came from families of comparative means. Strong, for example, was the first in a family of many daughters. When her brother, Caleb Junior, was born, the family threw its resources into his preparation for a profession. His Harvard education and legal and political training eventually won him the governorship of Massachusetts. With the bar and the route to the governor's office closed to her, Eleanor received training, too, in the tailoring trade. The wealthy Strong family, for example, owned ten slaves; Caleb and Phebe Strong could afford to do without their daughter's labor for the duration of her apprenticeship.[23] The parents of young apprentices apparently did not require that their daughters find some form of employment that generated more immediate rewards. A girl's apprenticeship in the needle trades was both proof and product of her family's success.

Upon arrival, female trainees usually possessed rudimentary needle skills, learned from their mothers at home. Some young women who hoped to master the tailor's trade had to struggle before gaining sufficient skill to practice their craft independently. Tailors sometimes tried to keep apprentices, whether male or female, insufficiently skilled to become competitors, assigning them routine chores or otherwise limiting their artisanal education. "Not one in ten" of the journeymen tailors in mid-eighteenth-century London, according to the *London Tradesman,* had learned how to cut a pair of breeches.[24] That trick was even more readily played on young women, since longstanding cultural prescription meant that they were more easily asked to perform household duties than were their male counterparts. Letters between an early nineteenth-century tailor's apprentice in New Hampshire and her sister reveal the latter's concern that her sibling was being cheated out of crucial information: "You have given him already 14 months time which is more than would be asked for larning to sew and put garments together a year being the usual time—I suppose you have only learned how to make vests pantaloons and coat trimmings & if he learns you to cut it will be nothing more than he ought to for the time you have staid with him."[25] This young woman constantly struggled "to learn . . . the whole of the trade."[26]

Hampshire County tailors were no more generous. A 1791 lawsuit between Ithamar Burt and the angry parents of Clarinda Colton reveals something of apprenticeship practices and pitfalls. In May 1788, Andrew Colton of Springfield (thirty-five miles south of Deerfield) had contracted with Burt to place his twenty-four-year-old daughter Clarinda with the craftsman, "to be his apprentice, to learn the art of a tailor . . . and to serve him the said Ithamar, after the manner of an apprentice, the full term of one year."[27] Colton paid half of the fee, thirty-six shillings, to the tailor, with the expectation that he would pay the remaining half upon completion of her service and training. But when Clarinda returned to Springfield at the end of her year-long term, she had apparently learned almost nothing of cutting clothing. In a scenario repeated in communities throughout New England, she had been more often used as a domestic servant to Burt's wife than an apprentice in Burt's shop.

As Clarinda testified before the courts: "I used generally to take work for the Wife of the said Ithamar and if she had none for me I used to take work out of the Shop but for the most part she found me with work." What's more, Colton added, her master "never in any instance taught or gave me any instruction, either how to measure any person or to Cut out any garment."[28] That final phrase is important; those two skills—the measure and the cut—were the essence of the craft, and Clarinda had not learned them. Diamond Colton, who later hired Clarinda to work in his Springfield tailor shop, testified before the court that he had found her wholly unable to complete even the simplest assignments: "I asked her to measure some Customer that came to the Shop and she told me that she could not do it for she knew nothing about it."[29] Colton made a second attempt, and asked her once again "to measure some person that came to have a garment made and to cut her notches on the measure, which she did and after she had done it she did not understand the notches she had made in the measure." Clarinda apparently had observed Burt often enough to mimic his actions, stretching her parchment along the client's sleeve, and notching the paper to note the lengths between shoulder and elbow, elbow and wrist, and so forth; but once she removed her tape, she was utterly at a loss about what that information represented, or how it might be applied. Diamond Colton felt justified in cutting her wages to below those "Common to give Girls who had been properly instructed in the Art of Cutting." Fortunately, however, before she began her training, Diamond added, she was already "a very good Symstress," and after he had provided some remedial instruction, she was finally able to go "out to work at the tailoring business and Cuts the garments mostly that she makes."[30] Her year of service at Burt's had done nothing to advance her training. When her father refused to pay the remainder of Burt's fee, Burt sued to recover what he believed to be a just debt.

The Colton-Burt entanglement tells us much about tailoring as a trade for young women in rural Massachusetts. A one-year term of service seems to have been as typical in the Connecticut River Valley as in New Hampshire, and girls who had been "properly instructed" in the art of cutting were commonly employed in the shops of male tailors. The responsibilities of these young women apparently extended to the measuring of clients (suggesting perhaps surprisingly intimate physical contact between girls and men) and, once working, these young artisans, still under the employ of masters like Colton, generally made up a client's garments from start to finish. Finally, Diamond Colton was apparently familiar with Clarinda's skills before she embarked on her Deerfield apprenticeship but for some reason did not choose to supervise her formal apprenticeship.

Several women in Catherine Phelps Parsons family, as we have seen, were noted local clothes makers. Her mother, Catherine King Phelps, was a widely recognized gown maker in Northampton and, during a subsequent marriage, shared her own particular skills with step-daughter Esther Lyman Wright, who became a busy gown maker herself at the close of the eighteenth century.[31] Meanwhile, one of Catherine Phelps Parsons's six daughters (if not more) took up her mother's trade: Experience could be found making surtouts and performing other sewing in local households before her 1805 marriage to Perez Graves and possibly after.[32] Toward the end of her long and productive life, Catherine King Phelps, a gown maker, moved in with her daughter Catherine Phelps Parsons, a tailor, and her granddaughter Experience Parsons, also a tailor, bringing three generations of clothes makers under one roof.[33]

To BETTER understand Catherine Phelps Parsons's experience as a woman in a trade dominated by men, it is helpful to examine aspects of the work itself—shops and seasons, products and profits, access to hired help, and circles of clients—in the light of those competitors. John Russell, working just sixteen miles north, in Deerfield, provides a useful point of comparison. Closely related to the formation and persistence of artisanal identity as it is usually discussed is a dedicated worksite, that is, a shop space clearly separate from domestic spaces.[34] But dedicated sites were less necessary for artisans in the clothing trades; both men and women regularly practiced their craft in the homes of employers, their tools were small and portable, and their ongoing projects and materials could easily be folded away. Although early maps of western Massachusetts towns routinely mark the sites of shops occupied by hatters and cabinetmakers, tailor shops appear more rarely, because tailors usually appropriated spaces in and around homes. Some tailors rented shops in commercial buildings; others erected small structures on their home lots or installed shops in ells attached to their houses. Such shops generally meant a well-lit room lined with broad tables on which to cut fabric. John Russell and his wife, Hannah Sheldon Russell, worked out of the ell of her parents' house for six years before they purchased a lot down the street and built a home with a shop space on the ground floor.[35]

Whether Catherine Phelps Parsons maintained a traditional tailoring shop is unclear. Sylvester Judd refers to Parsons's having "opened her shop," but no record of a shop structure on the house lot of Catherine and Simeon Parsons survives, nor do any deeds associated with Catherine Phelps Parsons. The 1798 Direct Tax indicates that Catherine and Simeon's wooden house was two stories high, with 1,340 square feet, and was lit by seventeen windows, suggesting that it may have been a two-over-two-room house with a lean-to addition, the New England "saltbox" typical of the period. No outbuildings are noted on the property.[36] Where Parsons and her "tailor girls" sewed from day to day remains unknown, but wherever they worked, Parsons certainly benefited from the location of her home, one door east of Northampton's Tontine building, a center of artisanal life in that community before the building burned—taking the Parsons house with it—in 1816.[37]

Parsons's work brought her into close physical contact with the town's male civic and commercial leaders, whom she measured and clothed. The height, weight, and shape of each one provided particular challenges for the tailor. Years later, her daughter Catherine Parsons Graves, who as a girl had helped make garments for these men, recalled, along with the personalities of her mother's clients and the houses they lived in, their body shapes. She remembered that Ebenezer Alvord was a "very corpulent" man with a "large belly," that Ephraim Wright was tall and broad shouldered but also "fat bellied," and that Noah Wright was merely "portly" and otherwise "good-looking."[38] The meaning that physical intimacies like these held for both client and craftswoman is almost certainly unknowable but certainly distinguished Parsons from her gown-making counterparts.

Working largely out of their homes enabled Parsons and John and Hannah Russell to blend family and artisanal life. Catherine Phelps Parsons sewed through ten pregnancies, bearing children every two or three years, between 1753 and 1778. Her seven daughters surely contributed to the success of her business, by either sewing or doing the household chores while their mother worked at her trade.[39] The Russells had five children between 1761 and 1769. When John died in 1775, Hannah's children were all still at home; the eldest daughter, also Hannah, now fourteen, surely stepped in to care for the four boys, who were between six and thirteen years old. Hannah Russell continued to serve the shop's clientele for another eighteen years, until the 1790s. By that time, she may have had the help of her daughter-in-law. The records do not show whether Orra Harvey worked as a tailor before she married Elijah Russell, but she did after her marriage and for many years was well known for her craft in Deerfield.[40]

Once established, tailors earned most of their income from simple alterations and mending. In this, they conform to other artisans of eighteenth-century rural New England, who derived much of their income from farm labor, not craft work, and whose artisanal skills were harnessed toward everyday maintenance more often than the production of masterworks.[41] Jane Nylander, in her analysis of the accounts of Asa Talcott, found that less than half of his work comprised the making of new garments. Instead, he spent most of his time "cutting and fitting garments that were then sewn and finished in owner's homes, and in cutting apart, turning over the fabric, and resewing or resizing old clothing to extend its period of usefulness."[42] Judd's assertion that the leading men of Northampton had their coats made by tailors in Boston but their vests and breeches by Parsons suggests that the bulk of her business came from the more mundane work of clothing production and maintenance. Parsons also, for example, regularly "turned" coats, extending the life of older garments by reversing the pieces for several additional years' wear.[43] The Russell accounts indicate that most days his work involved making and repairing men's work clothes: leather and buckram breeches, vests, and coats. This is not evidence of any lack of skill or training on the part of these artisans; Russell, for example, was on occasion employed to create silk suits. Rather, it seems that the gentlemen of means who could afford these articles preferred to have them made by urban tradesmen in Hartford or Boston.[44]

Tailoring was subject to seasonal variation. As Campbell warned in the *London Tradesman,* most tailors "are out of Business about three or four Months of the Year" (adding, with disdain, "and generally are as poor as rats").[45] The long respites may have been both welcome and worrisome to craftswomen, though they may have coped with them differently than their male counterparts. In Stoneham, Massachusetts, Polly Wiley cut, basted, made, and altered a variety of garments, including coats, pants, waistcoats and jackets, great coats, pelisses and spencers, slips and gowns, and even, occasionally, bonnets.[46] Her accounts, like John Russell's, suggest that she received most of her tailoring income in the winter; she might work on as many as forty-five garments in a busy January and lay her needle aside almost entirely in July, August, and September, when harvest time meant additional hired men had to be fed. February, March, and April—often devoted to making soap from the ashes, tallow, and grease accumulated over the winter, while calving cows launched the beginning of the dairy season—were also months in which Wiley spent little time sewing for others. Catherine Phelps Parsons may have appreciated such periods of ebbed demand, since she, too, had farm duties to attend to.

Earnings in tailoring varied with the season, the type of garment, and the skill of the artisan; gender played a role as well. For plain sewing, generally paid by the day, women fared poorly in comparison to their male competitors. One means by which to compare the compensation available to men and to women in the clothing trades, and to situate that income among other forms of labor, is the series of price controls established by the Massachusetts legislature and adopted by towns throughout the soon-to-be state to combat price gouging during the Revolutionary crisis. According to these standards,

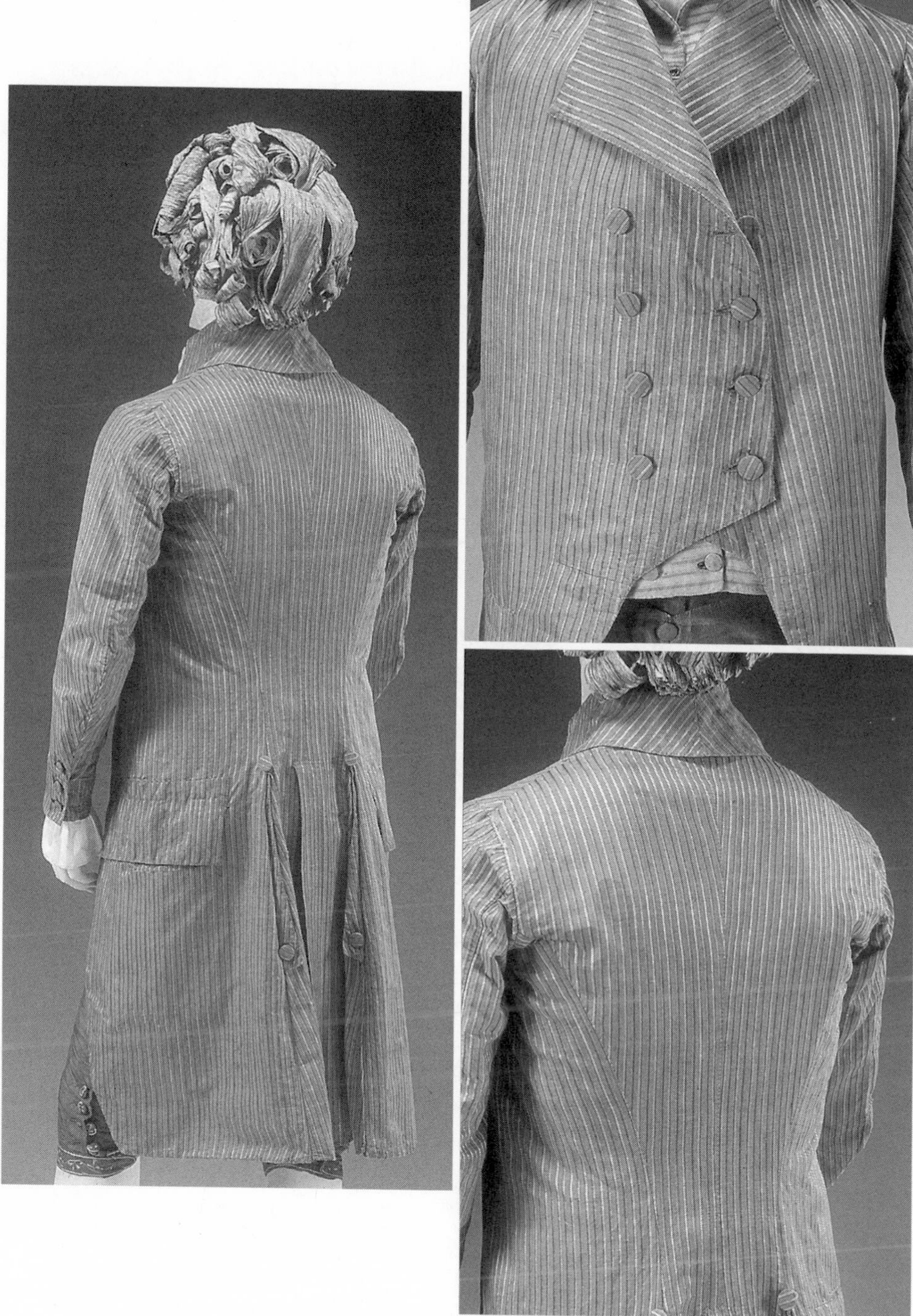

Silk frock coat, 1790–1800. Courtesy of Historic Deerfield, Inc., 200.34 (photographs by Penny Leveritt).

The tailor who made this double-breasted silk coat displayed considerable skill in manipulating the striped silk, which meets flawlessly at the seams. The height of fashion in its day, the high turned-down color is expertly cut to enhance the draping. The construction of the coat's shoulders helped the wearer achieve the period's preferred posture. Eight self-covered wooden buttons close the coat before it cuts away into the skirt, where matching buttons ornament decorative vents.

mowers and reapers, for example, could charge no more than three shillings a day, while masons could charge four shillings a day, and joiners ("in summer") three. Spinners could demand three shillings for a week's work. Three categories of clothing producers were also included in these price lists. Male tailors could ask two shillings eight pence for a day's labors, women tailors one shilling two pence a day, and women whose work was making women's clothes could ask just a shilling a day.[47] Thus, women working on men's apparel could earn just under half the men's rate, while women working on apparel for other women earned still less. These disparities are even greater than that between male and female farm laborers, in which the "weekly rates for 'maid's work' equaled the maximum daily rate received by farm laborers," or, approximately 40 to 42 percent of men's wages, once the additional value of room and board is factored in.[48] The list of price caps set by the town of South Hadley during the Revolution also supports these figures; in the comparative values assigned to men's and women's needlework, male tailors could command two shillings eight pence for a day's work, while women performing the same labor could receive one shilling two pence—again, less than half the men's rate.[49] Writing in the second quarter of the nineteenth century, Sylvester Judd also observed that Hampshire County "women formerly had for a week's work, but little more than a man had in a day, or variously from 1/5 to 1/3 as much as a man [though] sometimes near half as much."[50]

Such gaps close somewhat when we look at rates paid by the task. In the 1760s and 1770s, Catherine Phelps Parsons charged between six and ten shillings to make a coat, between four and six for breeches, and about four for vests.[51] In the 1760s, John Russell charged about five or six shillings for breeches, two to three for a vest, two to thirteen for a coat, and from seventeen to twenty-two shillings for a "sute of clothes."[52] Mending breeches might cost one shilling six pence; altering a coat, two shillings eight pence; turning a coat, fourteen shillings; seating breeches, one shilling. Russell charged ten shillings for a completed riding habit and just over three if he cut it out but did not make it up. Task for task, Parsons's and Russell's rates are comparable.[53] The evidence available suggests that men like Russell did not necessarily earn more for the same work as women like Parsons; rather, they were more likely to perform a wider variety of services with a wider variety of materials and so could command a wider variety of fees.

To supplement the uneven income that tailoring by its seasonal nature typically afforded, many tailors, like other rural artisans, did other work, sometimes related to their needle skills, sometimes not. In Deerfield, John Russell, for example, in addition to tailoring, sold imported foods, including rum, coffee, chocolate, sugar, salt, and molasses, earthenware and glassware, and shoe buckles and snuff, as well as scissors, pins, and needles. The probate inventory for Simeon Wells, also in Deerfield, reveals that assessors found his "tailor's tools" alongside a set of "woodworking tools" and some "saddlers tools."[54] In Hadley, Nathaniel Seymour also imported and sold ("cheap for cash or grain") rum, brandy, molasses, lump and brown sugar, and glassware and crockery; he also exchanged rum and salt for shipping horses, and salt for flax seed.[55] Almost all rural tailors maintained sidelines that for some eventually became primary sources of income. After Levi Dickinson, in Hadley, began to plant broom corn seed in 1797, he turned his attention full-time to the more lucrative production of brooms, which eventually became a major local industry.[56]

Tailors in commercial centers like Northampton also sought to supplement their income, often through retailing. Heman Pomeroy, in his shop opposite the Hampshire County courthouse, carried a small assortment of English goods, goods from Boston, and an ever-widening variety of fine fabrics.[57] After two years of tailoring in Northampton, Sylvester Lyman too began to advertise various goods; his first shipment was a "quantity of spanish brandy"—an inauspicious beginning, since alcoholism would eventually rob him of his own estate.[58] Lyman soon operated as a "merchant tailor," offering "articles selected with great care, from the latest importations, and equal in goodness to any in the country."[59] Cephas Clapp, in his "work shop," took orders for "fine suits or single garments executed on the shortest notice, and in the best and most fashionable manner," while he displayed a wide assortment of fine cloths and fashionable trimmings.[60]

Hampshire County women did not, it appears, pursue a similar route to financial security until the first quarter of the nineteenth century, when commercial opportunities for women expanded. In the 1810s, "A. Howard" opened up a shop in Sylvester Lyman's former tailoring stand, followed by "Miss Sprague's" "Fancy Goods and Milliner's Shop" in the same place. Sprague also offered "pelices, gowns, coats, habits, spencers and bonnets made in the newest fashion—All kinds of millinery made and plain sewing attended to."[61] In August 1816, a young Northampton mantua maker, milliner, and shopkeeper named Sarah Williams placed her first advertisement in the pages of the *Hampshire Gazette,* announcing that she had "received from Boston, and is now opening, a large assortment of <u>fancy goods</u>, among which: muslins, silks, gassimere and flannel shawls, bombazettes, scotch plaid, and a great variety of pelisse habits and bonnet trimmings. <u>Also</u> crockery, glassware, etc. offered at reduced price for Cash or most kinds of produce, as butter, cheese, grain, etc. <u>Millinery and Mantua-making</u>, in all their various branches, in latest Boston fashions."[62]

Both men and women artisans employed help during periods of peak demand, though their access to skilled help differed. In Deerfield, John Russell's relatively small operation required an occasional temporary employee who worked for several weeks at a time. On the first page of an account book, he records that in early 1768, "Bolton worked for me for 24 days. . . . James Shennan began to work for me Oct 8, 1758." Shennan stayed for just five days and was quickly replaced by Patrick Grimes, who worked for six weeks, settled his accounts, and then worked another few weeks before he left Deerfield in December of that year. Russell never hired more than one journeyman at a time, probably because demand did not justify it. In all, seven men's names appear as having been at one time or another short-term employees in Russell's shop.[63]

Likewise, Russell's competitors were in regular, if not constant, need of short-term, seasonal help. In the fall of nearly every year, advertisements seeking "good journeymen tailors" appeared in the pages of the *Hampshire Gazette.* In November 1795, Aaron Wright, a tailor in Northampton, sought two or three journeymen tailors that he hoped to engage for a period of "two or three months," that is, to help see him through the winter's work. In November 1799, Sylvester Lyman advertised for one or two journeymen, "to whom good encouragement will be given." Lyman occasionally needed more than one man at once, and in the fall of 1815, required six.[64] As his business expanded, he added more workmen to his seasonal staff: in November he regularly sought journeyman tailors who could find employment "for a few months, by applying immediately, to Sylvester Lyman." Lyman probably recognized the financial burden these men's wages would pose, for he sometimes followed this notice with another demanding immediate payment for services rendered, along with a warning that, "gentlemen are assured that no further notice will be given them except from the attorney."[65]

Tailors also sought the less experienced but often cheaper aid of apprentices. Notices seeking "likely," "active" boys about the age of fourteen, though sometimes as young as twelve or as old as sixteen, were common; occasionally an artisan sought two boys, one fourteen or fifteen and another slightly older.[66] Although male tailors also accepted young girls of about the same age as apprentices, their advertisements always specified boys. Unlike journeymen, who were almost always hired for the busy fall season, or occasionally in February to help with the winter's work, apprentices were sought throughout the year. The majority of advertisements seeking apprentices appeared, however, between July and November, maybe because tailors recognized the need to give boys as much training as possible before the seasonal demand for their services rose. Journeymen could be taken on as needed, but novices would need more time to learn their work.[67]

While men like Lyman and Pomeroy employed journeymen as circumstances demanded, there is no evidence in the pages of the local paper that Catherine Phelps Parsons ever sought to hire journeymen, or young boys as apprentices, and no evidence in other records that she ever employed such help. But apparently she did keep a constant stream of female apprentices, or "tailor girls," moving through her shop—three or four, as we have seen, at a time.[68] The two facts may be related: some inability to hire itinerant male artisans of advanced skill may have encouraged Parsons to keep a larger and steadier force of less experienced female apprentices on hand to help her meet her demand. While women were willing and allowed to work with and train under men without comment, men seemed less keen to take positions subordinate to female artisans like Parsons. Also significant here is the role of tramping in artisanal preparation. Moving from place to place was an essential means by which male journeymen in a variety of trades augmented their training, gaining exposure to new styles and techniques. Such travel, however, was not encouraged among young single women, limiting the supply of additional needlewomen with comparable levels of experience.[69]

Before the 1786 founding of the *Hampshire Gazette,* artisans in Hampshire County secured clients by referral alone.[70] Most tailors' clients there were drawn from the same community as the artisan, known to one another through networks of neighbors and kin. Among John Russell's more than three hundred clients, for example, ten extended families comprise most of the accounts.[71] After the *Gazette'*s appearance, male tailors regularly advertised in its columns for clients and in doing so increased the chances that client and craftsperson were initially unknown to each other.

As the demand for fashionable tailoring grew in the new republic, competition between tailors also grew.[72] In Hampshire County, such rivalry led Aaron Wright Jr. in the spring of 1798 to publish a sarcastic rebuttal to a competitor's claims in the *Hampshire Gazette.* And when Sylvester Lyman returned to town after having spent some years in New York and Philadelphia sharpening his skills, he flaunted his connections in the pages of the local press. Offering to "all gentlemen who wish" the "most fashionable work," he asserted his "superior advantages, [gained from his] working in the cities of Philadelphia and New York with the most approved workmen in the United States." His work, he said, was "equal to the best custom work in any seaport in America," and, further, he had "formed a correspondence with the principil [*sic*] tailors in Philadelphia and New York, to receive the fashions as they arrive from London."[73]

Wright responded forcefully to Lyman's claim. He was, he said, "returning thanks to his friends and old customers, who have resumed the patronage of his business." And he "assures them that, although he does not pretend to boast of any *extraordinary advantages* from *working in the cities of Philadelphia and New York* and *forming correspondence with the principil* [sic] *tailors* there . . . he flatters himself he shall always be able to gratify his customers with the newest, and will strive to make his work speak its own eulogy."[74] Lyman's boast and Wright's tart reply afford a glimpse into the tensions sparked as craftsmen both embraced and resisted forces that were altering their relationships to larger economic and cultural currents. For his part, the Hadley tailor Nathan Seymour stressed his ability to supply metropolitan style by informing "his customers and others" that he still carried on "the Tailoring business at his shop near the [Hadley] meeting house . . . [where he offered] cloathes made in the newest fashion, from Boston or New York, on the most reasonable terms."[75] At the turn of the nineteenth century, Lyman's hubris challenged and annoyed his colleagues. But some "eulogy" was in order, for Wright's world of reputation, personal connection, and local patronage was fading fast. Lyman was responding to phenomena that were reverberating throughout the United States and across the transatlantic world.

The same forces that transformed the economic environment of these Hampshire County tailors would eventually mean enlarged opportunities, too, for a small number of female entrepreneurs (like mantua maker and milliner Sarah Williams of Northampton), who used advertising in the local press in the nineteenth century to improve the prospects of their modest shops. In the Connecticut Valley, notices like those exchanged between Lyman and Wright and between Mary Gabiel and the Salmon sisters in the *Connecticut Courant* in 1775, while motivated by similar tensions, were rare among eighteenth-century craftswomen but became increasingly common among eighteenth-century craftsmen. For the first thirty years of its existence, no skilled needlewomen advertised in the pages of the *Hampshire Gazette.* Catherine Phelps Parsons was a notable member of Northampton's craft community, but not once did she turn to the pages of a local press to attract business. It may be that the founding of the county paper in 1786, when Parsons was in her fifties, simply came too late to be of any advantage to the well-established craftswoman. Perhaps also Parsons was not among the rising numbers of New England women to master literacy skills.[76] But another possibility is that the advent of the press, and of local advertising, reflected one expansion of commerce in the community and the region in which women did not easily participate. Hampshire County's female artisans continued to draw clients by word-of-mouth alone for a further thirty years.

THE CAREER of Catherine Phelps Parsons reminds us that tailoring could prove a worthwhile occupation for those women able to gain the training and means to practice the craft. Women's artisanal work in this aspect of clothes making was in many ways similar to men's: both men and women served apprenticeships through which they learned the "art and mystery" of the craft, both acted as masters who imparted skills to aspiring needleworkers, both recognized and asserted an artisanal identity in a variety of arenas, from (most narrowly) the courts to (most broadly) the community. But men's and women's experiences also diverged, largely in ways that reflect women's relatively restricted access to the skills of literacy and numeracy (which hampered some women's ability to manage a business) and capital (which inhibited women's ability to establish multiservice shops). Prevailing gender divisions of household labor may have brought female apprentices to their trades with greater preparation than men but may also have caused them to face greater obstacles in obtaining from masters the whole of their training, though some form of apprenticeship (formal, informal, or something in-between) was a critical component of female artisanal identity. Both men and women at some point pursued multiple income-earning strategies, supplementing artisanal work with other activities, though men had greater access to market alternatives for their labors, as well as greater access to commercial spaces and practices and more flexibility in the hiring of additional laborers. Evidence regarding the comparative income available to men and women is mixed but suggests that skilled needlework offered women one occupation in which they could compete, task for task, fairly well with their male counterparts, while the daily wages assigned to semi-skilled labor (the work of tailoresses like Easter Fairchild Newton and Tryphena Newton Cooke) disadvantaged women workers, indicating that the acquisition of special skills was critical if a woman hoped even to approach a living wage.

Considering Catherine Phelps Parsons together with other women skilled in the making of fitted clothing, gown makers like Rebecca Dickinson and Tabitha Clark Smith, also reminds us that the gender of the client matters as much as that of the craftsperson. Gown makers labored among a predominantly female clientele and work force. Tailors like Parsons competed in a world of male clients and craftsmen. In the physically intimate world of clothing construction, the gender of one's client determined not only the specific skills the artisan needed to master but also could influence elements from the site of the craft activity (for example, whether the client was measured in public or private) to the forms of payment and accounting that would document the exchange.

Catherine Phelps Parsons's career, beginning in the middle decades of the eighteenth century, was in some ways a harbinger. It is possible that she—along with Esther Graves, Martha Nash, and other female tailors in the Connecticut Valley—was among those women who Gloria Main has argued entered expanding trades in the middle decades of the century.[77] At present the evidence is more suggestive than conclusive, but the presence of women tailors like Catherine Phelps Parsons affords an opportunity to reflect on how they, as well as Robert Robinson, the Hartford tailor whose complaints open this chapter, might fit into the larger picture of occupational regendering in the eighteenth-century Atlantic world. Tracking the tensions that accompanied the creation of the first guilds for French craftswomen, Clare Crowston has remarked that the protracted disputes over who would be allowed to make what, in which women asserted their sexual identity to claim new rights and privileges, not only drew on gendered understandings of appropriate male and female labor but, moreover, "helped to propagate the notion of gender itself."[78] When conflict erupted in the pages of the 1769 *Connecticut Courant,* it reflected the arrival of a vastly larger renegotiation of gender roles and expectations long under way when Robinson fired this salvo, and one that would still be ongoing long beyond the end of his career. The beleaguered tailor had hoped to convince readers that women were ill-equipped to make fine apparel for men, but it was too late. In the United States, as in Europe, the making of clothing was increasingly associated with women, and gender divisions of labor in those trades substantially transformed. In time, needlework would be hailed not only as an "appropriate female trade" but as a "biologically innate female skill."[79]

But the story does not end there. In 1789, Abigail Woodman, a "man tailor" working on Boston's Creek Lane, appears to have produced clothing for a primarily male clientele, though she was the only woman among the eleven tailors listed in that year's city directory. Of thirty-one women listed as tailors in 1796, again just one, Martha Bowens on Sheaf Street, called herself a "man tailor," while none listed herself as such in 1798. Women had become involved in other aspects of the making of clothing for men—many listed "tailoress" as their occupation, and others noted their employment in the "slop shops" along Fish Street (shops in which rough, ill-fitting, ready-made clothing was produced for the sailors coming in and out of the city through the nearby wharves)—and by the turn of the nineteenth century there were no Boston women who identified themselves as "man tailors."[80] The women who gained a foothold in the tailoring trades in the last half of the eighteenth century would see their purchase collapse as the production of men's clothing was transformed in the early decades of the nineteenth century.

Parsons lived until 1798, the same year that tensions erupted among the town's male tailors, each anxious to secure his claim to the most fashionable cuts. An alternative reading of those events might suggest that the men were vying for the patronage of Parsons's clientele as the aging craftswoman withdrew from active trade. By the time Sylvester Judd interviewed Parsons's daughter in the second quarter of the nineteenth century, times had greatly changed, but Parsons's influence persisted: "most of the older female tailors in town are Mrs Parsons apprentices, or those who learned the trade of them."[81] In the 1830s, the multigenerational legacy of the tailor's skill was still recognizable. At the same time, however, Parsons's daughters had witnessed the transformation of their mother's trade, as thousands of New England women were drawn into outwork systems, while others learned to make men's clothing through the profusion of trade manuals published in the 1820s and 1830s.[82] Vast impersonal systems were replacing the world of custom production, prompting the antiquarian Sylvester Judd to undertake his researches in an effort to capture a world that seemed to be vanishing before his very eyes.

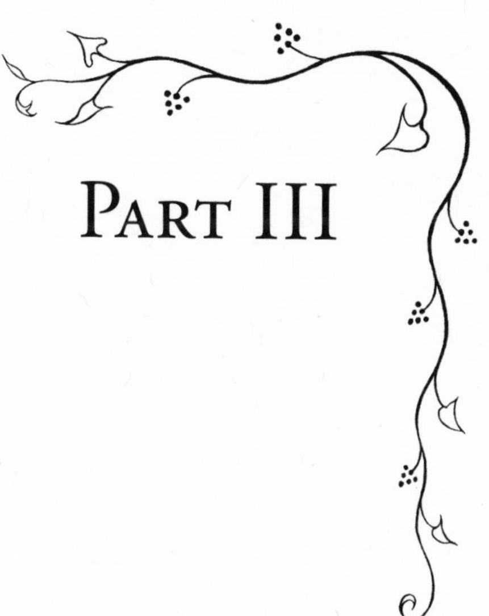

Part III

Chapter 7

Women's Artisanal Work in the Changing New England Marketplace

In 1776, while a gathering of planters and businessmen in Philadelphia declared one revolution, Adam Smith launched another. His *Inquiry into the Nature and Causes of the Wealth of Nations* would revolutionize economic thought and economic organization throughout the Atlantic world. At the outset of Smith's revolution lay a small, simple tool: pins. Smith's now-familiar exposition of efficiencies of labor, laid out in book 1, chapter 1 of his treatise, explicated the "trade of the pin-maker."[1] While a man working singly might produce fewer than twenty pins a day, Smith wrote, by dividing their labor into separate tasks, pin makers in shops could produce more than forty-eight thousand. Some fraction of those millions of well-produced pins made their way across the Atlantic, to western New England and into the hands of women like Rebecca Dickinson, Tryphena Cooke, and Catherine Phelps Parsons. Eventually Smith's treatise, too, found its way to the pages of the *Hampshire Gazette* and perhaps caught these needlewomen's notice—for pins lay at the center of their revolution as well.[2]

The year 1776 found the Hatfield gown maker Rebecca Dickinson and the Northampton tailor Catherine Phelps Parsons at the height of their careers. Born in 1738, Dickinson would die in 1815, by then an elderly aunt boarding in the home of her nephew, his wife, and their children. Born in 1731, Parsons, who was forty-five when Independence was declared, would live nearly to the age of seventy, dying in 1798, just before the turn of the new century. In 1776 the Hadley tailoress Easter Newton was struggling alongside her husband to provide for their growing family; she would spend the last forty years of her life alone, finding a new career as an innkeeper in her widowhood. Her daughter Tryphena was born to a generation rising in the midst of political turmoil; she died in 1805, of cancer, while a young wife and mother. Elizabeth Phelps, who employed the labors of each of these women over the years, was born in 1747; her gown maker, Tabitha Smith, was born about 1750; in their twenties when revolution broke out, both women lived to see yet another war with Britain before their deaths in 1817.

Over the course of their lifetimes, these women witnessed vast changes—the birth of a new nation, the advent of new styles, the evolution of new manners, the development of new forms and patterns of commerce, the emergence of a new economic culture. The world they left was vastly different from the one they entered. One can only wonder what they made of it all. At times the changes surely struck them as remarkable. During the spring of 1795, for example, Elizabeth and Charles Phelps, as well as their daughters, Thankful and Betsy, made a series of trips to survey the wondrous locks and canal under construction in South Hadley. A year later, Phelps and her children amused themselves with rides to see a new woolen manufactory and to view the goods offered for sale at a newly opened store. Meanwhile, the family's hired woman quit her job at Forty Acres to work instead at a spinning mill.[3] Did Phelps group these developments together in her mind, seeing them all as related manifestations of new economies taking root? Rebecca Dickinson observed that same season the large number of migrants moving round the countryside and paused to muse "how the inhabitence of the Earth are a walking and a stalking up and down the Earth."[4] Both women were noticing the coming of new social and economic orders that today we recognize as industrial and consumer revolutions. In Connecticut, 1776 had seen a young Polly L'Hommedieu flee with her family over the Long Island Sound to escape the chaos of revolution. Later, L'Hommedieu surely perceived the many ways in which the political upheaval had changed the course of her family's lives. But her own life would be just as keenly affected by the revolution of pins, the reorganization of the clothing trades in the early nineteenth century. In 1800, Polly L'Hommedieu Lathrop was earning a living as an independent artisan, constructing gowns for women in her community as a means by which to generate income; by the 1810s, she had abandoned the women's custom clothing trade to make men's shirts, moving, with thousands of other women across the Northeast, into the world of outwork.

The career of capitalism in the early modern and modern world—when and how it arrived, what constitutes it, who embraced it, who eschewed it, why, and when—has sparked a good deal of scholarly debate. While there is still much to be discovered and understood, historians have forged something like a consensus around a pivotal phase in that transformation, the decades immediately following 1776, when Americans brought forth their Revolution and Smith his treatise.[5] What once appeared to be competing schools of thought, between historians who emphasize the quick growth of a vigorous capitalistic economic culture and others who stress the longevity of premodern value systems, have edged closer to reconciliation, producing a new narrative that describes the steady growth of capitalistic social relations that were planted and took root along with the colonies and thrived throughout the eighteenth century, blossoming in the nineteenth century.

Having looked closely at Hampshire County's clothing trades as they appeared during the lifetimes of six of its practitioners, we step back here to take a broader view of women's work in the clothing trades and to track larger changes the trades experienced between the mid eighteenth century and the early nineteenth centuries. During these decades, as Laurel Thatcher Ulrich points out, the "transition to factory production involved more than a move of young women from the household. It, potentially at least, disrupted a multitude of connections within the female economy."[6] My aim here is to consider how such constellations of laborers may have weathered small and large transformations in community and regional economies. Putting these trades into motion, and contemplating how they may have intersected with larger developments across the Atlantic world, allows us to revisit the braided histories of women, work, and economic change with a fresh eye.

For eighteenth-century clothes makers in Hampshire County, the changing shape of their craft was closely tied to the region's almost constant state of war. The gown maker Catherine King Phelps, for example, grew up in the midst of Queen Anne's War; she was three years old when French, Mohawk, and other forces sacked Deerfield, some sixteen miles to the north, burning the village nearly to the ground in an effort to resist English encroachments in North America, and would turn twelve before she saw peace. By mid century, she had survived another war (King George's, in the 1740s), and two husbands as well. Her daughter, the tailor Catherine Phelps, reached her twenties as a more decisive conflict among European and native nations erupted and soon thereafter witnessed still another war as Britain's North American colonies sought their independence.

This constant state of conflict affected women's relationships to the larger economy, the general need for labor climbing as demands for large amounts of goods and services, generated by wartime exigencies, put more money in circulation.[7] As prices for livestock, farm products, and crops soared, farm families positioned to do so shifted their energies to agricultural production and away from craft activities, turning more often to the hiring of others to accomplish those tasks. At the same time, rising wages drew growing numbers of women into clothing and textile occupations. Women had already begun moving into tailoring and weaving, but the labor shortages created by the mid-century imperial struggle boosted demand for their services. Between the close of this conflict and the opening of the war for Independence, the number of girls and young unmarried women recorded as working for someone other than their parents nearly tripled. Both women's rising wages during these years and their larger numbers in the labor market marked an "important structural shift" in the region's economy. Women, like men, were pulled into the labor force.[8] But women's points of entry into those markets were the comparatively poorly remunerated occupations, like needlework, increasingly abandoned by men.

These developments in New England were embedded in a larger "industrious revolution" that was transforming the Atlantic world. Households that once expended considerable energy to produce goods for their own use chose to devote more energy to the production of goods for the market, altering "both the supply of marketed goods and labour and the demand for market-bought products."[9] The ensuing withdrawal of some households from certain tasks created new opportunities for others. As Jan de Vries has written, this "industrious" revolution "placed [women] in a strategic position, located, as it were, at the intersection of the household's three functions: reproduction, production and consumption."[10] Put another way, women, as wives and mothers, had long been making decisions about how best to spend money and time to provide for their families—what to make, what to buy, when and how. Thus, it was their changing assessments and preferences that transformed the early modern economy.

New England families participated in this larger sweep of economic change. Between about 1780 and 1820, the Connecticut River Valley, and the Northeast more generally, witnessed significant economic growth. Rural households anxious to participate in the burgeoning commercial opportunities "intensified" practices already in place.[11] Farmers and farm wives stepped up their respective productive activities; commerce expanded, and new occupations opened up; farm households began accepting outwork; rural families acquired more and more goods produced well beyond their communities, and even outside their region. These changes affected rural men and women differently. Men developed strategies that allowed them to take greater advantage of the mixed-crop economy already in place. Especially in towns along the Connecticut River, farmers hustled to meet the expanding need for fattened beef cattle. They planted larger crops of hay and corn in the summers to provide winter feed, while pasturing their cattle during the growing season in the uplands flanking the river. Upland farmers meanwhile spent winters maintaining and expanding those pastures.

At the same time, farm wives enlarged some forms of production and initiated others. The nonimportation movements of the 1760s and 1770s had encouraged women to amplify their roles in textile production. Some directed more effort to the making of butter and cheese for the market and also to the production of salted beef and pork. Elizabeth Porter Phelps devoted more and more time to her dairy, sending hundreds of pounds of cheese each year to market in Boston. She became so successful at her "making-cheese business" (as she called it) that her husband, Charles, wanted to expand the operation.[12] Between 1777 and 1806, the number of cows grazing Forty Acres rose from eight to thirteen. In 1797, when Charles and Elizabeth built a large ell stretching south from their house, they added a dairy room lined with shelves enough to store as many as seventy cheeses. The room's door retains its keyhole, evidence of the value of the contents stored therein.[13] Other families were apparently as eager to reap the rewards of a productive dairy as were the Phelpses; in the spring of 1807, Elizabeth recorded, "Mrs John Hibbard is here, she came last night and lodged here to see the whole process of cheese making, as they are setting out in the dairy line."[14]

This increased farm and household production was closely linked to the growing rural work force. Wage work expanded "as the number of people with insufficient resources to provide for themselves sought work with households keen to increase their own production."[15] Such aspirations brought Sarah Jackson, a free black woman living in the hill towns, to the Phelps farm. Born in 1761 in Colchester, Connecticut, Jackson was at least a second-generation African American. Her husband, Peter, was born in 1746 on a slave ship crossing from Africa to the Americas. He and his parents were purchased by planters in the southern colonies, and sometime, perhaps during the American Revolution, Peter escaped captivity. By 1800, he and Sarah Jackson were heads of a free black family in Shutesbury that included three children.[16] Jackson worked from time to time in the Phelps dairy, just as Tryphena Cooke sewed from time to time for the Phelps household. As Phelps, Hibbard, and women like them stood over churns and cheese ladders, they turned to women like Jackson and Cooke for help. At the same time, women like Jackson and Cooke (unable to invest in the livestock necessary for dairying) sought out that work in an effort to improve their own fortunes—in Cooke's case, to help the family afford the new home that would house her mother's tavern.

How such transformations affected women's lives depended on larger and more complex constellations of circumstances. Historians studying a number of occupations have observed a hardening over the course of the long eighteenth century as notions of what constituted appropriate women's work narrowed. These ideas moved in concert with other phenomena likewise reshaping women's relationships to the marketplace. Women's work in various clothing and textile trades, for example, expanded and deepened as the overall range of occupations available to them narrowed. During the eighteenth century, women's work in agriculture was reshaped and redirected; brewing, once a craft dominated by women, became an occupation associated with men, and dairying would follow a similar trajectory a century later. The emergence of professionally trained physicians was steadily relegating women to the margins of the healing arts. Certain trades (such as furniture making, blacksmithing, and other metalworking occupations) had never admitted large numbers of women. Shoemaking would come to involve large numbers of both women and men, though stages in the production were segregated by gender. Other eighteenth-century occupations saw the steady infiltration of female practitioners. Cloth making, for example, underwent a complete transformation; Laurel Ulrich has tracked the "feminization of weaving" in northern rural economies as this craft, once a trade largely reserved for men who possessed special skill, became the "foundation of local patterns of barter and exchange" that comprised a "female economy." Teaching, too, saw increasing numbers of female practitioners, particularly in the late eighteenth and early nineteenth centuries.[17]

At the same time, as people increasingly found themselves in commercial, economic, and social relationships with others largely unknown to them, authority accrued to institutions and practices that helped structure formal dealings among strangers (such as courts, the press, long-distance commerce, and institutions of higher learning), and the informal, interpersonal practices that had shaped women's exchanges lost ground. For example, men and women had once been visible as active participants on court days; by the end of the century, the flourishing "litigated economy" involved comparatively fewer women. Once, few men or women attained medical skills or credentials though formal educational channels; as physicians became more closely associated with professional training, women without access to that training could no longer attain the local prestige of their predecessors.[18] In other words, as access to economic opportunity became enmeshed within less personal, more formal institutions, women had a tougher time finding it.

Scholarship on shifting gender divisions of labor in trades closely related to the making of clothing help us define more precisely the issues at play as these developments unfolded. Even in occupations that at first glance may seem closely related, the character of artisanal work evolved in very different ways and at very different times. For example, after about 1780, the expansion of the ready-made industry encouraged shoemakers to recruit female labor in their own households to sew uppers. Women shoe binders learned only one part of the process and so were denied full craft status, preserving at least for a time the artisanal identities of their husbands and fathers.[19] Reorganization of the craft encouraged larger numbers of women to participate in production but without gaining artisanal identity. Almost a century earlier, New England cloth production had also begun to engage larger numbers of women without necessarily conferring artisanal identity. Elsewhere, European divisions of labor among cloth producers persisted in the New World, male weavers preserving the artisanal nature of their craft and restricting women's participation in craft processes.[20] In New England, however, weaving as an artisanal craft practiced by men "disappeared" into the household, and into the hands of women, as early as the late seventeenth and early eighteenth centuries.[21]

For the makers of both cloth and shoes, expanding production engaged female labor but did not necessarily admit women as full-fledged practitioners. Women did not infiltrate crafts that men had dominated; rather, within a wholesale transformation of the work itself, women gained only the limited skills necessary to execute some tasks. While female participation among New England shoemakers remained limited, women's role in weaving varied by region and was shaped by such factors as immigration and regional culture and economies. Adrienne Hood has shown that, in southeastern Pennsylvania, a booming economy, encompassing mixed farming practices and seasonal variation in labor, drew steady English, Irish, and German migration and provided residents with sufficient income to buy, rather than make, cloth. These factors and others combined to sustain European craft practices and traditional gender divisions of labor far longer than they did elsewhere; through the eighteenth century, cloth making here remained an artisanal skill largely controlled by men. By contrast, among New England weavers, apprentice-trained specialists were supplanted by "dutiful daughters and industrious wives scattered among dozens of rural households" who inherited "some but not all the tools of their predecessors."[22] By the turn of the nineteenth century, "cloth making was not only ubiquitous, it was the foundation of local patterns of barter and exchange" that comprised a "female economy."[23] Young women like Betty Newton of Hadley, whom we observed weaving for the Phelps household while her sister and mother sewed, became familiar figures on the New England landscape. Sometime in the first half of the eighteenth century, the balance had tipped in favor of female practitioners, and "cloth-making lost its artisan identity;" by the middle of the eighteenth century, New England's male weavers had been squeezed out, caught between commercial producers across the Atlantic and women who worked in the "anonymity of the household production system" across town.[24] Weaving no longer required any sort of sustained apprenticeship, as neighbors exchanged skill, time, and materials within local economies.

Textile production provides interesting points of comparison to changes in the clothing trades during those same decades. As Judith Coffin's and Clare Crowston's work on the clothing trades elsewhere in the eighteenth-century Atlantic world has shown, gender divisions of labor in the early modern clothing trades were "fluid and contentious."[25] Despite long-standing associations between women and the making of clothing, men had traditionally controlled the skilled labor essential to the construction of fitted apparel. When increasing numbers of women sought to enter these occupations in the seventeenth century, "no normative conceptions of femininity" had yet emerged to resolve disputes when aspiring female practitioners began to encroach on tailor's traditional territory. Clothes making, like other crafts involving soft materials, also saw amplified female participation over the course of the eighteenth century, but its artisanal character persisted far longer. In part, this resilience reflects significant differences between the production of cloth, a two-dimensional product not necessarily associated with its eventual user, and the production of clothing, custom-made until the early nineteenth century, meaning that it had to be fitted to the body in question. Cloth was easily imported; clothing was not. The shape that gender divisions of labor took in shoemaking also moved in concert with the advent of large ready-made inventories. But there could be no anonymity in clothes-making crafts while the custom trade and the specialized skills it demanded thrived; comparable transformations did not come until the advent of ready-made clothing—at the turn of the nineteenth century for men's clothing and, for women's, almost a century later.

In the decades prior to the Revolution, New England women entered low-wage occupations like tailoring.[26] By that time, men had—with both cultural and economic incentives—withdrawn from mantua making and millinery and had allowed women to participate in stay making (at least in the Connecticut Valley) without notable objection. By the early eighteenth century, the gown-making trade had taken on forms that would persist until the turn of the twentieth: small shops headed by female proprietors who worked alone or with a limited number of apprentices or assistants. Men's clothing experienced more volatile change. By the mid-eighteenth century, more and more of this work went to women like Tryphena Cooke, who, as we have seen, seized opportunities to take in plainwork. In an expanding economy, women sharpened certain skills to advantage but did not master the full range of knowledge that sustained artisanal identity. For men like

Robert Robinson, however, competition from skilled craftswomen like Catherine Parsons (as well as Esther Graves, Martha Nash, Lydia Kellogg, Mary Smith, and Jemima Woolworth) clearly became problematic in the years leading up the American Revolution, prompting the anxious craftsman to attempt to cast doubt on the ability of women to master the tailor's craft. Robinson's claims came too late; they had already lost their purchase in a world that had accepted the success of Parsons and her counterparts. However, the advent of ready-made apparel for men and large systems of outwork would reduce opportunities for female entrepreneurs.

While attending to differences between women's work in cloth and clothing production, one must also remember that, because of the significantly different construction techniques involved, women's clothing and men's clothing responded very differently to these developments, again in ways that correspond closely to the advent of large inventories for yet-unknown users. Here it might be helpful to compare each to other sorts of artisanal crafts that industrialized similarly. Men's clothing production traced a path akin to that of furniture making.[27] Anxious to even out the ebb and flow of demand in custom orders, furniture makers began devoting time, energy, and resources during slow seasons to the production of furniture for nonspecific consumers. Craftsmen were increasingly influenced by "scientific" principles of standardization and specialization that would alter the means and methods of production and acquisition.[28] "Ready-made" products in woodworking trades appeared in the Connecticut Valley by the 1790s, only slightly predating that same development in the clothing trade. Some craftsmen—like the eleven windsor-chair makers thriving in Northampton between 1790 and 1820-embraced specialization, building and marketing a single furniture form. Others took specialization a step further and engaged other craftsmen to produce standardized furniture elements, like the chair seats purchased by Ansel Goodrich.[29] Published pattern books enlarged access to technical skill and design while helping to homogenize the products of handiwork.

Each of these features—the advent of "scientific" principles to improve sizing patterns to fit all bodies, the use of down time to make garments for as-yet-unknown customers, the use of published sources of instruction and inspiration—also transformed the production of men's clothing, as it had the production of furniture, toward the mass marketing of ready-made apparel. At the turn of the nineteenth century, several innovations altered traditional practice. Through the eighteenth century, tailors employed no standard unit of measurement to record customers' dimensions; the introduction and acceptance of the tape measure replaced the "individualized intuitive art" of cutting with a standard means by which a man's size could be recorded and conveyed, heightening the importance of literacy and numeracy.[30] Drafting systems proliferated in the early nineteenth century, inspired at least in part by Enlightenment faith in reason and a revived interest in classical theories of human proportion.[31] Instruction manuals, supported by a booming publishing industry, transmitted craft knowledge from author to reader. And men's shirts and other garments became the work of anonymous makers first with the appearance of large and thriving slop shops and later with the advent of vast outwork networks.

Women's clothing production, in contrast, which continued to demand a custom fit to the body of the wearer, remained more akin to crafts like blacksmithing. Indeed, gown makers had more in common with Longfellow's "Village Smithe" than we might suppose, since the trades of both lingered on the rural landscape well into the nineteenth century.[32] In the early nineteenth century, neither blacksmithing nor gown making could be profitably transformed into large-scale enterprises. Instead, blacksmiths and gown makers both continued to make and to mend products used locally and continued to operate on small scales, retaining the form and organization of local service occupations. The divergent paths of the two forms of clothing production affected the women who worked in each industry differently. The custom production of women's clothing, on one hand, continued to encourage female enterprise into the twentieth century; the mass production of menswear, on the other hand, began to circumscribe opportunities for women workers almost a century earlier.[33]

Outwork and the Making of Clothing for Men

Ample opportunities for outwork in a variety of industries became available to women in the last quarter of the eighteenth century, and with the advent of the new century, those opportunities expanded and flourished. Throughout the eighteenth century, the increasing surplus of women workers in the needle trades on both sides of the Atlantic had facilitated the exploitation of cheap female labor. Slop shops and quilt warehouses, in particular, had taken advantage of the abundance of unskilled and semi-skilled laborers. Spurred by tremendous military expansion around the globe, the production of ready-made apparel became a "discernable and increasingly important part" of clothing production in England.[34] As tens of thousands of soldiers and sailors departed for ports of call from the Caribbean to Canada to Calcutta, the need for shirts, stockings, and other articles accelerated. The English clothes dealer Charles James, for example, sold more than half a million shirts, trousers, frocks, and drawers to the British Navy in the 1760s alone.[35]

Charitable institutions, orphanages, and hospitals also began to desire ready-made clothing for their residents, while the Hudson Bay Company and other firms shipped bales of finished clothing to British outposts around the world. And it was not just men's clothing that left London warehouses by the cartload: women's quilted petticoats, which bore only a slight relationship to the shapes of the bodies they eventually clothed, lent themselves particularly well to anonymous production systems. However, unlike the production of shirts, waistcoats, and other men's garments, easily carried out in garrets or other domestic spaces, quilting—which required long frames and lengths of fabrics—was more typically organized in large-scale workshops where quilters, seated along an assemblage of frames, could work under the supervision of others.[36] But, this quilting aside, English manufacturers looked not to factories but to expanded systems of household production. Fabric was cut into pieces in shop or factory settings and then shipped out to women working in their homes to assemble. Huge systems of outwork developed that engaged thousands of women. One slop maker guessed that his firm employed twelve hundred women each week but confessed that he "could not state the number within five hundred."[37]

As similar phenomena found their way to rural New England, the landscape of labor was likewise transformed. In the 1780s, Levi Shephard built a factory in Northampton for the manufacture of canvas cloth. Weaving was carried on in one part of the building and spinning in another, though most of the flax continued to be spun "in families."[38] In the 1790s William Porter distributed raw cotton to Hadley women who then spun it into yarn for his store, while Northampton merchants handed out knitting.[39] In the nineteenth century, women in Ashfield and Conway, Massachusetts, began manufacturing shirt collars and linen bosoms.[40] In Amherst, Massachusetts, the palm-leaf hat business, which employed women as braiders, grew into one of the region's most successful commercial enterprises, while button manufacturing grew into another important industry, especially in the western towns of Hampshire County.[41] Elizabeth Porter Phelps's hired woman Persis Leonard quit domestic work to "go to the mills to spin," while Polly Randall, despite her "very great wages," "could not support a family . . . and half-cloath herself," as Phelps's domestic servant, so she returned home to Pelham and began braiding straw hats.[42] Both women embraced new economic opportunities that did not require them to be subaltern members of other people's households. Even women with greater technical skill and training found outwork appealing: in the summer of 1835, Esther Goodell of Amherst went to Boston and "learned the dressmaker's trade," but by fall she had taken a job in a bonnet factory and by the winter she had returned home altogether and with her two sisters began braiding palm leaf.[43] Thousands of other New England women in the late eighteenth and early nineteenth centuries also embraced forms of outwork that enabled them to balance certain objectives, be it gaining greater autonomy or a steadier income, retaining familial privacy, or simply staying home.

Women in the southernmost communities of the Connecticut Valley, those who lived near coastal ports, and those within the orbit of America's fastest-growing metropolis, New York City, were likeliest to participate in the manufacturing of men's shirts. Sylvester Judd in the second quarter of the nineteenth century recorded that "farmer's wives and daughters in the vicinity of New York who have good homes, in order to get a little money," made four or more plain shirts a day, at a rate of six cents a shirt. Women picked up the garments "all cut out and ready" stitched them up "for 6d ea New York currency," and retailed for about 62 cents. "Wives and daughters of farmers and mechanics with homes and property," Judd further observed, "will work cheaper to get a little money or some good garments than those can afford to work, who depend wholly on their labor, and have no income of their own."[44]

Few careers illustrate these developments as clearly as that of the Connecticut needlewoman Polly L'Hommedieu Lathrop. At the turn of the nineteenth century, Lathrop had been earning a living making and altering gowns, a typical craftswoman in the custom clothing trade.[45] By 1810, however, something had changed. Lathrop was shifting occupations to enter the outwork system, an act symbolized at least in part by her flipping over her account book and beginning again from the opposite end. In that year, Lathrop records, "Rec'd the 8 day of Nov 25 twenty-five shirts." A week later, she received fifteen more, and on the twenty-first, another fifteen. Another set of entries from 1813 suggests the pace of the work. On 8 November, Lathrop received from Reynolds twenty-five shirts. On the sixteenth, she delivered twenty-one shirts—at 13.5 cents per shirt—-and received fifteen more. On the twenty-first, she delivered seven shirts, and received fifteen. In early December she received sixteen more, and during the month delivered thirty-six shirts. On the twenty-third, she received another twenty-five; for whatever reason Lathrop made a big push with these, delivering them just over a week later. Between mid November 1813 and early January 1814, Polly Lathrop produced eighty-nine shirts. Elsewhere, the accounts suggest that shirts comprised only part of Lathrop's output; in a list that appears to be an end-of-season inventory, Lathrop wrote "Began the 8th day of November 1813. Made 50 shirts, 17 frocks, 15 shirt, 1 pair corsets, 1 ruffle, 10 shirts, 9 frocks, 14 shirts." The year 1814 would bring more of the same; Lathrop opened the year with the notation: "rec'd the 26 day of January 100 frocks." Making custom dresses was no longer as attractive as churning out garments by the dozen.

Lathrop appears to have received the batches of sewing she completed through her sister-in-law, Sally Reynolds. When Lathrop opened her record, Reynolds had just passed her fiftieth birthday and was living in her family homestead with her widowed mother and a sister who, like she, had never married. Reynolds's position in the process represented yet another means by which women contributed to their household's upkeep; as a broker, she might have been responsible for monitoring the work of the women to whom she distributed materials, determining whether or not the work returned met her supplier's standards, and so whether or not the workers merited full compensation. Sea captain Giles L'Hommedieu was absent for long periods in an uncertain occupation. Outwork provided a steady income for the Reynolds, Lathrop, and the L'Hommedieu women. The advent of outwork in Norwich coincided with the expansion of the practice throughout the Northeast. The embargo and nonintercourse acts that preceded the War of 1812, together with the war itself and its outcomes, spurred innovation in manufacturing in the New England clothing trades as well as an array of other industries. Shut out from Caribbean ports, northeastern traders turned to the southeastern United States. Thousands of New England shirts made their way to New York City and then to southern plantations. Fine linen shirts intended for wealthy men in the South shipped alongside far larger numbers of coarser counterparts intended for the enslaved work force there.

As the nineteenth century wore on, shirt manufactories flourished. In Fairfield County, Connecticut, the Ridgefield Shirt Company produced thousands of shirts each year, largely destined for New York City, with the labor of hundreds of local women.[46] The firm was organized by George Hunt, whose father had launched the first stage line linking Ridgefield, a town in Connecticut's interior, with the Long Island Sound. Hunt began driving a stage for his father's company sometime in the late 1830s or early 1840s. While waiting to begin his return trip north, he sometimes took a steamer into Manhattan. On one such trip, Hunt was approached by someone in New York's garment industry, who suggested that he might be able to earn some extra income taking shirts to Connecticut women. Hunt embraced the idea, using his stage route to deliver materials and retrieve finished goods. As he traveled through Ridgefield, Redding, Danbury, Bethel, and other towns as far north as Putnam County, Hunt invited women along his route to participate in the outwork system. At each stop, the women met the stage to hand over completed shirts and pick up fresh materials. By the Civil

War, his firm employed a thousand women.[47] Sometimes entire families embraced the work; husbands, wives, sons, and daughters are listed together as delivering finished goods. More often, several women from a single family appear: of the hundreds of women workers listed in Hunt's accounts, just over half worked alongside women who shared the same surname.

In 1846, the first year that records of the company's work force are available, 350 women and a handful of men delivered finished articles of clothing. Of these, three-quarters appear at least twice in the ledgers. During the nine-month period recorded, most women returned work three or four times, participating fairly casually in the outwork system, but some women exchanged materials as often as twenty-five times, that is, almost weekly. Several women of the Keeler family of Ridgefield, for example—whose tavern was a natural stopping place for Hunt's stage—appear regularly in the accounts, Susan and Catherine returning shirts eight and nine times, respectively, while Esther, Hannah, and Mary completed between a dozen and sixteen batches of shirts during those months. Rachel Burt delivered eighteen batches, Fanny Dauchy seventeen, and Mary Gilbert more than two dozen. The number of exchanges alone, however, does not necessarily convey the number of shirts sewn; while the typical batch usually contained six shirts, some women picked up as many as twenty or thirty shirts at a time. Elizabeth Haines, for example, appears only a few times in the 1846 accounts, but on one occasion she delivered thirty shirts. Perhaps Haines lived at a distance from the stage route and so preferred to take away enough work to last her several weeks. Or perhaps she and the other women who delivered large batches like this took away shirts that they redistributed to women of their own families or neighborhoods. Thus, the two dozen shirts that Haines and others returned might have been made up by another circle of sewers for whom these women acted as agents, or brokers. Steamers and stages are often cited as evidence of a thickening of commercial relations in the first decades of the nineteenth century, alongside the growth of industrial systems like rural outwork. For the women of Litchfield County, steamers and stages made it possible for them to participate in New York's garment industry, producing shirts that made their way across even greater distances.[48]

Taking in shirts to sew was especially appealing to economically marginal families, for it provided an additional source of income and allowed them to participate in the acquisition of a tantalizing array of consumer goods. Outwork enabled the children of rural New England families to remain in their homes and communities, rather than migrating to factory towns. And though rural outworkers became enmeshed in ongoing credit relationships with merchant middlemen, outwork, at least as it initially appeared in rural

New England, was not necessarily onerous compared with the factory work of women in the urban clothing industry who faced miserable working conditions and poor compensation.[49]

While rural outwork produced record numbers of ready-made garments and provided occupations for thousands of women whose skills and aims were limited, other developments affected the custom trade in ways that benefited women who were looking for more advanced skills and sources of self-employment. Women of Catherine Phelps Parsons's generation had had to secure training—sometimes with difficulty—from a practicing tailor, but women of her daughters' generation saw their access to craft knowledge expanding at the same time that their ability to compete with male artisans was contracting. The nineteenth century, for example, saw an explosion of published instructions, allowing anyone reasonably adept with a pair of shears and "acquainted with figures" to enter the tailor's trade.[50] One of the earliest to appear in the United States was James Queen and William Lapsley's *The taylors' instructor,* published in Philadelphia in 1809.[51] A decade later, such treatises were being produced and published throughout the United States, in small towns as well as urban centers, as authors recycled old material, adding their own innovations. Amanda Jones of Vermont, for example, published *The tailor's assistant* in 1822 and again in 1823. In 1823, Erastus and Joseph Wrightman published *The tailor's assistant: being a new and complete system of cutting men's garments,* David Watson published Fielder Clark's *Easy and Correct Method of Cutting Men's Garments by Geometrical Rules,* in Woodstock, Vermont, and E. Eaton published John Moxley's *Every One His Own Tailor: The Improved Compass Rule, Now Called By The Third, to Cut Garments* in Danville, Vermont. By the end of the decade, Otis Madison and John B. Pendleton's *New System of Delineating, founded on True Principles,* had appeared from printers in both Boston and Worcester.[52] When William Sumner's edition of Jones's *The Tailor's Assistant* became available, promising that "in a few hours, a person may acquire such a knowledge of the art, as will enable him to cut all sizes and fashions, with the greatest accuracy," Julia Goodenough purchased her copy and proudly inscribed on its cover "Miss Julia Eliza Goodenough, tailoress," while Abigail Sheldon, another aspiring tailoress, purchased *A Guide to Cutting Men's Clothes by the Square Rule.*[53]

The availability of published guides gave aspiring needleworkers access to information they might not otherwise have had. For women who could not secure any sort of apprenticeship or whose apprenticeships, like Clarissa Burt's, were inadequate, guides created possibilities where they might not otherwise have existed, though the purchase of a book could not supplant careful training under a practiced artisan. In these same years, however, men with skills in clothing production expanded their businesses to include the sale of materials and sometimes finished apparel. Like house carpenters who in the early nineteenth century redirected their energies to general contracting, some tailors became less artisans than businessmen, opening stores with large inventories of ready-made garments.[54] As increasing numbers of men like Sylvester Lyman formed aesthetic and commercial ties with their urban counterparts, the generation of female artisans that followed Catherine Phelps Parsons may have found themselves unable to compete. By the second quarter of the century, then, many New England communities included a "village tailoress" who filled the role once supplied by tailors—women like those who, by the end of the century, had become stock figures in town histories such as that by Northampton's Jonathan Trumbull. Their abilities may have been uneven, but many such women found opportunities filling gaps left behind by the men who entered the world of ready-made apparel.

Fit, Fashion, and the Making of Clothing for Women

While men's clothing production became associated in the first half of the nineteenth century with rural tailoresses who entered the trade with the help of tape measures and trade manuals, as well as other needlewomen who entered it through systems of outwork, the production of women's clothing followed a very different trajectory. The highest echelon of women's work in the eighteenth and nineteenth centuries was and would remain gown making—or, as it gradually became known, dressmaking—and millinery work. The major technological changes that would transform the women's garment industry (sewing machines, sizing systems, and published patterns) were all phenomena of the mid-nineteenth century. But no ready-made or wholesale trade developed in women's apparel until the turn of the twentieth century. The generations of gown makers who followed Rebecca Dickinson and Tabitha Smith would have found much that was familiar in the work of their predecessors.

In the women's clothing industry as in men's, style shaped production. Throughout much of the eighteenth century, women's and men's fashions developed in tandem, "evolving toward a closer and closer fit."[55] Had such preferences endured, mantua makers, like tailors, would have been pressed earlier on to develop proportional drafting systems. But the appearance of the so-called empire or neoclassical style, with its high-waisted, fluid gowns, required different construction methods, pin-to-the-form techniques that persisted as long as the empire style in women's fashions endured.[56] New knowledge and skills were demanded, but the organization of the trade was not significantly altered.

In the final decades of the eighteenth century, the clothing trades, like woodworking trades and indeed the entire world of artisans whose work produced the objects now called the "decorative arts," witnessed a dramatic shift, a moving away from the effusive ornamentation of the rococo style and a growing preference for the neat, clean lines of the neoclassical. Reasons behind this development are multiple. In part, it was simply the familiar swing of the pendulum, the exuberance of the rococo popular in the middle decades of the century necessarily answered by new preferences for visual simplicity. Prevailing philosophical winds contributed as well, particularly Jean-Jacques Rousseau's emphasis on simplicity and closeness to nature, which encouraged elites to adopt plainer preferences. The excavations at Herculaneum and Pompeii earlier in the century fed fascination with classical antiquity and the visual culture associated with it. That America was in these same years at work forging a new government based on principles of republicanism and democracy made these new opportunities in design seem all the more appropriate; cultivating a neoclassical style was the perfect enterprise for a new nation eager to make its own claim as the inheritor of the legacies of Greece and Rome.

Men and women throughout New England embraced the new fashions with enthusiasm, creating particular challenges for artisans in the clothing trades. The large number of alterations undertaken during the 1790s and early 1800s to comply with changing tastes certainly generated activity for gown makers; in fall 1801, for example, Elizabeth Phelps hired Fanny Allen to make her lutestring gown "plumb"—that is, to revamp the gown to conform with the slimmer silhouette of the neoclassical style—an act that was repeated time and again in households throughout New England as extant wardrobes were brought into harmony with prevailing fashion.[57] The new aesthetic required alterations that were nothing short of architectural. As the advent of the mantua itself had done over a century earlier, the new style had the power to transform the clothing trades themselves. In the same way that the mantua, far simpler to create than the styles that preceded it, had enabled larger numbers of women to embrace prevailing fashion, creating opportunity for aspiring mantua makers, the neoclassical gown, simpler still and demanding less investment in both fabric and trimming, enabled yet larger numbers of women to participate in the new mode of dress. New skills in terms of construction would play a central role as well. We have already seen how shifting fashions may have affected the demand for stays and the skills required for their construction; in the same way, the construction of gowns changed dramatically in these years. In fact, just as housewrights and furniture makers cultivated new skills to form their traditional materials into the lighter, airier structures of the neoclassical style, so too did gown makers develop new methods by which to achieve the effect desired by growing numbers of consumers. Not only did construction change as the round fullness of the Georgian era was supplanted by the slender silhouettes of the neoclassical style, but the materials in which garments was rendered changed, too, the heavy silks of the mid-eighteenth century giving way by the turn of the nineteenth to light, sheer cottons.

The tasks involved in mastering the new fabrics and fashions were neither simple nor apparent, even to specialists in the clothing trades, much less the women across New England who sought out a fashionable appearance. As David Lazaro observes, "when introduced in the 1790s, rising waistlines challenged everyone in the clothing trades."[58] Consumers' desire for garments with waistlines just under the arms forced artisans—sometimes reluctantly—to devise and cultivate new abilities. *The Taylor's Complete Guide,* published in 1796, captured their complaint: in the early 1790s, tailors were accustomed to cutting waists nine inches long, close to the natural form, but by 1796, since the "quick transition of fashion," they were "obliged to cut them but three inches in the same place for the length, to figures of the same height and stature."[59] "Stripped" of "every guide that nature pointed out as a direction for fitting the body," tailors and gown makers scrambled to devise new ways to meet demand while maintaining the same levels of craftsmanship.[60]

For gown-making artisans, this radical shift in silhouette was a mixed blessing. On one hand, the simpler architecture of the neoclassical style meant that the steps required to create a fashionable garment were significantly reduced. Mid-century gowns had typically involved running stitches, backstitches, whip, and hemming stitches; fit might demand arrangements of pleats, gathers, and darts, and embellishments could include everything from robings, ruching, and fringe to multiple layers of ruffles that required additional effort, such as pinking or the application of trim. By contrast, neoclassical gowns were commonly constructed to accentuate the long, columnar drape of the skirt, meaning simple shaping at the bustline and small cap sleeves. The preference for simplicity reduced the need for elaborate trimmings. The gowns' fabrics were sometimes shockingly sheer, worn over pale slips to all but reveal the wearer's body.

Once mastered, the new style may have proved something of a boon to busy craftswomen. As one observer remarked, "the 'slips' worn at the Hartford assemblies" were so simple that "a dressmaker could cut and baste three in a day."[61] However, the long side seams, which once required only loose stitching to assemble, now demanded significantly greater attention; while just six or eight stitches per inch had sufficed for the heavier fabrics popular in previous years, the sheer, light-weight materials favored at the turn of the century required more like ten or twelve stitches per inch to be fastened securely, almost doubling a needlewoman's effort to assemble a gown's skirts.[62]

In part, and not surprisingly, gown makers striving to adapt to a new aesthetic atmosphere relied on tradition. For example, gowns in the neoclassical style no longer needed a neckpiece to secure the pleating that enabled the garment to hug the wearer's back. But gown makers, at least early on, continued to employ this element of the construction techniques they had long practiced, even when they ceased to be important to the garment's architecture.[63] Pleats, once the means by which gown makers produced a close fit, now created unsightly bulk that worked against the most desirable properties of the lighter fabrics, and so craftswomen adopted a different technique in which shoulder seams, dropped to the back, intersected with angled side and back seams; the resulting diamond-shaped panel could cling snugly to the wearer's back, achieving fit in a new way that was consistent with neoclassical styles and materials. Most important to the gown-making trades, however, was the introduction of techniques borrowed, for the first time, from their counterparts in the tailoring trades. Not before the advent of the neoclassical style at the turn of the nineteenth century did women's garments, apart from riding habits, employ seams rather than gathering techniques to achieve fit. Some gown makers, aware of the advent of seams among more skilled practitioners but unable to grasp altogether the techniques involved, developed strategies that used the traditional, and more time-consuming, method of achieving fit with stitched-down pleats to create the appearance of seams where none existed. This use of pleats suggests something interesting about the creators of these garments, that merely achieving a particular fit was not the entire goal: the garment's wearer may not have had a strong opinion about the method by which fit was achieved, as long as the proper silhouette resulted, but the makers wanted the finished object to reflect at least their awareness of the preference for seams, if not their ability to deploy them.

Clearly remodeling existing gowns to conform to new fashions generated income, but was constructing new gowns in this style as lucrative? Without more systematic evidence it is difficult to determine whether the greater simplicity of neoclassical garments meant reduced wages for skilled gown makers, who no longer devoted hours to careful cutting, fitting, and assembly, much less to the design and application of ornamentation like ruffles and lace, or whether it meant that more garments could be produced in less time, like the "three in a day" slips that supposedly could be cut and basted in Federal Hartford. Apparently some women decided not to make the change; in the same years that the neoclassical style reached Northampton, Sarah Clark, for example, quit making gowns and redirected her energies to making bonnets and hats. Mary Dwight, a mantua maker in Hartford, did what any entrepreneur might do: she diversified. In addition to "the business of mantua making in its various branches," Dwight wished potential clients to know that she "also makes curtains for high post and field beds"; several years later she again announced to readers of the local newspaper that she "also makes bed and window curtains and coverings for sofas and chairs."[64] Other craftswomen began maintaining inventories of shop goods, largely pertaining to millinery, in an effort to generate incomes beyond the sale of their particular skills.[65]

The same years that witnessed this radical reshaping of women's fashion saw a radical reshaping of the American economy. These transformations in society and commerce meant shifting fortunes for the Hartford mantua maker Chloe Filley. Filley had first opened a gown-making shop in the spring of 1809, in partnership with Mercy Tabor.[66] The two women carried on the "millinery and mantua-making business" on Burr Street, informing readers that they offered "the most modern and best approved fashions" and "as liberal terms as can be purchased in this city." They also invited the custom of women from the outlying towns, assuring them that "orders from a distance will be carefully and punctually attended to." A subsequent advertisement in the fall of the year elaborated on the sewing services provided, indicating that "they make habits, pelices, and all other kinds of mantua-making . . . at short notice."[67]

In May, Chloe Filley advertised herself as a "Milliner and Mantua-Maker" with a shop opposite William Imlay's store on Main Street, just south of the state house.[68] A notice placed in November informed readers that "the co-partnership between Chloe Filley and Mercy Tabor . . . dissolved 15 April last."[69] Just beneath this announcement was a larger notice for Filley's new shop, informing customers that an assortment of millinery goods had arrived, including lace veils and handkerchiefs, straw and winter bonnets, figured lustring, lace armlets, white and colored kid gloves, and an "elegant assortment of ribbons." She also reminded women in need of new clothing that the "newest styles, according to the most fashionable patterns from Boston and New York," would be "executed with taste and dispatch."

The following fall, anxious to secure customers, Filley placed an announcement hoping to attract clients in need of outerwear for the coming winter; the timing was fortunate, since Filley was about to endure a spate of competitors. A month later "Mrs Lincoln" purchased space to inform her "friends and public" that she has "resumed her business of mantua-making and millinery"; "Ladies Pelices, Habits, etc." would be "cut to order."[70] In January of the following year, Filley tried to improve her fortunes by moving to a new stand at the corner of Main and Theatre Streets. Her old spot was quickly taken by Catherine Seymour, "where she plans to carry on the business of mantua-making and millinery." Like Lincoln, Seymour seems to have been reentering a field previously abandoned; "her former success in pleasing her customers induces her to solicit a renewal of their favors."[71] In October 1812, Filley was on the move once more, relocating to a brick storefront just south of the Brick Meeting House.[72] By February 1813, Catherine Seymour had given up her business and moved in with Filley, where she took in plain sewing.[73]

Filley's story reflects both change and continuity in the work of New England gown makers. In her day, much like Rebecca Dickinson's decades earlier, artisanal women continued to weigh marriage and family against the demands of their crafts and would continue to operate within a largely female economy; these things changed little as the trade moved from the eighteenth to the nineteenth century. The organization of production also changed little. Small shops, headed by female proprietors, usually employed a small number of apprentices and assistants, as they would through most of the nineteenth century.[74] These shops were in many ways similar to their predecessors' home-based workshops. However, Filley also witnessed the erosion of relationships based on reciprocity in favor of others grounded in impersonal market forces. The lively exchange that pitted the Salmon sisters against Mary Gabiel was rare among craftswomen in the *Courant*'s advertising columns of 1776; after the turn of the century, such notices became commonplace. Though they continued to seek out a female clientele, those customers were no longer identified by word of mouth alone. At the same time, for some women, these changes moved them out of family circles and into communities of other working women. Chloe Filley, for example, lived not with her parents or a family at all but with a houseful of other single women on their own in early nineteenth-century Hartford.[75] In the decades to come, larger numbers of women would live and labor alongside other working women.

Also new for women of Filley's generation was the commercial context of the enterprise. In cities like Hartford and Boston, small shops were known throughout the eighteenth century but grew markedly in number in the early years of the nineteenth. The Boston city directory for 1789 lists only ten mantua makers, but by 1805, that number rose to thirty-four and by 1820, forty-two.[76] The pages of the *Connecticut Courant* capture part of that story as well: before 1805, only a handful of women, perhaps fewer than half a dozen, had ever advertised their skills in the local press; thereafter, new names entered their notices almost every year. In 1807, "M. Hinsdale" advertised that she "wishes to inform her friends" that she has opened a millinery and mantua-making shop opposite the printing office.[77] In 1808, H. Marsh and Co. announced its opening. A year later, as we have seen, Chloe Filley and Mercy Tabor opened a shop, and in 1811 Mrs. Lincoln also opened one.[78] Catherine Seymour tried her hand at the business the following year, but later, perhaps recognizing an insufficiency of skill or training in the art of fitting, she retreated to the Filley shop, where she took in plain sewing; she later opened a small boardinghouse.[79] In the fall of 1812, Mary Barnard and her sisters rented the house at the corner of Theatre and Main formerly occupied by Chloe Filley and "commenced the mantua-making and millinery business in all its branches."[80] "Mrs MacDonald" did the same in October 1815, a few doors from City Hall, and two months later "E. Howe" opened her own shop near Filley's old stand.[81] In March 1817, three more women—Philenda Skinner, Mary Spencer, and "Mrs Mather"—opened shops, and less than six months later, Sarah Merrill joined them in competition.[82] Dela Clark announced her ability to offer the latest fashions from New York in the spring of 1819, and by the fall of the following year she, too, had competition from the aspiring milliner and mantua maker Elizabeth Brace.[83] In the hurly-burly of the bustling county, women pursued commercial lives based in public shops, not private homes. Reputation and word of mouth were no longer sufficient. Women entrepreneurs adopted the practices of their male counterparts in an effort to secure the custom in and beyond their community. For women positioned to do so, opening a shop, and offering goods along with services, could be the first step to real economic advancement.

Between 1810 and 1820, women in smaller New England towns also began to open shops, both in their homes and in their communities' commercial districts, and to advertise those enterprises in the local press. Among the first of these in Hampshire County was a young Northampton mantua-maker, milliner, and shopkeeper named Sarah Williams.[84] In August 1816, Williams placed her first advertisement in the pages of the *Hampshire Gazette:* "Miss Williams has received from Boston, and is now opening, a large assortment of *fancy goods,* among which: muslins, silks, gassimere and flannel shawls, bombazettes, scotch plaid, and a great variety of pelisse habits and bonnet trimmings. *Also* crockery, glassware, etc. offered at reduced price for Cash or most kinds of produce, as butter, cheese, grain, etc. *Millinery and Mantua-making,* in all their various branches, in latest Boston fashions."[85] Soon after, other businesswomen purchased space in the *Hampshire Gazette and Public Advertiser* (tellingly renamed so in 1815), their increasing presence in the paper's advertising columns reflecting their increasing presence among Shop Row's proprietors.[86] Mary W. Lee, another Northampton mantua maker, was advertising in the *Hampshire Gazette* in 1818 and 1819, while milliner Nancy Best announced that she "has taken the shop formerly occupied by Col'l Breck," in which she carried fashionable accessories like bonnets, caps, ruffs, vandykes, and even ostrich feathers that she shipped in from New York.[87] In the emergent economy of the 1810s, reputation and word of mouth were no longer sufficient. Women entrepreneurs embraced the practices of their male counterparts in an effort to secure the custom in and beyond their community.

Although the society and economy of the Connecticut Valley underwent substantive transformations between the mid eighteenth century and the opening of the nineteenth, the gap between gown makers like Rebecca Dickinson, who learned her craft in the 1750s, and Chloe Filley, who came of age five decades later, was in other ways not especially large. The essential tasks of fitting, cutting, and stitching had, compared with changes in the men's clothing industry, changed comparatively little. Most scholars note that mistresses and masters in the early nineteenth-century assumed less of the burden of their apprentices' upkeep. Whereas Catherine Phelps Parsons had once boarded several of her apprentices, requiring of them slightly longer terms of service in exchange for their room and board, her latter-day counterparts expected parents to provide those needs.[88] On the surface, Filley's trade appears to have been less itinerant than Dickinson's. She enjoyed the stability of a dedicated site and the respectability that such a site conferred. That difference, however, had wider repercussions too. Her inventory of goods, and the diversification of her income-generating activities, meant that she was integrated more thoroughly into a commercialized, market-oriented economy than her earlier counterparts had been. Although the skills of gown making—or, now, dressmaking—had changed little, the world in which those skills were acquired and marketed had changed a good deal.

Given the demise of the local aristocracy's influence amid the rise of a commercial economy, craftswomen like Rebecca Dickinson, whose reputation and clientele depended on close personal associations with the women of the county gentry, may also have found themselves particularly disadvantaged by the redistribution of economic and political power and cultural authority.[89] Their young apprentices, however, took advantage of these shifts in the commercial landscape to establish in the growing market centers small businesses more akin to those of their male counterparts.[90]

TRANSFORMATIONS IN the eighteenth-century economy were prompted by women expanding their work in the clothing trades, and affected them as well, though just how depended on which skills they had mastered, whose clothing they made, where they lived, and a number of other factors. All of the women who grace these pages—Elizabeth Phelps, Easter Newton, Tryphena Cooke, Rebecca Dickinson and Tabitha Smith, Catherine Phelps Parsons, and many others—helped effect some reconfigurations and responded to others. When Elizabeth Phelps allocated energy to the dairy rather than the workbasket, she helped create the expansion of opportunity embraced by women like Tryphena Cooke, eager to add to her household's resources. Tabitha Smith mastered a skill that would nicely complement her husband's separate work as a merchant. The never-married gown maker Rebecca Dickinson saw craft skill as a means to preserve her independence; a generation later, Polly Lathrop may have, too, but ultimately exchanged self-employment for the more certain income of outwork.

For some New England women, their relationships to that expanding economy became attenuated. When Parsons sought training in the making of men's clothes, for example, she embraced and advanced new understandings about appropriate work for women; but when her male competitors turned to a nascent press to expand their business, she did not join them. Other women, of a later generation, embraced the advantages offered by advertising columns. Here we may recall the notices placed by the Hartford gown maker Mrs. Mather. Like Sylvester Lyman, who boasted of "superior advantages," having worked in the "cities of Philadelphia and New York with the most approved workmen," Mather, too, assured readers that she had cultivated her skills among the nation's best practitioners; just as Lyman sought to attract business having "formed a correspondence with the principle tailors in Philadelphia and New York, to receive the fashions as they arrive from London," so Mather emphasized her continuing connections to the capital city to suggest quicker access to rapidly changing fashion.[91]

But businesswomen like these were the exceptions in the early national Connecticut Valley. For many women, craft skill did not mean commercial opportunity. By the third quarter of the eighteenth century, for instance, women in Connecticut who continued to be active in their local economies were increasingly distanced from new credit relations of an expanding economy.[92] Women still participated in a vigorous female economy grounded in personal relationships, but the gap between the informal economies of women and the formal economies that engaged their fathers, husbands, and sons grew wider. As Cornelia Dayton writes, while women's contributions to their households and neighborhoods remained "crucial," "the worlds of commerce and credit in which their menfolk partook were increasingly unknown and alien to them."[93] For women and the evolution of the clothing trades, such developments meant that far fewer women, despite their enlarging numbers in an evolving industry, were likely to have the means to seize the reins of those transformations, to direct their course or to profit from them.

As the production of both men's and women's apparel changed shape in the late eighteenth and early nineteenth century, male artisanal culture acquired a distinctly political cast. During the American Revolution, political mobilization drew men in skilled trades together in actions that helped form and then reflected a shared craft consciousness.[94] In the years to follow, artisanal men continued to cultivate a sense of themselves based on their political and artisanal identities. Craft associations, too, began to emerge that crystallized a distinct artisanal identity among men. In 1792, for example, Connecticut artisans joined together to protest the state's tax system, the first political action undertaken specifically by craftsmen.[95] Although short-lived, the action was not isolated. As artisanal men gathered together in formal organizations with political and economic aims, an activity not comparably open to artisanal women, one gap between male and female artisanal experience widened.

The changes in male artisanal culture were not duplicated in female artisanal culture, which continued to embrace long-shared craft values that persisted amid industrial, commercial, and political transformations whose consequences were multiple, varied, and contradictory. Put another way, the changes these women experienced were not part of any single "revolution" in commerce or industry; they emerged from complex and closely intertwined processes that came to each woman differently, depending on where she was already standing. The men's clothing industry succumbed early on to the control of wholesale manufacturers, drawing women into systems of outwork that ranged in circumstances and conditions from harshly exploitative to benign to advantageous. The women's clothing industry resisted such encroachments much longer, but transformed, too, in ways that benefited women with access to education and capital. A certain bifurcation occurred during this period as some craftspersons succeeded in adapting their businesses to changing circumstances while others did not. The historian Paul Gilje writes that those artisans who continued in craft production "occupied an ambiguous class location" somewhere between mechanics who seemed increasingly trapped on the lowest rungs of the industrial ladder, and men who had enough capital to establish themselves as proprietors.[96] Likewise, gown and dressmakers with position and luck found themselves able to convert craft skill to social and economic success, while others joined the swelling ranks of failed entrepreneurs and became workwomen in the shops of others.

Throughout the Atlantic world, as the eighteenth century gave way to the nineteenth, the clothing trades had become associated with its female practitioners. A century earlier, women had pressed their way into the guilds of England and France, demanding the right to make clothing for women and appropriating the right to make clothing for men. A craft once regarded as a male preserve had become the "natural" province of women.[97] Those developments, however, would color the way later generations viewed their eighteenth-century ancestors. When James Russell Trumbull in 1902 concluded that "apparently everyone" in the eighteenth-century town "was her own dressmaker" because he found no flourishing "dressmaking establishments," he was responding to his own late Victorian conception of what dressmaking as a trade for women looked like. And likewise, when he conceded that some women may well have "made themselves useful" by sewing, he was responding to and helping to perpetuate a vision in which women's participation in the clothing trades was seen not as an exchange of skill but rather as a neighborly sharing of inherent abilities held among women.[98] In the late nineteenth and early twentieth centuries, such descriptions had a ring of easy familiarity that ushered readers away from the complex systems of production, consumption, and exchange that characterized early American women's economic culture and toward illusions of housewifery that would gain mythic proportions.

Conclusion

The Romance of Old Clothes

"Old letters and old garments bring us in close touch with the past; there is in them a lingering presence, a very essence of life." These words introduce the final chapter of Alice Morse Earle's 1903 publication *Two Centuries of Costume in America,* a survey of American clothing from 1620 to 1820.[1] To Earle's readers—middle-class Victorians unnerved by their rapidly changing world—her vision of early American hearths and homes offered a comforting model of social and cultural change, grounding an unsettling present in a virtuous past.[2]

Earle titled her concluding essay "The Romance of Old Clothes," and so do I. But while the "romance" of "old clothes" provided Earle and her readers with a tangible connection to their ancestry, for me, the romance assumes a fuller meaning. A century after Earle limned the clothing of distant generations, I wonder how our contemporary perceptions of early American women are to some degree still products of her historical creation, shaping subsequent history writing, and maybe history too. Given what we know about the character of needlework as a trade for women in early New England, it is worth considering why that history has become so difficult to see, how it was that early American needlework became so thoroughly suffused with romance. Tom Englehardt and Edward T. Linenthal have observed that our shared myths, our cultural fables, reveal what we as a nation "can and cannot bear to look at or consider at any moment, and why."[3] So what was it about early American women's work that became, over the nineteenth century and at the turn of the twentieth, sufficiently unbearable that romantic revisionings were embraced instead? What did Earle's vision of an idealized past mean at the close of the nineteenth century, and why does it still resonate, if now more familiar in the forms of Betsy Ross and Colonial Barbie, at the turn of the twenty-first? What does it illuminate, and what does it obscure?

Scholars have written persuasively about the rise of artisan republicanism and the aggressively masculine cast to that culture, so strong that it "utterly obliterated the presence of women in commerce and the trades."[4] At the founding of the republic, men whose economic independence was jeopardized by developments in commerce and industry successfully articulated a political vision grounded in male culture and male privilege, limiting women's actual role in artisanal activities while reshaping in dramatic and enduring ways public understanding of what constitutes artisanal life.[5] That story need not be retold here, but it provides critical context for another confluence of factors, specific to clothing and needlework, that clouded our historical view. Changes in the garment industry in the nineteenth century gradually took clothing production, first of men's garments and later of women's, out of homes and into factories, gradually removing working women from sight, consciousness, and imagination. Innovations in both home sewing and dressmaking during that same period—most notably, published drafting systems and the sewing machine—conflated the work of custom dressmakers and home sewing, blurring distinctions between professional and amateur sewing, and sewers. Finally, the colonial and craft revivals of the half-century following the 1876 Centennial, responding to those very changes along with others of industrializing America, selectively remembered and revived women's earlier work, celebrated the ornamental aspects of needlework, romanticized the tedious, and effaced the remunerative.

As EARLY as the second quarter of the nineteenth century, the notion that plain sewing was most appropriately performed by working-class women was firmly planted. Louisa Hall recalled that her aunt "kept a sempstress in the family, and a part of her duty was to make and mend my clothes." Hall was so far removed from the process by which her wardrobe was constructed that when she entered her twenties (in 1822), she "had a fashionable contempt for plain sewing" and could not, she said, "conjecture how a single garment that I wore was cut or made." Hall found such work beneath her; what's more, her "contempt" for plain sewing was "fashionable."[6] In 1831, a young Rachel Stearns, under pressure of necessity, recorded her willingness to sew for another household, although she had earlier "thought it quite too degrading" to go out sewing.[7] Art and literature echoed concerns voiced by economic and social reformers as they depicted the sewing women's vulnerability to prostitution.[8] In the nineteenth century, as greater amounts of sewing were relegated to waged laborers, clothing production became less a general category of work familiar to all women than an occupation associated with degradation, depravity, and chronic poverty.

While industrialization of the men's garment industry widened real and symbolic gaps between the women who produced clothing and the families that consumed it, changes in the women's garment industry muddied distinctions between producers and consumers. The creation of women's clothing, with its greater emphasis on tight fit, for most of the nineteenth century had proven nearly impossible to mechanize. While garments least dependent on a close fit (such as cloaks, petticoats, and chemises) shifted toward factory production by the 1860s and 1870s, blouses (known then as shirtwaists) and skirts did not follow until their more billowy silhouette came into vogue in the 1890s. Dresses were not mass produced until the 1910s. Small shops with female proprietors, then, survived far longer in the production of women's apparel; nevertheless, the effects of industrialization on the garment industries as well as home-sewing were felt, and in ways that conflated the work of custom dressmakers and home sewers.

Events in the nineteenth-century history of cloth production had transformed relationships between materials and labor. In 1774, the fabric used in a medium-quality gown accounted for 90 percent of its cost. As cloth production industrialized, the price of materials dropped steadily, while the cost associated with labor grew in comparison.[9] In revolutionary New England, hiring skilled artisans to insure successful outcomes was an obvious choice; as the cost of fabric plummeted, hiring well-trained craftspersons demanded the largest outlay, prompting larger numbers of individuals to try to master skills for themselves. Interest in acquiring such proficiencies helped drive the proliferation of drafting systems and other tools intended to facilitate home clothing production.

The introduction and adoption of the sewing machine had had surprisingly little effect on the actual work of home sewing, since the main problem for home sewers was never the stitching of seams but rather the cutting of a well-fitting garment.[10] The special levels of skill in cutting—expertise that had provided Rebecca Dickinson, Tabitha Clark Smith, and Catherine Phelps Parsons with their incomes—still lay beyond the reach of many home sewers. In the nineteenth century, however, the development of drafting systems and the appearance of published graded patterns radically altered clothing production, both among professionals and among home sewers. Consumers were inundated with innovations that promised to replace the "art and mystery" of clothing production with reliable, easy-to-use tools.

The appeal of these products as well as the income they promised were linked in no small part to the dramatic growth, in Victorian America, in the numbers of unmarried women in search of some source of economic support. The demographic catastrophe of the Civil War and the lure of westward migration skewed sex ratios in communities throughout the eastern United States. In Massachusetts in 1875, the three counties (Hampshire, Hampden, and Franklin) that comprised the former Hampshire County contained some 5,000 more women than men. Ten years later, women outnumbered men by more than 7,400.[11] In 1891, observing the 2,000 "surplus" women in Northampton, a writer for the *Hampshire Gazette* wondered "what our excess of female population does for a living." His investigation of life "among the dressmakers" estimated that "over 200 women . . . make a living by clothing and adorning the bodies of their sex and there must be many more." Urban centers experienced the same phenomenon on a larger scale. In 1828, 15 Hartford, Connecticut, women had worked as mantua makers and dressmakers; by 1890, that number had grown to 278 (or one dressmaker for every 190 residents), and by 1900 to 329. Similarly, Boston's 1875 city directory lists 270 dressmakers, with more in the neighboring towns of Charlestown and West Roxbury, serving a population of 250,000. Just five years later the number had nearly doubled, 456 dressmakers advertising in the directory's columns. By 1905, the number had climbed to 688; by 1910, to 853. And by 1915, the peak of the industry in that city, 1,189 women were practicing dressmakers.[12]

As home sewers with new tools and abilities encroached on territory once reserved for professional craftswomen, the work of artisans and amateurs edged closer. The "ideological conflation" of women's appropriate work in the marketplace (in which needle trades played a large role) and women's appropriate work in the home worked to the disadvantage of skilled needle workers. Tradeswomen lost work to customers who now fashioned their own clothes and faced growing competition from self-trained amateurs who marketed their own newly acquired skills. The means by which women's work in early American needle trades have receded from view was a long and complicated process, but certainly, as Wendy Gamber has observed, "by simultaneously recommending their systems 'to dressmakers' and 'to ladies in private life,' the makers of systems increasingly blurred the boundaries between home and workshop. . . . By identifying dress cutting with middle-class domesticity—by classifying it as a variant of the housewife's labor that 'all' women performed—systematizers obscured the artisanal origins of the dressmaking trade.[13]

Those changes in the garment and home sewing industries took place amid larger cultural dislocations that caused Americans to look longingly back to a preindustrial past that was just then slipping slightly beyond the reach of memory. Ornamental needlework, in its production and consumption, played a pivotal role in a culture discomforted by industrial capitalism. Throughout the nineteenth century, fancywork helped growing numbers of middle- and working-class women resist the encroachments of industrial capitalism, by allowing women to domesticate products of mass production as they selected and reworked them into artful reflections of a more personal aesthetic.[14] The same developments in production, consumption, and distribution that put more forms of needlework into the hands of larger numbers of women would help create the gulf between experience and memory on which all revivals rest. At the same time, the advent of ornamental needlework forms for the masses meant that, when the colonial and craft revivals took hold, women for whom fancywork was an important part of the present naturally took an interest in the fancywork of the past; that work, no longer the province of comparatively privileged women like Elizabeth Porter Phelps, was "revived" and remembered.

As a result of this confluence of forces, ever-larger numbers of women during these decades embraced hobbies like Berlin work (a craft developed for amateur stitchers involving embroidery patterns worked on canvas with brightly colored German wools, enormously popular in the first half of the nineteenth century) and those ubiquitous mottoes of the 1870s and 1880s with which we are today so familiar. While well-wrought eighteenth-century samplers and needlework pictures had required a good deal of talent, dedication, and training, the stitching of mottoes on preprinted perforated cardboard, products of another sort of deskilling elsewhere in industrializing America, demanded comparatively minimal time and effort, little money, and less expertise to complete.[15] Pale shadows of the finer ornamental needlework produced by eighteenth-century elites, these projects gave the parlors of the growing middle and even working classes a veneer of respectability by gesturing toward work historically associated with genteel women.

While industrialization altered the ways in which both practical and ornamental needlework was practiced, experienced, and remembered by both leisured and working American women, the broader cultural response to industrialization was having yet another effect on the way women and men imagined needlework in early America. As early as the second quarter of the nineteenth century, a complex web of myth, nostalgia, and wonder had come to surround preindustrial women's labor, as the grandchildren of the revolutionary generation looked back at hardy and persevering grandmothers and suffered, they feared, by the comparison. By the 1860s, hosts of fund-raising "Sanitary Fairs" celebrated the supposedly simple domesticity of the colonial kitchen and New England farmhouse life, reenacting apple parings, weddings, and bees. Women in mobcaps and long white aprons sat before spinning wheels, worked some knitting in front of huge faux hearths, or gathered around quilt frames. In an era of tension surrounding women's political rights, their access to education, and their roles in the workplace, coupled with unease over rapid immigration and class anxiety, white middle-class women created and then placed themselves within reassuring tableaux of female communality.[16]

While this sentimentalized domestic sphere—and the clothing and textiles produced there—became central to civic events, American public life gained a new feature in the last quarter of the nineteenth century with the introduction of Betsy Ross, the so-called seamstress who was said to have sewed the nation's first flag. The first printed reference to the Ross story appeared in the 15 March 1870 *Philadelphia Press.*[17] The legend spread throughout the United States in the last quarter of the nineteenth century, promoted vigorously among her descendants. Their interests are clear, but the story's warm reception is perhaps explained by women's struggle for suffrage, raging through those same years, since the Ross tale allowed Americans caught up in both Centennials and suffrage an opportunity to welcome a female character to the cast of the nation's origin story without challenging women's traditional relationship to the state. The Ross story suggested to Victorian Americans that knowledge of domestic skills answered an important need in Revolutionary America's social and political order, and that female patriotism was most appropriately expressed through household labors. In an era of gendered political tumult, that message comforted millions. After C. H. Weisgerber's popular painting "The Birth of Our Nation's Flag" (depicting a solemn George Washington, George Ross, and Robert Morris gathered in Ross's parlor, looking on as Betsy serenely stitches) was exhibited at the 1893 Columbian Exposition, interest in Ross revived, and a movement was launched to preserve the "American Flag House."[18]

Although Ross's work as seamstress was a crucial component of her characterization (she was an upholsterer, but this occupation held less emotional appeal), clothing production was not a large part of the Colonial Revival, although clothing was. Revivalists enjoyed dressing up in colonial costume, or at least what someone imagined colonial costume to be.[19] In Deerfield, the "Frary House," an eighteenth-century house restored by the Cambridge historian C. Alice Baker, opened in 1892 with a "colonial" ball. Town residents dug through their trunks and attics to find, or to cobble together, clothing from the wardrobes of their ancestors. New England archives teem with photographs of women in real eighteenth-century garments or fantasies of colonial costume, for pageants, parades, and private events. Descendants of Elizabeth Porter Phelps, like many of their privileged peers across the region, had photographs and even portraits taken in the clothing of their ancestors.

But few women active in the colonial revival took an interest in the intricacies of early clothing construction (though they could have; re-enactors today display a passionate interest in the smallest details of early clothing construction and design). Instead, what captured their interest were the sam-

Catherine Sargent Huntington wearing Elizabeth Pitkin Porter's wedding gown. PPHP. Courtesy of Amherst College Archives and Speial Collections.

Catherine Sargent Huntington (1887–1987) donned Porter's c. 1743 wedding gown for a Fourth of July costume party in the 1910s. In so doing, she joined other elite men and women who, at the turn of the century, found comfort and inspiration in the clothing of their ancestors as part of a larger sense of their role as descendents of the nation's founders. Arrested in 1927 for demonstrating in support of Sacco and Vanzetti outside Boston's State House, Huntington cited her ancient New England lineage in justification of her political activism: "When the liberties which my ancestors established are endangered . . . I consider it peculiarly my duty to protest." For Huntington and her peers, dressing in colonial clothing was not simply naïve, romantic indulgence but rather one way to embody their particular notion of heritage.

plers and crewelwork wrought by elite colonial women. In Boston, one of the first organized attempts to nurture and direct a general revival of early American crewelwork was the Needlework School of the Museum of Fine Arts.[20] Similar efforts sprung up in New York and Chicago. Among the most widely acclaimed groups to revive early needlework was the Deerfield Society for Blue and White Needlework. Founded in 1896 by two New York art students, Ellen Miller and Margaret Whiting, the society had its start when the two women were perusing pieces of early needlework preserved in Deerfield's Memorial Hall, the museum founded in the 1870s by George Sheldon and the Pocumtuck Valley Memorial Association to preserve and exhibit local heirlooms. The women observed the deteriorating condition of some of the antique crewelwork and attempted replicas, but, influenced by John Ruskin, William Morris, and the principles of the Aesthetic Movement, they quickly recognized an opportunity to create from these early examples new designs that conveyed the best of the colonial with a twist of the modern. Their Society of Blue and White Needlework, they hoped, in the tradition of Ruskin, "would be profitable materially and morally."[21]

Drawing on extant eighteenth-century needlework for their models (including that of the Hatfield gown maker Rebecca Dickinson) Miller and Whiting began designing and producing linen coverlets, bureau covers, curtains, bed hangings, and tablecloths, ornamented with designs wrought largely in indigo and inspired by examples culled from local attics and collections. Their enterprise quickly grew from four women to more than a dozen, and soon between twenty and thirty were employed in the production of domestic decorations from small table services to bed furnishings, screens, and door hangings. A parlor in the Miller home was dedicated to display and sales space, and the society attracted a thriving mail-order business as well.

Miller and Whiting set out to produce nothing but high-quality craftwork. They adopted a logo—a spinning wheel marked in the center with a *D*—affixing this symbol to a finished product only after it had been examined to ensure that it met their high standard of workmanship. And the society did produce truly spectacular pieces of needlework, many of which are now preserved in Deerfield's Memorial Hall Museum. In its day, their work sold in a range of values; at the upper end lay a fourteen-hundred-dollar tablecloth—a goodly sum today, and a fortune in 1910. The artistic achievement of Miller and Whiting as designers and the craft skill of the women whose work they oversaw are certainly impressive, as surviving examples make plain. The Society of Blue and White Needlework was awarded "master" status by the Boston Society of Arts and Crafts; members exhibited their

Margaret Whiting, drawing of Rebecca Dickinson's needlework, c. 1905. Courtesy of the Pocumtuck Valley Memorial Association, Memorial Hall Museum, Deerfield, Mass.

This sketch was drawn by Margaret Whiting (1860–1946), co-founder of the Deerfield Society of Blue and White Needlework. Society members both created original designs and adapted eighteenth- and nineteenth-century patterns. In this sketch, they adapted a new design from the wool-embroidered linen head cloth completed in 1765 by Hatfield, Mass., gownmaker Rebecca Dickinson (1738–1815). More than a century after Dickinson created the bed hangings on which this sketch is based (see plate 8), Whiting and co-founder Ellen Miller revived and reinterpreted her to appeal to turn-of-the-twentieth-century customers interested in the products of a thriving arts and crafts movement. The *D* in a flax wheel (at lower right corner and center) was the society's trademark.

work nationwide and earned medals for excellence at exhibitions like the 1915 International Panama-Pacific Exhibition and the Paris Exposition.[22]

Inspired by the past, Miller and Whiting were also instructed by the present. In the early years of the society, Whiting wrote to her friend Emily Green Balch, then professor of economics at Wellesley College: "The effort to establish an industry in Deerfield is leading Ellen Miller and myself a dog's life but . . . it is having some success, and we have a hope or two for its future. . . . There are seven women in what Ellen calls our 'Virtuous Sweatshop' every day."[23] Miller and Whiting controlled all aspects of production: they designed the patterns, assigned labor, chose exhibitions, supervised distribution, and set pay rates, twenty cents an hour for skilled labor. They assigned work to those women best suited to carry out a certain task or design element, and most finished products reflected this careful division of labor. Miller and Whiting also conducted time studies to determine the length of time a given element ought to require, and hence what a worker could hope to earn from her work.[24]

Some of the needlewomen of late-nineteenth-century Deerfield's revival were responding to a failing custom industry. The relationship between changes in the garment trades and the advent of the craft revivals was not merely reactive or symbolic. By the early twentieth century, custom shops had lost ground to vendors of ready-made clothes. Moreover, those not rendered jobless by the ready-made industry saw their daily wages drop precipitously. Dressmakers who in the 1850s had earned $1.33 a day by the 1860s earned just $.93. Over the next two decades that figure fell farther, bottoming out at just $.87. In the 1880s and 1890s the average daily wage climbed once more to over $1.00 a day, but it would never again reach its prewar level.[25] In Deerfield, women whose livelihoods once depended on the custom market turned to the craft revival to replace lost income. The dressmaker M. Anna Childs, for example, in 1901 earned $45 from the Society of Blue and White Needlework, representing some 225 hours of labor, and the seamstress Maria Stebbins earned $139 in that same year—the highest amount paid a single worker.[26] Since the society paid about $.22 an hour, Stebbins must have worked nearly seven hundred hours producing tablecloths and bed hangings for consumers of the craft revival. The revival of early American crewelwork helped Childs and Stebbins weather transformations in the garment industry that threatened the custom work that they practiced. The two women redirected their skills in clothes making to revival needlework, gladly embracing Miller and Whiting's "virtuous sweatshop."

The romantic revival of some forms of colonial needlework required that others, and especially the clothing-related chores that more accurately represent the work of eighteenth-century needles, be altered in collective historical imagination. As people gained other means by which to acquire clothing and perform needlework, they began to forget the huge amount of tedious sewing required to clothe entire households and the special skills required to create those suits, stays, and mantuas. In the age of "ready-to-wear," it was easy to romanticize (and conflate) preindustrial patterns of both cloth and clothing production, "especially as industrial progress was increasingly perceived to be a negative force."[27] Women employed in the making of garments were pushed aside in favor of hardy housewives entirely capable of providing for all of the needs, practical and aesthetic, of themselves and their families. Museums acquired spectacular examples of ornamental needlework, while the everyday wardrobes that occupied a large share of needlewomen's attention went largely unpreserved. As a result, Betty Foote's remarkable bed rug survives; none of the garments whose manufacture helped support herself and her family does.

In these same years, and not coincidentally, the ways in which these women entered the historical record were clouded by the haze of the colonial revival. For example, readers of George Sheldon's 1896 two-volume *History of Deerfield* found in it, among many other things, a brief panegyric to eighteenth-century goodwife Elizabeth Arms Field Wright. After the early death of her first husband, Ebenezer Field, Elizabeth Arms moved the few miles up to Northfield, where she earned her living by teaching children in her own home for twenty-two weeks a year, charging parents four pence each week. To supplement this income, Sheldon explains, Arms made "shirts for the Indians," at eight pence each, and sewed breeches for her brother-in-law, earning one shilling six pence a pair. Sheldon's account of Arms's labors does more than reveal the means by which she earned and disposed of her income; it also illuminates a perception that by the close of the nineteenth century had taken firm root. After her marriage to Azariah Wright, "with eight children, the youngest but a year old," Sheldon writes, Arms had "leisure to work at tailoring, as formerly; leisure to spin and weave tow cloth to be exchanged with the traders for crockery and a few luxuries," as well as, he adds, cash.[28] The pastoralization of housework that Jeanne Boydston has so deftly explicated, already under way not long after Arms's lifetime, permitted the late-nineteenth-century historian to perceive the eighteenth-century woman's work in clothing and textile production as "leisure," a perception that would endure among future generations of readers.[29]

To be sure, Arms did not confuse her labor with leisure; for Arms and women like her, the production of both clothing and textiles was serious business. The idea that respectable women should not perform artisanal work had been cultivated in a specific historical context, as male artisans sought to protect their interests by creating and enforcing gender ideologies that overturned generations of practice. They reserved craft skill and its privileges for men, while normalizing associations between women and unskilled work—powerful ideas that persist today. The notion that such women did not perform artisanal work was cultivated in another, specific historical context, as Victorians constructed a colonial past in which women's work was shielded from market forces. Women who acquired no formal training in the needle trades but possessed enough knowledge to work at the less demanding tasks that the trade involved are indeed among those "least susceptible to historical analysis," though they were found throughout every New England community, exchanging their time and labor with a needle for income and credit.[30] Those shirts Elizabeth Arms made "for the Indians" were not only trade goods on a tense international frontier; they were also early evidence of an industrious revolution, and those "few luxuries," heralds of revolutions in consumption to come.

WHAT IS added to our historical vision when we attempt to recover craft communities once familiar in early New England? A world of artisanal skill and pride, to be sure, along with a richer understanding of asymmetrical power relations, among women and between women and men, in early American households and communities, as well as new insight into early American labor and laborers more generally. To borrow an irresistible metaphor from Philip Zea, gender alone is not necessarily the best "seam to rip" when defining artisanal culture.[31] Artisanry and masculinity are not synonymous; family and craft identities are not oppositional. Although distinctions grounded in gender are crucial to understanding the full scope of artisanal culture, equally compelling are delineations related to the specific features of urban and rural settings, the size and character of local markets, sources of training and materials, population density, and a host of other factors. Rethinking the early American clothing trades in ways that encompass the larger scope of women's participation in them prompts us to reconsider how historical study might better accommodate the lives of everyday women in rural New England. Seeing artisanry as a relational quality that unfolds across communities of practice expands our view of early American craftwork in ways that include women as well as men, in rural as well as urban settings. At the same time, looking closely at women's work as it was embedded in the places they lived reminds us that communities in early America were as much about process as they were about place, that skill with a needle—like skills with a loom, wheel, or herb garden—both shaped and reflected relationships among New England women and their families. Gender and class, marriage and family, age and skill, all inflected women's work identities in complex and variable ways.

Women in the eighteenth-century Atlantic world had a variety of motives for seeking out wage-earning work, motives that need "wider historicisation"; while some historians have argued that women generally emphasized family responsibilities over economic opportunity, others have suggested that women sought to amplify their earnings to reach specific objectives, from household necessities to luxuries small and large.[32] The women whose work is considered here suggest a comparable range of objectives. Some girls and women were thrown into tailoring at the death of a father or husband; they sewed to keep food reliably on the table. Others, like Elizabeth Wright, worked to insure their family's access to everyday necessities as well as some occasional comforts. The tailoresses who worked toward their setting out were striving to acquire goods deemed necessary for their first home. And recall the gown maker Catherine King's effort to match her sister's refinement. Easter Newton and Tryphena Cooke sewed at least in part to help their families enlarge their own prospects as they built a home that would house a tavern. Other women obtained and deployed higher levels of skill to gain the whole of her livelihood. For Rebecca Dickinson, craftwork was her sole means of support and a resource that allowed her to make considered decisions about marriage and family. Tabitha Smith, Esther Wright, Catherine Phelps, and other married artisans contributed to their family's upkeep; however, without other evidence, we cannot know what kind of authority they wielded over these earnings within the family circle. Finally, though her work was unpaid, the contribution Elizabeth Phelps made to the creation of quilted petticoats was essential to her family's continuing prominence. All these aims and needs coexisted in the communities of early New England. Put another way, clothing production was a large arena in early America that witnessed a wide variety of objectives, opportunities, frustrations, and disappointments.

Any consideration of women and men in the marketplace requires an understanding of gender divisions of labor, among the most critical questions to confront historians of women, work, and labor in the past quarter-century. The men who worked as mantua makers in the first century of New England's settlement vanished from this trade as it became the province of women. Over time, women made inroads in the production of menswear, though these weakened as the commercial economy expanded in the nineteenth century. But women did not simply infiltrate occupations formerly practiced by men; along the way, they transformed them. Artisanal identity among European men was grounded in their status as heads of households; artisanal identity among women hinged on their sense of themselves as individuals in possession of craft skill. Men's artisanal culture flourished in the taverns frequented by tradesmen; Europe's craftswomen, Clare Crowston shows, saw piety and industry as central to their own, distinct culture.[33]

How these developments affected trades on this side of the Atlantic is less well understood. Not until the emergence of organized labor around the turn of the nineteenth century, and particularly of journeymen tailors objecting to the use of cheap female labor, do we have substantial bodies of evidence that articulate similar beliefs and values about women's appropriate role in the trades.[34] During the late seventeenth century and throughout the eighteenth, European women on both sides of the Atlantic reconfigured economic and cultural constructions to create new places for themselves in the production of fitted apparel. As Europe's North American communities gained momentum, men and women in the colonial clothing trades participated in that long and complex renegotiation of gender roles that involved artisanal identities for women that both conformed to and departed from those of their husbands, fathers, and sons. By the middle decades of the eighteenth century, those patterns and beliefs had been transformed once more as the exigencies of colonial life inflected European practices in distinct ways. In the absence of guilds, New England clothes makers experienced these changes as individuals as well as members and heads of households, rather than as mediated by a corporate association that controlled access to skill. Particularly in rural areas, local markets in agricultural economies governed all artisanal identity; craftwork among both men and women was usually one of several strategies embraced by households also engaged in farming. Clothes makers, whether male or female, considered themselves and each other skilled artisans whose patterns of work, though responsive to changing assumptions about gender, were in many ways similar to those of rural cabinetmakers, blacksmiths, and other workers in occupations primarily practiced by men. Close investigation of female needleworkers challenges traditional depictions of early American artisanry as a male preserve, since these women recognized in their craft the same range of tasks, skills, and practitioners, from the unskilled to the specialist, found in more commonly studied trades.

Looking closely at craftwork in occupations predominantly practiced by women accomplishes more than merely including women in an arena that has often appeared to exclude them. It helps trouble the categories of artisanry more generally by calling into question the hallmarks traditionally associated with artisanal work. The concept of artisanry itself has become so loaded that it obscures as much as it reveals. Several recent works have suggested that, to date, explorations of craftwork have been too narrowly construed. Christine Daniels and Wendy Gamber, for example, in very different studies, critique the "new labor history" for embracing tradition-bound definitions of artisanry.[35] As Gamber suggests, "despite abundant evidence to the contrary, . . . scholars have generally assumed that all artisans were men"; the trouble, she suggests, is that historians have attached qualities to "artisanal" life that necessarily exclude women altogether. "Women had no place in the male artisanal world so skillfully reconstructed by practitioners of the 'new' labor history for as females they were excluded from this political and cultural milieu. As far as we can tell, craftswomen failed to attend (nor, one suspects, were they invited to) the dramatic parades, political debates, and rowdy entertainments that helped define that work, and their absence from those arenas has rendered them invisible to subsequent historians." Daniels observes that the "outpouring of books and essays on craftsmen and their culture" reveals "gaps" and "untested assumptions" emphasizing the experience of urban craftsmen with the means to own their own shops and tools at the expense of a larger world of urban and rural artisans whose access to capital varied widely and whose work was affected by the size and sort of the markets they were able to serve. Explorations of artisanal lives that imagine mainly urban, politically active men necessarily overlook the broader contours of early American crafts, which involved men and women in a variety of economic, social, familial, geographic, and political settings.

Enlarging our understanding of artisanal practice also helps us rethink the multiple ways that skill could be acquired and defined in early America. Although hagiographical celebrations of individual craftsmen have largely been set aside, remnants of that approach persist in studies that emphasize linear relationships between masters and apprentices, when in fact most early American craft work was a necessarily collective enterprise carried out in communities of practice. Exchanging models of craft knowledge as specialized information transferred neatly from experts to novices for another in which aspiring artisans cultivate special abilities not widely shared in their communities, and so assume gradually larger roles in communities of practitioners, enables us to reconceptualize historical understanding of what constitutes artisanal labor.

A second set of questions shifts our attention from relations between men and women, within and across households and communities, to relations among different kinds of women in those communities. The pathbreaking work of Laurel Thatcher Ulrich on the "female economy" of early New England—in which women participated in economic networks that intersected with, though remained separate from, those of men—continues to advance significantly our understanding of women and work, their roles in the preindustrial economy, the sexual division of labor, and the nature of men's and women's "spheres" in early America and has shown how women's work for the market and the household was not necessarily markedly different.[36] Yet while that scholarship has amplified and complicated our picture of eighteenth-century rural life, our understanding is not yet complete. Ulrich's masterful explication of Martha Ballard's diary, for example, suggests that networks of exchange in Hallowell, Maine, obscured differences among women. As Ulrich puts it, "there is a consistent leveling in Martha's references to her female neighbors, a blurring of social rank, that contrasts with her usual manner of describing men."[37] Drawing out her metaphor of the loom's web, she posits that while "economic and social differences might divide a community, the unseen acts of women wove it together."[38] New research continues to gauge how men and women throughout Britain's North American colonies may have experienced the interlocking developments we now see in terms of consumer and industrial revolutions. Adrienne Hood in her study of artisanal weaving in southeastern Pennsylvania reminds us that the path by which cloth production industrialized in New England was by no means normative; at the same time, this study joins others that seek to show how, even within the region, the advance of the market affected different communities in very different ways.[39] Needlework in the vibrant female economy of Hadley, Massachusetts—a century older than Hallowell's by the Revolutionary era—highlights unequal relations among women, even as it brought them into sometimes close association. The production of clothing was complicated by differences in social rank, community cultures, and other sources of livelihood, cautioning us not to generalize too soon about the character of a "female economy."

A host of other factors influenced women's participation in local, regional, and national economies, patterns of women's work encompassing a wide variety of relationships and responding to a host of variables. Acknowledging women's work in clothing production necessitates a reevaluation of traditional interpretations of an important sector of a colonial economy that comprised both male and female artisans. Recognizing needlework as a female-dominated craft raises critical questions about women's place in the much-discussed expanding marketplace of eighteenth-century New England. We know, for example, that in the systems of local interdependence that sustained rural communities, men engaged in cooperative work with relatives, friends, and neighbors to accomplish tasks and to obtain goods, though at the same time they embraced a variety of market alternatives with which to obtain needed goods and labor. When examining early American women's work, historians have focused on the similarly communal aspects of that labor but have largely overlooked the market alternatives that women likewise used.

While women's work in the production and maintenance of clothing did require a great deal of collaboration and cooperation, it also required elaborate hierarchies, grounded in economic and social status to be sure, as well as skill, age, and, even in rural western New England, race. To borrow a notion from Evelyn Glenn, viewing any form of labor only in terms of gender extracts gender from its context, obscuring other "interacting systems of power." Glenn is writing here specifically about race, although her admonition holds more broadly, too.[40] Despite the relative homogeneity of the New England countryside, the need to produce, acquire, and maintain clothing created opportunities for women to interact as artisans, as consumers, as employers, and as employees, at different ages, skill levels, and points in their lives. The very appearance of homogeneity points up the real complexity of these relationships, in that it masked, and continues to mask, intricate and asymmetrical power relations among women. Examinations of differences among women, as part of a larger effort to deepen understanding of our multicultural past, has been an important project in recent years. Still, we cannot overlook, or underestimate, the complex power relationships that also exist among women who at first glance look very similar, and the multiple ways in which class and culture have intersected to shape women's working lives, sometimes in unexpected places.

Various forms of needlework continue to bring women together and set them apart. A kit from which women can reproduce the very piece of schoolgirl embroidery—the "Reclining Shepardess"—wrought by the eighteenth-century gentlewoman Esther Stoddard, is commercially available. The complete kit costs no less than two hundred dollars; the worked piece, when framed and displayed, continues to be, as it once was for the Stoddards, a sign of economic privilege and leisure. Home sewing, too, has become largely the province of privileged consumers. The core audience for home-sewing equipment and periodicals are "well-educated working women aged 25 to 44 who enjoy making high-quality fashionable clothes in their limited leisure time"; as one study reported, "the more highly educated the woman, the more likely she is to sew: Now that the American homemaker has gone to work, the only people who sew are those who like to."[41]

Of course, the vast majority of women who are sewing on any given day in the United States, or for Americans, are not "those who like to" but women crowded into sweatshops both here and abroad. Since the 1960s, globalizing markets have brought massive reorganization to the garment industry. Early in the twentieth century, manufacturers moved production first out of the Northeast and into the South, and then out of the South and abroad, outsourcing production to subcontractors in Central American nations such as Honduras, Nicaragua, and El Salvador, and to Asian competitors in Bangladesh, Malaysia, and Singapore.[42] Americans consume billions of dollars' worth of apparel each year from manufacturers in China, Hong Kong, and Mexico, and millions of dollars' worth from India, Indonesia, the Philippines, South Korea, Sri Lanka, Taiwan, Thailand, Costa Rica, and Haiti. In recent years hourly wages in those nations have ranged from $4.51 in Hong Kong to $.62 in the Philippines.[43] The exploitative conditions under which so many laborers work have been of increasing concern to consumers worldwide, as images of women and children bent over machines in crowded, unsafe workplaces producing high-profile consumer goods have drawn media attention and prompted boycotts.

Sweatshops also continue to flourish in the United States. When inspectors of the California Department of Industrial Relations and the U.S. Department of Labor in August 1995 raided an apartment complex in El Monte, California, and discovered there seventy-two illegal Thai immigrants, mostly women, captive and sewing under appalling conditions, they drew the attention of a shocked American public to the persistence of exploitative labor practices in the domestic clothing industry.[44] In the decade that has followed, various celebrities—most famously Kathie Lee Gifford—were accused of endorsing clothing lines made with sweated labor, heightening public and corporate consciousness on these issues, while a number of U.S. cities and states passed legislation aimed at eliminating sweated labor. California, Maine, New Jersey, and Pennsylvania have established no-sweat standards for the procurement of state clothing (such as uniforms), while the municipalities of San Francisco and Los Angeles in California; Milwaukee and Madison, Wisconsin; Newark, New Jersey; and Albuquerque, New Mexico, have pledged not to purchased products of sweated labor.[45] Nevertheless, to cite just one example, the Union of Needle Trades and Industrial Textile Employees found that 75 percent of all apparel manufacturing firms in New York City—the center of the U.S. apparel industry, encompassing thousands of workers—met the definition of sweatshops.[46]

That certain kinds of needlework are associated in popular imagination with advantaged white women, while other kinds lie outside public definitions of sewing, raises important questions about how we understand needlework, and needleworkers, in the present and in the past. Myths, the novelist Jeanette Winterson writes, "explain the universe while allowing the universe to go on being unexplained."[47] Much more has been written about "reshaping the past to persuade the present" than can or need be recounted here.[48] Most important for my purposes is that, to thrive, myths must affirm ideas that are of continuing value to society.[49] Images of early American women gathered around a quilt frame, or nestled by the hearth, constructing clothing for loved ones, reaffirm notions of women's role in creating the home as haven, no small thing when women's roles in the workplace have been the source of so much political, cultural, economic, and international tension.

Our contemporary dependence on distant laborers for the construction of our clothing today is very different from the relationships observed in the 1780s by the members of the Hartford Ladies Association, but their understanding of themselves as intimately tied to laborers across town and around the globe is as appropriate today as it was then. The world of needleworkers captured within the account books, letters, and journals of Connecticut Valley families is characterized by a strong sense of interconnectedness alongside asymmetry. The lives and fortunes of women, whatever their economic and social position, were bound up with those of their neighbors, attached by enduring ties of neighborhood and kinship.[50] New relationships sprang from the old and persisted over generations. Consumers contemplated the effect of specific acts of clothing acquisition on producers, whether they were the daughters of indebted families across town or the makers of "gewgaws and frippery" abroad. Craftswomen and clients, employers and employees, consumers and producers recognized the uneven scaffolds on which their relationships rested, sustaining a "precarious interlocking equilibrium."[51] In the give and take of rural exchange, New England needleworkers, as much as cabinetmakers, housewrights, and headstone carvers, created and sustained communities of commerce imperative to the continued health of that equilibrium, to systems as important to continuity and change in the social, economic, and cultural order as that which existed in the larger commercial world.

Alice Morse Earle recalled lovingly the lives of some of those early American women and the evidence they have left behind:

> Old letters and old garments bring us in close touch with the past; there is in them a lingering presence, a very essence of life. Here the hand pressed that held the pen; here it lingered in dainty stitches. . . . There still clings to the firm all-wool stuff, unfaded hand-stamped calico, the lustrous homespun linen, something of the vitality of the enduring women who raised the wool, the cotton, the flax, even the silk; who prepared each for the wheel by many exhausting labors; who spun the yarn and thread, and wove the warp and woof; who bleached and dyed; who cut and sewed these ancient garments. All these honest stuffs, with their quaint fashionings, render them a true expres-

sion of old-time life; and their impalpable and finer beauty through sentiment puts me truly in touch with the life of my forbears.[52]

What Earle missed here is that the hand that composed those letters was not necessarily the one that created those garments. To be sure, there is in both a "lingering presence," although old letters and old garments are two very different sorts of sources, and they help us remember different sorts of women. Ever since Anne Dudley Bradstreet in 1650 dismissed "each carping tongue / who says my hand a needle better fits," we have naturally linked pens and needles, and rightly so; the two instruments were clearly linked in the minds of educated women. As Elizabeth Porter's cousin Sarah Hillhouse wrote her daughter, "Could you see or know the quantity of work before me you would be astonish'd that I should leave it for the pen, [nevertheless] for a few hours I lay by the needle for the quill."[53] However, some care must also be taken to recognize those women who had less need for pens, and whose livelihood depended on their needles. Cracks in the unified icon of the goodwife of popular historical imagination have begun to appear, and scholars of women's history, labor history, and early America have nearly dismantled her altogether, but more work is required before we can finally discard that picture in favor of another more encompassing one. Extending our view of quilting, for example, to laboring women employed in eighteenth-century London warehouses as well as their consumers on the western fringe of the British empire, rural women who quilted for themselves, and the women whose labor in other rooms within and beyond the house made quilting possible helps us to see quilts as the products of intersecting revolutions in manufacturing, in consumption, and in social and labor relations. Quilting can remain an effective metaphor for interconnectedess among women, if we can overcome the implication that that it comes on even footing.[54] Radka Donnell is persuasive when she observes that metaphors of the seam most appropriately signify connections grounded in tension.[55] Every stitch reflects tensions—between producers and consumers, employers and employees, men and women, clients and craftswomen.

In 1949, Elizabeth Phelps's descendant James Lincoln Huntington, like Alice Morse Earle, sensed ghosts of the colonial past. Huntington recorded that, every once in a while, the faint sound of a spinning wheel had been heard coming from the house's attic. But the soft hum of an ethereal wheel is not necessary to help us remember the dozens of working women who passed through the halls of Forty Acres.[56] The halls themselves remind us, as do the shears, needles, and thimbles, the old letters and old garments they left behind. Through them we remember the past and present tensions that together shape our communities. We are reminded of the full interconnectedness of our lives, how we too are closely involved with our neighbors' lives and fortunes, even when those neighbors are a continent away. Women's economic culture has long encompassed relationships both personal and commercial, social and professional. Over the last half of the eighteenth century the shapes that those relationships assumed, and the degree to which they intertwined, supported, competed with, undercut, or became disentangled from one another, shifted along with the changing economic, social, and cultural landscapes. In the end, new systems took root that altered permanently the ways in which rural New England women encountered one another, in a marketplace that had redefined the work they did in their own homes and reorganized the work that they did in and for the homes of others. Sewing lay at the center of these reconfigurations. Close examination of early American women's needlework—part, rightly said, of nearly every woman's life—reveals how these women thought about their work and how they thought about their world.

Abbreviations

Repositories

CHS	Connecticut Historical Society, Hartford, Connecticut
CSL	Connecticut State Library, Hartford, Connecticut
FL	Forbes Library, Northampton, Massachusetts
HCMRP	Hampshire County [Massachusetts] Registry of Probate
HHS	Hadley Historical Society, Hadley, Massachusetts
HN	Historic Northampton, Northampton, Massachusetts
JDC	Joseph Downs Collection of Manuscripts and Printed Ephemera, Henry Francis du Pont Winterthur Museum Library, Winterthur, Delaware.
MHS	Massachusetts Historical Society, Boston, Massachusetts
PPHP	Porter Phelps Huntington Papers, Archives and Special Collection, Amherst College, Amherst, Massachusetts*
PVMA	Pocumtuck Valley Memorial Association, Deerfield, Massachusetts
VHS	Vermont Historical Society, Montpelier, Vermont.

Publications

CC	*Connecticut Courant*
HG	*Hampshire Gazette*

Proper Names

TNC	Tryphena Newton Cooke
EFN	Elizabeth "Easter" Fairchild Newton
CPP	Catherine Phelps Parsons
EPP	Elizabeth Porter Phelps
EWPH	Elizabeth Whiting Phelps Huntington
RD	Rebecca Dickinson

* Most references to this collection in the notes are to letters between Elizabeth Porter Phelps and her daughter, Elizabeth "Betsy" Whiting Phelps Huntington, all housed in boxes 5 and 13 and filed chronologically. Citations to the PPHP materials assume these locations unless materials from elsewhere in the collection are cited, in which case box and folder numbers are provided as well. The full Finding Aid is available online at http://www.amherst.edu/library/archives/index.html.

Notes

Introduction. Early American Artisanry: Why Gender Matters

1. Scot M. Guenter, *The American Flag, 1777–1924: Cultural Shifts from Creation to Commodification* (London: Associated University Presses, 1990), 101–3; Karol Ann Marling, *George Washington Slept Here: Colonial Revivals and American Culture, 1876–1986* (Cambridge: Harvard University Press, 1988), 13–20; David Hackett Fischer, *Liberty and Freedom: A Visual History of America's Founding Ideas* (New York: Oxford University Press, 2005), 158–62. On the evolution of the Ross legend, see Allan E. Peterson, "Cherished and Ignored: A Cultural History of Betsy Ross" (master's thesis, San Diego State University, 2001).

2. William Timmins, *Betsy Ross: The Griscom Legacy* (Woodstown, N.J.: Salem County Cultural and Heritage Commission, 1983), 125–58, esp. 142–43.

3. Ken Ames, *Death in the Dining Room and Other Tales of Victorian Culture* (Philadelphia: Temple University Press, 1992).

4. Important work that has challenged notions of self-sufficiency includes Joan Jensen, *Loosening the Bonds: Mid-Atlantic Farm Women, 1750–1850* (New Haven: Yale University Press, 1986); Carole Shammus, "How Self-Sufficient Was Early America?" *Journal of Interdisciplinary History* 13, no. 2 (1982): 247–72; Adrienne D. Hood, *The Weaver's Craft: Cloth, Commerce, and Industry in Early Pennsylvania* (Philadelphia: University of Pennsylvania Press, 2003).

5. Joy Parr, "Gender History and Historical Practice," *Canadian Historical Review* 76 (1995): 354–76, esp. 367; Steven Maynard, "Rough Work and Rugged Men: The Social Construction of Masculinity in Working-Class History, *Labour/Le Travail* 23 (1989): 159–69.

6. Harry R. Reubenstein, "With Hammer in Hand: Working-Class Occupational Portraits," in *American Artisans: Crafting Social Identity, 1750–1850*, ed. Howard B. Rock, Paul A. Gilje, and Robert Asher (Baltimore: Johns Hopkins University Press, 1995), 184.

7. Lisa Lubow, "Artisans in Transition: Early Capitalist Development and the Carpenters of Boston, 1787–1837" (Ph.D. diss., University of California at Los Angeles, 1987), xiii, 593. See also Joshua R. Greenberg, "Advocating 'the Man': Masculinity, Organized Labor, and the Market Revolution in New York, 1800–1840" (Ph.d. diss., American University, 2003). Of course, the increasingly masculine resonance of artisanal trades was also bound up in changing gender conventions of those decades; especially relevant here is Catherine E. Kelly, *In the New England Fashion: Reshaping Women's Lives in the Nineteenth Century* (Ithaca: Cornell University Press, 1999).

8. Laurel Thatcher Ulrich, "Martha Ballard and Her Girls: Women's Work in Eighteenth-Century Maine," in *Work and Labor in Early America*, ed. Stephen Innes (Chapel Hill: University of North Carolina Press for the Institute of Early American History and Culture, 1988), 71.

9. The literature here is extensive. Among the most useful works are Judith M. Bennett, " 'History That Stands Still': Women's Work in the European Past," *Feminist Studies* 14, no. 2 (1988): 269–83; Judith G. Coffin, "Gender and the Guild Order: The Garment Trades in Eighteenth-Century Paris," *Journal of Economic History* 54 (1994): 768–93; Natalie Zemon Davis, "Women in the Crafts in Sixteenth-Century Lyon," in *Women and Work in Preindustrial Europe,* ed. Barbara Hanawalt, 167–97 (Bloomington: Indiana University Press, 1986); Pamela Sharpe, *Adapting to Capitalism: Working Women in the English Economy, 1700–1850* (London: Macmillan, 1996). Katrina Honeyman and Jordan Goodman observe the longstanding effort among women's historians to understand wage disparities, past and present, in "Women's Work, Gender Conflict, and Labour Markets in Europe, 1500–1900, *Economic History Review,* n.s., 44 (1991): 608–28.

10. Honeyman and Goodman, "Women's Work," 608.

11. Gloria Main, "Gender, Work, and Wages in Colonial New England," *William and Mary Quarterly* 51 (1994): 39–66; Laurel Thatcher Ulrich, *The Age of Homespun: Objects and Stories in the Creation of an American Myth* (New York: Knopf, 2001), and "Wheels, Looms, and the Gender Division of Labor in Eighteenth-Century New England," *William and Mary Quarterly,* 3rd ser., 55 (1998): 3–38; Winifred Barr Rothenberg, *From Market-Places to a Market Economy: The Transformation of Rural Massachusetts, 1750–1850* (Chicago: University of Chicago Press, 1992), and "The Emergence of Farm Labor Markets and the Transformation of the Rural Economy: Massachusetts, 1750–1855," *Journal of Economic History* 48 (1988): 537–66.

12. See, e.g., Rebecca J. Tannenbaum, *The Healer's Calling: Women and Medicine in Early New England* (Ithaca: Cornell University Press, 2002); Laurel Thatcher Ulrich, *A Midwife's Tale: The Life of Martha Ballard, Based on Her Diary, 1785–1812* (New York: Alfred A. Knopf, 1990), and "Wheels, Looms"; Hood, *Weaver's Craft;* Martin Breugal, "Work, Gender, and Authority on the Farm: The Hudson Valley Countryside, 1790s–1850s," *Agricultural History* 76, no. 1 (2002): 1–27; Jensen, *Loosening the Bonds;* Anne Yentsch, "Engendering Visible and Invisible Ceramic Artifacts, Especially Dairy Vessels," *Historical Archaeology* 25, no. 4 (1991): 132–55; Mary H. Blewett, "Work, Gender, and the Artisan Tradition in New England Shoemaking, 1780–1860," *Journal of Social History* 17, no. 2 (1983): 221–48; JoAnn Preston, "Domestic Ideology, School Reformers, and Female Teachers: School Teaching Becomes Women's Work in 19th-Century New England," *New England Quarterly* 66 (1993): 531–661; Joel Perlman, Silvana R Siddali and Keith Whitescarver, "Literacy, Schooling, and Teaching among New England Women, 1730–1820," *History of Education Quarterly* 37, no. 2 (1997): 117–39.

13. See Richard Bushman, "Markets and Composite Farms in Early America," *William and Mary Quarterly* 55 (1998): 364.

14. Judith M. Bennett, *Ale, Beer, and Brewsters in England: Women's Work in a Changing World, 1300–1600* (New York: Oxford University Press, 1996); Katrina Honeyman, *Women, Gender, and Industrialisation in England, 1700–1870* (New York: St. Martin's Press, 2000); Martha C. Howell, "Women, the Family Economy, and the Structure of Market Production in Cities of Northern Europe during the Late Middle Ages," in Hanawalt, *Women and Work,* 198–222; Margaret R. Hunt, *The Middling Sort: Commerce, Gender, and the Family in England, 1680–1780* (Berkeley: University of California Press, 1996); Elizabeth Sanderson, *Women and Work in Eighteenth-Century Edinburgh* (New York: St. Martin's Press, 1996); Sharpe, *Adapting to Capitalism,* and the essays collected in Pamela Sharpe, ed., *Women's Work: The English Experience, 1650–1914* (London: Arnold,

1998); K. D. M. Snell, *Annals of the Labouring Poor: Social Change and Agrarian England, 1660–1900* (New York: Cambridge University Press, 1986); Jan de Vries, "Between Purchasing Power and the World of Goods: Understanding the Household Economy in Early Modern Europe," in *Consumption and the World of Goods,* ed. John Brewer and Roy Porter, 85–132 (New York: Routledge, 1993).

15. There is a thriving literature on women in artisanal crafts in other parts of the early modern Atlantic world. Some notable contributions that are particularly relevant here include Ilana Krausman Ben-Amos, "Women Apprentices in the Trades and Crafts of Early Modern Bristol," *Continuity and Change* 6, no. 2 (1991): 227–52; Anne Buck, "Mantua-makers and Milliners: Women Making and Selling Clothes in Eighteenth-Century Bedfordshire," *Publications of the Bedfordshire Historical Society* 72 (1993): 142–55; Judith Coffin, *The Politics of Women's Work: The Paris Garment Trades, 1750–1915* (Princeton: Princeton University Press, 1996), and "Gender and the Guild Order"; Clare Haru Crowston, *Fabricating Women: The Seamstresses of Old Regime France, 1675–1791* (Durham, N.C.: Duke University Press, 2001); Natalie Zemon Davis, "Women in the Crafts in Sixteenth-Century Lyon," in Hanawalt, *Women and Work,* 167–97; Madeline Ginsburg, "The Tailoring and Dressmaking Trades, 1700–1850," *Costume* 6 (1972): 64–71; Gay L. Gullickson, *Spinners and Weavers of Auffay: Rural Industry and the Sexual Division of Labor in a French Village, 1750–1850* (New York: Cambridge University Press, 1986); Jennifer Jones, "Coquettes and Grisettes: Women Buying and Selling in Ancien Regime Paris," in *The Sex of Things: Gender and Consumption in Historical Perspective,* ed. Victoria de Grazia (Berkeley: University of California Press, 1996); Beverly Lemire, "Redressing the History of the Clothing Trade in England: Ready-Made Clothing, Guilds, and Women Workers, 1650–1800," *Dress* 21 (1994): 61–74, " 'In the Hands of Work Women': English Markets, Cheap Clothing, and Female Labour, 1650–1800," *Costume* 33 (1999): 23–35, and *Dress, Culture and Commerce : The English Clothing Trade before the Factory, 1660–1800* (New York : St. Martin's Press, 1997); Nancy Lynne Locklin, "Women in Early Modern Brittany: Rethinking Work and Identity in the Traditional Economy" (Ph.D. diss., Emory University, 2000); Elizabeth Musgrave, "Women and the Craft Guilds in Eighteenth-Century Nantes," in *The Artisan and the European Town, 1500–1900,* ed. Geoffrey Crossick, 151–71 (Aldershot: Ashgate, 1997); Jean H. Quataert, "The Shaping of Women's Work in Manufacturing: Guilds, Households, and the State in Central Europe, 1648–1870," *American Historical Review* 90 (1985): 1122–48; Elizabeth Sanderson, " 'The New Dresses': A Look at How Mantua Making Became Established in Scotland," *Costume* 35 (2001): 14–23; Margaret Spufford, *The Great Reclothing of Rural England: Petty Chapmen and Their Wares in the Seventeenth Century* (Ronceverte, W.V.: Hambledon Press, 1985); Merry Wiesner, "Spinsters and Seamstresses: Women in Cloth and Clothing Production," in *Rewriting the Renaissance: The Discourses of Sexual Difference in Early Modern Europe,* ed. Margaret W. Ferguson, Maureen Quilligan, and Nancy J. Vickers, 191–205 (Chicago: Chicago University Press, 1986).

16. Linda Baumgarten, *Eighteenth-Century Clothing at Williamsburg* (Williamsburg, Va.: Colonial Williamsburg Foundation, 1986), *What Clothes Reveal: The Language of Clothing in Colonial and Federal America* (Williamsburg, Va.: Colonial Williamsburg Foundation, 2002), and, with John Watson and Florine Carr, *Costume Close-Up: Clothing Construction and Pattern* (Williamsburg, Va.: Colonial Williamsburg Foundation, 1999); Claudia B. Kidwell and Margaret C. Christman, *Suiting Everyone: The Democratization of Clothing in America* (Washington, D.C.: Published for the National Museum of

History and Technology by the Smithsonian Institution Press, 1974); Nancy E. Rexford, *Women's Clothing in America, 1795–1930* (New York: Holmes and Meier, 1994) and *Women's Shoes in America, 1795–1930* (Kent, Ohio: Kent State University Press, 2000); Aileen Ribeiro, *The Art of Dress: Fashion in England and France, 1750 to 1820* (New Haven: Yale University Press, 1995), and *Dress in Eighteenth-Century Europe, 1715–1789* (New York: Holmes & Meier, 1985, ca. 1984).

17. See Marla R. Miller, "Dressmaking as a Trade for Women: Recovering a Lost Art(insanry)," in *A Separate Sphere: Dressmakers in Cincinnati's Golden Age, 1877–1922*, ed. Cynthia Amnéus, 1–6 (Cincinnati: Cincinnati Museum of Art, 2003).

18. Polly L'Hommedieu Lathrop account book (ca. 1803–17), CHS.

19. Main, "Gender, Work, and Wages in Colonial New England," 46. Laurel Thatcher Ulrich also writes "Judging only from the account books, one might conclude that most married women were seldom involved in trade even on the village level," though "account books represent but one strand of the village economy;" see *Good Wives: Image and Reality in Northern New England, 1650–1750* (New York: Knopf, 1980), 45.

20. George Sheldon, *History of Deerfield, Massachusetts*, 2 vols. (Greenfield, Mass.: Press of E. A. Hall and Co., 1895–96), 2:111.

21. Patricia Cline Cohen suggests that women in the eighteenth century were indeed less numerate than men, but given the general paucity of mathematical training, "relatively few people noticed." Cohen, "Reckoning with Commerce: Numeracy in Eighteenth-Century America," in *Consumption and the World of Goods*, ed. John Brewer and Roy Porter (New York: Routledge, 1993), 331.

22. Solomon Wright account book (1787–1810), HN.

23. Reuban and Lydia Duncan Champion ledger (1753–77), Champion-Stebbins Papers, Family Account Books, Special Collections and Archives, W. E. B. Du Bois Library, University of Massachusetts Amherst. That Reuban began the account book in 1753, at the time of his marriage to Lydia Duncan, also hints at the book's larger purpose.

24. Sylvester Judd, "Miscellaneous," 14:244, FL.

25. Nathaniel Phelps account book (1730–43), PVMA.

26. Joseph and Submit Williams account book (1802–41), Williamsburg Historical Society, Williamsburg, Mass., described in Christopher Clark, *The Roots of Rural Capitalism: Western Massachusetts, 1780–1860* (Ithaca: Cornell University Press, 1990), 98. An example of Williams's needlework survives in the collections of the Society for the Preservation of New England Antiquities, now known as Historic New England; my thanks to costume specialist Lynne Z. Bassett for bringing this to my attention.

27. The Cooke accounts are preserved in the collections of HHS.

28. On Solomon Cooke as an innkeeper, see, for example, the Massachusetts Historical Commission cultural resource survey form for the house today at 1 West Street in Hadley. Elizabeth Newton's annual petitions for a tavern license can be found in the Hampshire County Court Records, Clerk of the [Hampshire County] Superior Court's Office, Northampton, Mass. and are discussed in Chapter Four.

29. Toni Morrison, "The Site of Memory," in *Out There: Marginalization and Contemporary Cultures* (New York: The New Museum of Contemporary Art, 1990): 302. For a less metaphorical investigation of the archaeology of needlework, see Mary C. Beaudry, *Findings: The Material Culture of Needlework and Sewing* (New Haven: Yale University Press, 2006).

30. Sylvester Judd, *History of Hadley* (Springfield, Mass.: H. R. Huntting and Co., 1905), 380; See also James Russell Trumbull, *History of Northampton, Massachusetts, from its founding in 1654,* 2 vols. (Northampton: Press of the Gazette Printing Co., 1898–1902), 2:11. William N. Hosley Jr. discusses the Connecticut River Valley as a subregion with its own distinct culture in the introduction to *The Great River: Art and Society of the Connecticut Valley, 1635–1820* (Hartford: Wadsworth Atheneum, 1985), xiii–xiv.

31. Jay Mack Holbrook, *Vermont 1771 Census* (Oxford, Mass.: Holbrook Research Institute, 1982), ii.

32. Thomas R. Lewis, "The Landscape and Environment of the Connecticut River Valley," in Hosley, *Great River,* 3–15.

33. Joseph Haynes interleaved almanac, 1762, n.p., MHS.

34. Lewis, "Landscape and Environment of the Connecticut River Valley," 11.

35. Ellsworth Grant and Marie Grant, *The City of Hartford, 1784–1984: An Illustrated History* (Hartford: CHS, 1986), 8.

36. J. Hammond Trumbull, ed., *Memorial History of Hartford County, Connecticut, 1633–1884,* 2 vols. (Boston: Edward L. Osgood, 1886), 1:598.

37. Sarah Pitkin to Frances Pitkin, 10 December 1812, Ms. 69985, CHS.

38. Stephen Jay Gould, "The Creation Myths of Cooperstown; or, Why the Cardiff Giants Are an Unbeatable and Appropriately Named Team," *Natural History,* November 1989, 14.

39. See, for example, Carol Shammas, "Early American Women and Control over Property," in *Women in the Age of the American Revolution,* ed. Ronald Hoffman and Peter Albert, 134–54 (Charlottesville: University of Virginia Press, 1989); Bushman, "Markets and Composite Farms," 351–74.

40. There is very little scholarship on eighteenth-century New England milliners. Patricia Cleary's excellent biography of a Boston shopkeeper, *Elizabeth Murray: A Woman's Pursuit of Independence in Eighteenth-Century America* (Amherst: University of Massachusetts Press, 2000), touches on eighteenth-century milliners in that city; see also her "She-Merchants of Colonial America: Women and Commerce on the Eve of the Revolution" (Ph.D. diss., Northwestern University, 1989). For excellent recent work on milliners in the nineteenth century, see Glendyne Wergland, "Designing Women: Massachusetts Milliners in the Nineteenth Century," in *Textiles in Early New England: Design, Production, and Consumption,* Proceedings of the 1997 Dublin Seminar for New England Folklife, ed. Peter Benes, 203–21 (Boston: Boston University, 1999); Melinda Talbot, "Mary Anne Warriner, Rhode Island Milliner," in *Textiles in New England II: Four Centuries of Material Life,* Proceedings of the 1999 Dublin Seminar for New England Folklife, ed. Peter Benes, 69–83 (Boston: Boston University, 2001). Also critically important, though it takes up a later period, is Wendy Gamber, *Female Economy: The Millinery and Dressmaking Trades, 1860–1930* (Urbana: University of Illinois Press, 1997). See also Christina Bates, "Women's Hats and the Millinery Trade, 1840–1940: An Annotated Bibliography," *Dress* 27 (2000): 49–58. For a rare look at American women's work producing one category of a milliner's typical goods, see Marta Cotterell Raffel, *The Laces of Ipswich: The Art and Economics of an Early American Industry, 1750–1840* (Hanover, N.H.: University Press of New England, 2003).

41. EPP's memorandum book (referred to by other historians as her diary, though "memorandum book" is her own term and clarifies the record's purpose), extending from 1766 to 1812, is in PPHP, box 7 (with typescripts and other copies in boxes 8 and 9). Most

of EPP's record (1766–1805) has been published in segments in the *New England Historical and Genealogical Register,* 118–22 (January 1964–October 1968). Citations provide the date of the relevant entries. Laurel Thatcher Ulrich notes the extraordinary richness and potential of these papers in "Of Pens and Needles: Sources for Early American Women's History," *Journal of American History* 77 (1990): 200–207. For a biography of Phelps, see Elizabeth Pendergast Carlisle, *Earthbound and Heavenbent: Elizabeth Porter Phelps and Life at Forty Acres (1747–1817)* (New York: Scribner, 2004).

42. Sylvester Judd, "Northampton," 1:326, FL.

43. For a brief biography of Judd and a discussion of the nature and value of his manuscripts, see Gregory H. Nobles and Herbert L. Zarov, *Selected Papers of the Sylvester Judd Manuscript* (Northampton, Mass.: Forbes Library, 1976). Differentiation of dress for morning and afternoon was firmly in place among fashionable upper- and middle-class Americans by the 1790s; see Marguerite A. Connolly, "Dressing for the Occasion: The Differentiation of Women's Costume in America, 1770–1910" (master's thesis, University of Delaware, 1987).

44. Catharine Anne Wilson, "Reciprocal Work Bees and the Meaning of Neighbourhood," *Canadian Historical Review* 82 (2001): 431

45 Wilson, "Reciprocal Work Bees," 455. Daniel Vickers also comments on the role of work bees in healing inter-household tension in "Competency and Competition: Economic Culture in Early America," *William and Mary Quarterly* 47 (1990): 26–27.

46. Judd, *Hadley,* 424. In 1790, the first federal census found 143 families living in 132 houses, the population totaling 882.

47. Gregory Nobles, "A 'Class Act': Redefining Deference in Early American History," paper presented to the Georgia Workshop in Early American History and Culture, University of Georgia–Athens, 26 September 2003. www.uga.edu/colonialseminar/Nobles%202.

48. On "hidden transcripts," see James Scott, *Domination and the Arts of Resistance: Hidden Transcripts* (New Haven: Yale University Press, 1990).

Chapter 1. Clothing and Consumers in Rural New England, 1760–1810

1. Sylvester Judd, "Northampton," 1:104, FL. Judd does not name his informant here; the attribution is based on similar topics discussed with Catherine Graves and entered on nearby pages 94 and 101. Other possibilities include Mrs Kingsley (who comments on the Stoddard clothing in "Northampton," 1:332) and Mrs Samuel Wright (who comments on fashion among the Edwards women in "Northampton," 1:492).

2. Important work on fashion, self-fashioning, and the marketplace includes T. H. Breen, " 'Baubles of Britain': The American and Consumer Revolutions of the Eighteenth Century," *Past and Present* 19 (1988): 73–104, "An Empire of Goods: The Anglicization of Colonial America, 1690–1776," *Journal of British Studies* 25 (1986): 467–99, "Narratives of Commercial Life: Consumption, Ideology, and Community on the Eve of the American Revolution," *William and Mary Quarterly* 50 (1993): 471–501, and *The Marketplace of Revolution* (New York: Oxford University Press, 2004); Richard Bushman, *The Refinement of America: Persons, Houses, Cities* (New York: Alfred A. Knopf, 1992); John Brewer and Roy Porter, eds., *Consumption and the World of Goods* (New York: Routledge, 1993); Cary Carson, "The Consumer Revolution in Colonial America: Why Demand?" and the other excellent essays collected in Cary Carson, Ronald Hoffman, and

Peter J. Albert, eds., *Of Consuming Interests: The Style of Life in the Eighteenth Century* (Charlottesville: University Press of Virginia, 1994), 483–697; Catherine Anna Haulman, "The Empire's New Clothes: The Politics of Fashion in Eighteenth-Century British North America" (Ph.D. diss., Cornell University, 2002); Gilles Lipovetsky, *The Empire of Fashion: Dressing Modern Democracy* (Princeton: Princeton University Press, 1994); Ann Smart Martin, "Buying into the World of Goods: Eighteenth-Century Consumerism and the Retail Trade from London to the Virginia Frontier" (Ph.D. diss., College of William and Mary, 1993); Neil McKendrick, John Brewer, and J. H. Plumb, *The Birth of a Consumer Society: The Commercialization of Eighteenth-Century England* (Bloomington: University of Indiana Press, 1982); Jonathan Prude, "To Look Upon the 'Lower Sort': Runaway Ads and the Appearance of Unfree Laborers in America, 1750–1800," *Journal of American History* (1991): 124–59; Daniel Roche, *The Culture of Clothing: Dress and Fashion in the ancien regime* (Cambridge: Cambridge University Press, 1994).

3. Josiah Pierce almanacs, 29 April and 2 May 1755, HHS.

4. "The Poor of the Town," receipts, 1800–1820, Kent Public Library, Suffield, Conn.

5. EPP memorandum book, 19 June 1785, PPHP.

6. *Middlesex Gazette, or Federal Advertiser,* 17 March 1791.

7. Philemon Stacy, account of vendue sale, Marlboro [Vt.] District Registry of Probate, vol. 1, 1781–95, 112.

8. John Lamson inventory, 29 January 1805, Essex [Vt.] District Registry of Probate, vol. 1, 1791–811, 206–8.

9. Mary Sedgwick inventory, 1743, Hartford [Conn.] District Registry of Probate, 14:454.

10. EPP memorandum book, 27 February 1791, 26 August 1804, PPHP.

11. Rebeckah Ashley inventory, 17 October 1781, HCMRP, 13:550, box 6, no. 5; Elizabeth Gunn inventory, 9 July 1761, HCMRP, 10:117, box 65, no. 27. My thanks to Diane Cameron for providing the information about Katherine Russell.

12. For a good introduction to the second-hand trade in England, see Beverly Lemire, *Dress, Culture, and Commerce: The English Clothing Trade before the Factory 1660–1800* (New York : St. Martin's Press, 1997); Anne Buck, "Mantuamakers and Milliners: Women Making and Selling Clothes in Eighteenth-Century Bedfordshire," *Publications of the Bedfordshire Historical Society* 72 (1993): 142–55.

13. *CC,* 7 November 1780.

14. *Middlesex Gazette, or Federal Advertiser,* 28 January 1792.

15. *CC,* 15 August 1780.

16. Ibid., 5 September 1780.

17. But see Michael Zakim, "Sartorial Ideologies: From Homespun to Ready-Made," *American Historical Review* 106 (December 2001): 1553–86.

18. *CC,* 6 November 1786;.

19. Samuel Wolcott, *Memorial of Henry Wolcott* (New York: Anson D. F. Randolph & Co., 1881), 156–57. Wolcott claims to be publishing from an undated text titled "Resolutions of the Ladies of Hartford" in the Governor Oliver Wolcott Papers (now held by CHS), but that document could not be located. Wolcott believed that the resolutions were drawn up in the 1770s, and his version of the text is distinct enough from the 1786 resolutions published by the "Economical Society" to suggest that they may date from a

different time. But given the similarities between the two texts and the absence of evidence that two such associations emerged, I treat Wolcott's transcribed text as related to the documented 1786 association.

20. J. Hammond Trumbull, ed., *Memorial History of Hartford County, Connecticut, 1633–1884*, 2 vols. (Boston: Edward L. Osgood, 1886), 1:586.

21. Sylvester Judd, *History of Hadley* (Springfield, Mass.: H. R. Huntting and Co., 1905), 326; Polly Wiley account book, 1815–29, JDC. The collections of Old Sturbridge Village, Sturbridge, Mass., include the portrait of Rev. Howe (1764–1837) of Hopkinton, Mass., as well as the wig and cocked hat that he is said to have worn well into the 1820s and 1830s. My thanks to Aimee Newell, Curator of Textiles and Fine Arts, for bringing these objects to my attention.

22. Elizabeth Mankin Kornhauser, *Ralph Earl: The Face of the Young Republic* (New Haven: Yale University Press, 1991), with costume notes by Aileen Ribeiro, 188–89. See also Robert Blair St. George's provocative discussion of these portraits as ideological gestures in *Conversing by Signs: Poetics of Implication in Colonial New England Culture* (Chapel Hill: University of North Carolina Press, 1998), 297–378.

23. Thomas Dwight to Mrs Hannah Dwight, 31 January 1796, Dwight-Howard Papers, MHS. I was alerted to this lively collection by Nicola Shilliam's "The Sartorial Autobiography: Bostonians' Private Writings about Fashionable Dress, 1760s–1860s," in *Textile and Text* 13, no. 3 (1990): 5–22.

24. David Selden Jr. to David and Cynthia Selden, 23 March 1807, Ms. 89970, CHS. On men's styles, see also 23 July 1807.

25. Carson, "Consumer Revolution in Colonial America," 548.

26. Bushman, *Refinement of America*, 66.

27. *CC*, 14 November 1780.

28. Lewis Tappan, "Reminiscences of Northampton," 25 October 1854, in *HG*, 23 January 1855.

29. Hawley's appearance was consistent with a practice observed by Robert Blair St. George: "Only part of the Connecticut River Valley gentry's longevity in power was due to their assertions of social difference. The rest was due to their success in assuring their poorer neighbors that they had their best interests at heart." In acts "more practical than altruistic," elites consciously restrained their consumption and display to avoid alienating the members of their communities, the sources of their influence. Hawley then balanced his need to assert his superiority with another to reassure his neighbors of his commonality. St. George, "Artifacts of Regional Consciousness in the Connecticut River Valley, 1700–1780," in *The Great River: Art and Society of the Connecticut Valley, 1635–1820*, ed. William N. Hosley Jr. (Hartford: Wadsworth Atheneum, 1985), 33.

30. Carole Turbin, in "Class Dressing: Gender, Fashion, and the Changing Landscape of Class in the U.S., 1860–1940," Tenth Berkshire Conference on the History of Women, Chapel Hill, North Carolina, 9 June 1996, observed that in the nineteenth century, the middle and working classes came to be understood linguistically through a metaphor of clothing, as "white-" and "blue-collar" workers. Tappan's reminiscence about the white and blue shirts that marked Northampton's professional and laboring people makes clear that this distinction had firm eighteenth-century roots.

31. [Elizabeth Heath?] to [Susanna Craft Heath?], 24 February 1799, Heath Family Papers, Correspondence, (1736–1887), MHS.

32. Alice Morse Earle, ed., *Diary of Anna Green Winslow: A Boston Schoolgirl of 1771* (Boston: Houghton, Mifflin and Co., 1894), 7.

33. Claudia B. Kidwell, "Riches, Rags, and In-Between," *Historic Preservation* 28, no. 5 (1976): 28–33, esp. 30. For a good introduction to eighteenth-century clothing construction in England, see Janet Arnold, *Patterns of Fashion: Englishwomen's Dresses and Their Construction, c. 1660–1860* (New York: Drama Book Specialists, 1972); Nora Waugh, *The Cut of Women's Clothes, 1600–1800* (New York: Theatre Arts Books, 1969), and *The Cut of Men's Clothes, 1600–1800* (New York: Theatre Arts Books, 1969); C. Willet and Phillis Cunnington, *Handbook of English Costume in the Eighteenth Century* (London: Faber and Faber, 1957); Aileen Ribeiro, *A Visual History of Costume: The Eighteenth Century* (London: B. T. Batsford, 1983). For the American side of the Atlantic, see Peter F. Copeland, *Working Dress in Colonial and Revolutionary America* (Westport, Conn.: Greenwood Press, 1977); Linda Baumgarten, *Eighteenth-Century Clothing at Williamsburg* (Williamsburg, Va.: The Colonial Williamsburg Foundation, 1986), *What Clothes Reveal: The Language of Clothing in Colonial and Federal America* (Williamsburg, Va.: The Colonial Williamsburg Foundation, 2002), and, with John Watson and Florine Carr, *Costume Close-Up: Clothing Construction and Pattern* (Williamsburg, Va.: The Colonial Williamsburg Foundation, 1999). See also Meridith Wright, *Put on Thy Beautiful Garments: Rural New England Clothing, 1783–1800,* with illustrations by Nancy Rexford (East Montpelier, Vt.: Clothes Press, 1990).

34. Connecticut Valley Clothing File, a database created by the author in spring and summer 2001, documenting almost twelve thousand articles of apparel owned by all decedents whose inventories (taken 1760–1810) enumerated apparel in eighteen selected Connecticut Valley towns. I am grateful to the University of Massachusetts Office of Research Affairs for funding this project and for David E. Lazaro's capable work as a research assistant. That the number of examples of garments made from home-woven textiles described as "homespun" or "homemade," though never large, rises as one moves from the 1760s to the 1790s may reflect the effects of the American Revolution and increased use of domestically produced textiles for clothing. Readers should note that this figure does not speak in any way to household textiles (e.g., bed curtains, blankets and other coverings, and table linens, including cloths and napkins) produced domestically; the relative proportion of domestically produced compared with imported fabric surely was markedly different in wardrobes than it was among household textiles. Adrienne D. Hood, in *The Weaver's Craft: Cloth, Commerce, and Industry in Early Pennsylvania* (Philadelphia: University of Pennsylvania Press, 2003), postulates a relationship between references to "homespun" cloth and the absence of artisanal weavers (126–37). For useful critiques of probate inventories as sources of historical insight, see Peter Benes, ed., *Early American Probate Inventories,* Proceedings of the 1987 Dublin Seminar for New England Folklife (Boston: Boston University, 1989).

35. George Howard memoir, 5–6, Windsor Historical Society, Windsor, Conn. Patricia Anne Trautman includes a fascinating discussion of the particular garments associated with college life and some men's professions in "Colonel Edward Marrett: A Gentleman Tailor" (Ph.D. diss., University of Colorado, 1982), 87–93.

36. EPP memorandum book, 23 May 1790, PPHP.

37. See David Lazaro, "Something Old, Something New, Something Borrowed . . . : A Beloved Wedding Gown's Many Lives," in *Historic Deerfield Magazine,* Spring 2002, 34–39.

38. For more on the gown originally owned by Betsey Barker, see Jane C. Nylander, "Textiles at Old Sturbridge Village," *Antiques,* September 1979, 600–606, esp. 603. For another discussion of early American maternity wear, see Baumgarten, *What Clothes Reveal,* 152–56, and "Dressing for Pregnancy: A Maternity Gown of 1780–96," *Dress* 23 (1996): 16–24.

39. EWPH to EPP, 27 March 1803, PPHP.

40. John Ellery will, 1744, Hartford [Conn.] Registry of Probate, 15:544.

41. EPP memorandum book, 22 July 1787; see also July 14, 1814, PPHP.

42. See the day books of the Miles & Lyons firm, PVMA. Among the few scholarly considerations of graveclothes makers in the eighteenth-century Atlantic world is Elizabeth Sanderson, *Women and Work in Eighteenth-Century Edinburgh* (New York: St. Martin's Press, 1996), 64–71.

43. Martha Newton inventory, 6 September 1799, Windsor [Vt.] District Registry of Probate, vol. 3, 1797–1804, 69–72.

44. Miriam Warner inventory, 6 April 1773, HCMRP, 12:83–84, box 154, no. 22.

45. Rev. Justus Forward account book (1777–86), 51 and 75, Joseph Allen Skinner Museum (archival collections housed at Mount Holyoke College Art Museum), South Hadley, Mass.

46. EPP memorandum book, 28 December 1806, PPHP. William Pierson discusses the clothing of African Americans in New England and especially how it circulated, second hand, through this community, in *Black Yankees: The Development of an Afro-American Subculture in Eighteenth-Century New England* (Amherst: University of Massachusetts Press, 1988).

47. *HG,* 30 April 1788, 5 December 1787.

48. John Barber inventory, 5 April 1774, HCMRP, 12:157.

49. Sylvester Judd, "Connecticut," 10:394, FL.

50. Contract, 24 July 1778, Dwight Family Papers, 2:47, Norman Rockwell Museum, Stockbridge, Mass.

51. *Middlesex Gazette and Federal Advertiser,* 28 July 1792.

52. Indenture, Thomas Calkins to Samuel Calkins, 7 January 1763, CSL.

53. James Russell Trumbull, *History of Northampton, Massachusetts, from its founding in 1654,* 2 vols. (Northampton: Press of the Gazette Printing Co., 1898–1902), 2:10.

54. Gill indenture, 8 February 1762, Bartlett Family Papers, box 1, folder 1, PVMA.

55. Cotes indenture, 15 September 1761, Nims Family Papers, box 1, folder 25, PVMA.

56. Connecticut Valley Clothing File.

57. Hannah Miller inventory, 23 December 1762, HCMRP, 10:153–54, box 98, no. 1.

58. For close examination of the construction and use of short gowns as an article of apparel, see Claudia Kidwell, "Short Gowns," *Dress* 4 (1978): 31–65.

59. *Greenfield Gazette, or, Massachusetts and Vermont Telegrapher,* 16 April 1795.

60. Lydia Ellsworth inventory, 1 August 1808, Hartford [Conn.] District Registry of Probate, 28:322.

61. Thirty-two percent, or nearly 1 in 3, of the short gowns observed in the Connecticut Valley Clothing File were not described in any way by court-appointed assessors.

62. Ibid. Dark fabrics were favored over light 3 to 1.

63. Beverly Lemire, *Fashion's Favourite: The Cotton Trade and the Consumer in Britain, 1660–1800* (New York: Oxford University Press, 1991), 96–200.

64. For critiques of emulation theses, see, e.g., Lorna Weatherill, "The Meaning of Consumer Behavior in late Seventeenth- and Early Eighteenth-Century England," in John Brewer and Roy Porter, eds., *Consumption and the World of Goods* (London: Routledge, 1993), 207–27; Amanda Vickery, The *Gentleman's Daughter: Women's Lives in Georgian England* (New Haven: Yale University Press, 1998), 162–64; Margaret R. Hunt, *The Middling Sort: Commerce, Gender, and the Family in England, 1680–1780* (Berkeley: University of California Press, 1996), 205.

65. Thomas Dwight to Mrs Hannah Dwight, 20 January 1799, Dwight-Howard Papers, MHS.

66. Wendy Kenerson, "A Suit of Clothes: Men's Clothing in the Deerfield Probate Inventories Taken from 1674–1820" (seminar paper, Historic Deerfield, Inc., 1987); Lynne Zacek Bassett, "Cloathes of his own Wareing: A Study of Clothing Listed in the Probate Inventories of Deerfield, Massachusetts, 1650–1750" (seminar paper, University of Connecticut, 1986), and "The Sober People of Hadley: A Study of Clothing in the Probate Inventories of Hadley, Massachusetts, 1663–1731" (master's thesis, University of Connecticut, 1991); and Wright, *Put on Thy Beautiful Garments.*

67. Matthew Patrick inventory, 8 September 1789, Windsor [Vt.] Registry of Probate, vol. 1, 1787–89, 52.

68. Charles Evans inventory, 12 June 1790, Marlboro [Vt.] Registry of Probate, vol. 1, 1781–1795, 188–93.

69. See Kristin Janea Whitacre, "What Did She Wear?" (paper presented at the symposium Women's Dress, 1750–1780, University of Delaware, 13 February 1993); Alexandra Deutsch, "In Search of the Connecticut River Goddess" (seminar paper, Historic Deerfield, Inc., 1992) and Connecticut Valley Clothing File.

70. Rachel Parmenter inventory, 1 March 1799, Marlboro [Vt.] Registry of Probate, 2, 1795–1804, 186.

71. Abigail Wells inventory, 3 November 1772, HCMRP, box 156, no. 53.

72. Elizabeth Lyman inventory, 13 September 1793, HCMRP 18:197, box 91, no. 15.

73. Lois Morton inventory, 3 December, 1800, HCMRP, 21:166–67, box 102, no. 14; Florence M. Montgomery, *Textiles in America, 1650–1870* (New York: W. W. Norton, 1984).

74. For another discussion of texture, color, and fit within elite wardrobes, see Bushman, *Refinement of America,* 69–74.

75. Ibid., 71.

76. Ibid., 70.

77. Robert Blair St. George discusses the meaning of artificiality in *The Wrought Covenant: Source Material for the Study of Craftsmen and Community in Southeastern New England, 1620–1700* (Brockton, Mass.: Brockton Art Center-Fuller Memorial, 1979), 14–15.

78. Carrie Rebora and Paul Staiti, *John Singleton Copley in America* (New York: Harry N. Abrams, 1995), 312–14; Kornhauser, *Ralph Earl,* 188–91. Aileen Ribiero contributed substantive notes on costume to each of these publications.

79. See Karin Calvert, "The Function of Fashion in Eighteenth-Century America," in Cary Carson, Ronald Hoffman, and Peter J. Albert, eds., *Of Consuming Interests: The Style of Life in the Eighteenth Century* (Charlottesville: University Press of Virginia and United States Capital Historical Society, 1994), 270–81.

80. Wolcott, *Memorial of Henry Wolcott,* 117.

81. Elizabeth Newberry inventory, ca. 1776, Hartford [Conn.] District Registry of Probate, 13:215.

82. Sarah Porter inventory, 12 October 1784, HCMRP, 14:229–30, box 117, no. 30.

83. [Susannah Craft Heath] to Eliza [Heath?], 3 September 1786, Heath Family Papers, Correspondence (1736–1887), MHS.

84. Earle, *Diary of Anna Green Winslow,* 14

85. Martin, "Buying into the World of Goods," 66; for more on "cultural capital," see chap. 2, "Consumerism, Material Culture, and the Meaning of Goods," 45–89.

86. Kevin M. Sweeney, "From Wilderness to Arcadian Vale: Material Life in the Connecticut River Valley, 1635–1760," in William Hosley, ed., *The Great River: Art and Society of the Connecticut Valley, 1635–1820* (Hartford: The Wadsworth Atheneum, 1985), 17–27.

87. EPP memorandum book, 17 February 1771, PPHP.

88. Journal of Abigail Brackett Lyman, 11 March 1800, quoted in Helen Roelker Kessler, "The Worlds of Abigail Brackett Lyman" (master's thesis, Tufts University, 1976), 184. I am grateful to Helen Kessler for sharing her work on Lyman with me. On the need for moderation, see also St. George, "Artifacts of Regional Consciousness," 34.

89. Connecticut Valley Clothing File.

90. Ibid. Interestingly, of over one thousand gowns listed in Connecticut Valley probate inventories from 1760 to 1805, fewer than thirty are described as "homespun" or "homemade." For more on the relative importance of imported and domestically produced cloth for use in the construction of clothing, see Carol Shammas, *The Pre-Industrial Consumer in England and America* (Oxford: Clarendon Press, 1990); Laurel Thatcher Ulrich, "Wheels, Looms, and the Gender Division of Labor in Eighteenth-Century New England," *William and Mary Quarterly,* 3rd ser., 55 (January 1998): 3–38.

91. Elisha Pomeroy inventory, 5 April 1762, HCMRP, 10:11, box 115, no. 43.

92. Nathan Bolles inventory, n.d., in Bolles account book, 1779–1810, State Historical Society of Wisconsin, Madison. Ann Smart Martin has suggested that this wealth of choice helped render the task of shopping a pleasurable leisure activity; browsing enabled consumers to experience the world of goods vicariously, looking and handling without necessarily purchasing. But browsing may have occurred less often in smaller establishments. On shopping as a leisure activity, see Martin, "Buying into the World of Goods," 211; Richard Bushman, "Shopping and Advertising in Colonial America," in Carson, Hoffman, and Albert, *Of Consuming Interests,* 233–51.

93. The American press did not become a major disseminator of fashion until the mid-nineteenth century, and then, largely through the pages of *Godey's Lady's Book* and similar publications. Publications available earlier in the Connecticut Valley (usually British), however, did contain images of fashionable dress. In Northampton, Abigail Brackett Lyman's *The Ladies Remembrancer; or, Polite Journal for the year 1800* (London: W. Wilson, 1800) contained engravings of fashionable for that year. See Lipovetsky, *Empire of Fashion,* 68; Madeleine Ginsberg, *An Introduction to Fashion Illustration* (London: Her Majesty's Stationary Office, 1980); and Erin Skye Mackie, *Market a La Mode: Fashion in "the Tatler" and "the Spectator"* (Baltimore: Johns Hopkins University Press, 1997).

94. These comments are derived from Richard D. Brown, *Knowledge Is Power: The Diffusion of Information in Early America, 1700–1865* (New York: Oxford University Press, 1989); Gloria L. Main, "An Inquiry Into When and Why Women Learned to Write in Colonial New England," *Journal of Social History* 24 (1990–91): 579–89; Martin, "Buying

into the World of Goods;" David D. Hall, "Books and Reading in Eighteenth-Century America," in Carson, Hoffman, and Albert, *Of Consuming Interests,* 354–72; and William J. Gilmore, *Reading Becomes a 'Necessity of Life': Material and Cultural Life in Rural New England 1780–1930* (Knoxville: University of Tennessee Press, 1988).

95. Brown, *Knowledge Is Power,* 160–96.

96. Sylvester Judd, "Miscellaneous,"1:146, FL.

97. Memorandum, 25 January 1786, Dwight-Howard Papers, MHS.

98. Thomas Dwight to Mrs Hannah Dwight, 19 January 1795, Dwight-Howard Papers, MHS.

99. Thomas Dwight to Mrs Hannah Dwight, 20 January 1799, Dwight-Howard Papers, MHS.

100. Samuel Eliot to Thomas Williams, 1 January 1774, Papers of Thomas Williams, Williams Family Papers, box 8, folder 6, PVMA. Mourning was proscribed during the political crisis to discourage the accompanying purchases of appropriate cloth and funeral objects.

101. Because of the amount of purchasing that was done on behalf of others, it was not unusual for the selection of fabric to be left up to a merchant, or the surrogate shopper, with some direction from the actual purchaser. For example, in September 1780, David Field wrote to Jos. Barnard, asking him to "go to Doctor Williams' wife at Roxbury and git four pounds sixteen shillings money she has of mine and git some sort of fashionable silk for gown and gimp for trimming the same. Let it be all of a colour except it be flowered, and you will oblige your humble servant. N.B. The colour must not be black, red or yellow." Barnard obliged, and purchased nine yards of lustring for ten shillings six pence, and three and one-half yards of gimp at one shilling two pence. See "Buying a Gown 120 Years Ago," *HG,* 3 January, 1888.

102. Abigail Brackett Lyman to Erastus Lyman, 18 October 1801, in Kessler, "Worlds of Abigail Brackett Lyman," 224.

103. EWPH to Sarah Parsons Phelps, 9 November 1800, PPHP.

104. Patience Langdon to Sophronia Beebe, 22 May 1804, quoted in Judith Knight's 1995 notes on needlework in the Beebe Family Papers, Old Sturbridge Village. My thanks to Lynne Bassett for making these notes available to me during her tenure as curator of textiles and fine arts.

105. Eliza Southgate Browne to her parents, 16 December 1798, in *A Girl's Life Eighty Years Ago: The Letters of Eliza Southgate Browne* (Williamstown, Mass.: Corner House Publishers, 1980), 20. For a discussion of Browne's correspondence and the fan back style described here, see David E. Lazaro, "Construction in Context: A 1790s Gown from Medford, Massachusetts" (master's thesis, University of Massachusetts at Amherst, 2001), 48–49.

106. Eliza Southgate Browne to her parents, 14 July 1803, in Browne, *A Girl's Life Eighty Years Ago,* 167.

107. Literacy skills were pertinent to the success of artisans as well. Roche, *Culture of Clothing,* 322–26, notes a high level of literacy among Parisian tailors, dressmakers, and linen drapers and a lower level among journeymen and wage-earners. In part, Roche points out, the difference reflects the educational advantages of urban living but also suggests that this trade, "more than most," required craftspersons to be able to maintain accounts and correspond with clients.

108. See Abigail Brackett Lyman to Erastus Lyman, 18 October 1801, in Kessler, "Worlds of Abigail Brackett Lyman," 224.

109. Kessler observes Abigail Brackett Lyman's taste, and haste, in "Worlds of Abigail Brackett Lyman," 88–89.

110. *CC,* 8 May and 30 October 1775.

111. Judd, "Miscellaneous," 1:146. The years during and after the French Revolution brought large numbers of émigrés from France's working class, including members of the needle trades, as well as dancing instructors and fencing masters, to northeastern cities, amplifying French influence on American fashion; see Michele Majer, "American Women à la Française": French Influence on Federal Dress," Costume Society of America, Region I Fall Symposium, Portsmouth, New Hampshire, 2000.

112. J. Ritchie Garrison, "Builders and the Myth of Deskilling: The Case of Calvin and George Stearns" (paper presented at the Eighth Symposium of the George Meany Memorial Archives, Building History and Labor History: Toward an Interdisciplinary Dialogue, Washington, D.C., 11–12 February 1992).

113. Judd, "Northampton," 1:492. An interesting passage in the letters of the Hadley native Sarah Porter Hillhouse suggests the role of such women as arbiters of taste for their communities. Once she had married and moved to Georgia, Sarah Porter Hillhouse received fashion instruction from a relative (perhaps a sister-in-law) in New Haven: "I thought there was no prospect of getting any person of better judgment than Miss Stoddard to select [a hat] if I sent to New York. . . . I hope the Leghorn will please you—they are very fashionable." Stoddard delivered further instruction on whether or not the hat should be turned up. See M. L. H. to Sarah Porter Hillhouse, 22 July 1810, folder 62, Alexander and Hillhouse Family Papers, Southern Historical Collection, Chapel Hill, N.C.

114. EPP to EWPH, 4 November 1797, PPHP.

115. EWPH to EPP, 27 March 1803, PPHP.

116. See also Hannah Williams Heath diary (1771–1832), 27 March 1805, Heath Family Collection, MHS, which describes a spring evening when "Mrs Ingersoll went home at dark [and] the girls went with her to borrow a robe to cut one by." My thanks to Elisabeth Nichols for passing this citation along to me.

117. EPP memorandum book, 15 July 1798, PPHP.

118. The Boston directories for 1796 and 1798, published by Manning and Loring, and Rhoads and Laughton, respectively, together list nineteen women who may have been working in 1797: Lucy Atkins, Maria Ayres, Hannah Boyd, Mildred Byles, Ann Flinn, Elizabeth Goddard, Rachel Hall, Ann Hatch, Anna Hearter, Hannah Hunt, Elizabeth Lanman, Mary Laughton, Hannah Milliquet, Betsy Nichols, Madam Poher, Sarah Snow, Hannah Tileston, Mary Todd, and Sarah Walker.

119. Lois Morton inventory, 30 December 1800, HCMRP, 21:166–67, box 102, no. 14.

120. EPP to EWPH, 4 November 1797, PPHP.

121. Betsy continued, "If should ever visit Boston again, I should want a good one—I think a green Sattin, made in imitation of those, would look very well." Elizabeth Whiting Phelps [EWPH] to Charles Phelps Jr., 20 April 1797, PPHP. Elsewhere, Betsy joked to her brother that he would be glad not to have his "country cousins" [his family] visit, suggesting that their rough rural edges might embarrass him. See EWPH to Charles Porter Phelps, 12 July 1797, PPHP.

122. Elizabeth Whiting Phelps [EWPH] to Charles Phelps Jr., 18 December 1797, PPHP.

123. Theodore Gregson Huntington, "Sketches of Family Life in Hadley," 1881, box 21, folder 5, PPHP.

124. Trumbull, *Memorial History of Hartford County,* 595; the maker, Trumbull further suggests, may have been Sally Tripper of Hartford's Draw Lane, who in 1766 advertised "Female Aprons, for Ladies from eighteen to fifty."

125. Solomon Clarke, *Historical Catalogue of the Northampton First Church* (Northampton: Gazette Printing Co., 1891), 109.

126. "Miss Lucy Watson's Memory and Account of New Settlers in the American Woods—1762, chiefly at Walpole, N.H.," JDC, Winterthur Library, Winterthur, Del.

127. See Deane Lee, ed., *History of Conway [Massachusetts], 1767–1967* (Town of Conway, 1967), 55–56.

128. Chauncey Goodrich to Fredrick Wolcott, 25 January 1790, in Samuel Wolcott, *Memorial of Henry Wolcott* (New York: Anson D. F. Randolph & Co., 1881), 324.

129. Edward Augustus Kendall, *Travels Through the Northern Parts of the United States in the years 1807 and 1808* (New York: I. Riley, 1809), 6.

130. Hannah H. Smith, Glastonbury, to her mother, Abigail Mitchell, Southbury, Conn., 26 April 1796, Correspondence of Smith and Mitchell Families (1796–1819), CSL.

131. Sarah Pitkin to Frances Pitkin, 10 December 1812, Ms. 69985, CHS.

132. Brown, *Knowledge Is Power,* 163–67. Cary Carson has suggested that the advance of the consumer revolution occurred through a number of stages, including "instruction, preparation, rehearsal, performance, acclamation (or not), and acceptance (or rejection)," which always "to a certain extent bowed to local customs." Carson, "Consumer Revolution," 619, 650. Clearly, those stages are at work here: Betsy was instructed in the new fashion, prepared and rehearsed it in Boston, and performed it in Hadley. She received the acclamation of others, after which the style was accepted, either directly or with some alteration, into local custom.

133. Elisha Pomeroy, 5 April 1762, 10:118. My attention was drawn to the significance of mirrors by Ann Smart Martin's insightful paper "Sukey's Mirror: Consumption, Commodities, and Cultural Identity in 18th-Century Virginia," Tenth Berkshire Conference on the History of Women, Chapel Hill, N.C., 9 June 1996; see also Martin, "Buying into the World of Goods; Eighteenth-Century Consumerism and the Retail Trade from London to Virginia (Ph.D. diss., College of William and Mary, 1993).

134. EWPH to EPP, 20 August 1797, PPHP.

135. My thinking about Elizabeth Whiting Phelps Huntington's maturing sense of self and her ongoing effort to construct an identity, or identities, for herself in both rural and urban communities in Massachusetts and Connecticut have been greatly influenced by Elisabeth Nichol's work on gender, reading, writing, and identity in early America; in particular, two conference papers have analyzed Huntington's correspondence: " 'Attached and Loving Sister,' 'Constant and Unalterable Friend,' and 'Loving and Dutiful Daughter': Elizabeth Phelps Huntington Conceptualizes Her Identity" (paper presented at the symposium Through Women's Eyes: The Porter Phelps Huntington Museum Reinterpretation Initiative, Phase II, Hadley, Mass., 24 September 1995); and "Daughters of the Early Republic: Girlhood and Identity in Rural New England" (paper presented at the Fifth Conference on Rural and Farm Women in Historical Perspective, Chevy Chase, Md., 1–4 December 1994).

Chapter 2. Needle Trades in New England, 1760–1810

1. Isaac Green account book (1800–1801) (Windsor), Nathan Stone Papers, VHS.

2. For a biography of another eighteenth-century New England tailor, see Patricia Anne Trautman, "Colonel Edward Marrett: A Gentleman Tailor" (Ph.D. diss., University of Colorado, 1982). For a suggestive study exploring how one craftsman can be understood in the context of his community, see Robert Tarule, *The Artisan of Ipswich: Craftsmanship and Community in Colonial New England* (Baltimore: Johns Hopkins University Press, 2004).

3. Isaac Green account book, VHS.

4. Claudia Kidwell, "Short Gowns" *Dress* 4 (1978): 47.

5. J. Ritchie Garrison, "Builders and the Myth of Deskilling: The Case of Calvin and George Stearns" (paper presented at the Eighth Symposium of the George Meany Memorial Archives, Building History and Labor History: Toward an Interdisciplinary Dialogue, Washington, D.C., 11–12 February 1992).

6. This overview of women's work in European clothing trades relies heavily on the following works: Alice Clark, *Working Life of Women in the Seventeenth Century* (1919; repr., London: Routledge, 1992); Judith G. Coffin, *The Politics of Women's Work: The Paris Garment Trades, 1750–1915* (Princeton: Princeton University Press, 1996); Gay L. Gullickson, *Spinners and Weavers of Auffay: Rural Industry and the Sexual Division of Labor in a French Village, 1750–1850* (Cambridge: Cambridge University Press, 1986; Martha C. Howell, "Women, the Family Economy, and the Structure of Market Production in Cities of Northern Europe during the Late Middle Ages," in *Women and Work in Preindustrial Europe,* ed. Barbara A. Hanawalt (Bloomington: Indiana University Press, 1986); Ivy Pinchbeck, *Women Workers and the Industrial Revolution, 1750–1850* (1930; repr., London: Virago, 1981); K. D. M. Snell, *Annals of the Labouring Poor: Social Change and Agrarian England, 1660–1900* (Cambridge: Cambridge University Press, 1986): 270–319; Merry Wiesner, "Spinsters and Seamstresses: Women in Cloth and Clothing Production," in *Rewriting the Renaissance: The Discourses of Sexual Difference in Early Modern Europe,* ed. Margaret W. Ferguson, Maureen Quilligan, and Nancy J. Vickers, 191–205 (Chicago, Chicago University Press, 1986), and *Women and Gender in Early Modern Europe* (Cambridge: Cambridge University Press, 1993).

7. Wilfried Reininghaus, "Artisans: Comparative-Historical Explorations," *International Review of Social History* 47 (2002): 101–13.

8. Nancy Lynne Locklin, "Women in Early Modern Brittany: Rethinking Work and Identity in the Traditional Economy" (Ph.D. diss., Emory University, 2000), 46, 121.

9. Clare Crowston traces this "Revolution in Women's Apparel" in *Fabricating Women: The Seamstresses of Old Regime France, 1675–1791* (Durham, N.C.: Duke University Press, 2001), 36–41.

10. Judith G. Coffin, "Gender and the Guild Order: The Garment Trades in Eighteenth-Century Paris," *Journal of Economic History* 54 (1994): 777. See also Daniel Roche, *The Culture of Clothing: Dress and Fashion in the ancien regime* (Cambridge: Cambridge University Press, 1994), 315.

11. James R. Farr, *Artisans in Europe, 1300–1914* (Cambridge: Cambridge University Press, 2000), 41.

12. R[obert] Campbell, The *London Tradesman* (1747; repr., New York: David and

Charles Reprints, 1969) lists twenty trades as appropriate for women, thirteen of which are related to needlework.

13. For more on tensions between tailor's guilds and aspiring needlewomen, see Clare Crowston, "Engendering the Guilds: Seamstresses, Tailors, and the Clash of Corporate Identities in Old Regime France," *French Historical Studies* 23 (2000): 339–71, esp. 346.

14. E.g., Geoffrey Crossick observes that "female access to the formal practice of artisanal crafts was being restricted from at least the fifteenth century in much of Europe, with increasingly precise definitions of which women . . . were acceptable in artisanal trades and the task they might perform." Crossick, "Past Masters: In Search of the Artisan in European History," in *The Artisan and the European Town, 1500–1900*, ed. Crossick (Aldershot: Ashgate Publishing, 1997), 14.

15. Daphne Spain, *Gendered Spaces* (Chapel Hill: University of North Carolina Press, 1992), 86.

16. L. D. Schwarz, *London in the Age of Industrialization: Entrepreneurs, Labour Force, and Living Conditions, 1700–1850* (Cambridge: Cambridge University Press, 1992), 58.

17. Campbell, *London Tradesman*, 191. The evidence is anecdotal, but there also may have been a relationship between tailoring and disability. I noticed an unusual incidence of crippled children, and men injured later in life, in the tailor's trade. Jacob Lockwood is typical. He earned his living as a sailor out of Rhode Island until a shipboard case of frostbite necessitated the amputation of one foot. Once disabled, he moved near his family in Springfield, Vermont, and learned the tailor's trade, which he then practiced for the remainder of his life. C. Horace Hubbard and Justus Dartt, *History of the Town of Springfield, Vermont* (Boston: George Walker and Co., 1895), 380. Isaac Lane, a tailor in Chatham, Connecticut, had one leg that was much shorter than the other, the result of either a birth defect or a later injury. See *CC*, 24 May 1774. That tailoring often was undertaken by men who could not perform other, more vigorous kinds of labor likely contributed to the disparagement of the trade.

18. Sylvester Judd, "Miscellaneous," 9:162, and 4:149, FL.

19. Ibid., 4:162.

20. The best discussion of the tasks involved in textile production is Adrienne Hood, *The Weaver's Craft: Cloth, Commerce, and Industry in Early Pennsylvania* (Philadelphia: University of Pennsylvania Press, 2003).

21. Much of Elizabeth Fuller's diary is published in Francis Everett Blake, *History of the Town of Princeton*, 2 vols. (Princeton: Published by the Town, 1915), 1:302–23.

22. Edward Strong Cooke Jr., *Making Furniture in Preindustrial America: The Social Economy of Newtown and Woodbury, Connecticut* (Baltimore: Johns Hopkins University Press, 1996), 13.

23. Christopher Zeeman, "Mathematics Applied to Dressmaking," *Costume* 28 (1994): 97–102.

24. Esther Wright account book (1787–1810), HN.

25. Patience Langdon to Sophronia Beebe, n.d. [ca. 1800], Old Sturbridge Village, Sturbridge, Mass.

26. Ginsburg, "The Tailoring and Dressmaking Trades, 1700–1850," *Costume* 4 (1972): 64–71, esp. 68.

27. Invoice, box 4, folder 20, PPHP; Judd, "Miscellaneous," 9:162.

28. *Greenfield Gazette,* 18 February 1799. See also Trautman, "Colonel Edward Marrett," 72.

29. See Sarah Clark's work for Elijah Clark in 1789, in Judd's notes on the work of the gown maker Sarah King Root Clark. Judd, "Miscellaneous," 11:62, and "Northampton," 2:244, FL. Claudia Kidwell writes that, in 1774, "as much as 90 percent of the price of a medium-quality gown was for the material; 200 years later, the fabric represented only 7 percent of the cost." Kidwell, "Riches, Rags, and In-Between," *Historic Preservation* 28, no. 5 (1976): 28.

30. Patience Langdon to Sophronia Beebe, n.d. [ca. 1800], as quoted and cited in Judith Knight's 1995 notes on needlework in the Beebe Family Papers, Old Sturbridge Village. I thank Lynne Bassett for making Knight's notes available to me.

31. See notes for Burrage Dimock, as well as for John Fairchild, Elisha Hamilton, and William and Eliphalet Hill, in William N. Hosley, *The Great River Archives: Inventories, House Surveys, Manuscript Files, Photo Files, Cultural Histories* (Guilford, Conn.: Opus, 1989). The emphasis on speed may well be related to travel, that one could obtain a piece of apparel while visiting a given community and know that it would be ready by the time of departure.

32. Claudia B. Kidwell and Margaret C. Christman, *Suiting Everyone: The Democratization of Clothing in America* (Washington, D.C.: Published for the National Museum of History and Technology by the Smithsonian Institution Press, 1975), 27. Probate inventories regularly contain references to "homemade" garments, to distinguish them from others in the inventory. This word could well refer to the construction of the garment but more likely refers to the production of the cloth. See, for example, the following inventories in HCMRP: Mary Cole, 17 May 1742, 6:189, box 34, no. 45; Hannah Miller, 28 December 1762, 10:153–54, box 98, no 1; Mary Bond, 13 April 1791, 17:53

33. Though one might assume that a woman's ability to purchase the services of a needleworker varied in direct proportion to her income, it was not necessarily true that poorer families assumed more of their own clothing-related chores. The social critic Frederick M. Eden recorded in 1797 that the working people of London "content themselves with a cast-off coat, which may usually be purchased for about 5 [shillings] and second-hand waistcoats and breeches. Their wives seldom make up any article of dress, except making and mending cloaths for the children." The same may have held true for the working people of Boston and of western New England. As we have seen, for example, slaves and servants received cast-off clothing from their employers, as well as clothing procured for them as recompense for their labor. See Eden, *State of the Poor* (1797), 1:554; quoted in Schwarz, *London in the Age of Industrialisation,* 186.

34. See Anne Buck, "Mantuamakers and Milliners: Women Making and Selling Clothes in Eighteenth-Century Bedfordshire," *Publications of the Bedfordshire Historical Society* 72 (1993): 142–55.

35. Richard Bushman, The *Refinement of America: Persons, Houses, Cities* (New York: Alfred A. Knopf, 1992), 65; Meridith Wright, *Put on Thy Beautiful Garments: Rural New England Clothing, 1783–1800,* with illustrations by Nancy Rexford (East Montpelier, Vt.: Clothes Press, 1990), 25–28; Peter MacTaggart and Ann MacTaggart, "Ease, Convenience, and Stays, 1750–1850," *Costume* 13 (1979): 41–51.

36. Campbell, *London Tradesman,* 224–25.

37. Nathaniel Phelps account book, PVMA; Sylvester Judd, "Northampton," 2:140; Judd, "Miscellaneous," 14:242–45; EPP memorandum book, 14 August 1768, PPHP; ac-

count books of Jerijah Barber Sr. (1770–93), February 1784, 86, Windsor Historical Society, Windsor, Vt.

38. EPP to EWPH, 27 March 1805, 13 November 1810, 20 April 1815 and 4 May 1815, EWPH to EPP, 11 January 1801 and 14 February 1801, PPHP; "Peggy Browing," clipping from "Old Days in Hartford" series, Mary Kingsbury Talcott scrapbook (1884–85), Ms. 95131, CHS.

39. EPP to EWPH, 20 April 1815, EPP memorandum book, 21 April 1810, EPP to EWPH, 28 August 1805, EPP to Sally, 17 March 1802, EPP to EWPH, 4 April 1807, 27 March 1805, EPP memorandum book, 30 May 1812, PPHP; George Sheldon also mentions "Jenny," an African American women "frequently employed in the families of our citizens as a washerwoman" in his essay "Slavery in the Connecticut Valley," in *Papers and Proceedings of the Connecticut Valley Historical Society, 1876–1881* (Springfield, Mass.: Connecticut Valley Historical Society, 1881), 207–18. Jane C. Nylander describes the tasks involved in laundering clothing in *Our Own Snug Fireside: Images of the New England Home, 1760–1860* (New York: Alfred A. Knopf, 1993), 130–42.

40. Kevin M. Sweeney, "River Gods and Related Minor Deities: The Williams Family and the Connecticut River Valley, 1637–1790" (Ph.D. diss., Yale University, 1987), 604.

41. These preliminary sewing lessons would come to be communicated through children's literature. See, e.g., [Mary Ann Kilmer], *The Adventures of a Pincushion* (London: J. Marshall, [ca. 1812]); Sarah Trimmer, *The Silver Thimble* (Philadelphia: B. & J. Johnson, 1801); Oliver Optik, *The Adventures of a Bodkin* (Boston: Cotton and Barnard, 1832). I am extremely grateful to Laura Wasowicz, curator of the American Children's Book Project at the American Antiquarian Society, Worcester, Mass., for directing me to these materials.

42. Nylander, *Our Own Snug Fireside,* 143–62. Young boys were occasionally tutored in sewing as well, though perhaps more for novelty's sake than to make them productive assets to this aspect of a household's provisioning. On one occasion EWPH records having made a shirt for Edward, "of which he himself did all the sewing up and filing down—and hemming—excepting the bosom." EWPH to EPP, 12 December 1812, PPHP.

43. Elizabeth Fuller diary, April 1791, in Blake, *History of the Town of Princeton,* 1:311.

44. Sarah Snell Bryant (1766–1847) diary (1794–1835), Houghton Library, Harvard University, Cambridge, Mass., volumes from 1794 to 1804.

45. Spencers were close-fitting, just-below-the-waist jackets with collars and lapels and were among the more complicated garments a tailor constructed.

46. Ibid., volumes from 1794 to 1804, and entries for 22 April 1800, 5 September 1802, 26 and 28 April, 1803, 8 December 1796, 20 April 1798, 17 January 1798, 20 October 1798.

47. Anna Green Winslow, *Diary of Anna Green Winslow: A Boston School Girl of 1771, with an introduction and notes by Alice Morse Earle* (Boston: Houghton, Mifflin and Co., 1894), 47.

48. Huldah Sheldon to Lucy Sheldon, December 1803, quoted in David E. Lazaro, "Construction in Context: A 1790s Gown from Medford, Massachusetts" (master's thesis, University of Massachusetts at Amherst, 2001), 51. See also Lazaro and Patricia Campbell Warner, "The All-Over Pleated Bodice: Dressmaking in Transition, 1780–1805," *Dress* 31 (2004): 15–24.

49. EWPH to Charles Phelps Jr., 12 July 1797, PPHP. Likewise, when Anna Williams

Partridge sent her sister Esther Williams Williams five and one-half yards of check linen for shirts, she specified that that yardage, "according to her measure will be sufficient to make two shirts." Oliver Partridge to Esther Williams Williams, 6 August 1777, Williams Family Papers, box 8, folder 8, PVMA.

50. See, e.g., W. J. Rorabaugh, *The Craft Apprentice: From Franklin to the Machine Age in America* (New York: Oxford University Press1986).

51. My use of the term "communities of practice" is drawn from the anthropology of learning and teaching, a useful survey of which is found in Catherine Pelissier, "The Anthropology of Teaching and Learning," *Annual Review of Anthropology* 20 (1991): 75–95.

52. Snell, *Annals,* 276–85; Wiesner, *Women and Gender in Early Modern Europe,* 129.

53. Robert Blair St. George, *The Wrought Covenant: Source Material for the Study of Craftsmen and Community in Southeastern New England, 1620–1700* (Brockton, Mass.: Brockton Art Center-Fuller Memorial, 1979), 16.

54. James Richard Farr makes a similar observation about the "relational quality" of skill in *Artisans in Europe,* 42.

55. RD diary, 9 October 1788, and 26 September 1787, PVMA.

56. Judd, "Miscellaneous," 11:62; see also Judd, "Northampton," 14:244.

57. Judd, "Northampton," 1:94.

58. See, e.g., Barry Levy, "Girls and Boys: Poor Children and The Labor Market in Colonial Massachusetts," *Pennsylvania History* 64 (Summer 1997): 287–307, and "Born to Run: White Runaway Servants and the Labor Systems of Massachusetts and the Delaware Valley, 1700–1780" (paper prepared for the McNeil Center for Early American Studies Seminar, 9 September 2005).

59. For Anna Graham, see Connecticut State Library RG 62, Wethersfield, box 3; for Clarinda Colton, see Burt Family Papers, PVMA.

60. Indenture, 1 July 1770, Middlesex County Historical Society, Middletown, Conn.

61. Elizabeth Fisher indenture, 1788, and Lucinda Cone indenture, 1804, Middlesex County Historical Society.

62. Likewise, only 3 percent of the boys (33) went to tailors, while 60 percent were bound to crafts in general, and 40 percent to husbandry. See Lawrence W. Trainer, ed., "The Indentures of Boston's Poor Apprentices: 1734–1805," in *Transactions 1956–1963, Publications of the Colonial Society of Massachusetts* (Boston, 1966), 43:417–68.

63. Kathy A. Ritter, *Apprentices of Connecticut* (Salt Lake City: Ancestry Publishing, 1986), 54.

64. See Judd, "Northampton," 1:101b.

65. The "Directory of Craftsmen in the Connecticut Valley" compiled by Daniel Lombardo and housed at Deerfield's Memorial Libraries asserts that Margaret Booth was a dressmaker, though I have not been able to locate a source for the attribution. Booth's account book (1800–1810), is held by the Longmeadow Historical Society. It is also possible that these young women were hired help.

66. In 1770, his estate was valued at £120 14s., when the average in Hadley was £71; the mean value of Hadley estates was just £48 9s. These figures are based on the valuations published in Judd, *History of Hadley* (Springfield, Mass.: H. R. Huntting and Co., 1905), 423. His probate inventory assessed his wealth at the time of his death in 1802 at over $4,000—a healthy sum by the standards of the day. His house and outbuildings

were alone worth $598, in addition to another lot on Hadley's "back street," perhaps the site of his shop, worth another $555.

67. See EPP memorandum book, 15 November and 29 December 1799, 26 January 1800, PPHP.

68. Cooke, *Making Furniture,* 35.

69. EPP memorandum book, 15 July 1798, PPHP.

70. Philip Zea, "Rural Craftsmen and Design," in *New England Furniture: The Colonial Era,* by Brock Jobe and Myrna Kaye, with the assistance of Zea (Boston: Houghton Mifflin, 1984), 55, 56.

71. See Scott LaFrance, "Work Habits of Rural Massachusetts Cabinetmakers: A Study of Account Books, 1770–1840" (seminar paper, Historic Deerfield, Inc., 1982), 9.

72. Joshua Lane, "Breeches and Rum: An Investigation of Rural Economy through the Account Books of John Russell" (seminar paper, Historic Deerfield, Inc., 1984), 21.

73. Josiah Pierce accounts, HHS. See also Trautman, "Colonel Edward Marrett," 76.

74. Wright account book (1787–1810), HN.

75. RD diary, 23 November 1787, PVMA.

76. Wright account book (1787–1810), HN.

77. Ruth Pease diary, 13–14 February 1812, PVMA.

78. E.g., EPP memorandum book, 2 December 1792, PPHP records Tabitha Smith altering a calico gown of EPP's to fit her nearly fifteen-year-old daughter Betsy.

79. Ibid, 23 May 1790, 27 March 1803.

80. Ibid., 6 September 1801.

81. Ibid., 3 June 1770, 3 August 1788, 12 January 1812, PPHP. Historic Northampton possesses another good example: a gown (accession number 66.197) made in 1762 was remade in 1805, reviving the life of the garment more than forty years after its construction and probably extending it well over ten years more, since it corresponded loosely to prevailing fashion. The wedding gown of Prudence Punderson, now in the collections of CHS, was also altered many years after its original construction for the wedding of Punderson's daughter. Though the pattern of the fabric was well out of date by the latter occasion, the exceptional quality of the material would still have been plain to all. Evidence on the garment suggests one or more subsequent alterations as well. I am grateful to Lynne Bassett for bringing this additional example to my attention.

82. Esther Edwards Burr, *The Journal of Esther Edwards Burr, 1754–1757,* ed. Carol F. Karlsen and Laurie Crumpacker (New Haven: Yale University Press, 1984), 13 October 1755, 158.

83. Burr to Sarah Prince, 10–11 November 1755, quoted in ibid., 165.

84. Jane C. Nylander, *Our Own Snug Fireside: Images of the New England Home, 1760–1860* (New York: Alfred A. Knopf, 1993), 164–66.

85. Thaddeus Leavitt's book (1784–94), Kent Public Library, Suffield, Conn.

86. Homer White's Granby shop at 12 Common Street still stands and is illustrated in the *Granby Bicentennial: 1768–1968* (Granby: Town of Granby, 1968), 101. The home and shop room of the Cambridge tailor Edward Marrett is illustrated in Trautman, "Colonel Edward Marrett," 62–63.

87. Judd, "Miscellaneous," 13:231.

88. Clare Crowston uses the probate inventories of gown makers in France to describe domestic workspaces in *Fabricating Women,* 121–23.

89. Robert Corsill inventory, 5 January 1773, HCMRP, 12:61.

90. See Christine Daniels, "From Father to Son: The Economic Roots of Craft Dynasties in Eighteenth-Century Maryland," in *American Artisans: Crafting Social Identity, 1750–1850,* ed. Howard B. Rock, Paul A. Gilje, and Robert Asher (Baltimore: Johns Hopkins University Press, 1995), 5. George Herbert's 13 February 1786 probate inventory is in HCMRP, 16:7, box 70, no. 47.

91. Joseph Stack, 1 December 1787, Windsor [Vt.] District Registry of Probate, vol. 1, 1787–1789, 21.

92. Thomas Gross, 1773, Hartford [Conn.] District Registry of Probate, #2479.

93. Jonathan Root, 1812, Hartford [Conn.] District Registry of Probate, no file #.

94. Nehemiah Street, 1791, Farmington, [Conn.] District Registry of Probate #2647.

95. See, for example, HCMRP inventories of Peletiah Hitchcock, saddler, 10 December 1761, 10:55, box 72, no. 26; David Bliss, saddler, 12 January 1762, 10:57, box 16, no. 5; and Moses Bliss, shoemaker, 14 May 1762, 10:98, box 16, no. 33.

96. Jonathan Day, 14 October 1761, HCMRP, 10:47; James Warner 26 January 1762, HCMRP 10:107.

97. Scissors were even rarer, appearing in only four of three hundred Hampshire County inventories taken between 1760 and 1808. As small goods typically used by women, they are surely underrepresented in probate inventories, but scissor ownership, too, may have been on the rise during the eighteenth century. Elisha Pomeroy's Northampton shop had more than a hundred pairs of scissors in three grades in its 1762 inventory, but scissors do not begin to appear with any regularity in Hampshire County inventories until 1800.

98. See, e.g., Charles Clapp, 6 August 1791, HCMRP, 11:243–44.

99. This discussion of the processes involved in clothing construction relies heavily on the material cited below as well as extended conversation with Jane Whitacre, who oversees the mantua-maker's shop at Colonial Williamsburg, and Doris Warren and Brooke Barrows, who staff the shop. I am extremely grateful to them for allowing me to spend a day with them in February 2002 producing a replica of an eighteenth-century mantua. The New England costume historians and curators Lynne Bassett, Pat Warner, David Lazaro, Edward Maeder, and Aimee Newell have also been enormously helpful in helping me understand construction imperatives and techniques.

100. Linda Baumgarten and John Watson, *Costume Close-Up: Clothing Construction and Pattern* (Williamsburg, Va.: The Colonial Williamsburg Foundation, 1999), 7.

101. For discussion of how evidence from extant garments reveals construction on the body, see *ibid.,* 11–28.

102. Lazaro, "Construction in Context," 31–32.

103. EPP memorandum book, 14 June 1789, PPHP.

104. Ibid., 25 May 1788, PPHP. Thankful would have some gowns altered that fall as well; see 20 September 1789.

105. Claudia Kidwell, *Cutting a Fashionable Fit: Dressmaker's Drafting Systems in the United States* (Washington, D.C.: Smithsonian Institution Press, 1979), 11–13.

106. Baumgarten and Watson, *Costume Close-Up,* 9, 8.

107. Ruth Pease diary, 13–14 February 1812, Pease-Hyde Family Papers, box 1, folder 8, PVMA.

108. Ibid., 2 June 1812.

109. Oliver Talcott account book, Elizur Burnham account, 18 May 1776, and Ephraim Baker account, 1783, Wethersfield Historical Society, Wethersfield, Conn.

110. Judd, "Miscellaneous," 14:244–45.

111. EPP memorandum book, 29 March 1807, PPHP.

112. EWPH to EPP, 7 June 1803, PPHP.

113. Susannah Craft Heath to Elizabeth Craft White, 22 October 1797, Heath Family Papers, (1736–1887), MHS.

114. Lazaro, "Construction in Context," 33, traces ways in which artisans struggled to adapt to the challenges that accompanied the shift toward neoclassical style, developing new technical skills along the way.

Chapter 3. Needlework of the Rural Gentry: The World of Elizabeth Porter Phelps

Portions of this chapter appeared in earlier form in Marla R. Miller, "And others of our own people": Needlework and Women of the Rural Gentry," in *What's New England about New England Quilts? Proceedings of a Symposium at Old Sturbridge Village, 13 July 1998,* ed. Lynne Z. Bassett and Jack Larkin, 19–33 (Old Sturbridge Village, Mass., 1999).

1. EPP memorandum book, 13 August 1769, PPHP.

2. This description of the process involved in the making of a quilted petticoat is based on the following material: Patsy Orlofsky and Myron Orlofsky, *Quilts in America* (New York: Abbeville Press, 1992), 91–148; Ruth Finley, *Old Patchwork Quilts and the Women Who Made Them* (Newton Centre, Mass.: Charles T. Branford, 1970), 41–46; Jane C. Nylander, *Our Own Snug Fireside: Images of the New England Home, 1760–1860* (New York: Alfred A. Knopf, 1993), 228–30; Sylvester Judd's interview with Mrs. Moses Kingsley, in Judd, "Northampton," 1:487, FL.

3. "In describing a quilting . . . Martha [Ballard] mentioned that she 'helpt break the wool' that was used to fill the quilt and that a neighbor came to 'Chalk' or mark the design to be stitched." Laurel Thatcher Ulrich, *A Midwife's Tale: The Life of Martha Ballard, Based on Her Diary, 1785–1812* (New York: Alfred A. Knopf, 1990), 389–90, n. 11.

4. Elaine Hedges analyzes the use of quilt imagery, especially among feminist literary critics, in a highly insightful paper entitled "Romancing the Quilt: Feminism and the Contemporary Quilt Revival" (1993), a draft of which I was able to read in the collections of Old Sturbridge Village. My thanks to Sarah LeCount, Curator of Textiles and Fine Arts at the time, for making me aware of Hedges's manuscript, and to her successors, Lynne Bassett and Aimee Newell, for making it available to me.

5. See Radka Donnell, *Quilts as Women's Art: A Poetics* (North Vancouver, B.C.: Gallerie Publications, 1990); Judith Helen Elsley, "The Semiotics of Quilting: Discourse of the Marginalized" (Ph.D. diss., University of Arizona, 1990).

6. The 1995 film *How to Make an American Quilt* (Universal Studios and Amblin Entertainment, 1995), based on Whitney Otto's best-selling novel by the same title, is among the best-known examples of this particular form of mythmaking: through the quilting circle, women of different races, ages, and backgrounds come together around the quilt frame, their differences receding as they worked. Not surprisingly, the book offers a more sophisticated treatment of these issues than the film. Otto's narrator, Finn, in the end observes that it was the quilters's "recognition of their differences that allowed the group to survive, not pretending to transcend them." She adds, "The impulse to unify and separate, rend and join, is powerful and constant." Whitney Otto, *How to Make and American Quilt* (New York: Villard Books, 1991).

7. Hedges, "Romancing the Quilt," 1–2. Radka Donnell asserts that "quilts counteract separation anxiety" in *Quilts as Women's Art,* 67. I by no means wish to suggest, however, that all scholarship regarding early American quilting is colored by romantic longing; the American Quilt Study Group, which publishes the journal *Uncoverings,* is an excellent resource for information on the history of this work.

8. In a discussion of quilts and their use in historic tableaux, Jeanette Lasansky writes that "starting first in Brooklyn in 1864 . . . and then going on to New York, Philadelphia, Indianapolis, St. Louis and Poughkeepsie 'New England Kitchens' . . . with their regional variations . . . all had certain elements: the large and central fireplace, a gun over the mantel and candlesticks on it, a nearby string of dried apples, a tall clock and a spinning wheel. The women always wore mobcaps and a quilting bee was often part of the view." Lasansky, "The Colonial Revival and Quilts, 1864–1976," in *Pieced by Mother: Symposium Papers,* an Oral Traditions Project, ed. Lasansky (Philadelphia: University of Pennsylvania Press, 1988), 98.

9. Robert Shaw, *Quilts: A Living Tradition* (Hong Kong: Hugh Levin Associates, 1995), 7–8.

10. Sally Garoutte, "Early Colonial Quilts in a Bedding Context," *Uncoverings* 1 (1980): 18–27, esp. 18. Garoutte's article was first delivered as a paper to the American Quilt Study Group at its 1980 organizational meeting; though the article is now more than twenty-five years old, the myths she describes concerning early American quilts as artifacts of economic need common throughout colonial households still thrive.

11. HCMRP, 1770–1800. Of course, probate inventories are an imperfect source: in several instances, assessors lumped these textiles together as "bed and bedding," or "bed furnishings." A handful of inventories listed no textiles at all. Silvia Maulini found similar results in her study of Amherst; while no family possessed more than one quilt, blankets were owned in abundance. That many were homemade is suggested by one assessor's distinction, "boughten blanket." Maulini, "Women and the Paradox of Patriarchy in Eighteenth-Century Amherst" (honors paper, Mt. Holyoke College, 1980). In the twenty-four yeoman households Laura L. Tedeschi tracked between 1786 and 1810, nine contained no quilts (of those, four list no bedding of any sort, suggesting that something else had happened to all of these textiles before the inventory was taken). Typically these households owned eight sheets (the most held thirty-three), three blankets (the number ranged from one to thirteen), and two or perhaps three quilts. Some households without quilts possessed a number of coverlets (also called "coverlids") and bed rugs. Tedeschi, "Yeoman Farmers in Post-Revolutionary Deerfield: Class Status and Material Possessions" (seminar paper, Historic Deerfield, Inc., 1992). See also Roderick Kiracofe, *The American Quilt: A History of Cloth and Comfort, 1750–1950* (New York: Clarkson Potter, 1993), 48; Adrienne D. Hood, "The Material World of Cloth Production and Use in Eighteenth-Century Rural Pennsylvania, *William and Mary Quarterly* 53 (1996): 43–66, esp. 62.

12. Catharine Anne Wilson, "Reciprocal Work Bees and the Meaning of Neighbourhood," *Canadian Historical Review* 82 (2001): 431–64. Wilson points out that most participants in bees "would have been baffled to find twentieth-century writers casting the bee as the embodiment of the communal ideal and the polar opposite of the capitalistic spirit of individualism and material gain. Instead, most farm families understood that the work was a commodity and also a means to foster neighborly relations" (461).

13. The enormously popular book by Pat Ferrero, *Hearts and Hands: The Influence of Women and Quilts on American Society* (San Francisco: Quilt Digest Press, 1987) and ac-

companying film of the same name (San Francisco: Hearts and Hands Media Arts, 1988) associate quilting with the process of democratization, a theme resonant through much quilt scholarship. And quilting has indeed become a site of political action: for example, the NAMES project has produced a gigantic quilt to commemorate the lives of victims of AIDS and to call for greater commitment to defeating the disease. The Boise Peace Quilters have produced dozens of quilts to promote international understanding. But this association of quilting with forces of democratization is a legacy of nineteenth-century quilting traditions and is less appropriately applied to earlier periods; indeed, as a later discussion reveals, quilting in the eighteenth century can be seen as one means by which elite women helped resist those forces. See G. Julie Powell, *The Fabric of Persuasion: Two Hundred Years of Political Quilts* (Chadds Ford, Pa.: Brandywine River Museum, 2000); Linda Pershing, "The Ribbon around the Pentagon: Women's Traditional Fabric Arts as a Vehicle for Social Critique" (Ph.D. diss., University of Texas at Austin, 1990).

14. Elaine Hedges makes the excellent point that feminist invocations of quilt imagery often themselves disseminate misinformation about the history of quilts and quilting: "Too few feminist scholars are doing primary research into quilt history," she observes, perhaps because, "despite the appeal of the quilt as metaphor, researching the actual material objects is still seen as low-status work." Hedges, "Romancing the Quilt," 5–6.

15. Susan Burrows Swan, *Plain and Fancy: American Women and Their Needlework, 1700–1850* (New York: Holt, Rinehart and Winston, 1977); Suzanne Flynt, *Ornamental and Useful Accomplishments: Schoolgirl Education and Deerfield Academy, 1800–1830* (Deerfield: PVMA, 1988); Betty Ring, *Girlhood Embroidery: American Samplers and Pictorial Needlework, 1650–1850,* 2 vols. (New York: Alfred A. Knopf, 1993).

16. Nancy Cott, *The Bonds of Womanhood: "Woman's Sphere" in New England, 1780–1835* (New Haven: Yale University Press, 1977), 52.

17. Abigail Wadsworth's gown is in the collections of the Wadsworth Atheneum, Hartford, Conn.; two identical panels, supposedly the work of Abigail's mother, reside in the collections of the Webb-Deane-Stevens house in Wethersfield, Conn. See J. Herbert Callister, *Dress from Three Centuries: Wadsworth Atheneum* (Hartford: Wadsworth Atheneum, 1976), 10. Fragments of Mary Wright Alsop's embroidered gown can be found in the collections of the H. F. du Pont Winterthur Museum, Winterthur, Del.

18. For studies of crewelwork, see Swan, *Plain and Fancy;* also Ann Pollard Rowe, *Crewel Embroidered Bed Hangings in Old and New England* (Boston, Museum of Fine Arts, 1974); Mary Taylor Landon and Susan Burrows Swan, *American Crewelwork* (New York: Macmillan, 1970); Abbott Lowell Cummings, *Bed Hangings: A Treatise on Fabrics and Styles in the Curtaining of Beds, 1650–1850* (Boston: Society for the Preservation of New England Antiquities, 1961).

19. As Laurel Thatcher Ulrich has correctly observed, "Bending over their embroidery frames, little girls added value to themselves as well as to the silk their parents purchased." Ulrich, *The Age of Homespun: Objects and Stories in the Creation of an American Myth* (New York: Alfred A. Knopf, 2001), 147.

20. *Interesting Family Letters to the Late Mrs Ruth Patten* (Hartford, 1845), 18–20, quoted in Suzanne Flynt, *Ornamental and Useful Accomplishments: Schoolgirl Education and Deerfield Academy, 1800–1830* (Deerfield: PVMA, 1988), 17.

21. The best starting place is Ring, *Girlhood Embroidery.*

22. Betty Ring, "Heraldic Embroidery in Eighteenth-Century Boston," *Antiques,* April 1992, 622–31, and "Heraldic Needlework of the Neoclassical Period," *Antiques,* Oc-

tober 1993, 484–93. On the appeal of opportunities to demonstrate an Anglo-American identity, see Timothy Breen, "An Empire of Goods: The Anglicization of Colonial America, 1690–1776" *Journal of British Studies* 25 (1986): 467–99.

23. The Stoddard coat of arms is now in the collection of HN; Anne Grant's work is in the collections of Historic Deerfield. On Grant's schooling, see Henry R. Stiles, *The History of Ancient Windsor,* 2 vols., a facsimile of the 1892 edition (Somersworth: New Hampshire Publishing Company, 1976), 311–12.

24. The Mather coat of arms, now in the collection of the Longmeadow Historical Society, Longmeadow, Mass., is described in Jane C. Nylander, "Textiles, Clothing, and Needlework," in *The Great River: Art and Society of the Connecticut Valley, 1635–1820,* ed. William Hosley (Hartford: Wadsworth Atheneum, 1985), 407; and Ring, "Heraldic Needlework of the Neoclassical Period," 484.

25. Mary Porter to Jonathan Edward, 23 September 1770, Edwards Family Papers, folder 1439, Beinecke Library, Yale University, New Haven, Conn.

26. Mary Edwards Hoyt to Jonathan Edwards, 9 January 1796, Edwards Family Papers, folder 1446, Beinecke Library.

27. Jerusha Pitkin's work is preserved among the collections of CHS.

28. Harry Beckwith of the New England Historic Genealogical Society (hereafter NEHGS) Committee on Heraldry reviewed the needlework and a watercolor image of the Porter heraldry and observed in a letter to Betty Ring, 8 September 1993, that the watercolor appears to have been copied from the embroidery and not the reverse, as has been generally assumed. My thanks to Betty Ring for corresponding about this embroidery and sharing this exchange with me.

29. Journal of Abby Wright, 5 August 1805, in "Abby Wright Allen: A Record of Her Letters, etc., 1798–1842," Mount Holyoke College Special Collections and Archives, South Hadley, Mass.

30. Journal of Abigail Brackett Lyman, 3, 4, and 6 February 1800, in Helen Roelker Kessler, "The Worlds of Abigail Brackett Lyman" (master's thesis, Tufts University, 1976), 124–25.

31. Ibid., 141–42; see also 81.

32. On Snow, see Ring, *Girlhood Embroidery,* 1:74.

33. Journal of Abigail Brackett Lyman, 23 March 1800, in Kessler, "Worlds of Abigail Brackett Lyman," 81–83.

34. Sarah Porter Hillhouse to Sarah H. Gilbert, ca. 1795, Alexander and Hillhouse Family Papers, Southern Historical Collection, Chapel Hill, N.C.

35. The following discussion of Alsop draws on Glee Krueger, "A Middletown Cameo: Mary Wright Alsop and Her Needlework," *Connecticut Historical Society Bulletin* 52 (Summer/Fall 1987): 125–224.

36. See, e.g., Sylvester Judd, *History of Hadley* (Springfield, Mass.: H. R. Huntting and Co., 1905), 46, 261, 418; James Avery Smith, *The History of the Black Population of Amherst, 1728–1870* (Boston: NEHGS, 1999); Joseph Carvalho III, *Black Families in Hampden County, Massachusetts, 1650–1855* (Boston: NEHGS, 1984); Kevin M. Sweeney, "River Gods and Related Minor Deities: The Williams Family and the Connecticut River Valley, 1637–1790" (Ph.D. diss., Yale University, 1987), 82–83; Alain C. White, *History of the Town of Litchfield* (Litchfield, Conn.: Enquirer Print, 1920), 151.

37. EPP's memorandum book (PPHP) contains seventy-nine references to quilting.

Of these, twelve describe petticoats and twenty-two describe bed quilts; the remainder are unspecified. The majority of these references are in the summer months, suggesting that women took advantage of the extended daylight to complete such projects. For a discussion of eighteenth-century quilting in the Connecticut River Valley, including that in the Phelps household, see Nylander, "Textiles, Clothing and Needlework," 371–413. HN holds several quilted petticoats in its clothing collection like those made by Phelps and her peers, including a pink silk coat worn by Prudence Chester Stoddard (1699–1786), her daughter Esther (1738–1816), or her daughter-in-law Martha Partridge Stoddard (1739–1772).

38. The role of ornamental textiles in defining status has been amply documented. Key works include Swan, *Plain and Fancy,* and Ring, *Girlhood Embroidery.* See also Grant McCracken, *Culture and Consumption* (Bloomington: University of Indiana Press, 1982), 57–70.

39. See Nylander, "Textiles, Clothing, and Needlework," 378; Tandy Hersh, "Quilted Petticoats," in *Pieced by Mother,* ed. Jeannette Lasansky (Lewisburg, Pa.: Oral Traditions Project of the Union County Historical Society, 1988), 5–11; Linda Baumgarten and John Watson, *Costume Close-Up: Clothing Construction and Pattern* (Williamsburg: The Colonial Williamsburg Foundation, 1999), 29–38; Linda Baumgarten, *What Clothes Reveal: The Language of Clothing in Colonial and Federal America* (Williamsburg: The Colonial Williamsburg Foundation, 2002), 89.

40. Connecticut Valley Clothing File, a database created by the author in the spring and summer of 2001, documenting almost twelve thousand articles of apparel owned by all decedents whose inventories (taken 1760–1810) enumerated apparel in eighteen Connecticut Valley towns. Since probate inventories disproportionately record the wardrobe of older women, they likely misrepresent the spectrum of color that would have been present in any gathering of women. Michele Boardman, however, also found a preponderance of black clothing in her study of clothing in New England portraiture. She suggests that the popularity of black stems not only from its practicality, since dark fabrics are less likely to show stains, but also from its connotation of seriousness, and religiosity. She cites prescriptive literature that recommends dark colors for older women, only black for the truly elderly, and white for young women. Boardman, "Picturing the Past: Studying Clothing through Portraits" (research report, Old Sturbridge Village, 1990), 17–18.

41. Connecticut Valley Clothing File.

42. Sally Garoutte, "Early Colonial Quilts in a Bedding Context."

43. R[obert] Campbell, *London Tradesman* (1747; repr., New York: David and Charles Reprints, 1969), 213; see also Ivy Pinchbeck, *Women Workers in the Industrial Revolution, 1750–1850* (London: Cass, 1969), 288, 289.

44. Beverly Lemire, "Redressing the History of the Clothing Trade in England: Ready-Made Clothing, Guilds, and Women Workers, 1650–1800," *Dress* 21 (1994): 61–74. A beige quilted silk skirt in the collection of HN (1979.20.80) has been identified as a product of this London trade. The skirt has no batting, and its drawstrings can be either gathered evenly around the waist, producing a bell-shaped silhouette, or gathered all at the sides, producing the wide-at-the-hips appearance also created in the eighteenth century by panniers.

45. See Sylvester Judd, "Miscellaneous," 14:178, 190, 300, 17: 410, FL.

46. E.g., *Boston Gazette,* 22 August 1757, advertising "Quilted Petticoats, from 4 to 9

Breadths" and "Hoop Petticoats of various dimensions." Judd records "white quilting for petticoats" available in 1767 and "marseilles quilting for ladies coats" in 1772. "Miscellaneous," 14:300–301.

47. Kay Staniland, "An Eighteenth-Century Quilted Dress," *Costume* 24 (1990): 52.

48. Campbell, *London Tradesman,* 213.

49. Elizabeth Foote diary, 8 July 1775, CHS; Jonathan Judd diary, 22 June 1772, 20 November 1772, FL.

50. Several such frames with a Hadley, Massachusetts, provenance can be examined at the Hadley Farm Museum. I am grateful to Karen Parsons, then the volunteer curator of the HHS collections, for helping me to examine them.

51. Porter inventory, 1760, Hartford [Conn.] District Registry of Probate, vol. 18; Elisha Pomeroy inventory, 5 April 1762, HCMRP, 10:117–8.

52. Esther Williams Williams papers, Ashley Family Papers, PVMA; for her 29 May 1799 will, see also HCMRP, box 161, no. 20.

53. The Philadelphia' Loyalist and gentlewoman Grace Growden Galloway recorded being galled at seeing others ride in her family's confiscated carriage while she walked to quilting gatherings "like a common woman." Gunderson, *To be Useful to the World,* 161.

54. Judd, *Hadley,* 383.

55. EPP memorandum book, 13 and 20 May 1770, PPHP.

56. Ibid., 17 May 1795, PPHP; Judd, *Hadley,* 383.

57. Judd, *Hadley,* 382–83.

58. Ibid., 384.

59. Lemire, "Redressing the History of the Clothing Trade in England," 67.

60. EWPH to EPP, 9 September 1802, PPHP; and Lynn A. Bonfield, "Diaries of New England Quilters before 1860," *Uncoverings* 9 (1988): 171–98, esp. 177. According to Orlofsky and Orlofsky in *Quilts in America,* 64, a housewife might participate in twenty-five to thirty bees each year, but Hampshire County sources, including EPP's memorandum book, suggests that the number there was far fewer. Lynne Zacek Bassett's research supports the latter finding as well, and suggests, moreover, that quilting in groups was a largely seasonal affair, while solitary quilting was more common during winter months. See Bassett and Jack Larkin, *Northern Comfort; New England's Early Quilts, 1780–1850* (Nashville, Tenn.: Rutledge Hill Press, 1998), 102–4.

61. Ruth Henshaw Bascom diary, 28 June 1789, AAS.

62. Kevin M. Sweeney, "From Wilderness to Arcadian Vale: Material Life in the Connecticut Valley, 1635–1760," in *The Great River,* ed. William Hosley, 24; see also Sweeney, "Mansion People: Kinship, Class and Architecture in Western Massachusetts in the Mid Eighteenth Century," *Winterthur Portfolio* 19 no. 4 (Winter 1984): 231–55, esp. 234. The *Oxford English Dictionary* dates the usage of *quilting* as a noun to refer to a social event to just about this time—1768, the year before the quilting that opens this chapter.

63. Esther Edwards Burr, *The Journal of Esther Edwards Burr, 1754–1757,* ed. Carol F. Karlsen and Laurie Crumpacker (New Haven: Yale University Press, 1984), 101 (18 March 1755), 191 (5 April 1756). Some fifty years later, in Northampton, Mass., Abigail Brackett Lyman tried to avoid the "inconveniences of entertaining at one time a large collection" and chose instead to entertain only a handful of select friends at a time. Journal of Abigail Brackett Lyman, 5 March 1800, in Kessler, "Worlds of Abigail Brackett Lyman," 138.

64. On the comparative time demanded by plain and ornamental quilting, see Judd, "Miscellaneous," 15:423–24.

65. Wilson, "Reciprocal Work Bees," 443, 451–53.

66. Sarah was accustomed to supervising slaves; her father, Eleazer Porter, held at one time at least six: Thankful, Tab, Agnes, Boston, Simeon, and Josh, each of whom eventually claimed the surname "Boston." Eleazer Porter's January 1758 inventory can be found in the HCMRP, box 117, no. 10.

67. In his 13 November 1753, Chester Williams bequeaths to his wife Sarah a "negro woman, Phillis," and a "negro girl" appears in his 13 February 1754 inventory; see HCMRP, box 161, no. 8; Bill of Sale, Samuel Kent to Israel Williams, 22 May 1734, and Bill of Sale, Hezekiah Whitmore to Israel Williams, 20 May 1753, quoted in George Sheldon, "Negro Slavery in Old Deerfield," *New England Magazine,* March 1893, 58.

68. The classic work on slavery in New England is Lorenzo Greene, *The Negro in Colonial New England, 1620–1776* (Port Washington, N.Y.: Kennikat Press, 1966); other important studies include William D. Piersen, *Black Yankees: The Development of an Afro-American Subculture in Eighteenth-Century New England* (Amherst: University of Massachusetts Press, 1988); Robert J. Cottrol, ed., *From African to Yankee: Narratives of Slavery and Freedom in Antebellum New England* (Armonk, N.Y.: M. E. Sharpe, 1998). Genealogical information on blacks in western Massachusetts can be found in Carvalho, *Black Families in Hampden County, Massachusetts;* and Smith, *History of the Black Population of Amherst.*

69. Jonathan Ashley will, 16 June 1780, HCMRP, box 5, no. 45; Jennifer Moon, "Master and Servant: Slavery in Eighteenth-Century Deerfield (seminar paper, Historic Deerfield, Inc., 1987). See also Sheldon, "Negro Slavery in Old Deerfield," where Jenny's last name is given as "Cole," though as yet that surname cannot be confirmed in other sources. My thanks to Robert Romer for clarifying these naming issues for me.

70. Sweeney, "River Gods," 82–83.

71. See Richard Crouch account book, vol. 3 (1745–61), 25, FL.

72. Crouch account book, vol. 3, FL; see 20 January 1754, 25 and 28 June 1754.

73. EPP to EWPH, 28 October 1802, PPHP.

74. See Karen V. Hansen, " 'Social Work': Visiting and the Creation of Community," in *A Very Social Time: Crafting Community in Antebellum New England,* 79–113 (Berkeley: University of California Press, 1994),

75. Susan Geib, "Changing Works: Agriculture and Society in Brookfield, Massachusetts, 1785–1820" (Ph.D. diss., Boston University, 1981), 168.

76. Interleaved almanacs of Sarah Porter, Jones Library, Amherst, Mass.; Journal of Abigail Brackett Lyman, 1 January 1800, in Kessler, "Worlds of Abigail Brackett Lyman," 105.

77. Wilson, "Reciprocal Work Bees," 439.

78. Considering the probability of omissions, this estimate, based on my analysis of several selected years of EPP's memorandum book is, I suspect, low. On the character and purpose of EPP's records, it is worth noting that, though dairying occupied a good deal of EPP's time and attention, it is never once mentioned in her memorandum book. Phelps apparently had no need to record labor performed wholly within her own household or labor she herself performed; perhaps she recorded them elsewhere, in a document or by some other means that has not survived. The volume was indeed largely a record of women who crossed her threshold, logging productive labor and "social" exchanges.

79. EWPH to EPP, 10 April 1801, PPHP.

80. Ibid., 29 August 1802.

81. Description of objects as the "best sort" are common; the example quoted here is from the inventories of Timothy Woodbridge, 7 January 1771 and 27 March 1772, HCMRP, box 163, no. 43. The notion of the public exchange of the "goods of the world at large" is drawn from Gerald L. Pocius, *A Place to Belong: Community, Order, and Everyday Space in Calvert, Newfoundland* (Athens: University of Georgia Press, 1991). See also Rodris Roth, "Tea-Drinking in Eighteenth-Century America: Its Etiquette and Equipage," in *Material Life in America, 1600–1860,* ed. Robert Blair St. George, 439–62 (Boston: Northeastern University Press, 1988); first published in *United States National Museum Bulletin* 225 (1961): 61–91

82. Kevin Sweeney suggests that the "quantity of furniture also documents the role entertaining played in the life of the River Gods." On average, these families owned about thirty chairs each, while their neighbors owned, on average, between six and twelve chairs. The number of tables, and specialized forms, such as tea tables, also "attest[s] to a polite style of life." Sweeney, "Mansion People," 246. See also Sweeney, "Furniture and the Domestic Environment in Wethersfield, Connecticut 1639–1800," in St. George, *Material Life in America,* 261–90.

83. Roth, "Tea-Drinking in Eighteenth-Century America," 439–62.

84. Tara Louise Gleason, "The Porter Phelps Huntington Family: The Social Position and Material Wealth of an Elite Family in Eighteenth-Century Hadley, Massachusetts" (honor's thesis, Amherst College, 1994), 20.

85. Elizabeth Porter/Moses Porter, 10 December 1755 Guardianship, HCMRP, box 117, no. 19. Phoebe Marsh (1719–1779) was widowed in 1760; she lived just below the Middle Highway in Hadley, on the east side of what is now West Street, not far from the Eleazer Porter household. See EPP memorandum book, 26 July 1767, PPHP.

86. Wilson, "Reciprocal Work Bees," 459.

87. EPP memorandum book, 3 July 1768, PPHP.

88. Likewise, Sarah Snell Bryant of Cummington participated in three to five quiltings a year until 1803, "but none during the next ten years when her house was full of very young children and her elderly parents needed care." Nylander, *Our Own Snug Fireside,* 228. See also Martha Ballard Moore's references to quilting, concentrated in the 1790s when Ballard, then in her fifties, helped her grown daughters make bed quilts, discussed in Ulrich, *Midwife's Tale,* 143–46.

89. Sarah Porter Hopkins, interestingly, was in her early forties when she acquired this quilted petticoat with the help of her young relatives. Biographical information on these women is culled from Judd, *Hadley;* Daniel White Wells, *A History of Hatfield, Massachusetts* (Springfield, Mass.: Published under the direction of F. C. H. Gibbons, 1910); James Russell Trumbull's "Northampton Families," typescript in FL; NEHGS, *Vital Records of Conway, Massachusetts, to the Year 1850* (Boston: NEHGS, 1943).

90. See, e.g., the EPP memorandum book, 18 August 1793, 7 December 1794, 19 October 1794, 23 July 1797, and 14 June 1799, PPHP. EPP's second "daughter" was Thankful Richmond, taken in by the family in December 1776 when she was two weeks old; Thankful's mother had died in childbirth, and Elizabeth had just lost her newborn son. After some agonizing, Elizabeth and Charles decided to keep the child. She stayed with them until her marriage to Enos Hitchcock in 1796. Throughout this work I treat Betsy and Thankful as equal members of the household, as I believe they were treated during their youth, though later correspondence suggests that over the years after her marriage, Thankful drifted somewhat from her former intimacy with the family.

91. Wilson, "Reciprocal Work Bees," 440.
92. Judd, "Miscellaneous," 15:423–24.

Chapter 4. Family, Community, and Informal Work in the Needle Trades: The Worlds of Easter Fairchild Newton and Tryphena Newton Cooke

Portions of this chapter appeared in earlier form in Marla R. Miller, "The Accounts of Tryphena Newton Cooke: Work, Family, and Community in Hadley, Massachusetts, 1780–1805," in *Textiles in New England: Four Centuries of Material Life,* Proceedings of the 1999 Dublin Seminar for New England Folklife, ed. Peter Benes, 161–72 (Boston: Boston University, 2001).

1. Mrs. John Barstow recorded this piece of family lore in a paper entitled "Baker's or Cook's Tavern," found in the "Historians Record of the Doings of the Old Hadley Chapter of the Daughters of the American Revolution," HHS.
2. Josiah Pierce Accounts, Interleaved Almanack, HHS.
3. EPP memorandum book, 28 November 1779, PPHP.
4. Ibid., 24 December 1786, 23 October 1791; 9 June 1805, 19 January 1812.
5. See the probate files for Francis Newton in HCMRP, box 105, no. 20; and innholder licenses for Francis Newton (1778–80) and Elizabeth Newton (1781–97, 1808 and 1810). Hampshire County Court of Common Pleas, Northampton, Mass.
6. Elijah Williams account book, 1747, PVMA
7. Unidentified account book, Longmeadow, vol. 3, Springfield City Library, Springfield, Mass.
8. Apollos King account book (1791–1803), Kent Public Library, Suffield, Conn.
9. Reuban and Lydia Duncan Champion Ledger (1753–1777), Champion-Stebbins Papers Family Account Books, Special Collections and Archives, W. E. B. Du Bois Library, University of Massachusetts Amherst.
10. John Hollister account book (1792–1818), Glastonbury [Conn.] Historical Society, 10.
11. Jane C. Nylander, "Textiles, Clothing, and Needlework," in *The Great River: Art and Society of the Connecticut Valley, 1635–1820,* ed. William Hosley, 371–413 (Hartford: Wadsworth Atheneum, 1985), 392.
12. See Jane C. Nylander, *Our Own Snug Fireside: Images of the New England Home, 1760–1860* (New York: Alfred A. Knopf, 1993), 149–59. I am also grateful to Anne Digan Lanning for sharing with me insights and information from her own work with this source.
13. EPP to EWPH, December 1802, EPP to EWPH, 27 March 1805, EPP to EWPH, 13 November 1810, EPP to Sally Parsons, 17 March 1802, EPP memorandum book, 30 May 1812, 24 January 1813, 16 April 1815, EWPH to EPP, 11 January 1801, EWPH to EPP, 22 October 1802, PPHP.
14. EPP to EWPH, 22 October 1802, PPHP.
15. Hannah H. Smith to Abigail Mitchell, 2 August 1800, Correspondence of Smith and Mitchell Families (1796–1819), Connecticut State Library, Hartford, Conn.
16. EWPH to EPP, 16 November 1804, PPHP.
17. Mary Graves Miller, "Articles and essays by Mrs Mary Esther Graves Miller of Hatfield Mass," Miller Family Papers, box 1–122, PVMA; clipping, "Old Times in the Connecticut Valley," 15 May 1889.

18. Faye Dudden, *Serving Women: Household Service in Nineteenth-Century America* (Middletown, Conn.: Wesleyan University Press, 1983), 14.

19. EPP to EWPH, 2 March 1801, PPHP; and Dudden, *Serving Women.*

20. EPP to EWPH, 9 March 1803, PPHP.

21. William Stoddard Williams in Stockbridge to Patty Williams in Deerfield, 22 August 1784, in the papers of William Stoddard Williams, Williams Family Papers, PVMA.

22. EPP to EWPH, 17 December 1801, PPHP.

23. Ibid., 13 June 1801.

24. Ibid., 22 October 1802, 1 November 1805.

25. EWPH to Charles Phelps Jr., 12 July 12 1797, PPHP.

26. Ibid., 1 July 1796, [?] April 1797; 19 May 1797; 30 May 1797.

27. Ibid., 12 July 12 1797.

28. Similarly, the only reference in EWPH's correspondence that makes clear the home of a tailoress notes that she came from EWPH's own community: "Tomorrow your son goes to New Haven. I shall not be quite alone as I expect a girl to help me about sewing—Bethia Mason, she is a very pretty girl the daughter of a farmer in the east part of the town." EWPH to EPP, 8 September 1803, PPHP.

29. EPP memorandum book, 5 August 1792, PPHP.

30. Aileen Agnew's investigation of women and their local economies in eighteenth-century upstate New York has yielded some fascinating insights into the economic activities of African Americans living in Albany—a community near the western border of Massachusetts with which Connecticut Valley towns had much commercial intercourse. The black customers who traded with the merchant Elizabeth Schuyler Sanders bought items similar to those purchased by whites and paid for them largely in cash and garden produce. But "no blacks offered work of any kind as a payment," since, as slaves, their labor was not theirs to sell. In eighteenth-century Albany, at least, "Black women thus never sewed for credit, as white women did." Aileen B. Agnew, "Silent Partners: The Economic Life of Women on the Frontier of Colonial New York" (Ph.D. diss., University of New Hampshire, 1998); I am grateful to the author for sharing her work with me at an early stage in her project. See also Aileen B. Agnew, "The Retail Trade of Elizabeth Sanders and the 'Other' Consumers of Colonial Albany," *Hudson Valley Regional Review* 14, no. 2 (1997): 35–55

31. William Porter Papers, box 1, folder 6 (1803), Old Sturbridge Village, Sturbridge, Mass.

32. Indenture, Simon Baker to Charles Phelps, 1 May 1766, PPHP. Likewise, in October 1802, EPP in her diary recorded that Polly Seymour had come "to make Zerviah's silk gown" one week before Zerviah left EPP's employ. See EPP memorandum book, 10 and 17 October 1802, PPHP. In Northampton, when Saul Alvord was obliged to supply the hired man Hendrick Sleighter with two linen shirts, a frock, overall, and a pair of trousers, as well as a woolen shirt, a checked shirt, and a pair of stockings, the needlewoman Sarah King Root Clark provided both the cloth for the frock and checked shirts and the labor to make them up; for the overalls and trousers, she provided at least the labor and thread. See Sylvester Judd, "Miscellaneous," 11:62, and "Northampton," 2:244, FL.

33. EPP memorandum book, 24 May 1778, PPHP.

34. Solomon Cook account book (1789–1807), Hadley [Mass.] Historical Society, 23.

35. Reuban and Lydia Duncan Champion Ledger (1753–1777), Champion-Stebbins Papers Family Account Books.

36. Josiah Pierce account book, Moses Gunn account, entry for 13 November 1753, HHS. In November 1754 and November 1759, Gunn's accounts are once again settled by the making of leather breeches, 12/4 (a pair for Josiah and another for Samuel), and by the making (in 1759) of a banyan for William and cutting out a pair of breeches for Josiah, 1/10.

37. Jerijah Barber Sr. account books (1770–1793), November 1786, Windsor [Conn.] Historical Society.

38. Sylvester Judd, *History of Hadley* (Springfield, Mass.: H. R. Huntting and Co., 1905), 423. The average value of Hadley estates in 1770 was £70. Judd further records that Bartlett "came from Amherst in 1755, and had the care of the farm of the widow of Captain Moses Porter a few years" (425).

39. Nash Petition, December 1782, HCMRP, box 104, no. 11. It seems possible that Porter's awareness of the Nash family's circumstances prompted Lucy's employment at Forty Acres.

40. Robert Blair St. George, "Artifacts of Regional Consciousness in the Connecticut River Valley, 1700–1780," in Hosley, *Great River*, 29–39, esp. 32.

41. William Hosley, "Regional Furniture/Regional Life," in Luke Beckerdite and Hosley, eds., *American Furniture 1995* ([Milwaukee, Wisc.]: Chipstone Foundation; Hanover, N.H.: University Press of New England, 1995), 25, citing Philip Zea, "The Emergence of Neoclassical Furniture Making in Rural Western Massachusetts," *Antiques* 142 (December 1992): 842–51.

42. For a similar pattern elsewhere in the Atlantic World, see Olwyn Hufton, "Women and the Family Economy in Eighteenth-Century France," *French Historical Studies* 9 (1975): 1–22.

43. On Marsh, see EPP memorandum book, e.g., 22 March 1778, 26 December 1779, 15 July 1781, 9 September 1781, 13 July 1782. PPHP; on Kellogg, see 5 January, 19 January, 20 April, 4 May, 18 May, and 2 November 1783, PPHP.

44. Judd, "Northampton," 1:91. Jane C. Nylander analyzes the content of the Lane assemblages in "Provision for Daughters: The Accounts of Samuel Lane," in *House and Home,* Proceedings of the 1988 Dublin Seminar for New England Folklife, ed. Peter Benes, 11–27 (Boston: Boston University, 1990).

45. See Hampden County [Mass.] Registry of Deeds, vol. 18/68; K/176, L/174.

46. These figures are derived from the valuations attached to 104 Hadley heads of household in Sylvester Judd, *Hadley,* 423.

47. Peter Benes offers this definition in his introduction to *Itinerancy in New England and New York,* Proceedings of the 1984 Dublin Seminar for New England Folklife (Boston: Boston University, 1986), 7.

48. Josiah Pierce almanacs, September–October 1764, 11, 15, 19 and 22 March 1765, 30 May 1765, Jones Library, Amherst, Mass.

49. EPP memorandum book, 6 October 1816, PPHP.

50. Francis Newton Widow Allowance, 9 August 1785 , HCMRP, box 105, no. 20.

51. EPP memorandum book, 21 November 1779, 18 June, 27 August, and 3 December 1780, 14 October, 11 and 18 November, 23 December 1781, 13 and 27 January, 9 and 23 June, 7 July, 28 December 1782, 5 and 19 January, 2 March, 20 April, 4 and 18 May 1783. See also Josiah Pierce account book and interleaved almanac, March 1771, HHS.

52. EPP memorandum book, 2 March, 20 April, 4 May, and 18 May 1783, PPHP.

53. TNC account book, HHS.

54. William Porter Papers, box 1, folder 3 (1800), Old Sturbridge Village.

55. The source and amount of the Cooke family's debts are not recorded in this ledger, unfortunately, but are carried over from an earlier and apparently no longer extant account.

56. It seems quite possible that the additional labor expended in the early 1790s was related to the expenses incurred during the construction of the Cooke tavern.

57. In June 1791, for example, Parker was charged for fifty yards of cloth, "finding thread," and the making of two shirts, a pair of trousers, overalls, a fine holland shirt, a coat, a jacket, and one other item that is illegible. The fabric, perhaps produced by TNC, was worth 8 shillings 4 pence. The sewing was together valued at £1 4s. 10d. Cooke account book, HHS, 10.

58. See Anne Digan Lanning, "Women Tavernkeepers in the Connecticut River Valley," in *New England Celebrates: Spectacle, Commemoration and Festivity,* Proceedings of the 2000 Dublin Seminar for New England Folklife, ed. Peter Benes, 202–14 (Boston: Boston University, 2002).

59. When Epaphrus Hoyt in 1790 traveled from Deerfield to Philadelphia, he records having put up at "Mrs Newton's tavern at the end of Hadley." See the Epaphras Hoyt diary, 17 July 1790, PVMA.

60. *HG,* 12 October 1796.

61. Hadley Historical Commission survey forms, Goodwin Memorial Library, Hadley, Mass.; John Barstow, "Baker's or Cook's Tavern," HHS.

62. EPP to EWPH, 1 April 1804, PPHP.

63. Ibid., 4 April 1804.

64. EPP memorandum book, 9 December 1804, 2 and 9 June 1805, PPHP.

65. Barstow, "Baker's or Cook's Tavern," 127–29.

66. The shirt and bonnet worn by Samuel Cook were examined by researchers in preparation for the Wadsworth Atheneum's 1985 Great River exhibition by Mrs. Charles Cook. See William N. Hosley, *The Great River Archives: Inventories, House Surveys, Manuscript Files, Photo Files, Cultural Histories* (Guilford, Conn.: Opus Publications, 1989), reel 6.

67. Main, "Gender, Work, and Wages," 58.

Chapter 5. Family, Artisanry, and Craft Tradition: The Worlds of Tabitha Clark Smith and Rebecca Dickinson

Acknowledgments: Some of this material appears in my articles " 'My Part Alone': The World of Rebecca Dickinson," *New England Quarterly* 71, no. 3 (September 1998): 1–38, and "Gownmaking as a Trade for Women in Eighteenth-Century Rural New England," *Dress* 29–30 (2002–2003): 15–25.

1. EPP memorandum book, 20 November 1768, PPHP.

2. RD diary, 10 September 1787, PVMA.

3. See, for example, EPP memorandum book, 23 June 1782, PPHP.

4. See Christopher Zeeman, "Mathematics Applied to Dressmaking," *Costume* 28 (1994): 97–102.

5. R[obert] Campbell, *The London Tradesman* (1747; repr., London: David and Charles Reprints, 1969), 227.

6. *The Book of Trades or Library of the Useful Arts* (London: Tabart & Co., 1806), 34, 31.

7. Sylvester Judd, "Miscellaneous," 14:244, FL; Wright account book (1787–1810), HN.

8. The Elizabeth Foote bed rug is in the collections of CHS; bed rugs attributed to her sisters Abigail and Mary are in the collections of Historic Deerfield, Deerfield, Mass., and the Winterthur Museum, Winterthur, Del., respectively. For further discussion of the Foote rugs, see Laurel Thatcher Ulrich, Lynne Z. Bassett, Iona Lincoln, and Jessie A. Marshall, "Four Perspectives on a Bed Rugg," in *Textiles in New England II: Four Centuries of Material Life,* Proceedings of the 1999 Dublin Seminar for New England Folklife, ed. Peter Benes, 13–26 (Boston: Boston University, 2001). Ulrich also discusses the Foote sisters and their needlework in *The Age of Homespun: Objects and Stories in the Creation of an American Myth* (New York: Alfred A. Knopf, 2001), 221–28.

9. Elizabeth Foote diary, CHS.

10. Experience Wight Richardson diary, November 26, 1759, MHS; Susannah Heath to Elizabeth White, 22 October 1797, Heath Family Papers, Correspondence (1736–1817), MHS.

11. See indentures of Ann Cromartie, bound 7 June 1769 to Ruth Decosta, Boston, and Ann Wilkinson, 3 December 1784 to Martha Mellens, Boston, Records of the Boston Overseers of the Poor, Boston Public Library; Lawrence W. Trainer, "The Indentures of Boston's Poor Apprentices, 1734–1805," in *Publications of the Colonial Society of Massachusetts,* vol. 43 (1956–63), 417–68.

12. Fisher indenture, 13 October 1788, Middlesex County Historical Society, Middletown, Conn.

13. Sylvester Judd, "Northampton," 2:140, FL.

14. Judd, "Miscellaneous," 14:244–45, FL.

15. Wright account book (1787–1810), HN.

16. EPP memorandum book, 1 August 1784, 11 April 1790, PPHP; see also 19 June 1791.

17. See Judd, "Miscellaneous," 14:242. No recipient is specified for 25 percent of the entries; adult men are specified as recipients for roughly 10 percent of the entries.

18. Wright account book (1787–1810), HN.

19. Nathaniel Phelps account, PVMA; Judd, "Northampton," 2:140. For staymaking, see Campbell, *London Tradesman,* 224–26.

20. Judd, "Miscellaneous," 14:242.

21. Ibid., 245.

22. Wright account book (1787–1810), HN.

23. *CC,* 8 May and 30 October 1775.

24. Ibid., 27 November 1775.

25. See Chapter 1 for a discussion of the founding of the Economical Association.

26. Suffolk County [Mass.] Registry of Deeds, 141:12.

27. On Mather, see *CC,* 17 July 1799; on the Lincoln family, see *CC,* 11 December 1811, 28 April 1812, 6 April 1813, 11 January 1814, 3 January and 7 November 1815; on Barnards, see *CC,* 8 September 1812, 7 December 1813.

28. Philip Zea, "Rural Craftsmen and Design," in *New England Furniture: The Colonial Era,* by Brock Jobe and Myrna Kaye, with the assistance of Zea (Boston: Houghton Mifflin, 1984), 56–57; Joshua Lane, "Breeches and Rum: An Investigation of Rural Economy through the Account Books of John Russell" (seminar paper, Historic Deerfield, Inc., 1984). See also Patricia Anne Trautman, "Colonel Edward Marrett: A Gentleman Tailor" (Ph.D. diss., University of Colorado, 1982), 68.

29. RD's journal records only the very end of her career; when she was a younger and more vigorous artisan, such travels may well have taken up a greater portion of her business.

30. RD diary, 5 October 1787, PVMA.

31. Catherine Phelps Parsons was the first daughter of Nathaniel Phelps and Catherine King, though Nathaniel Phelps had been married once before and had children, including at least one daughter.

32. Because of the scarcity of sources about trades for early American women, I was unable to research further the question of what trades the younger sisters may have learned and practiced. Of RD's younger siblings, I know only that her sister Miriam was greatly occupied with the running of her family's tavern.

33. By comparison, Wendy Gamber found that female partnerships accounted for almost 14 percent of Boston women's businesses between 1853 and 1887, with individual proprietors accounting for 75.9 percent of the trade, and husband-and-wife teams accounting for 10.3 percent. Gamber, *Female Economy: The Millinery and Dressmaking Trades, 1860–1930* (Urbana: University of Illinois, 1997), 32.

34. *CC,* 8 September 1812.

35. Ibid., 6 April 1813.

36. Ibid., 11 December 1811.

37. Ibid., 28 April 1812.

38. Judd, "Northampton," 1:332; for the relevant probate materials, see HCMRP, box 83, no. 3, box 83, no. 40, and box 113, no. 45.

39. Judd, "Northampton," 1:332.

40. Wright account book (1787–1810), HN. It is also possible that the Esther Wright, to whom these accounts belonged, was Solomon Wright's sister, the fifth child and third daughter of Selah and Esther Wright, born in 1763. She never married and died in December 1813 at the age of fifty. It is possible that the gown-making accounts contained in this record are hers, since she was an unmarried woman in her thirties at the time. Another possibility is that the entries recorded reflect the work of both mother and daughter, each of whom was an unmarried woman in need of income at the time the accounts were recorded. At present, it is simply impossible to tell. Because of the relationship of the mother, Esther, to a documented artisan, I have attributed the accounts to her, though of course there is a likelihood that she in turn passed those skills on to her daughter, who may have found them useful as a never-married woman in late eighteenth-century New England.

41. On the Phelps family, see especially John Phelps, *Family Memoirs* (Brattleboro, Vt.: Selleck and Davis, 1886); Kevin Graffagnino, "Vermonters Unmasked: Charles Phelps and the Patterns of Dissent in Revolutionary Vermont," *Vermont History* 57 (1989): 133–61; James Lincoln Huntington, "The Honorable Charles Phelps," in *Publications of the Colonial Society of Massachusetts,* vol. 32 (1933–37), 441–60; Benjamin H. Hall, *History of Eastern Vermont* (Albany: J. Munsell, 1865).

42. RD diary, 19 April 1789, PVMA.

43. Recent work by Christine Daniels draws important distinctions between trades and helps illuminate more precisely possible relationships between gender and the creation of familial craft identities. Though gender was not a particular focus of her work, she argues convincingly that craft skills were less likely to be passed down through generations in trades like needlework that required little capital investment. In other words, the more difficult to enter, the more likely a given craft was to encourage the development of familial "dynasties," while comparatively accessible crafts, such as clothing construction, did not demand a comparable intergenerational commitment. Daniels, "From Father to Son: The Economic Roots of Craft Dynasties in Eighteenth-Century Maryland," in *American Artisans: Crafting Social Identity, 1750–1850,* ed. Howard B. Rock, Paul A. Gilje, and Robert Asher, 3–16 (Baltimore: Johns Hopkins University Press, 1995).

44. Ibid., table 1.3, 9.

45. For genealogies, see James Russell Trumbull, "Northampton Genealogies," typescript in FL.

46. Edward Strong Cooke Jr., *Making Furniture in Preindustrial America: The Social Economy of Newtown and Woodbury, Connecticut* (Baltimore: Johns Hopkins University Press, 1996), 46.

47. EPP memorandum book, 16 July 1769, PPHP.

48. Ibid., e.g., 4 June 1769, 19 April 1772, 4 April 1773.

49. Ibid., 30 April 1775.

50. *HG,* ca. 28 May 1800, 14 July 1800, 23 December 1800.

51. Windsor Smith to Andrew Cooke, Hampshire County [Mass.] Registry of Deeds, 10:449.

52. EPP memorandum book, 1 August 1784, PPHP.

53. Ibid., 11 April 1790; see also 19 June 1791.

54. There is a large literature on this subject; the best place to begin is Thomas Dublin, *Transforming Women's Work: New England Lives in the Industrial Revolution* (Ithaca: Cornell University Press, 1994).

55. EPP memorandum book, 26 February 1792.

56. Judd, "Northampton," 1:571, 574; Solomon Clark, *Antiquities, Historical and Graduates of Northampton* (Northampton, Mass.: Steam Press of Gazette Printing Company, 1882), 151; Trumbull, "Northampton Genealogies."

57. See, for example, *HG* advertisements on 29 December 1800, 16 July 1800, and 6 January 1802.

58. EPP memorandum book, 15 July 1798, PPHP; see also Chapter One for a discussion of this visit by Gaylord to the Phelps home.

59. Philip Zea, catalogue entry 123, *The Great River: Art and Society of the Connecticut Valley, 1635–1820,* ed. William Hosley (Hartford: Wadsworth Atheneum, 1985), 239–40, and "Rural Craftsmen and Design," 65–67. See also Samuel Gaylord Jr. ledger (1763–90), PVMA.

60. EPP memorandum book, 10 September 1809, 11 December 1814, 24 September 1816, PPHP.

61. See bills and receipts from 1792 to 1801 in the Papers of William Porter, box A, folders 1–4, Old Sturbridge Village, Sturbridge, Mass..

62. Sylvester Judd, "Hadley," 3:302, FL.

63. On the growing relationship between the Phelps girls and Tabitha Clark Smith,

see EPP memorandum book, 2 September 1792, 7 October 1792, 14 July 1793, 27 December 1795, and EPP to EWPH, 28 March 1810, PPHP. Regarding Smith's possible second marriage, it appears that the mother followed the daughter; in January 1799, the widow Lucretia Smith Gaylord married Samuel Dexter Ward of Brimfield.

64; Hampden County [Mass.] Registry of Deeds, 26:738, 28:3.

65. RD diary, 21 June 1789, PVMA.

66. Ibid., [1–8] June 1789.

67. Ibid., [15–22] September 1787.

68. Abby Wright Allen letterbook, 27 September 1803, microfilm of transcription in the archives of Mount Holyoke College, South Hadley, Mass.

69. This tendency to use local craftspeople is no doubt linked as well to the heavy reliance of the region on credit. See Christopher Clark, *The Roots of Rural Capitalism: Western Massachusetts, 1780–1860* (Ithaca: Cornell University Press, 1990); Gregory Nobles, "The Rise of Merchants in Rural Market Towns: A Case Study of Eighteenth-Century Northampton, Massachusetts," *Journal of Social History* 24 (1991): 5–23.

70. RD diary, 26 September 1787, PVMA

71. Bridget Hill, *Women, Work, and Sexual Politics in Eighteenth-Century England* (Oxford: Basil Blackwood, 1989), 96. Wendy Gamber suggests that this motivation continued to influence mid-nineteenth-century parents. Gamber, "A Precarious Independence: Milliners and Dressmakers in Boston, 1860–1890," *Journal of Women's History* 4 (1992): 61–88, esp. 73.

72. EPP memorandum book, 14 August 1768, PPHP.

73. RD diary, 22 August 1787, PVMA.

74. See, for example, EPP, memorandum book, 17 July 1768, 14 August 1768, 20 November 1768, 3 June 1770, 11 August 1771, PPHP. For examples of tailoring, see 17 February 1771, 12 November 1775, 26 May 1776, and 26 January 1777. Jonathan Judd Jr. also noted in his diary that, at one wedding he attended, a woman named Lucy Clapp was "there to dress the bride." Judd diary, 24 November 1774, FL.

75. EPP memorandum book, 11 November 1770, PPHP.

76. Ibid., 15 May 1768.

77. Oliver Smith account book, 27, FL.

78. Polly L'Hommedieu Lathrop account book (1803–17), CHS.

79. RD diary, 23 November 1787, PVMA.

80. Ibid., 5 September 1787.

81. EPP memorandum book, 3 August 1806, PPHP.

82. RD diary, 30 November 1787, PVMA.

83. Ibid., 27 October 1787, [third Sunday in] July 1789.

84. Ibid., 10 September 1787.

85. Ibid., 13 September 1787, and [25 May–8 June] 1788.

86. Wills of Moses, Anna, Samuel, and RD are held in the HCMRP, box 48, no. 3, box 48, no. 13, and box 48, no. 49, respectively.

87. RD diary, 23 November 1787, PVMA.

88. Ibid, 22 November 1787, PVMA.

89. Ibid., 22 August 1787.

90. For more RD's attitude toward marriage, see Marla R. Miller, " 'My Part Alone': The World of Rebecca Dickinson," *New England Quarterly* 71, no. 3 (September 1998): 1–38.

91. The name "Aunt Beck" first occurs in a letter from EPP to EWPH, 9 June 1808, PPHP, on the occasion of the death and funeral of Silas Billings, RD's brother-in-law.

92. See, e.g., Polly Warren to David Wells, Deerfield Overseers of the Poor, Deerfield I-V Town Office, Overseers of the Poor, Indentures L–Z, 1764–1828, PVMA.

93. Excerpts from Sylvester Judd's interview with Catherine Parsons Graves, 1832, in Judd, "Northampton," 1:334.

94. See, e.g., Elizabeth Keckley, *Behind the Scenes; or, Thirty Years as a Slave and Four Years in the White House* [1868] (New York: Arno Press, 1968).

95. Karen V. Hansen calls such unmarried women "obviously essential" features of community life. See the discussion of gossip and "the community jury" in her book *A Very Social Time: Crafting Community in Antebellum New England* (Berkeley: University of California Press, 1994), 114–36, esp. 116. RD believed herself to be the subject of vicious gossip because of her status as an "old maid"; perhaps she employed gossip to gain some control over the reputations of those whom she believed gossiped about her, to "equalize social relations" despite a "subordinate position in society" (133).

96. Ibid., 116.

97. RD diary, [15–18] November 1787. RD may have had reason to believe that she, too, was the subject of gossip, since she seems to have been privy to gossip about other unmarried women in the community. Once she recorded having "heard of the death of the aged mrs white of this town She was formerly hannah meekins an old maid above forty years of age when she married mr white of Sprinkfeald [*sic*]." Hannah Meekins White was born in January 1698; when she, "an old maid above forty years of age," married, RD was a toddler and never knew her as other than married. But clearly her late marriage had been brought to RD's attention, and it was this sole fact that RD recorded upon White's death. RD diary, 21 June 1789, PVMA.

98. Ibid., [15–18] November 1787. Daniel White Wells, *A History of Hatfield, Massachusetts (*Springfield, Mass., Pub. under the direction of F. C. H. Gibbons, 1910), 205.

99. Wells, *Hatfield,* 256. RD's "eccentricity" is especially interesting in the light of the tendency in nineteenth-century novels to cast never-married women as peculiar, quirky, or quaint figures. These posthumous characterizations may be as reflective of Wells's and Partridge's cultural context as RD's actual personality.

100. As Wendy Gamber observes concerning nineteenth-century dressmakers, "evidence suggests that customers could confide in their dressmakers precisely because the latter were social inferiors; 'ladies' could divulge secrets that pride and propriety forbade them from telling their peers." Gamber, *Female Economy,* 106.

101. RD diary, 13 July [August] 1787, PVMA.

102. Ibid., 5 September 1787.

103. Ibid., [17–25] August 1794, 12 August 1792, 5 August 1787 31 May 1794.

104. Margaret Miller, "An Old Maid's Diary," *New York Evening Post,* 9 January 1892, 1.

105. EPP memorandum book, 8 and 22 July 1787, PPHP.

106. RD diary, 15 November 1787, PVMA

107. Ibid., 3 August 1794.

108. EPP recorded: "Satt: I jest rode to Hatfield to see Becca Dickinson, who has fall[en]down & hurt her hip badly," on 25 March 1815, PPHP.

Chapter Six. Gender, Artisanry, and Craft Tradition: The World of Catherine Phelps Parsons

This discussion of Catherine Phelps Parsons forms the basis of my article "Gender, Artisanry, and Craft Tradition in Early New England: The View through the Eye of a Needle," *William and Mary Quarterly* 60 (October 2003): 743–76.

1. J. Hammond Trumbull cites Robinson's admonition, further observing that "it was not many years before he had several competitors." Trumbull, *Memorial History of Hartford, Connecticut,* 2 vols. (Boston: Edward L. Osgood, 1886), 2:596. See also James Russell Trumbull, *History of Northampton, Massachusetts, from its founding in 1654,* 2 vols. (Northampton, Mass.: Press of the Gazette Printing Co., 1898–1902), 11; Henry B. Fearon, *Sketches of America,* in, *Career Women of America, 1776–1840 by* Elisabeth Anthony Dexter (c. 1950; repr., Clifton, N.J.: A. M. Kelley, 1972), 163.

2. Sylvester Judd records that "for many years after mrs Parsons was married, there was no man tailor in the place; Mr Hodge came before the revolution and was the first which Mrs Graves [Catherine Phelps Parsons' daughter] remembers." See Interview with Catherine Parsons Graves in Judd, "Northampton," 1:94, 101b, FL.

3. Ibid., 1:101b.

4. Judd records excerpts from "Town Expenses" in ibid., 2:106–17.

5. Whether CPP apprenticed formally is a matter of conjecture. The work Catherine King Phelps performed—making and altering gowns and mantuas, making stays, and making coats for children—suggests that CPP would not necessarily have been able to learn her skills from her mother, or to gain credibility as a local tailor from that training. But since Catherine King Phelps did on one occasion produce a "suit of clothes" for the tailor Samuel Pomeroy, it is possible. See ibid., 2:140.

6. Ibid., 1:101b.

7. Massachusetts would pass legislation to allow feme sole traders (that is, the right to own and operate a business independently from one's husband, conferred on women under specific circumstances defined by law) in 1787, but the benefits were narrowly construed and limited to women living apart from their husbands for extended periods. On both coverture and feme sole traders; see Mary Lynn Salmon, *Women and the Law of Property in Early America* (Chapel Hill: University of North Carolina Press, 1986), esp. 45–56.

8. Gloria L. Main, "Gender, Work, and Wages in Colonial New England," *William and Mary Quarterly* 51 (1994): 39–66; Sylvester Judd, "Women's Pay as Makers of Garments For Men," in "Miscellaneous," 9:161–63, FL. For Esther Graves, see Deed, 1755; Martha Nash, see Franklin County Registry of Deeds, 1792; Lydia Sawtelle Kellogg, see 1757 deed; Mary Smith, see Deed, 1777; Jemima Woolworth, see Deed, 1778. See also Elizabeth Southwick, New Salem, 1762 Deed; Anne Warriner Ely, New Salem, Deed, 1777, as cited in Daniel Lombardo, "A Directory of Craftsmen in the Connecticut Valley of Massachusetts to 1850," print-out of database on deposit at Memorial Libraries in Deerfield, Massachusetts.

9. Judd, "Northampton," 1:94; Susanna Allen, Writ of execution of judgment, 1772, Allen Family Papers, box 1, file 9, PVMA.

10. Daniel Lombardo, "A Directory of Craftsmen in the Connecticut Valley of Massachusetts to 1850," vol. 3, For other examples see Main, "Gender, Work and Wages," 59–60.

11. Suffolk sessions III, 133–34 and 314, quoted in Lawrence William Towner, "A Good Master Well Served: A Social History of Servitude in Massachusetts, 1620–1750" (Ph.D. dissertation, Northwestern University, 1954), 65.

12. See Christine Daniels, "From Father to Son: The Economic Roots of Craft Dynasties in Eighteenth-Century Maryland," in *American Artisans: Crafting Social Identity, 1750–1850,* ed. Howard B. Rock, Paul A. Gilje and Robert Asher, 3–16 (Baltimore: Johns Hopkins University Press, 1995).

13. R[obert], Campbell, *The London Tradesman* (1747; repr., New York, 1969), 190–94.

14. Samuel Foote, *The Tailors: A Tragedy for Warm Weather, in Three Acts* (London: T. Sherlock, 1778), 41, American Antiquarian Society, Worcester, Mass.

15. Campbell, *London Tradesman,* 192.

16. Ibid. On the importance of posture in this period, see Richard Bushman, *The Refinement of America: Persons, Houses, Cities* (New York: Alfred A. Knopf, 1992).

17. For Anna Graham, see Wethersfield, box 3, Connecticut State Library, Hartford, RG 62; for Clarinda Colton, see Burt Family Papers, PVMA.

18. Judd, "Northampton," 1:101b.

19. Ibid., 1:94; see also Trumbull, *History of Northampton,* 2:615.

20. Judd, "Northampton," 1:101b.

21. Ilana Krausman Ben-Amos found that among young female craft apprentices in early modern Bristol, nearly half were the daughters of craftsmen. Just under one-fifth were the daughters of merchants or professionals, of which one-third were drawn from the "landed and agricultural classes." Daughters of gentlemen accounted for 7 percent of the town's female craft apprentices. Only three girls were drawn from the laboring classes. Ben-Amos, "Women Apprentices in the Trades and Crafts of Early Modern Bristol," *Continuity and Change* 6 (1991): 227–52, esp. 230–31.

22. Bridget Hill, *Women, Work, and Sexual Politics in Eighteenth-Century England* (Oxford: Basil Blackwell, 1989), 95.

23. See "Caleb Strong," in John Langdon Sibley, *Biographical Sketches of Graduates of Harvard University, in Cambridge, Massachusetts* (Cambridge, Mass., Charles William Sever, 1873–85); Emily L. Myers, "Caleb Strong" (master's thesis, Smith College, 1938).

24. Campbell, *London Tradesman,* 193; see also Madeleine Ginsburg, "The Tailoring and Dressmaking Trades, 1700–1850," *Costume* 6 (1972): 64–71.

25. Quoted in Jo Anne Preston, " 'To Learn Me the Whole of the Trade': Conflict Between a Female Apprentice and a Merchant Tailor in Ante-Bellum New England," *Labor History* 24 (Spring 1983): 268–69; see also Mary Anne Poutanen, "For the Benefit of the Master: The Montreal Needle Trades during the Transition, 1820–1842" (master's thesis, McGill University, 1985), who cites efforts to restrict the use of apprentices as servants through clauses in their indentures.

26. Preston, " 'To Learn Me the Whole of the Trade,' " 268.

27. Writ, 24 September 1791, Burt Family Papers, PVMA.

28. Clarinda Colton deposition, Burt Family Papers, PVMA.

29. Diamond Colton deposition, Burt Family Papers, PVMA. Diamond and Clarinda were distant cousins; see *Proceedings at the General Celebration of the Incorporation of the Town of Longmeadow* (Longmeadow, Mass., 1884). Interestingly, Coltons were heavily intermarried with Burts, though no direct connection to Ithamar is apparent,

30. Diamond Colton deposition.

31. See James Russell Trumbull, "Northampton Families," typescript in FL. The work of Esther Wright is documented in the Solomon and Esther Wright account book, HN. Solomon was Esther Lyman Wright's son; her daughter, Esther Wright, may also have performed the gown making recorded in this volume.

32. EPP memorandum book, 27 November 1791, 8 December 1793, PPHP.

33. Judd, "Northampton," 1:332.

34. Daniels, "From Father to Son," 3, 15–16.

35. Lane, "Breeches and Rum: An Investigation of Rural Economy Through the Account Books of John Russell" (unpublished seminar paper, Historic Deerfield, Inc., 1984), 5.

36. See Judd, "Northampton, Land & Dwelling Houses and Various Owners," FL. At 1,340 square feet, the Parsons house was well over the median of 1,080, and in the top 15 percent of the 117 houses valued at more than $100 surveyed by Judd. (His records as a surveyor for the 1798 direct tax describe just under half of the 242 Northampton properties for which assessments are found among the surviving official records; for those records, see *Massachusetts and Maine Direct Tax Census of 1798,* microform compiled by the New England Historic Genealogical Society, 1979). Although the 17 windows in the Parsons house, comprising 136 square feet of glass, exceeded the medians of 12 and 96, respectively, the amount of glass per square foot was no more than typical for a home of that size, suggesting that the structure itself did not include any unusual accommodations to Parsons's work as a tailor.

37. Judd, "Northampton," 1:120.

38. Ibid., 1:134.

39. Laurel Thatcher Ulrich discusses the relationship between daughters and their mother's trade in *A Midwife's Tale: The Life of Martha Ballard, Based on Her Diary, 1785–1812* (New York: Alfred A. Knopf, 1990), 80–81; see also "Martha Ballard and Her Girls: Women's Work in Eighteenth-Century Maine," in Stephen Innes, ed., *Work and Labor in Early America* (Chapel Hill: University of North Carolina Press for the Institute of Early American History and Culture, 1988), 70–105.

40. See George Sheldon, *History of Deerfield, Massachusetts,* 2 vols. (Greenfield, Mass.: Press of E. A. Hall and Co., 1895–96), 623. Orra Harvey Russell eventually shared a shop with the shoemakers Ebenezer Saxton and Lyman Frink; she would live on this lot for some "thirty or forty years."

41. Edward Strong Cooke Jr., *Making Furniture in Preindustrial America: The Social Economy of Newtown and Woodbury, Connecticut* (Baltimore: Johns Hopkins University Press, 1996), 69–90; Philip Zea, "Rural Craftsmen and Design," in *New England Furniture: The Colonial Era,* by Brock Jobe and Myrna Kaye, with the assistance of Zea (Boston: Houghton Mifflin, 1984), 55–63; and Scott LaFrance, "Work Habits of Rural Massachusetts Cabinetmakers: A Study of Account Books, 1770–1840" (seminar paper, Historic Deerfield, Inc., 1982).

42. Jane Nylander, *Our Own Snug Fireside: Images of the New England Home, 1760–1860* (New York: Alfred A. Knopf, 1993), 165.

43. Judd, "Northampton," 1:101b.

44. John Russell account books (1763–91), PVMA; Lane, "Breeches and Rum," 14.

45. Campbell, *London Tradesman, 193.*

46. Wiley account book (1815–29), JDC.

47. Judd, "Miscellaneous," 12:26.

48. See ibid., 9:160; Main, "Gender, Work, and Wages," esp. 43. Main examined the ceilings imposed by Westboro and Belchertown. I also use data from the ceilings imposed by South Hadley, recorded in the Judd, "Miscellaneous," 12:26. See also Barbara Clark Smith, "The Politics of Price Control in Revolutionary Massachusetts, 1774–1780" (Ph.D. diss., Yale University, 1983).

49. Judd, "Miscellaneous," 9:159.

50. Ibid., 160.

51. Ibid., 1:101b.

52. Russell account books (1763–91), PVMA.

53. Gloria Main finds the same to be true among men and women weavers in "Gender, Work, and Wages," 61.

54. Simeon Wells inventory, 5 April 1774, HCMRP, 12:159, box 157, file 27.

55. *HG,* 5 March 1800.

56. Sylvester Judd, "Hadley," 1:222, FL, and *History of Hadley* (Springfield, Mass.: H. R. Huntting and Co., 1905), 361.

57. *HG,* 2 and 25 March 1803.

58. Ibid., 31 December 1800. See HCMRP, box, 92 no. 22, 7 May 1822, in which Lyman, "a tipler," "who by excessive drinking is so wasting and lessening his estate and thereby to expose himself and his family to want and the Town of Northampton to expense," was appointed a guardian.

59. *HG,* 29 October 1806. See also 22 November 1815: "Six journeyman tailors can find employment for a few months, by applying immediately, to Sylvester Lyman."

60. Ibid., 23 August 1815.

61. Ibid.,30 May 1810 and 22 May 1811.

62. Ibid., 14 August 1816, 29 October 1817.

63. Lane, "Breeches and Rum, 15–16.

64. *HG,* 6 November 1799, 28 May 1806, 22 November 1815.

950. Ibid., 29 October 1806, 22 November 1815.

66. Ibid., 27 July 1808. An interesting notice regarding a runaway apprentice appeared in a 1794 edition of *HG:* "Ran away from Heman Pomeroy, a boy indentured to the Tailoring business, Thomas Curtis, 17 years old, 5' 7'', his "complexion rather resembling the American Native, roguish eyes and dark hair." The Native American populations who once flourished in the Connecticut Valley were largely scattered by the end of the eighteenth century, but notices like this one remind us that their descendants lingered in the area. See ibid., 16 December 1794.

67. It is also possible that tailors sought to hire apprentices in the summer months when, in addition to their work in the shop, they might also be able to assist with chores on the farm, suggesting some parallels to the challenge female apprentices faced regarding domestic service. I am grateful to Edward Strong Cooke Jr. for making this suggestion to me.

68. Judd, "Northampton," 1:94, 101b.

69. On tramping as an essential part of a craftsmen's training, see J. Ritchie Garrison, "Builders and the Myth of Deskilling: The Case of Calvin and George Stearns" (paper presented at the Eighth Symposium of the George Meany Memorial Archives, Washington, D.C., 11–12 February 1996).

70. Other Connecticut Valley newspapers include *CC,* founded in 1764, and the *Middlesex Gazette and Federal Advertiser* of 1785.

71. Lane, "Breeches and Rum," 20.

72. Karin Calvert, "The Functions of Fashion," in *Of Consuming Interests: The Style of Life in the Eighteenth Century,* ed. Cary Carson, Ronald Hoffman, and Peter J. Albert (Charlottesville: University Press of Virginia, 1994), 252–83., esp. 274.

73. *HG,* 9 May 1798.

74. Ibid.,17 July 1799. Kevin M. Sweeney has observed that in the mid eighteenth century, the orientation of trade switched from Boston to New York, the result of increasing difficulties in currency transactions with Boston merchants and also New York's influence as the site of a "major staging area for British troops in the Seven Years' War." Interestingly, this shift can be in part observed, it appears, in the notices of tailors, whose references to a familiarity with the "latest fashion" of Boston are increasingly countered with references to an ability to provide the same from New York. Sweeney, "From Wilderness to Arcadian Vale: Material Life in the Connecticut Valley, 1635–1760," in *The Great River: Art and Society of the Connecticut Valley, 1635–1820,* ed. William Hosley Jr. (Hartford: Wadsworth Atheneum, 1985), 23; see also *HG,* 10 October 1798, 11 September 1799, 10 November 1802.

75. *HG,* 21 August 1799.

76. Ibid., 10 October 1798.

76. See Gloria L. Main, "An Inquiry into When and Why Women Learned to Write in Colonial New England," *Journal of Social History* 24, no. 3 (1991): 579–89; but see also Ruth Wallis Herndon, "Literacy Among New England's Transient Poor, 1760–1800," *Journal of Social History* 29, no. 4 (1996): 963–65.

77. Main, "Gender, Work, and Wages"; Judd, "Miscellaneous," 9:161–63.

78. Clare Crowston, "Engendering the Guilds: Seamstresses, Tailors, and the Clash of Corporate Identities in Old Regime France," *French Historical Studies* 23 (2000): 343.

79. Clare Haru Crowston, *Fabricating Women: The Seamstresses of Old Regime France, 1675–1791* (Durham, N.C.: Duke University Press, 2001), 11–12.

80. See the Boston city directories published by John Norman in 1789; Manning and Loring in 1796; Rhoads and Laughton in 1798, and John Russell in 1800.

81. Judd, "Northampton," 1:94, 101.

82. The early nineteenth-century transition to industrial production in the clothing industry is described in several excellent studies, including Claudia Kidwell and Margaret C. Christman, *Suiting Everyone: The Democratization of Clothing in America* (Washington, D.C.: Smithsonian Institution Press, 1974); Joan Jensen and Sue Davidson, eds., *A Needle, a Bobbin, a Strike: Women Needleworkers in America* (Philadelphia: Temple University Press, 1984); Thomas Dublin, *Transforming Women's Work: New England Lives in the Industrial Revolution* (Ithaca: Cornell University Press, 1994).

Chapter Seven. Women's Artisanal Work in the Changing New England Marketplace

1. Adam Smith, *Inquiry into the Nature and Causes of the Wealth of Nations* (Dublin: Whitestone, 1776).

2. Smith's work was excerpted in the *Hampshire Gazette,* 5 March 1788.

3. EPP memorandum book, 30 May, 21 June 1795; 15 May, 29 May, 10 and 17 July 1796, PPHP.

4. RD diary, 14 June 1795, PVMA.

5. See Winifred Barr Rothenberg, *From Market-Places to a Market Economy: The Transformation of Rural Massachusetts, 1750–1850* (Chicago: University of Chicago Press, 1992); Christopher Clark, *The Roots of Rural Capitalism: Western Massachusetts, 1780–1860* (Ithaca: Cornell University Press, 1990).

6. Laurel Thatcher Ulrich, "Martha Ballard and Her Girls: Women's Work in Eighteenth-Century Maine," in *Work and Labor in Early America,* ed. Stephen Innes (Chapel Hill: University of North Carolina Press for the Institute of Early American History and Culture, 1988), 105.

7. Gloria Main, "Gender, Work, and Wages in Colonial New England," *William and Mary Quarterly* 51 (1994): 39–66.

8. Ibid., 44, 51.

9. Jan de Vries, "Between Purchasing Power and the World of Goods: Understanding the Household Economy in Early Modern Europe," in John Brewer and Roy Porter, eds., *Consumption and the World of Goods,* 85–132 (New York: Routledge, 1993), 107; and de Vries, "The Industrial Revolution and the Industrious Revolution," *Journal of Economic History* 54 (1994): 249–70.

10. De Vries, "Between Purchasing Power and the World of Goods," 119.

11. Clark, *Roots of Rural Capitalism.*

12. EPP to EWPH, 4 April 1807; 7 February 1803, PPHP. See also Elinor Oakes, "A Ticklish Business," *Pennsylvania History* 47 (1980): 195–212, esp. 209–10.

13. On the expansion of EPP's dairying, see Anne Poubeau, " 'You did not mention whether you had a cow . . . ': Cheese Making at the Porter Phelps Farm, Hadley, MA, 1770–1815" (seminar paper, University of Massachusetts Amherst, Fall 1999).

14. EPP to EWPH, 7 February 1803 and 21 May 1807, PPHP.

15. Christopher Clark, "Household Economy and Labor in Rural Massachusetts: The Connecticut Valley, 1750–1830," in *Travail et Loisiz: Dans les societies pre-industrielles,* ed. Barbara Karsky and Elisa Marienstras (Nancy: Presses Universitaires de Nancy, 1991), 20.

16. CPP to EPP, 15 May 1803, PPHP, box 4 folder 4; James Avery Smith, *The History of the Black Population of Amherst, 1728–1870* (Boston: New England Historic and Genealogical Society, 1999).

17. Relevant scholarship on shifting gender division of labor among a range of occupations includes Laurel Thatcher Ulrich, *The Age of Homespun: Objects and Stories in the Creation of an American Myth* (New York: Alfred A. Knopf, 2002); Judith Bennett, *Ale, Beer, and Brewsters in England: Women's Work in a Changing World, 1300–1600* (New York: Oxford University Press, 1996); Martin Bruegel, "Work, Gender, and Authority on the Farm: The Hudson Valley Countryside, 1790s–1850s," *Agricultural History* 76 (2002): 1–27; K. D. M. Snell, *Annals of the Labouring* Poor: Social Change and Agrarian England, 1660–1900 (New York : Cambridge University Press, 1985); Deborah Valenze, *The First Industrial Woman* (New York: Oxford University Press, 1995); Laurel Thatcher Ulrich, *A Midwife's Tale: The Life of Martha Ballard, Based on Her Diary, 1785–1812* (New York: Alfred A. Knopf, 1990); Rebecca J. Tannenbaum, *The Healer's Calling: Women and Medicine in Early New England* (Ithaca: Cornell University Press, 2002); Mary H. Blewett, "Work, Gender, and the Artisan Tradition in New England Shoemaking, 1780–1860," *Journal of Social History* 17 (1983): 221–48; Joel Perlman, Silvana R Siddali, and Keith Whitescarver, "Literacy, Schooling, and Teaching Among New England Women, 1730–1820," *History of Education Quarterly* 37, no. 2 (1997): 117–39.

18. Cornelia Hughes Dayton, *Women Before the Bar: Gender, Law, and Society in Connecticut, 1639–1789* (Chapel Hill: University of North Carolina Press, 1995); Tannenbaum, *The Healer's Calling.*

19. Mary H. Blewett, "Work, Gender, and the Artisan Tradition in New England Shoemaking, 1780–1860," *Journal of Social History* 17 (1983): 221–48. Female cordwainers were present in New England before that time; in Northampton, for example, CPP's aunt Abigail Phelps Lankton was a well-known shoemaker in Northampton. See Sylvester Judd, "Northampton," 2:139, FL.

20. See Adrienne D. Hood, *The Weaver's Craft: Cloth, Commerce, and Industry in Early Pennsylvania* (Philadelphia: University of Pennsylvania Press, 2003).

21. Ulrich, *Age of Homespun,* and "Wheels, Looms, and the Gender Division of Labor in Eighteenth-Century New England," *William and Mary Quarterly,* 3rd ser., 55 (January 1998): 3–38.

22. Hood, *Weaver's Craft, and* Ulrich, "Wheels, Looms," 6.

23. Ulrich, *Age of Homespun,* 4.

24. Ulrich, "Wheels, Looms," 13.

25. Judith Coffin, "Gender and the Guild Order: The Garment Trades in Eighteenth-Century Paris," *Journal of Economic History* 54, no. 4 (December 1994): 770. See also Clare Haru Crowston, *Fabricating Women: The Seamstresses of Old Regime France, 1675–1791* (Durham, N.C.: Duke University Press, 2001; Gay L. Gullickson, *Spinners and Weavers of Auffay: Rural Industry and the Sexual Division of Labor in a French Village, 1750–1850* (New York: Cambridge University Press, 1986).

26. Main, "Gender, Work, and Wages," 44.

27. For the evolution of the making of men's clothing, see Michael Zakim, *Ready-Made Democracy: A History of Men's Dress in the American Republic, 1760–1860* (Chicago: University of Chicago Press, 2004); Claudia Kidwell and Margaret C. Christman, *Suiting Everyone: The Democratization of Clothing in America* (Washington, D.C.: Smithsonian Institution Press, 1974).

28. William Hosley Jr., "Architecture," in *The Great River: Art and Society of the Connecticut Valley, 1635–1820,* ed. Hosley, 63–72 (Hartford: Wadsworth Atheneum, 1985); Philip Zea, "Furniture," in ibid., 185–91.

29. Leigh Keno, "The Windsor-Chair Makers of Northampton, Massachusetts," *Antiques,* May 1980, 1100–107; Zea, "Furniture," 189, 267.

30. Claudia Brush Kidwell, *Cutting a Fashionable Fit: Dressmakers' Drafting Systems in the United States* (Washington, D.C.: Smithsonian Institution Press, 1979), 3–4.

31. Ibid., 6–7.

32. On blacksmiths, see Barbara McLean Ward, "Metalwares," in Hosley, *Great River,* 277.

33. See Gamber, *Female Economy,* 8, 125–26. For the best work on the nineteenth- and early twentieth-century trade, in addition to Gamber, see Cynthia Amnéus, ed., *A Separate Sphere:* Cincinnati Dressmakers, 1880–1920 (Cincinnati: Cincinnati Museum of Art, 2003); Susan Hay, ed., *From Paris to Providence: Fashion, Art, and the Tirocchi Dressmakers' Shop, 1915–1947* (Providence: Museum of Art, Rhode Island School of Design, 2000).

34. Beverly Lemire, *Dress, Culture, and Commerce: the English Clothing Trade before the Factory 1660–1800* (New York: St. Martin's Press, 1997), 43.

35. Ibid., 19.

36. For a fuller discussion of both commercial and local quilting, see Chapter Three.

37. Quoted in Lemire, *Dress, Culture, and Commerce,* 71.

38. James Russell Trumbull, *History of Northampton, Massachusetts, from its founding in 1654,* 2 vols. (Northampton, Mass.: Press of the Gazette Printing Co., 1898–1902), 2:527. See also Agnes Hannay, "A Chronicle of Industry on the Mill River," *Smith College Studies in History* 21 (1935–36): 9–57.

39. See Clark, *Roots of Rural Capitalism,* 176; Elisabeth Anthony Dexter, *Career Women of America, 1776–1840* (c. 1950; repr., Clifton, N.J.: A. M. Kelley, 1972).

40. Ashfield, with a combined male and female population of just over sixteen hundred in 1845 produced some ninety-two thousand collars and bosoms. See Marjorie Ruzich Abel, "Profiles of Nineteenth Century Working Women," *Historical Journal of Massachusetts* 14 (1986): 43–52, esp. 44.

41. On braiding, see Caroline Sloat, " 'A Great help to many families': Straw Braiding in Massachusetts Before 1825," in *House and Home,* Proceedings of the 1988 Dublin Seminar for New England Folklife, ed. Peter Benes, 89–100 (Boston: Boston University, 1990).

42. EPP memorandum book, 17 July 1796, EPP to EWPH, 13 August 1801 and 19 December 1810, PPHP; Clark, *Roots of Rural Capitalism,* 181–90.

43. Stephen Aron, "The Mind of Hands: Working People of Amherst in the Mid-Nineteenth Century" (honors thesis, Amherst College, 1982), 102.

44. Sylvester Judd "Miscellaneous," 14:163, FL; for more on outwork in New York, see Christine Stansell, *City of Women: Sex and Class in New York, 1789–1860* (New York: Knopf, 1986), esp. chap. 6, on the "harrowing truths" of manufacturing.

45. Polly L'Hommedieu Lathrop account book (1803–17), CHS.

46. George V. K. Hunt account book (1846–52), Fairfield County Clothing Trade, CHS.

47. Silvio A. Bedini, *Ridgefield in Review* (Ridgefield, Conn.: 250th Anniversary Committee, 1958), 195; George L. Rockwell, *History of Ridgefield, Connecticut* (Harrison, N.Y.: Harbor Hill Books, 1979), 77.

48. Hunt account book, CHS.

49. Gregory Nobles, "An Overview of the Outwork Network of Rural New England," in Karsky and Marienstras, *Travail et Loisiz,* 31–42, esp. 34–35.

50. Fielder Clark, *Easy and Correct Method of Cutting Men's Garments by Geometrical Rules adapted to the faculties of any person acquainted with figures* (Woodstock, Vt.: David Watson, 1823). W. J. Rorabaugh describes the ways in which growing literacy and the publication of trade secrets undermined many crafts in *The Craft Apprentice: From Franklin to the Machine Age in America* (New York: Oxford, 1986), 33.

51. Winifred Aldrich traces the appearance of published manuals in Europe in "Tailor's Cutting Manuals and the Growing Provision of Popular Clothing, 1770–1870," *Textile History* 31, no. 2 (2000): 163–201.

52. Amanda Jones, *The Tailor's Assistant: Comprising rules and directions, for cutting men's clothes, by the square rule; by which, in a few hours, a person may acquire such a knowledge of the art, as will enable him to cut all sizes and fashions, with the greatest accuracy* (Whitehall, Vt.: William Sumner, 1823); Otis Madison and John B. Pendleton, *A New system of delineating, Founded on True Principles . . .* (Boston: John Cotton, 1829; and Worcester, Moses W. Grout, 1830).

53. Goodenough's volume is held by VHS; Sheldon's is housed among the Winchester-Ingram Papers, VHS.

54. Lisa Lubow, "From Carpenter to Capitalist: The Business of Building in Postrevolutionary Boston," in Conrad Edick Wright and Katheryn P. Viens, eds., *Entrepreneurs: The Boston Business Community, 1700–1850* (Boston: MHS, 1997), 181–210.

55. Kidwell, *Cutting a Fashionable Fit,* 12.

56. Ibid.

57. EPP memorandum book, 6 September 1801, PPHP.

58. David E. Lazaro, "Construction in Context: A 1790s Gown from Medford, Massachusetts" (master's thesis, University of Massachusetts, 2001), 34–35. See also Lazaro and Patricia Campbell Warner, "The All-Over Pleated Bodice: Dressmaking in Transition, 1780–1805," *Dress* 31 (2004): 15–24.

59. *The Taylor's Complete Guide* (1796), as quoted in R. L. Shep, *Federalist and Regency Costume: 1790–1819* (Mendocino, Calif., 1998), 101, and discussed in Lazaro, "Construction in Context," 35.

60. Lazaro, "Construction in Context," 35.

61. J. Hammond Trumbull, ed., *Memorial History of Hartford County, Connecticut, 1633–1884,* 2 vols. (Boston: Edward L. Osgood, 1886), 2: 596.

62. Lazaro, "Construction in Context," 22.

63. This discussion of construction challenges is developed from ibid., 19, 21, 24, 26, 104–16.

64. *CC,* 16 February 1795, 15 January 1803.

65. See, e.g., ibid., 10 December 1807, 26 October 1808, and 26 April 1809, for three different millinery and mantua-making firms.

66. Ibid., 26 April 1809.

67. Ibid., 15 November 1809.

68. Ibid., 2 May 1810.

69. Ibid., 7 November 1810.

70. Ibid., 27 November 1811.

71. Ibid., 22 January 1812.

72. Ibid., 13 October 1812.

73. Ibid., 9 February 1813.

74. See, e.g., Hay, *From Paris to Providence.* For a close study of one shop, see Amy Simon, " 'She is so Neat and Fits so Well': Garment Construction and the Millinery Business of Eliza Oliver Dodds, 1821–1835" (master's thesis, University of Delaware, 1993).

75. Hartford census, 1810; I thank Sharon Steinberg of CHS for providing this information on Filley.

76. *Boston Directory* (Boston: John Norman, 1789); *Boston Directory* (Boston: John Russell, 1805); *Boston Directory* (Boston: Frost & Stimpson, 1820).

77. *CC,* 10 December 1807.

78. Ibid., 26 April 1809, 15 November 1809, 2 May 1810, 7 November 1810, 22 November 1811, 21 April 1812, 13 October 1812, 9 February 1813. On Lincoln, see ibid., 11 December 1811, 28 April 1812.

79. Ibid., 22 January 1812, 9 February 1813, 16 February 1813.

80. Ibid., 8 September 1812, 7 December 1813.

81. Ibid., 11 October 1815, 19 December 1815.

82. Ibid., 11 March 1817, 18 November 1817, 2 December 1817.

83. Ibid., 27 April 1819, 31 October 1820.

84. Before Williams opened her shop, two women opened what appear to be millinery shops. In 1811, "A. Howard" opened a shop in Sylvester Lyman's former tailoring stand; the following year "Miss Sprague" opened a "Fancy Goods and Milliner's Shop," also in Sylvester Lyman's former space. Sprague also offered "pelices, gowns, coats, habits, spencers and bonnets made in the newest fashion—All kinds of millinery made and plain sewing attended to." See *HG,* 30 May 1810, 22 May 1811.

85. Ibid., 14 August 1816, 29 October 1817.

86. Ibid., 1 January, 13 May and 16 June 1818, and 12 October 1819. For the change to the newspaper's title, see 26 July 1815.

87. *HG,* 13 May 1818 and 12 October 1819; for Best, see *HG,* 1 January and 16 June 1818.

88. Mary Anne Poutanen, "For the Benefit of the Master: The Montreal Needle Trades During the Transition, 1820–1842" (master's thesis, McGill University, 1985), 136–39, 148–49.

89. Robert Blair St. George, "Artifacts of Regional Consciousness in the Connecticut River Valley, 1700–1780," in Hosley, *Great River,* 29–40; Richard D. Brown, "Regional Culture in a Revolutionary Era: The Connecticut Valley, 1760–1820," in ibid., 41–61.

90. Margaret Pabst, "Agricultural Trends in the Connecticut Valley Region of Massachusetts, 1800–1900," *Smith College Studies* 26 (October 1940–July 1941), esp. 1–44, cited in J. Ritchie Garrison, "Tradition and Change in the Agriculture of Deerfield, Massachusetts, 1760–1860" (manuscript prepared for Historic Deerfield, Inc., in the collection of Memorial Libraries, Deerfield, Mass., [1978]).

91. *CC* 17 July 1799.

92. Dayton, *Women Before the Bar,* 69–104.

93. Ibid., 102.

94. See, e.g., Charles G. Steffen, *The Mechanics of Baltimore: Workers and Politics in the Age of Revolution* (Urbana: University of Illinois Press, 1984); Ronald Schultz, *The Republic of Labor: Philadelphia Artisans and the Politics of Class, 1720–1830* (New York: Oxford University Press, 1993); Sean Wilentz, *Chants Democratic: New York City and the Rise of the American Working Class, 1788–1850* (New York: Oxford University Press, 1984). See also L. Diane Barnes, "Fraternity and Masculine Identity Among White and Black Artisans in the Upper South" (paper presented at the annual meeting of the Society for Historians of the Early Republic, Baltimore, July 2001).

95. James P. Walsh, " 'Mechanics and Citizens: The Connecticut Artisan Protest of 1792," *William and Mary Quarterly,* 3rd ser., 1 (1985): 66–89.

96. Paul A. Gilje, "Identity and Independence: The American Artisan, 1750–1850," in *American Artisans: Crafting Social Identity, 1750–1850,* ed. Howard B. Rock, Paul A. Gilje, and Robert Asher (Baltimore: Johns Hopkins University Press, 1995), xv; see also Richard Stott, "Artisans and Capitalist Development," in Gilje, *Wages of Independence: Capitalism in the Early Republic* (Madison, Wis.: Madison House, 1997), 101–117.

97. Crowston, *Fabricating Women,* 4–31.

98. Trumbull, *History of Northampton,* 2:13.

Conclusion: The Romance of Old Clothes

1. Alice Morse Earle, *Two Centuries of Costume in America,* 2 vols. (New York: Macmillan Company, 1903), 2:797.

2. This discussion of Earle's work is largely informed by Susan Reynolds Williams's excellent study "In the Garden of New England: Alice Morse Earle and the History of Domestic Life" (Ph.D. diss., University of Delaware, 1992).

3. Tom Englehardt and Edward T. Linenthal, eds., *History Wars: The Enola Gay and Other Battles for the American Past* (New York: Metropolitan Books, 1996), 6. For a particularly thoughtful consideration of history, memory, and the preservation of American textiles, see Laurel Thatcher Ulrich, *The Age of Homespun: Objects and Stories in the Creation of an American Myth* (New York: Knopf, 2001).

4. Jeanne Boydston, "The Woman Who Wasn't There: Women's Market Labor and the Transition to Capitalism in the United States," in *Wages of Independence: Capitalism in the Early American Republic,* ed. Paul Gilje (Madison, Wis.: Madison House, 1997), 35.

5. Important works include Mary H. Blewett, *Men, Women, and Work: Class, Gender, and Protest in the New England Shoe Industry, 1780–1910* (Urbana: University of Illinois Press, 1988); Howard B. Rock, *Keepers of the Revolution: New Yorkers at Work in the Early Republic (*Ithaca : Cornell University Press, 1992); Howard B. Rock, Paul A. Gilje, and Robert Asher, eds., *American Artisans: Crafting Social Identity, 1750–1850 (*Baltimore: Johns Hopkins University Press, 1995); Ronald Schultz, *The Republic of Labor: Philadelphia Artisans and the Politics of Class, 1720–1830* (New York: Oxford University Press, 1993) Sean Wilentz, *Chants Democratic: New York City and the Rise of the American Working Class, 1788–1850* (New York: Oxford University Press, 1984).

6. Louisa J. Hall, *My Thimbles* (Boston: John Wilson and Son, 1852), 23.

7. Quoted in Nancy Cott, *The Bonds of Womanhood: "Woman's Sphere" in New England, 1780–1835* (New Haven: Yale University Press, 1977).

8. On images of impoverished and vulnerable needlewomen in the nineteenth century, see T. J. Edelstein, " 'They Sang the Song of the Shirt': The Visual Iconology of the Seamstress," *Victorian Studies* 23 (1980): 183–210; Lynn Mae Alexander, "The Forgotten Icon: The Seamstress in Victorian Fiction" (Ph.D. diss., University of Tulsa, 1981); Beth Harris, " 'The Works of Women are Symbolical': The Victorian Seamstress in the 1840s" (Ph.D. diss., City University of New York, 1997); Carol Shiner Wilson, "Pricking Our Conscience: The Needle, Gender, Race, and Utopia," *Annals of Scholarship* 9 (1992): 403–26. For a more recent iteration of this well-established genre, see Emma Donaghue's novel *Slammerkin* (London: Virago, 2001).

9. By America's bicentennial, fabric would represent just 7 percent of the cost; see Claudia Kidwell, "Riches, Rags, and In-Between," *Historic Preservation* 28, no. 5 (1976): 28.

10. See Ava Baron and Susan E. Klepp, " 'If I didn't have my Sewing Machine . . . ': Women and Sewing Machine Technology," in *A Needle, a Bobbin, a Strike: Women Needleworkers in America,* ed. Joan M. Jensen and Sue Davidson, 30–37 (Philadelphia: Temple University Press, 1984). On the European adoption of this technology, see Judith G. Coffin, "Credit, Consumption, and Images of Women's Desires: Selling the Sewing Machine in Late Nineteenth-Century France, *French Historical Studies* 18 (1994): 749–83.

11. *Census of Massachusetts: 1875,* 3 vols. (Boston: A. J. Wright, State Printer, 1876); *Census of Massachusetts: 1885,* 3 vols. (Boston: Wright and Potter, State Printers, 1887).

Some of that number includes young working women who had relocated to the county's industrial centers.

12. "Among the Dressmakers," *HG,* 12 January 1891; Lynne Z. Bassett, "To Sew a Fine Seam: Northampton Dressmakers, 1880–1905," *Historic Northampton,* 3 March–20 June 1993; for Hartford, see Bassett, "Dressmakers in Hartford, Connecticut, 1870–1910" (unpublished seminar paper, University of Connecticut, 1988). The figures for Boston craftswomen are taken from city directories through those years.

13. Wendy Gamber, " 'Reduced to Science': Gender, Technology, and Power in the American Dressmaking Trade, 1860–1910," *Technology and Culture* 36 (1995): 473–74.

14. Nancy Dunlap Bercaw, "Solid Objects/Mutable Meanings: Fancywork and the Construction of Bourgeois Culture, 1840–1880," *Winterthur Portfolio* 26 (1991): 231–48.

15. As Kenneth L. Ames points out, "the ease with which they could be crafted was a critical factor in their popularity." Ames, *Death in the Dining Room and Other Tales of Victorian Culture* (Philadelphia: Temple University Press, 1992), 143.

16. See David R. Proper, "The Fireplace at Memorial Hall, Deerfield, Massachusetts: 'Picturesque Arrangements, Tender Associations,' " in *Foodways in the Northeast,* Proceedings of the 1982 Dublin Seminar for New England Folklife, ed. Peter Benes, 114–29 (Boston: Boston University, 1984); Rodris Roth, "The New England, or 'Old Tyme' Kitchen Exhibits at Nineteenth Century Fairs," in *The Colonial Revival in America,* ed. Alan Axelrod, 159–83 (New York, W. W. Norton, 1985).

17. *Philadelphia Press,* 15 March 1870, 6, as cited in Theodore Gottlieb, *The Origin and Evolution of the Betsy Ross Flag Legend or Tradition* (Newark, N.J.: Privately published, 1938), 1.

18. Scot M. Guenter, *The American Flag, 1777–1924: Cultural Shifts from Creation to Commodification* (London: Associated University Presses, 1990), 101–3.

19. On this point, see Beverly Gordon, "Dressing the Colonial Past: Nineteenth Century New Englanders Look Back," in Patricia A. Cunningham and Susan Voso Lab, *Dress in American Culture* (Bowling Green, Ohio: Bowling Green University Popular Press, 1991), 109–39.

20. Catherine Hedlund, *A Primer of New England Crewel Embroidery* (Sturbridge, Mass.: Old Sturbridge Village, 1973), 16.

21. [Margaret Whiting], "The Deerfield Blue and White Embroidery," draft of talk delivered to the Woman's Club of Nashua New Hampshire, 1905, in Deerfield Town Papers, Business and Commerce, Society of Blue & White Needle Work, 2–III, box 4, folder 9, PVMA.

22. Margery B. Howe, "Deerfield Blue and White Needlework," *Bulletin of the Needle and Bobbin Club* 47 (1963): 43–53.

23. Margaret Whiting to Emily Green Balch, as quoted in Margery Burnham Howe, *Deerfield Embroidery* (New York: Charles Scribner's Sons, 1976). Eileen Boris compares craft and sweated labor in "Crafts Shop or Sweatshop? The Uses and Abuses of Craftsmanship in Twentieth-Century America," *Journal of Design History* 2 (1989): 175–92.

24. See Whiting, "Some Observations on Village Industries," text of a talk, in Deerfield Town Papers, Business and Commerce, Society of Deerfield Industries, 2–III, box 1, folder 9, PVMA. For the time studies, see Margaret Whiting's notebook, on display at the PVMA's Memorial Hall Museum.

25. U.S. Department of Labor, *History of Wages in the United States from Colonial Times to 1928* (Washington, D.C.: Government Printing Office, 1934), 219–20.

26. These women's occupations are listed in Deerfield's 1900 census returns; see U.S. Bureau of the Census, *12th Census of the United States, taken in the year 1900: Population,* pt. 1 (Washington, D.C.: U.S. Census Office, 1901).

27. Adrienne Hood, "The Organization and Extent of Textile Manufacture in Eighteenth-Century Rural Pennsylvania," (Ph.D. diss., University of California at San Diego, 1988), 2.

28. George Sheldon, *History of Deerfield, Massachusetts, 2 vols.* (Greenfield, Mass.: Press of E. A. Hall and Co., 1895–96), 2:31–32. Sheldon concludes his account: "in the annals of our town little can be learned of our foremothers, and Elizabeth Arms must stand as one of their best representatives."

29. Jeanne Boydston, *Home and Work: Housework, Wages, and the Ideology of Labor in the Early Republic* (New York: Oxford University Press, 1990).

30. L. D. Schwarz, *London in the Age of Industrialisation: Entrepreneurs, Labour Force, and Living Conditions, 1700–1850* (Cambridge: Cambridge University Press, 1992), 183.

31. Philip Zea, "Rural Craftsmen and Design," in *New England Furniture: The Colonial Era,* by Brock Jobe and Myrna Kaye, with the assistance of Zea (Boston: Houghton Mifflin, 1984), 50.

32. Pamela Sharpe, *Adapting to Capitalism: Working Women in the English Economy, 1700–1850* (New York: St. Martin's Press, 1996), 9, summarizing Maxine Berg, "Women's Work, Mechanization and the Early Phases of Industrialisation in England," in *On Work: Historical, theoretical and Comparative Approaches,* ed. R. E. Pahl, 61–94 (Oxford: B. Blackwell, 1988); Olwyn Hufton, "Women and the Family Economy in Eighteenth-Century France," *French Historical Studies 9 (1975): 1–22;* Neil McKendrick, "Home Demand and Economic Growth: A New View of the Role of Women and Children in the Industrial Revolution," in *Historical Perspectives: Studies in English Thought and Society,* ed. McKendrick, 152–210 (1974); and Jan de Vries, "Between purchasing power and the world of goods: understanding the household economy in early modern Europe," in *Consumption and the World of Goods,* ed. John Brewer and Roy Porter, 85–132 (New York: Routledge, 1993).

33. Clare Crowston, "Engendering the Guilds: Seamstresses, Tailors, and the Clash of Corporate Identities in Old Regime France," *French Historical Studies* 23 (2000): 339–71.

34. See, e.g., Charles G. Steffen, "Changes in the Organization of Artisan Production in Baltimore, 1790–1820," *William and Mary Quarterly* 36 (1979): 101–17. In 1825, the United Tailoresses of New York, a trade union for women, organized in New York City; see Michael Zakim, *Ready-Made Democracy: A History of Men's Dress in the American Republic, 1760–1860* (Chicago: University of Chicago Press, 2004), 157–58.

35. Wendy Gamber, *The Female Economy: The Millinery and Dressmaking Trades, 1860–1930* (Urbana: University of Illinois, 1997), 5; Christine Daniels, " 'WANTED: A Blacksmith who Understands Plantation Work": Artisans in Maryland, 1700–1810," *William and Mary Quarterly* 50 (1993): 743.

36. See the following works by Laurel Thatcher Ulrich: "Housewife and Gadder: Themes of Self-Sufficiency and Community in Eighteenth-Century New England," in *To Toil the Livelong Day: America's Women at Work, 1780–1980,* ed. Mary Beth Norton, 21–34 (Ithaca: Cornell University Press, 1987); "Martha Ballard and Her Girls: Women's Work in Eighteenth Century Maine," in *Work and Labor in Early America,* ed. Stephen Innes, 70–105 (Chapel Hill: University of North Carolina Press for the Institute of Early American History and Culture, 1988); *Good Wives: Image and Reality in the Lives of*

Women in Northern New England, 1650–1750 (New York, Knopf, 1982); and *A Midwife's Tale: The Life of Martha Ballard, Based on Her Diary, 1785–1812* (New York: Alfred A. Knopf, 1990). Patricia Cleary's *Elizabeth Murray: A Woman's Pursuit of Independence in Eighteenth-Century America* (Amherst: University of Massachusetts Press, 2000) is another important discussion of women's participation in commerce and also depicts a "female economy" that exists apart from, yet in concert with, a "male economy." See also Cleary, " 'She Will Be In the Shop': Women's Sphere of Trade in Eighteenth-Century Philadelphia and New York," *Pennsylvania Magazine of History and Biography* 119, no. 3 (1995): 181–203.

37. Ulrich, *Midwife's Tale,* 98.

38. Ibid., 96. The picture that has emerged from these and other studies is one in which men conceived of their economic interactions as discrete exchanges within the marketplace, while women worked within an informal economy outside the market, grounded in "long-term, reciprocal relationships of mutual aid." See Nancy Grey Osterud, "Gender and the Transition to Capitalism in Early America," *Agricultural History* 67, no. 2 (Spring 1993): 11–29, esp. 24. Karen V. Hansen has investigated community life in antebellum New England and observes that "economic relations pervade social activities, overlapping and intertwining with social relations. It was not unusual for social exchanges to be assigned economic value and for economic exchange to be embedded in a social context." See Hansen, *A Very Social Time: Crafting Community in Antebellum New England* (Berkeley: University of California Press, 1994), 10.

39. Adrienne D. Hood, *The Weaver's Craft: Cloth, Commerce, and Industry in Early Pennsylvania* (Philadelphia: University of Pennsylvania Press, 2003); for a study that compares differing experiences among communities, see Cooke, *Making Furniture in Preindustrial America: The Social Economy of Newtown and Woodbury, Connecticut* (Baltimore: Johns Hopkins University Press, 1996).

40. Evelyn Nakano Glenn, "From Servitude to Service Work: Historical Continuities in the Racial Division of Paid Reproductive Labor," *Signs* 18 (1992): 33.

41. Margaret Ambry, "Sew What," *American Demographics* 10 (1988): 36–37.

42. See Philip Kahn Jr., *A Stitch in Time: The Four Seasons of Baltimore's Needle Trades* (Baltimore: Maryland Historical Society, 1989).

43. "Between a Rock and a Hard Place: A History of American Sweatshops, 1820–Present," http://www.americanhistory.si.edu/sweatshops/intro/intro.htm, accessed 11 February 2005.

44. See, e.g., Miriam Ching Yoon Louie, *Sweatshop Warriors: Immigrant Women Workers Take on the Global Economy* (Cambridge, Mass.: South End Press, 2001).

45. "S[an] F[rancisco] Pledges to Use Purchasing Power to Produce Sweatshop Reform," *Associated Press,* 14 September 2005, and "Sweat Free: A Movement Towards Ending Sweatshops," 1 April 2005, both posted on Global Exchange, http://www.global exchange.org/index.html, and accessed 23 September 2005. See also www.unitehere.org/news.

46. Ellen Israel Rosen, *Making Sweatshops: The Globalization of the U.S. Apparel Industry* (Berkeley: University of California Press, 2002), 227.

47. Jeanette Winterson, *Boating for Beginners* (London: Methuen, 1985), 66.

48. One especially important contributor to this effort has been Michael Kammen. The quotation here titles chap. 4 of Kammen's *A Season of Youth: The American Revolution and the Historical Imagination* (New York: Knopf, 1978); see also his *Mystic Chords of*

Memory: The Transformation of Tradition in American Culture (New York: Knopf, 1991), and *Selvedges and Biases: The Fabric of History in American Culture* (Ithaca: Cornell University Press, 1987). See also David Lowenthal, *The Past Is a Foreign Country* (New York: Cambridge University Press, 1985).

49. Virginia Gunn, "From Myth to Maturity: The Evolution of Quilt Scholarship," *Uncoverings* 13 (1992): 194.

50. Barbara Clark Smith, *After the Revolution: The Smithsonian History of Everyday Life in the Eighteenth Century* (New York: Pantheon Books, 1985), 12.

51. Robert Blair St. George, "Artifacts of Regional Consciousness in the Connecticut River Valley, 1700–1780," in *The Great River: Art and Society in the Connecticut Valley, 1620–1820,* ed. William Hosley Jr. (Hartford: Wadsworth Athenaeum, 1985), 36.

52. Earle, *Two Centuries of Costume in America,* 2:806–7.

53. Sarah Porter Hillhouse to Sarah H. Gilbert, 12 November 1795, folder 62, Alexander and Hillhouse Family Papers, Southern Historical Collection, Chapel Hill, North Carolina. On Bradstreet, see "Anne Dudley Bradstreet (1612–1672)," prologue to *The Tenth Muse Lately sprung up in America. By a Gentlewoman in those parts* (London: Stephen Bowtell, 1650): 3–4. One notable linkage is Laurel Thatcher Ulrich's excellent article "Of Pens and Needles: Sources for Early American Women's History," *Journal of American History* 77 (1990): 200–207.

54. Elaine Hedges suggests that feminist invocations of quilt imagery often disseminate misinformation about the history of quilts and quilting: "Too few feminist scholars are doing primary research into quilt history," she observes, perhaps because, "despite the appeal of the quilt as metaphor, researching the actual material objects is still seen as low-status work." Hedges, "Romancing the Quilt: Feminism and the Contemporary Quilt Revival" (1993), 5–6, Curator of Textiles and Fine Arts research files, Old Sturbridge Village, Sturbridge, Mass.

55. Radka Donnell, *Quilts as Women's Art: A Quilt Poetics* (North Vancouver, B.C.: Gallerie Publications, 1990), 25, 85.

56. James Lincoln Huntington, *Forty Acres: The Story of the Bishop Huntington House* (New York: Hastings House, 1949), 47.

Index

Page numbers in italics refer to illustrations.

MARLA R. MILLER teaches early American history at the University of Massachusetts Amherst and directs the Public History Program there. She attended the University of Wisconsin–Madison and the University of North Carolina at Chapel Hill, where she earned her Ph.D. in 1997. Her articles have appeared in the *New England Quarterly,* the *Proceedings of the Dublin Seminar on New England Folklife, Dress,* and the *William and Mary Quarterly.* Miller's work has been recognized by the Organization of American Historians with a Lerner-Scott dissertation prize and by the Colonial Society of Massachusetts with a Walter Muir Whitehill prize. She lives in Hadley, Massachusetts.